国际贸易实务：汉英对照

宋秀峰　王　芳　陈　忠　陈　婷　主　编
林琼慧　苏锦红　何守超　陈　俊　副主编

中国财经出版传媒集团
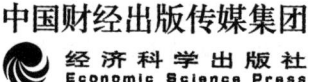
经济科学出版社
Economic Science Press

图书在版编目（CIP）数据

国际贸易实务：汉英对照/宋秀峰等主编．—北京：经济科学出版社，2018.6（2022.2 重印）

ISBN 978 - 7 - 5141 - 9470 - 8

Ⅰ．①国… Ⅱ．①宋… Ⅲ．①国际贸易 - 贸易实务 - 高等学校 - 教材 - 汉、英 Ⅳ．①F740.4

中国版本图书馆 CIP 数据核字（2018）第 141539 号

责任编辑：李　雪　赵　岩
责任校对：李淑敏
版式设计：齐　杰
责任印制：邱　天

国际贸易实务：汉英对照

宋秀峰　王　芳　陈　忠　陈　婷　主编
林琼慧　苏锦红　何守超　陈　俊　副主编
经济科学出版社出版、发行　新华书店经销
社址：北京市海淀区阜成路甲 28 号　邮编：100142
总编部电话：010 - 88191217　发行部电话：010 - 88191522
网址：www.esp.com.cn
电子邮件：esp@esp.com.cn
天猫网店：经济科学出版社旗舰店
网址：http://jjkxcbs.tmall.com
固安华明印业有限公司印装
787×1092　16 开　23.25 印张　570000 字
2018 年 6 月第 1 版　2022 年 2 月第 2 次印刷
ISBN 978 - 7 - 5141 - 9470 - 8　定价：50.00 元
(图书出现印装问题，本社负责调换。电话：010 - 88191510)
(版权所有　侵权必究　打击盗版　举报热线：010 - 88191661
QQ：2242791300　营销中心电话：010 - 88191537
电子邮箱：dbts@esp.com.cn)

本教材得到了闽江学院教改项目（编号为 MJJG20171003）与北京智欣联创科技有限公司联合开发产教融合项目（编号为 CJRH20170045）、闽江学院"闽都学者"奖励计划教学骨干成果项目、闽江学院国际经济与贸易类应用型本科教学"十三五"规划项目（编号为 MJGH20171006）、2016 年福建省高校提升办学水平专项跨境电商专业群项目（编号为 115001041209）和福建省高等学校精品资源共享课项目《跨境电商运营实训》（闽教高（2017）27 号文件）的共同资助与支持，在此，编者一并表示感谢！！！

前　　言

据中国海关统计，2017 年，我国货物贸易进出口总值 27.79 万亿元人民币，其中，出口 15.33 万亿元，增长 10.8%；进口 12.46 万亿元，增长 18.7%；贸易顺差 2.87 万亿元，仍旧保持世界第一大贸易国地位。与此同时，我国高等教育特别是地方本科院校也在迅速扩展，入学学生的特点发生了很大变化，他们将面临中国对外贸易大发展的良好机遇和挑战。为适应上述形势发展和变化的需要，我们组织编写了适合本科应用型技能培养要求的《国际贸易实务：汉英对照》教材。

本书内容涵盖面广、体系完整。全书分十一章。本书内容新颖，深入浅出，对重点、难点问题进行了深刻挖掘，突出了理论性、政策性、应用性和实践性；在内容上注重理论与实践相结合，力求原理清晰明确、实务通俗易懂，有利于培养学生综合应用能力和实际操作能力，与地方本科应用型人才培养目标相吻合。为突出上述特点的要求，我们在编写过程中，适当地增加了实训、实践和英文参考教材的内容。

本书既可以作为国际贸易、国际商务、电子商务等专业的专业课教学用书，又可以作为经济类、管理类专业的专业基础课教材，还可以作为经济类、管理类干部、职工培训教材以及社会各界人士了解国际贸易综合知识和基础业务技能的参考读物。根据本书的体系，教师还可以结合课程的需要，有侧重地讲授国际贸易实务的实训或英文教程。

本书由闽江学院国际经济与贸易专业负责人、中国国际贸易学会国际贸易实务教学委员会副主任宋秀峰副教授担任总审稿，吉林工程技术师范学院国际经济与贸易专业带头人王芳教授和福建师范大学经济学院国贸系陈忠教授担任副总审稿，并和温州大学瓯江学院陈婷教授共同起草写作大纲并负责对全书修纂定稿。闽江学院宋秀峰副教授、吉林工程技术师范学院王芳教授、福建师范大学陈忠教授、温州大学瓯江学院陈婷教授共同担任主编，林琼慧副教授、苏锦红、何守超、陈俊讲师担任副主编。该教材为闽江学院教改项目（编号为 MJJG20171003）与北京智欣联创科技有限公司联合开发产教融合项目（编号为 CJRH20170045），闽江学院"闽都学者"奖励计划教学骨干成果项目、闽江学院国际经济与贸易类应用型本科教学"十三五"规划项目（编号为 MJGH20171006）、2016 年福建高校提升办学水平专项跨境电商专业群项目（编号为 115001041209）和福建省高等学校精品资源共享课《跨境电商运营实训》（闽教高（2017）27 号文件）（创新创业教育与专业教育融合类）的阶段性成果。本书分工如下：王芳撰写第三章、第四章，宋秀峰撰写第六章、第七章、第八章、第十一章；陈忠撰写第五章；林琼慧撰写第二章，何守超、陈俊撰写第十章。

本书在编写过程中还广泛参考了多位专家、学者和同仁的研究成果，在此致以真诚的谢意。由于编者水平有限，本书难免存在一些疏忽和不足，敬请有关专家和读者批评指正。

目　　录

第一章　绪论 ··· 1
　　英文参考教程 ·· 9
　　理论思考 ·· 10

第二章　合同的磋商与签订 ·· 11
　　本章指导 ·· 11
　　第一节　交易磋商前的准备 ··· 11
　　第二节　交易磋商的一般程序 ·· 14
　　第三节　国际商务谈判的策略 ·· 20
　　第四节　合同的签订 ··· 27
　　英文参考教程 ·· 30
　　本章小结 ·· 46
　　本章名词 ·· 47
　　理论思考 ·· 47
　　实训习题 ·· 47

第三章　国际贸易术语和商品的价格 ··· 51
　　本章指导 ·· 51
　　第一节　国际贸易术语概述 ··· 51
　　第二节　六种主要贸易术语 ··· 54
　　第三节　其他贸易术语 ··· 64
　　第四节　商品的价格 ··· 67
　　第五节　买卖合同中的价格条款 ··· 73
　　英文参考教程 ·· 74
　　本章小结 ·· 91

本章名词 ··· 92
理论思考 ··· 92
实训习题 ··· 92

第四章 商品的描述 ··· 96
本章指导 ··· 96
第一节 商品的品名、品质 ··· 96
第二节 商品的数量 ··· 99
第三节 商品的包装 ··· 101
英文参考教程 ··· 104
本章小结 ··· 121
本章名词 ··· 121
理论思考 ··· 121
实训习题 ··· 121

第五章 国际货物运输 ··· 128
本章指导 ··· 128
第一节 国际海上货物运输 ··· 128
第二节 集装箱运输 ··· 131
第三节 其他运输方式 ··· 132
第四节 海运提单 ··· 134
第五节 买卖合同中的运输条款 ··· 138
英文参考教程 ··· 140
本章小结 ··· 154
本章名词 ··· 154
理论思考 ··· 155
实训习题 ··· 155

第六章 国际货物运输保险 ··· 159
本章指导 ··· 159
第一节 海洋货物运输保险的风险、损失与费用 ··· 159
第二节 我国海洋运输保险条款与险别 ··· 162
第三节 我国陆、空、邮货物运输保险 ··· 168
第四节 伦敦保险协会的海运货物保险条款 ··· 170

第五节　保险实务与合同中的保险条款 …………………………… 173
　　英文参考教程 ……………………………………………………… 178
　　本章小结 …………………………………………………………… 191
　　本章名词 …………………………………………………………… 191
　　理论思考 …………………………………………………………… 191
　　实训习题 …………………………………………………………… 192

第七章　国际货款的结算 …………………………………………… 194
　　本章指导 …………………………………………………………… 194
　　第一节　货款结算的支付工具 ……………………………………… 194
　　第二节　支付方式 …………………………………………………… 200
　　第三节　支付方式的选用及贸易合同中的支付条款 ……………… 220
　　英文参考教程 ……………………………………………………… 224
　　本章小结 …………………………………………………………… 242
　　本章名词 …………………………………………………………… 243
　　理论思考 …………………………………………………………… 243
　　实训习题 …………………………………………………………… 243

第八章　争议的预防和处理 ………………………………………… 247
　　本章指导 …………………………………………………………… 247
　　第一节　商品检验 …………………………………………………… 247
　　第二节　索赔 ………………………………………………………… 250
　　第三节　不可抗力 …………………………………………………… 251
　　第四节　仲裁 ………………………………………………………… 253
　　英文参考教程 ……………………………………………………… 254
　　本章小结 …………………………………………………………… 263
　　本章名词 …………………………………………………………… 264
　　理论思考 …………………………………………………………… 264
　　实训习题 …………………………………………………………… 264

第九章　出口合同的履行 …………………………………………… 266
　　本章指导 …………………………………………………………… 266
　　第一节　备货 ………………………………………………………… 266
　　第二节　落实信用证 ………………………………………………… 268

第三节　安排运输 ··· 272
　　第四节　制单结汇 ··· 275
　　第五节　对违约的处理 ··· 281
　　英文参考教程 ··· 281
　　本章小结 ··· 293
　　本章名词 ··· 294
　　理论思考 ··· 294
　　实训习题 ··· 294

第十章　进口合同的履行 ·· 297

　　本章指导 ··· 297
　　第一节　开证、托运和投保 ··· 297
　　第二节　审单和付款 ··· 300
　　第三节　报关、提货 ··· 301
　　第四节　进口索赔 ··· 304
　　英文参考教程 ··· 306
　　本章小结 ··· 308
　　本章名词 ··· 308
　　理论思考 ··· 308
　　实训习题 ··· 308

第十一章　国际贸易方式 ·· 318

　　本章指导 ··· 318
　　第一节　经销和代理 ··· 318
　　第二节　寄售与展卖 ··· 324
　　第三节　拍卖与招标投标 ··· 329
　　第四节　国际加工贸易 ··· 334
　　第五节　国际电子商务 ··· 342
　　英文参考教程 ··· 349
　　本章小结 ··· 360
　　本章名词 ··· 361
　　理论思考 ··· 361

参考文献 ·· 362

CHAPTER 1
第一章　绪　　论

国际贸易实务可分为广义和狭义，广义的国际贸易实务包含国际贸易买卖、加工贸易、租赁贸易、技术贸易和劳务输出业务等；狭义的国际贸易实务则专指国际货物买卖业务。国际贸易实务课是高等教育国际经贸类专业一门必修的主要专业基础课，在整个专业课程体系中处于极其重要的地位，学好国际贸易实务这门课是国际经贸类专业学生的基本任务。该课程又是一门实践性很强的对外贸易综合性课程，对于市场营销、企业管理、会计、国际商务等专业的学生以及从事外经贸业务的人员而言，掌握国际贸易实务方面的知识也是十分必要的。那么，怎样才能掌握这门课程呢？必须对下列问题有所了解。

一、国际贸易实务课程的研究对象

按照商务部和教育部审定的全国统编教材大纲要求，《国际贸易实务》这门课程的研究对象是指狭义的国际贸易实务，是国家间有形商品交换的具体运作过程，包括国家与国家之间货物买卖的有关原理，实际进出口业务过程所经历的环节，操作方法和技能，以及应遵循的法律和惯例等行为规范。

目前，国际贸易的三大支柱是货物贸易、技术贸易和服务贸易，而技术贸易和服务贸易所占的比重已经很大，并且该比重还在不断地上升。但货物进出口仍然是国际贸易最基本和最重要的部分，这不仅因为货物贸易在国际贸易中占有最大的比重，而且许多有关技术贸易和服务贸易操作方法都是从货物贸易演变而来的，甚至有的直接沿用了货物贸易的基本做法。所以本教材阐述的国际贸易实务的原理、知识、方法和技能都是对国际货物贸易而言的。

国际货物贸易的具体过程是通过进出口业务的各个环节来完成的，由于不同国家间的法律、文化、习俗以及贸易习惯上存在差异，因此，在贸易过程中，当涉及双方的利害关系时经常会出现矛盾和争议，研究如何既能很好地协调贸易各方的关系，又以平等互利、公正合理为基础达成约定的进出口交易，实现利益的双赢是本课程学习的中心问题。

二、国际贸易实务课程的主要内容

国际贸易实务是一门综合性应用课程，涉及的范围比较广泛，它包括商品的一般描述、商品的价格术语、国际货物运输与保险、国际货款的结算、争议的预防和处理、合同的磋商与签订、合同的履行和国际贸易方式等方面的内容，概括地说，主要有以下几个方面。

1. 国际货物买卖的合同条款

国际货物买卖合同应具备合同的标的、货物的价格、买方的义务、卖方的义务、争议的预防和处理五个方面的内容。合同条款是交易双方当事人在交接货物、收付货款和解决争议等方面的权利和义务的具体体现，也是双方履行合同的法律基础和依据。由于各国法律都规定，买卖双方可以根据"契约自主"的原则，在不违反法律的前提下，规定符合双方意愿的条款。因此，合同内容的多样性就不可避免了。这就要求我们必须把合同中各项条款的法律含义及其所体现的权利义务关系作为国际贸易实务课程的基本内容来研究。

针对内容多样的国际货物买卖合同，除订明采用何种贸易术语成交外，主要还应对商品名称、品质、数量、包装、价格、运输、保险、支付、检验、索赔、不可抗力、仲裁等交易条件做出明确规定。在了解各种合同条款的基本内容及其规定办法的同时，还应重视其法律和实践意义。

2. 合同的商定和履行

买卖双方通过函电或面对面形式经过磋商就各项交易条件取得一致协议后，交易即告达成，双方之间就构成了合同关系。国际贸易的任何交易都是从磋商合同开始的，商务谈判是订立合同的前提。交易磋商前的准备一般包括谈判人员的选配，目标市场、交易对象的选择，进出口商品经营方案的制定等。交易磋商的一般程序包括询盘、发盘、还盘和接受四个环节，其中发盘和接受是合同成立不可缺少的基本环节和法律步骤。在合同商定的过程中，采取正确的谈判策略和技巧非常重要。合同成立以后，订约双方应信守合同，在享有合同规定的权利的同时也要承担约定的义务，即履行合同。合同的履行，是实行货物和资金按约定方式转移的过程。由于履行合同的过程很复杂，经常会出现争议或法律纠纷，因此我们不仅要了解合同成立的法律步骤和履行合同的基本程序，还要掌握合同履行中产生争议的解决办法，保障当事人的合法权益。

3. 国际贸易方式

据不完全统计，国际贸易方式有几十种，并且随着世界经济一体化的发展，国际间的经济合作日益加深，国际贸易方式也日益呈现出多样化和综合化趋势，除了通常使用的单边进口和单边出口这种逐笔售定的贸易方式外，还出现了融货物、技术、劳务和资本移动为一体的新型国际贸易方式，如包销、代理、寄售、商品期货交易、租赁贸易、转口贸易和加工装配贸易等。近年来，电子商务也越来越多地应用到国际贸易领域，促使国际贸易发生了深刻的变化，形成了新的贸易业态——跨境电子商务，因此必须了解各种国际贸易方式的特点，在实际业务中，将各种贸易方式有机结合，灵活运用。

4. 进出口业务操作技能训练

国际贸易实务理论知识学习的最终目的是应用到实际业务中去。进出口业务操作技能训练是在掌握国际贸易实务基本理论的前提下，通过模拟实际操作训练来提高学生的实际动手能力，该技能训练主要包括下列内容：建立业务关系、出口报价核算、出口发盘、出口还价核算、出口还盘、合同签订、开证审证、制单结汇、报检、储运、报关、保险等。

三、国际货物买卖关系的适用法律

国际货物买卖是一种跨越国界的经济活动，同时，也是跨越国界的法律行为。因此，它的法律关系调整要比在同一法律制度下国内货物买卖的法律关系复杂得多。国际货物买卖合同的订立和履行，必须符合有关法律规定，主要包括三个方面。

1. 各国有关国际贸易法律

西方国家多拥有高度发达的商品经济，为了调整商品买卖过程中的买方和卖方之间的权利、义务关系，保障商品交换的顺利进行，他们制定了一套比较完备的有关商品买卖的法律。由于西方各国的经济大多数是市场经济，与国际市场有许多共同之处，无论是大陆法系还是英美法系，他们的买卖法一般既适用于国内贸易，又能适用于国际贸易。我国市场经济发展得比较晚，制定的有关法律在同国际接轨方面还存在一定的差距，特别是加入世界贸易组织（WTO）以后，这方面的矛盾更加突出。自1999年10月1日施行的《中华人民共和国合同法》是我国有关货物买卖的根本法律，同以前的有关法律相比，新《合同法》更尊重市场经济规律和国际商务惯例。

由于国际货物买卖合同的当事人所在的国家不同，所在国的国内法对他们又都具有约束力，而不同国家有时对同一问题在法律上的规定又存在诸多的差异，一旦出现争议引起诉讼究竟以哪国法律为依据呢？《中华人民共和国合同法》第126条作出原则规定："涉外合同的当事人可以选择处理合同争议所适用的法律，但法律另有规定的除外。涉外合同的当事人没有选择的，适用与合同有密切联系的国家法律。"据此，除法律另有规定外，我国当事人只要与国外当事人取得协议，可在合同中选择处理合同争议所适用的法律，例如，既可选择按我国法律，也可选择按对方所在国法律，或双方同意的第三国法律，或者有关的国际条约来处理本合同的争议。如果当事人未在合同中作出选择的，则当发生争议时，由受理合同争议的法院或仲裁机构，依照法院或仲裁机构视交易具体情况认定的"与合同有最密切联系的国家"的法律进行处理。

2. 国际贸易惯例

国际贸易惯例（International Trade Practice）或称国际商务惯例（International Commercial Practice），也是国际货物买卖合同应当遵循的重要法律规范。它是指在长期国际贸易实践中逐渐形成和发展起来的，为大多数国家所认可和遵循的一些习惯做法和解释。国际贸易惯例通常是由国际性组织或商业团体制定的有关国际贸易成文的通则、准则和规则。

国际贸易惯例有以下几个特点。

（1）它是在长期的国际贸易活动中逐渐形成的。

（2）它具有确定的内容而且被许多国家和地区认可。

（3）它不具有法律强制性，只有当事人双方经过协商选用某一国际贸易惯例，并在合同中明确规定时，这一国际惯例才具有法律约束力。

（4）它的内容随国际贸易实践的发展不断更新壮大。

3. 国际条约

国际条约是两个或两个以上主权国家为确定彼此的政治、经济、贸易等方面的权利和义务而缔结的诸如公约、协定、议定书等各种协议的总称。国际货物买卖合同的订立和履行还必须符合当事人所在国缔结或参加的与合同有关的双边或多边的国际条约。目前与我国对外贸易有关的国际条约，主要是我国与其他国家缔结的双边或多边的贸易协定、支付协定、贸易议定书，以及我国缔结或参加的有关国际贸易、海运、陆运、空运、商标、工业产权、知识产权、仲裁等方面的协定或公约。

在各种国际贸易条约中，《联合国国际货物销售合同公约》是与我国货物进出口贸易关系最紧密和最重要的一项国际条约。该公约于1980年3月在维也纳召开的国际外交会议上通过，并于1988年1月1日生效。我国是该公约的最早缔约国之一，1986年12月我国向联合国秘书长递交了《国际货物销售合同公约》核准书，成为该公约的缔约国。因而，我国的涉外企业在与其他缔约国进行货物买卖时，该公约将自动适用。

从某种意义上来说，中国缔结或参加的国际条约是构成我国法律的一部分，具有国家法律效力。国际条约优于国家法，即当中国缔结或者参加的国际条约与中华人民共和国法律有不同规定时，适用于有关国际条约的规定，但我国声明保留的条款除外。

四、国际货物贸易的基本做法

国际货物贸易从一个国家的角度来看可分为进口贸易和出口贸易。尽管进口贸易和出口贸易的程序相反，其业务运作的侧重点也各不相同，但都分别包括交易前的准备、商订合同和履行合同三个阶段。现将进出口贸易的一般业务程序、贸易方式和预防与处理合同争议的办法，分别概述如下。

（一）进出口贸易的一般业务程序

1. 出口贸易的程序

（1）交易前的准备。

出口交易前的准备工作，主要包括：落实货源和做好备货工作；加强对国外市场与客户的调查研究选择适销的目标市场和资信好的客户；制订出口商品经营方案或价格方案，以便对外洽商交易时胸有成竹；开展多种形式的广告宣传和促销活动。

（2）商订出口合同。

在做好上述准备工作之后，即通过函电联系或当面洽谈等方式，同国外客户磋商交易，当一方发盘被另一方接受后，交易即告达成，合同关系订立。

（3）出口合同的履行。

出口合同订立后，交易双方要根据重合同、守信用的原则，履行各自承担的义务。如按 CIF 条件和信用证付款方式达成的交易，就卖方履行出口合同而言，主要包括下列各环节的工作：认真备货，按时、按质、按量交付约定的货物；落实信用证，做好催证、审证、改证工作；及时租船订舱、安排运输、保险，并办理出口报关手续；缮制、备妥有关单据，及时向银行交单结汇和收取货款。

2. 进口贸易的程序

（1）交易前的准备。

进口交易前的准备工作，主要包括：制订进口商品经营方案或价格方案，以便对外洽商交易和采购商品时，做到心中有数，避免盲目行事；在对国外市场和外商资信情况调查研究的基础上，并经过货比三家，选择适当的采购市场和供货对象。

（2）商定进口合同。

商定进口合同与商定出口合同的程序与做法基本相同，但应强调指出的是，如属购买高新技术、成套设备或大宗商品交易，更应注意选配好洽谈人员，组织一个包括有各种专长的专业人员的、精明能干的谈判班子，并切实做好比价工作。

（3）进口合同的履行。

履行进口合同与履行出口合同的程序相反，工作侧重点也不一样，如按 FOB 条件和信用证付款方式成交，买方履行合同的程序，一般包括下列事项：按合同规定向银行申请开立信用证；及时派船到对方口岸接运货物，并催促卖方备货装船；办理货运保险；审核有关单据，在单证相符时付款赎单，办理进口报关手续，并验收货物。

（二）各种国际贸易方式的灵活运用

在国际贸易中，除上述通常使用的单边进口和单边出口贸易这种逐笔售定的贸易方式外，根据市场环境、商品流通渠道、交易条件和贸易习惯等方面的不同，还可采用其他各种贸易方式，如经销、代理、寄售、展卖、招标与投标、拍卖、期货交易、对销贸易和加工贸易等。近年来，随着电子技术的发展和贸易方式、方法的改变，又兴起了电子商务这种新型的贸易方式。每种贸易方式，都有各自的特点，学会灵活运用和结合使用各种贸易方式，对发展对外贸易具有重要的意义。

实践表明，我国灵活运用各种贸易方式是很有成效的。例如，为了利用外商的销售渠道，我国生产的轻纺产品、机电产品和工艺品等，采用经销、代理和寄售等方式，有效地扩大了销路。我们利用招标与投标以及对销贸易的方式，既采购了我国急需的建设物资、生产设备器材，又扩大了我国产品的出口能力。为了增加外汇收入，我们还开展了各种形式的加工贸易。此外，期货交易、无纸贸易以及电子商务也相继发展起来，其运用范围正在扩大。上述这些贸易方式，将在本书有关章节中分别加以阐述。

（三）预防与解决合同争议的办法

在国际货物买卖中，无论通过何种贸易方式达成的交易，在订立合同后，如果合同没有履行或履约当中一方出现违约情况，致使对方蒙受经济损失，则受损害方有权采取各种必要的救急方法，这就会产生索赔、理赔与处理纠纷的问题。针对合同订立后可能出现的这些问题，当事人在订立买卖合同时，应约定异议与索赔、违约金与定金、不可抗力和仲裁条款，以明确处理争议的依据和办法。

五、本课程的研究对象与学习方法

（一）本课程的研究对象

本课程的研究对象主要是，针对国际贸易的特点与要求，从实践和法律的角度，分析研究国际贸易使用的有关法律与惯例，国际货物贸易买卖过程的实际运作和总结国内外实践经验，并吸收国际上一些行之有效的贸易习惯做法，以便掌握国际货物贸易的"生产经"，学会在进出口业务中，既能正确贯彻我国对外贸易的方针政策和企业经营意图，确保最佳经济效益，又能按国际规范办事，使我国的贸易做法能为国际社会普遍接受，同国际市场接轨。

国际间商品交换的具体过程，从一个国家的角度来看，具体体现在进出口业务活动的各个环节。在这些环节中，由于存在彼此法律上的不同规定和贸易习惯上的差异，所以涉及买卖双方的利害关系时，往往会出现矛盾和斗争。研究如何协调这种关系，在平等互利、公平合理的基础上达成交易，完成约定的进出口任务，这就是本课程研究的中心课题。具体地说，本课程研究对象，主要包括下列几个方面。

1. 国际货物贸易有关法律与惯例的运用

国际货物贸易必须按照国际货物买卖的有关法律和惯例进行，在洽商交易、订立合同、履行合同和处理贸易争议时，都离不开国际货物买卖的相关法律和惯例。这些相关的法律与惯例，是本课程必须研究的主要内容。

鉴于完成每笔交易，不仅需要销售合同，还需要运输合同、保险合同和融资合同，国际商会国际贸易术语解释通则（Incoterms）专门针对销售合同中买卖双方交接货物所承担的责任、风险和费用的划分作了具体解释。因此，我们将有关贸易术语的惯例及其解释与运用单独作为一篇加以详细阐述，而其他国际贸易惯例，则结合其他章节的内容分别予以介绍和说明。

2. 国际货物买卖合同条款的约定

合同条款是交易双方当事人在交接货物、收付货款和解决争议等方面的权利与义务的具体体现，也是交易双方履行合同的依据和调整双方经济关系的法律文件。按照各国法律规定，买卖双方可以依据"契约自主"的原则，在不违反法律的前提下，规定符合双方意愿的条款，这就必然导致合同内容的多样性。因此，研究合同中各项条款的法律含义及其所体现的权利与义务关系，是本课程研究最基本的内容。

在国际货物买卖合同中，除订明采用何种贸易术语成交外，应就合同的主体和成交商品的名称、品质、数量、包装、价格、运输、保险、支付、检验、索赔、不可抗力与仲裁交易条件作出明确具体的规定。由于这些交易条件的内涵及其在法律上的地位和作用不同，所以了解各种合同条款的基本内容及其规定办法，有着重要的法律和实践意义。

鉴于合同条款的重要性及其涵盖的内容很广泛，故本书以较大的篇幅将各项条款的内容分别加以介绍和说明。

3. 国际货物买卖合同的商定与履行

在国际货物贸易中，交易双方通过函电洽商和当面谈判就各项交易条件达成一致协议后，交易即告达成，一般地说，合同即告成立，买卖双方当事人就存在了合同关系，彼此应重合同、守信用，各自履行约定的义务。

合同的履行，是实现货物和资金按约定方式转移的过程。在履约过程中，环节很多、程序繁杂、情况多变，如稍有不慎或某些环节出问题，或合同当事人违约，都会影响合同的履行，甚至可能引起争议或法律纠纷。因此，外经贸人员不仅要了解合同成立的法律步骤和履行合同的基本程序，还应当了解如何处理履约当中产生的争议，并掌握违约的救济方法，以保障合同当事人的合法权益。

鉴于订立、履行合同和处理合同争议，都涉及合同当事人的正当权益，故研究如何依法订立合同、正确履行合同和妥善处理合同争议，就成为本课程不可缺少的一项重要内容。

4. 国际贸易方式的运用

随着国际经济关系的日益密切和国际贸易的进一步发展，国际贸易方式、渠道日益多样化和综合化。除传统的贸易方式外，还出现了融货物、技术、劳务和资本移动为一体的新型的国际贸易方式。在国际贸易方式中，除单边进口和单边出口外，还包括包销、代理、寄售、展卖、商品期货交易理论、对销贸易、加工贸易、无纸贸易与电子商务等。介绍和阐述各种贸易方式的性质、特点、作用、基本做法与选用时的注意事项，也属本课程研究的一个重要方面。

（二）学习本课程的方法

根据本课程的性质、研究对象及其涵盖的内容，在学习过程中，需要掌握下列基本学习方法。

1. 必须贯彻理论联系实际的原则

在学习本课程时，要以国际贸易基本原理和国家对外方针政策为指导，将国际贸易理论、中国对外贸易政策理论等先行课程中学到的基础理论和基本政策，在本学科中加以具体运用，以便将理论与实践、政策与实务有效地结合起来，不断提高分析、解决实际问题的能力。

2. 必须注意业务与法律的联系

国际贸易法律课的内容同本课程内容关系密切。因为，国际货物买卖合同的成立必须经过一定的法律步骤，国际货物买卖合同是对合同当事人双方有约束力的法律文件，履行合同是一种法律行为，处理履约当中的争议实际上是解决法律纠纷问题。在学习本课程时，应同有关法律课程的内容联系起来考虑，即要求从实践和法律两个方面来研究本课程的内容。

3. 认真贯彻"洋为中用"的原则

为了适应国际贸易发展的语言，国际商会等国际组织相继制定了一系列有关的国际惯例与规则，这些惯例与规则，已成为当前国际贸易中公认的一般国际惯例，并被人们普遍接受和经常使用，成为国际贸易界从业人员共同遵守的行为准则。因此，学习本课程时，我们必须根据"洋为中用"的原则，密切结合本国国情来研究国际上一些通行的惯例和普遍实行的原则，并学会灵活运用国际上一些行之有效的贸易方式和贸易习惯做法，按国际规范办事，力求在商务运作上做到同国际市场接轨。

4. 坚持"学""用"结合的原则

由于本课程是一门实践性很强的综合性应用学科，在教学过程中，要注重实例案例教学和平时操作演练，开展模拟教学与现场教学活动，并结合现场参观、实习，增加感性知识，加强基本技能的训练，提高业务素质和商务运作能力，把"学"和"用"结合起来，以体现"学用一致"的原则。

总之，针对上述国际贸易的特点，按照国际贸易的有关法律、惯例与国际上公认的准则，并采取正确的学习方法，切实掌握本课程所阐述的基本原理、基本知识与基本技能，就能达到"学以致用"的预期效果。

英文参考教程

Introduction
Reasons for International Trade

Most nations of the world export goods to other counties. Likewise, most of them import goods from other nations. Why do countries of the world engage in international trade? Why can't they be self-sufficient, capable of living exclusively on the goods and services produced within their own borders? Various reasons can be cited. In general, however, the reasons for international trade can be classified as resource reasons and economic reasons.

Resource Reasons

Some countries in the world have certain conditions or resources that provide them with a basis for international trade. Illustrations include favorable climate conditions and terrain, natural resources, skilled workers, and capital resources.

Favorable Climate Conditions and Terrain

Some countries have year-round or seasonal weather conditions that make them ideally suited for the raising of particular crops. For example, Colombia and Brazil have just the right climate for growing coffee beans. The United States, with the exception of Hawaii, does not. Therefore, the United States must import coffee. On the other hand, the United States grows so much wheat that it is able to export wheat to other nations abroad. Thus, climate and terrain help determine some of the goods a nation can produce and trade internationally.

Natural Resources

If a country has an abundance of natural resources, it is common to find some of these resources being exported. Among developing countries raw materials may be sold before being processed. Tin from Bolivia and oil from some of the Middle East countries are examples. On the other hand, in many highly industrialized nations raw materials are often sold in finished form. For example, the United States sells its iron ore in the form of steel products, such as automobiles and machinery. Yet, regardless of how they are sold, raw materials play a major role in determining a country's involvement in international trade.

Skilled Workers

If a nation has great many skilled workers, it can produce sophisticated equipment and machinery, such as computers, jet aircraft, and electric generators. The United States, Japan and Western European countries are illustrations. On the other hand, some nations have basically unskilled work forces and must confine their activities to the manufacture of simple products. Ethiopia, Uganda, and Guinea are illustrations. The skill of a country's work force helps determine what it will be able to produce and trade with other countries.

Capital Resources

Another important factor in international trade is that of capital resources. These include things such as plant, machinery, and equipment. The more capital resources a nation has, the better its chance to free its workers from manual jobs and allow them to work on more important tasks. In these countries, while the machines do the busy work people concentrate their attention on "Think" jobs, such as developing technological breakthroughs that will result in a higher standard of living for the nation. Poor countries, of course, lack these capital resources and must rely heavily on manual labor and on certain goods from other countries.

Economic Reasons

Another reason why nations engage in international trade is to secure some kind of economic benefit. It is the simple truth that for two nations to trade with each other voluntarily, both nations must gain. If one nation gained nothing or lost, it would simply refuse to trade. But how does this mutually beneficial trade take place and form where do these gains from trade come? Here are the tow important principles—that sere to illustrate the point and can be explained in detail in some other specific books, not here.

（资料来源：宋秀峰. 国际贸易（双语版）[M]. 北京：中国发展出版社，2010.）

> **理论思考**

1. 国际贸易实务课程的研究对象是什么？
2. 国际贸易实务课程的主要学习内容是什么？
3. 国际贸易实务课程学习中应注意哪些问题？

CHAPTER 2

第二章　合同的磋商与签订

▶本章指导

通过对本章的学习，要求能够了解进出口交易前的必要准备，进出口交易磋商的一般程序，进出口交易磋商的策略，重点掌握进出口交易磋商的主要环节以及《联合国国际货物销售合同公约》（以下简称《公约》）对此的相关规定，能够运用相关知识进行如下操作：

1. 询盘；
2. 发盘；
3. 还盘；
4. 接受；
5. 组织简单的商务谈判。

第一节　交易磋商前的准备

一、选配贸易谈判人员

为了国际商务谈判及交易能够顺利进行，配备精明强干的谈判人员至关重要，一场国际商务谈判或交易应配备几个谈判人员才合适，应根据谈判及交易内容的繁简、技术性的强弱、时间的长短及己方谈判人员和对方谈判人员的素质等因素来确定。

对于较小型的国际商务谈判，谈判人员多由2~3人组成，有时甚至由一人全权负责；内容复杂、较大型的磋商或谈判，因为内容繁多、专业性强、涉及面广和组织协调工作量大等特点，配备的人员相对要多一些，有的甚至多达数十人。在大中型的国际磋商或谈判中，必须配备一名负责人、律师、经济师、工程师及译员，在特大型谈判中有时还可根据实际需要把谈判班子再分为若干个小组，如商务小组、技术小组、法律小组等，各个小组负责不同方面的谈判工作，谈判班子不但要有专门人才，而且还应注意选拔复合型人才参加。

二、选择目标市场

这里所说的选择目标市场是加强对已经选定的目标市场和谈判进行进一步的调查，着重调查谈判目标在目标市场上的需求、销售、竞争等方面的情况。

（一）需求情况

对谈判目标的需求情况进行调查应包括该产品的市场需求总量、需求结构、需求的满足程度、潜在的需求量和消费群体及消费者的心理倾向等方面，客观地估计该产品的竞争力，为以后的磋商提供有力的保证，同时还可以达到在出口时主动积极适应国外市场的需要，在商品进口时，以最合适的价格选择我们最需要的商品。

（二）销售情况

对谈判目标的销售情况的调查应包括该类产品过去几年在当地的销售量、销售总额以及价格变动情况，了解该类商品在当地的生产规模、销售趋势，以便我们选择最佳的销售和采购市场和时机。

（三）竞争情况

对谈判目标的竞争情况的调查应包括目标市场的主要竞争对手的生产规模、价格水平、产品性能、竞争对手可能使用的销售渠道和网络，以及市场占有率等，了解竞争对手所具有的优势和劣势，预测己方产品的竞争能力，扬长避短。

三、选择交易对象

在谈判之前，对客户的情况要进行全面调查，通过分析比较，选出成交可能性最大的客户。

（一）资信情况

关于谈判对方的资信情况，主要包括以下两个方面。
（1）对方是否具有授权签订合同的资格，谈判者可以要求对方提供有关的证明文件，如法人资格证明或营业执照。谈判代表的被委托书等。
（2）对方是否具有资本、信用和履约能力。关于这方面的调查，资料来源可以是公共会计组织对该企业的年度审计报告，也可以是银行、资信征询机构出具的证明文件等。

(二) 客户的政治经济背景及其对我们的态度

谈判时了解对方的政治经济形势及其变动情况十分重要，它将会对交易产生很大的影响。所以尤其是要对对方的政治、经济的现状和发展情况进行调查。客户对己方的经营能力、财务状况、支付能力、商业信誉、谈判能力的认可程度以及是否信任尤为重要。

(三) 客户的经营范围

主要是指客户企业的经营品种、经营性质、服务范围以及是否同我国做过交易等。

(四) 客户的谈判作风

是指谈判者在多次谈判中表现出来的一贯风格。谈判作风因人而异，千差万别，可分为强硬型、温和型和原则型三种，了解对方的谈判作风，对预测谈判的发展趋势和对方可能采取的策略以及制定好己方的谈判策略等提供重要的依据。

(五) 客户的经营能力

是客户企业活动能力、购销渠道、联合网络、贸易关系和经营做法等。了解客户的渠道有很多，如在业务往来过程中，逐渐考察；通过举办的交易会、展览会等主动接触；通过国际商会咨询民间组织及国际友人进行了解；通过企业名录、国内外专业报刊去查询。

四、制订进出口经营方案

(一) 出口商品经营方案

出口商品经营方案主要包括：国内货源情况，国外市场情况，出口经营情况，营销计划和措施。

(二) 进口商品经营方案

在落实和审核了进口许可证和外汇、进口订货卡片以后，进口商品经营方案主要还包括：商品数量的掌握，采购市场的安排，交易对象的选择，贸易方式的运用，交易条件的掌握等。

第二节 交易磋商的一般程序

一、交易磋商的方式

交易磋商的方式有面对面谈判、电话谈判和函电谈判三种。

(一) 面对面谈判

面对面谈判是上述三种谈判方式中应用得最广泛、最普遍、最经常的一种方式。即使在信息技术较发达的今天,面对面谈判仍因其综合优势全面而在三种谈判方式中居首要位置。该种谈判方式的特点是比较正式、正规,谈判的内容深入细致,便于施展谈判的策略和技巧,及时了解交易对方的态度和诚意,尤其适合于谈判内容复杂、涉及问题较多的交易。

(二) 电话谈判

电话谈判是随着电话通讯的广泛采用和日益普及而产生的,现在越来越多的为人们所认识和采用,该种谈判方式的优势是快速方便、联系广泛,在当今生活、工作节奏不断加快的社会时代,为现代人所青睐。但电话磋商也有一定的缺陷,电话谈判双方相距较远,只能听到,不能看到对方的表情、手势等,容易造成磋商双方的误解。某些事情很容易被遗漏和删除,注意力难以集中,有时还增加了谈判的风险。

(三) 函电谈判

函电谈判是国际营销商务和地区营销商务中进行业务沟通、磋商交易的一种谈判方式,这种谈判方式在各国进出口公司、外贸部门和涉外企业用户中使用最普通、最频繁。它包括电报、传真、电子邮件等。一方通过函电发盘或还盘,另一方以函电的形式表示接受,从而双方达成交易,签订协议或者合同。我们把这种函电谈判的过程称作函电谈判。函电谈判有快速、准确无误、材料齐全、有据可查的优点,特别需要指出的是函电具有法律效力。

二、交易磋商的内容

该内容涉及拟签订买卖合同的各项条款,包括品名、品质、数量、包装、价格、装运、保险、支付以及商品检验、索赔、仲裁和不可抗力等。从理论上讲,只有就以上条件逐一达成一致意见才能充分体现"契约自由"的原则,然而在实际业务中,并非每次磋商都需要把这些条款一一列出,逐条商讨,因为在普遍的商品交易中一般都使用固定格式合同,合同中对商检、索赔、仲裁、不可抗力等一般交易条件,要求己方事先印成一份书面文件,或印在合同格式背面,或在老客户之间已经形成一些习惯做法,只要对方没有异议,这些条件也成为双方进行交易的共同基础而不必每次重复磋商。

三、交易磋商的一般程序

每笔交易磋商的程序不完全相同,但每一笔交易的磋商从建立业务关系到达成交易,不外乎以下四个环节,询盘—发盘—还盘—接受。

(一) 询盘

询盘(enquiry/inquiry)又叫询价,也称邀请发盘(invitation to offer),是指交易的一方为了购买或销售商品,向对方询问买卖该商品的有关交易条件。询盘可由卖方提出,也可由买方提出。询盘可只询问价格,也可询问其他一项或几项交易条件,直至要求对方发盘,在实际业务中由买方询盘的较多。询盘时,除品名外,有时还包括价格、规格、品质、数量、包装、交货期等。询盘可采用口头方式,亦可采用书面方式。书面方式除采用书信、电报、传真询价外,还经常利用询价单进行询盘。下面是询盘的实例:

买方询盘:

中国松香WW级1 000吨,8月装船,请报CIF伦敦价。

Please offer Chinese rosin ww grade 1,000M/T August Shipment CIF London.

卖方询盘:

可供中国松香WW级,8~9月装船,请递盘。

We can supply Chinese rosin WW grade shipment Aug. /Sept. , Please bid.

在国际贸易中询盘虽对询盘人没有约束力,但也要慎重不要乱发询盘。特别是在进出口业务中,以免引起不良后果。特别是自己的询盘往往被另一方用作调查研究,摸清市场行情,刺探商业秘密的一种手段。

(二) 发盘

1. 发盘的含义

发盘(offer,quotation,报盘、发价、报价)是指买卖双方的一方(发盘人—offeror)向对方(受盘人—offeree)提出各项交易条件,并愿按照这些条件与对方达成交易、订立合同的一种肯定的表示,发盘在法律上称为要约,既属商业行为,又属法律行为。

2. 发盘的形式

在实际业务中，发盘通常是一方在收到对方的询盘之后提出的，但也可以未经过对方询盘而直接向对方发盘。发盘多由卖方发出，这种发盘称为售货发盘（selling offer），也可以由买方发出，称为购货发盘（buying offer）或递盘（bid）。下面是电报发盘的实例：

兹发盘1 000打运动衫规格按3月15日样品每打CIF纽约85美元，标准出口包装5月至6月装运，以不可撤销信用证支付，限20日复到。

Offer 1,000 dozen sport shirts sampled march 15, USD85 Per dozen CIF New York Export standard packing May June shipment irrevocable sight L/C subject reply here March 20.

发盘可以是口头进行，也可以是书面进行，无论是买方发盘，还是卖方发盘。在发盘的有效期内，发盘人不得任意撤销或修改其内容。发盘一经对方在有效期限内表示无条件接受，发盘人将受其约束并承担按照发盘条件与对方订约合同的法律责任。

3. 发盘的构成条件

（1）发盘要有特定的受盘人。发盘必须向特定的人提出，只有发盘中特定的人才能作为受盘人对有关发盘表示接受而成立合同，特定的受盘人可以是自然人也可以是法人，可以是多个人也可以是一个人，但以广大公众为泛指时不可以。因此，有时交易是在报刊杂志或其他媒体所做的商业广告，即使内容完整，由于没有特定的受盘人，也不能构成有效的发盘，只等同于邀请发盘。

（2）发盘的内容必须十分确定。即发盘的条件是完整的、明确的和终局的。一般来说，一项条件完整的发盘应包括商品的品名、品质、数量、包装、价格、交货和支付等主要条件，但也有例外。例如，在有些业务中也有一次发盘不是以上述所有主要交易条件完整形式出现，尽管如此，一旦对方接受，便可拟定详细的书面合同，既可减少事后的争议，又有利于合同的订立和履行。

（3）表明发盘人愿意承受约束的意旨。即发盘人必须表明发盘人愿意按照发盘中的条件同对方签订合同的意思，即发盘人在发盘时向对方表示，在得到有效接受时，双方即可按发盘的内容订立合同。

（4）送达受盘人才生效。因为受盘人必须在收到发盘时才能决定是否可以接受。所以发盘也必须到达受盘人时才能生效。这里的"送达双方"是指将发盘内容通知对方或送交对方本人或其营业地址或通信地址。

4. 发盘的有效期

发盘的有效期是指可供受盘人作出接受的期限，凡是发盘都是有有效期的，一般都明确做出规定。

例：

Offer subject reply here 15 May（发盘限5月15复到）

这类明确规定有效期的发盘，从发盘被送达受盘人时开始生效，重叠规定的有效期满为止。但也有不明确规定有效期的发盘，是指在一般合理时间内有效，所谓"合理时间"国际上也并无明确的规定或解释。一般与买卖货物的性质密切相关。一些在国际市场上价格频繁波动的，发盘有效的合理时间应理解为短一些。而对市价比较稳定的货物，合理时间可理解为相对要长一些。

5. 发盘的撤回与撤销

如果一项发盘还没到达受盘人，发盘人为了使该项发盘不发生效力以一种较快的通讯方式先于发盘到达受盘人以通知受盘人，取消将要到达的发盘。这种行为称作发盘的撤回。如果一项发盘已经到达受盘人，但受盘人在发盘规定的有效期内进行考虑，尚未表示接受，发盘人为了使该项发盘不发生效力而及时通知受盘人，宣布取消自己发出但对方还未接受的发盘，该行为则被称为发盘的撤销。

关于发盘的撤回问题，《公约》第15条第2款规定："一项发盘，即使是不可撤销的也可以撤回，如果撤回的通知在发盘到达受盘人之前或同时到达受盘人，也是可以撤回的"，也就是说，只要发盘还未生效，对发盘人就还未产生约束力，所以发盘是可以撤回的，但需要在发盘到达受盘人之前通知受盘人，否则就不是发盘撤回的问题了，而是发盘撤销了。

关于发盘的撤销，世界各国的法律规定上存在很大的差异。英美法律认为，在发盘被接受之前，发盘人有权力撤销发盘或变更发盘的内容，例外的情况是受盘人给予了"对价"（consideration）或者发盘人以签字蜡封的特殊形式发盘。但美国在《统一商法典》中对上述原则做了修改，规定凡是商人以书面形式作成的发盘，在规定的有效期内不得撤销，未规定有效期的发盘在合理时间内不得撤销，但最长时间不得超过三个月。

而大陆法系国家的法律认为：发盘在有效期内不得撤销，例如德国法认为，发盘原则对发盘人有约束力，除非他在发盘中已表明不受约束、法国虽然允许发盘人在有效期内撤销其发盘，但判例表明他必须承担赔偿责任。

《公约》第16条对大陆法和英美法在此问题的分歧进行了协调，并提出：

（1）发盘可以撤销，如果撤销的通知于受盘人发出接受通知之前送达受盘人。

（2）但在下列情况下，发盘不得撤销。

①发盘中写明了发盘的有效期或其他方式表明发盘是不可撤销的；

②受盘人有理由信赖该发盘是不可撤销的，而且受盘人已本着对该发盘的信赖行事。

6. 发盘的失效

所谓发盘的失效，简单地说，是指在一定条件下的发盘对发盘人的约束力将得以解除。即发盘失去了法律效力，发盘人不再受发盘的约束，受盘人也失去了接受发盘的权力，发盘失效经常有以下几种情况。

①在有效期内未被接受而过期。明确规定有效期的发盘,在有效期内如未被受盘人接受即失效;未明确规定有效期的发盘,在合理时间内未被接受也在失效之列。

②受盘人表示拒绝或还盘。

③发盘人对发盘依法及时撤回或撤销。

④发盘因内容违法而失效。

⑤发盘因受盘人对发盘的内容作实质性的修改而失效。

(三) 还盘

还盘(counter-offer)是指受盘人不同意或不完全同意发盘人在发盘中提出的条件,为了进一步协商,对发盘提出修改意见,还盘既是受盘人对发盘的拒绝,也是受盘人以发盘人的地位所提出的新发盘,一方的发盘经对方还盘以后即失去效力,除非得到原发盘人同意,受盘人不得在还盘后反悔。

还盘只有受盘人才可以做出。一项还盘等于是受盘人向原发盘人提出的一项新的发盘,还盘做出后,还盘的一方与原发盘人在地位上发生了变化,还盘人由原来的受盘人变成了新发盘的发盘人,而原发盘人则变成了新发盘的受盘人。

还盘可以用口头方式或者其他方式表达出来,一般与发盘采用的方式相符。还盘可以是针对价格也可以是针对商品的品质、数量、交货的时间及地点、支付方式等主要条件提出修改意见。

例如:"你 5 日电收悉,还价每打 60 美元 CFR 纽约。"

(Your cable 5th counter-offer USD 60 Per dozen CFR New York.)

新受盘人有权针对还盘的内容进行考虑决定接受、拒绝或是再还盘,新受盘人(原发盘人)如果是对受盘人发出的还盘提出新的修改意见并再发给受盘人,其效果与还盘一样。在进出口业务中,一笔交易的达成往往要经过多次还盘和再还盘的过程。这也是合同法的主要过程。

(四) 接受

接受(acceptance)一词在法律上称承诺,在进出口上叫接受,是指受盘人接到对方的发盘或还盘后同意对方提出的条件愿意与对方达成交易,并及时以声明或行为表示出来。

接受像发盘一样既属于商业行为,也属于法律行为,接受产生的法律后果是双方达成交易,订立合同。在实际业务中,接受的形式一般都是用函电、口头等形式表示,但在某些情况下,接受也可以用行为表示出来,但该方式的前提必须是发盘规定允许的方式,或双方当事人之间业已形成这样做的惯例。

1. 接受构成的条件

(1) 接受必须由特定的受盘人做出。发盘是向特定的人做出的。因此,只有特定的人才能对发盘做出接受,而不能是其他人,其他人即使通过其他途径了解了发盘的内容而向发盘人表示接受,合同也不能成立,这种"接受"只能被认为是向原发盘人完成了一项新的发盘。

(2) 接受必须以某种方式表示出来。接受的方式有两种:第一种是用声明来表示,即受盘人用口头或书面形式向发盘人表示同意发盘内容;第二种是用行为来表示,即在发盘明确规定的有效期内,或在合理时间之内(特指发盘未规定有效期),根据发盘的要求或依照当事人之间确定的习惯做法(如卖方备货或发运货物,买方支付价款等)行事。值得注意的是,我国在批准《公约》时对《公约》承认合同可以用书面以外形式订立的规定声明保留(参见《公约》第12条),因此在实际业务中,意愿上已同意接受对方的发盘,保持沉默或者没有用任何行为予以表示出来,是不能构成接受的。

(3) 接受必须在发盘的有效期内传达到发盘人。按《公约》采用的"到达生效"原则的规定,接受只有在发盘有效期内到达发盘人时才生效。这种规定对于面对面口头谈判或电报谈判,进行磋商时,比较切实可行,而在用信件或电报方式进行磋商以及用行动表示接受时,接受的表示没有立即送达到发盘人,对此,接受应于何时生效的问题,国际上不同法系的规定有较大的分歧。

英美法系的国家采用"投邮生效"的原则作为一般规则,即接受必须传达到发盘人才生效。但是如果接受是用信件或电报做出时,法律例外地承认,当信件投邮或电报交发,接受即告生效,即使接受的函电在邮递途中延误或遗失,发盘人未能在发盘有效期内收到,也不影响合同的成立,但如果发盘人在发盘中规定接受必须于有效期内传达到发盘人,则接受的函电传达到发盘人的接受方才能生效。

大陆法系的国家采用"到达生效"原则。即接受必须到达发盘人时才生效,即使用信件或电报做出表示也不例外,如果表示接受的函电,在邮递过程中延误或遗失,合同不能成立,其传递延误或遗失的风险由受盘人承担。

《公约》采用"到达生效"的原则,第18条第2款中规定:接受于到达发盘人时生效。如果接受在发盘的有效期内,或者如发盘未规定有效期,在合理的时间内未到达发盘人,接受即为无效。

(4) 接受的内容必须与发盘相符。如果要达成交易,成立合同,根据传统的法律规则,受盘人必须无条件地全部同意发盘的条件。即接受必须是绝对的、无保留的,与发盘人的发盘条件必须完全相符。

根据英美法的"镜相规则",接受必须像照镜子一样照出发盘。大陆法系也有类似的原则,要求接受必须"纯净"(pure)并与发盘"完全相符"。但这样严格的规定,难以适应国际贸易实际业务的需要,所以在国际贸易的实际业务中受盘人在表示接受时,往往对发盘作出某些添加、限制或其他更改,为了不影响合同的成立,尽量促成交易的达成,《公约》将接受中对发盘的条件所作的变更分为:一是在实质上变更发盘的条件,即实质性变更;二是在实质上并不变更发盘条件即非实质性变更。凡对货物的价格、付款、质量、数量、交货地点和时间赔偿责任范围或解决争端等的添加、限制或更改,均视为实质上变更发盘的条件,包括这些内容的添加或变更是对发盘的拒绝,发盘人对此不予确认。而接受中含有非实质性变更的接受,例如,要求提供重量单、装箱单、商检证书和产地证书等单据或要求分两批装运等,除发盘人及时向受盘人表示反对其间的差异外,将构成接受,合同得以成立,并且合同的条件以该项发盘的条件以及所接受中变更为准。

2. 逾期接受

逾期接受(late acceptance)是指接受通知到达发盘人的时间已经超过了发盘所规定的有效期,或在发盘中未规定有效期时,已超过了合理的时间。逾期接受在一般情况下无效。只能认为是新的发盘。但为了有利于双方合同的成立,对逾期接受采取一些灵活的处理方式,使它在符合某些条件的情况下,仍然具有接受的效力。据此,《公约》规定:如果发盘人于收到逾期接受后,毫不迟延地通知受盘人,确认其为有效,则该逾期接受仍具有接受的效力。

对于另一种情况,一项接受由于传递不正常而未能及时送达发盘人,造成了延误。在如果传递正常的情况下,可以及时送达发盘人,《公约》对此的规定是:该逾期接受仍是有效的。除非发盘人毫不迟延地用口头或书面通知受盘人,他的发盘已经失效。

3. 接受的撤回

接受必须在合同生效之前才能撤回。如果接受生效,合同即告成立,受盘人也就不可能撤回其接受,因为接受已经生效了。但撤回的通知如果能在该项接受到达发盘人之前或和该项接受同时到达发盘人时,接受时可以撤回的,因为此时接受尚未生效。

但是按照英美法律的投递生效原则,情况则不同,其法律规定,接受一经投邮立即生效,合同就此成立,所以不存在接受的撤回问题。接受通知一经到达发盘人即不能撤销。因为接受一经生效,合同即告成立,如果允许撤销,这实际上无异于允许毁约的行为。

第三节 国际商务谈判的策略

谈判:从某种意义上说,谈判就是有利害关系的双方为寻求一致而进行磋商的一种行为,谈判双方互有所求都希望从对方获得能使己方所需的利益,之所以有谈判,这种人们寄希望获得的利益驱动起了十分重要的作用。

商务谈判:商务谈判有着悠久的历史。第二次社会大分工,即农业与手工业分离后，出现了原始性的商品交换—物物交换。人们在物物交换的过程中，为了各自的目标利益所进行的洽谈协商，即为商务谈判。商务谈判活动随着商业活动的发生而发生，但商务谈判为一门独立的学科被广泛重视和研究则是在第二次世界大战以后。

国际商务谈判：是指跨越国界的当事人之间为实现一定的经济目的、明确相互的权利与义务关系而进行协商的行为。

一、国际商务谈判主要包含的含义

（1）参加谈判的当事人起码有一方是跨越国界的。
（2）其内容一定是跨越国界的。
（3）其手段是当事人为了各自的商业目标、利益而采取洽谈协商的方法。
（4）其目的是明确当事人相互之间的权利与义务。

二、国际商务谈判策略

国际商务谈判策略是指国际商务谈判人员为取得预期的谈判目标而采取的措施和手段的总和。国际商务谈判的策略很多，这里只是对商务谈判的不同阶段以及经常出现的策略做简要介绍。

（一）国际商务谈判开始阶段的策略

国际商务谈判的开始阶段一般包括准备阶段和始谈阶段，在这一阶段，下面一些策略常被采取。

1. 知己知彼

俗话说，"知己知彼，百战不殆"，该策略最主要的是搜集信息、谈判准备等。谈判中要搜集哪些信息？做哪些准备？这要根据谈判的内容及谈判对象而定，要做到谈判开始之前既要了解谈判对方的情况，掌握对方信息，又包括了解对方的谈判目的，参加谈判人员的权限，对该次谈判的重视程度以及技术方面的情况。同时对己方的实际情况要清楚。

2. 感情投资

谈判中进行感情投资是推进谈判的"润滑剂"。纽约著名语言学家李斯特（List）说过，"人们都愿意说自己只受理智支配，但其实整个世界都被感情所左右"。要注意积累感情，多接触，多交往，加深双方相互了解非常重要。进行感情投资时，一方面不可操之过急，只宜采取逐步推进的方式；另一方面是采取有时间差的感情投资，即感情投资的时间应早于谈判开始时间，感情投资的收回时间应晚于感情投资时间。切记不可平时不烧香，临时抱佛脚。

3. 察言观色的策略

在谈判开始阶段，双方就当次谈判的内容，陈述各自的观点、立场及建议。在谈判中通常被称为开局陈述或开场陈述。开局陈述的内容主要包括以下两方面。

（1）己方的立场，即己方希望通过谈判取得哪些利益，己方可以采取何种方式为双方共同获得利益作出贡献。

（2）己方对该次谈判问题的理解。即己方认为当次会谈应涉及的主要问题，以及对这些问题的看法或建议、想法等。作为谈判的一方，我们不能忽略对对方开局陈述的深入细致的观察，通过对方的形体语言，如表情、手势、目光等来分析判断其态度、意向等深层次的内容。

（二）国际商务谈判摸底阶段的策略

实际的谈判过程，是从摸底阶段开始的。在这一阶段，下面一些策略常被采用。

1. 投石问路

"投石问路"这个策略是取得资料的一种绝好办法，在谈判中，作为买方常采用这个策略获取商品的成本、价格等方面的资料，以使自己做出绝好的选择。例如用下列方法来获得对方有价值资料时经常运用。

（1）假如我方订货数量增加呢？

（2）假如我方一次性全额付款，你方还能优惠多少呢？

投石问路的策略，使卖主进退两难，对付投石问路的最佳办法是不要对对方提出的"假如"问题立刻回答，有时需要认真准备之后才可回答。

2. 统计魔术

在谈判的摸底阶段，谈判当事人经常向对方出示统计数字，以证明自己的观点，对于对方所运用的统计数字，应时时小心，因为数字是权利的一项很微妙的来源，搜集数字的人常常控制着决策。这些数字本身就难免发生重大错误，加之有时运用统计数字为自己的某种目的服务时，错误的统计数字就会出现得更多。例如，某人是销售商，在做价格涨跌预测时，他总是在努力寻找有关对他本人有利的数字。由此提示我们对于统计数字要保持审慎的怀疑态度，防止在对方的数字里，故意隐藏一些制造出来的"事实""解释""假设"和有利于个人价值的判断等错误。

3. 浑水摸鱼

国际商务谈判中的"浑水摸鱼"策略是指谈判者故意把水搅混，从中取利，这也称为"搅和"的策略。采用此策略时，谈判者先东鳞西爪地乱扯一通，把众多的问题搅和在一起，扰乱对方思路，等对方筋疲力尽、使一个简单的洽谈变得十分复杂时，乘机达到自己的目的。对付"搅和"策略，首先，要具备信心，要有勇气对对方提出自己没有把握回答的问题说"我不了解"；其次，在你真正了解之前，要继续说"我不了解"，等到自己完全弄清楚之后再同对方谈判。

（三）国际商务谈判僵持阶段的策略

1. 勃然大怒

世界文明发展到今天的地步，文明的人们在日常生活中早已学会了忍耐，习惯于将恐惧、愤怒等情绪埋藏于心中，当谈判中有人毫无顾忌地发泄愤怒时，对方往往感到震惊，难以抵抗愤怒巨浪的冲击，有时也认为若不是自己在谈判中提出十分不合理的要求或建议，对方绝对不会发怒，如果自己又真的在谈判中，提出了非分之想，此时被迫退步，降低要求是可能的。

2. 欲擒故纵

在谈判的过程中，不露出自己的真正意图甚至把对方误导到其他方向，并竭力创造一个良好的谈判气氛，以取得对方的信任与合作，使对方逐渐放松警惕，在探知对方薄弱环节和底细以后再转向发动攻势，甚至达不到要求就没有离开谈判桌的可能，采用该种策略必须是在已经充分地了解谈判对方，已摸清对方底细，做好充分准备的情况下才能有效。

3. 虚张声势

该策略一般在商谈商品交易价格时采用，对谈判当事人来说，主要运用于交易双方互相不甚了解与信任，或者对方对物品的性能和竞争力不甚了解的场合。例如，在市场情况不变的前提条件下，卖方往往开价稍高一些，买方往往把价压得稍低一些，为进一步谈判留有余地，这就是谈判中通常出现的卖方喊价偏高，并大肆宣传鼓动，如何货有所值，买方杀价较狠，并再三挑剔商品的缺陷的原因，这实际上就是虚张声势策略的运用。

4. 黑白脸策略

该策略又称为"坏人与好人"策略，也叫做"黑脸与白脸"策略。谈判时先由扮黑脸的人（坏人）出场表现出傲慢无礼。苛刻无比、僵化强横，让对手感到难以合作，极其反感，然后此人退场。由扮白脸的人（好人）出场，此人谦逊有礼，易于合作，以合情合理的态度对待谈判对方，当你对他的要求表示难以接受时，扮白脸的人则暗示自己的权力有限。若谈判陷入僵局，那位"黑脸人"会再度登场。因此绝大多数谈判者在"好人"的礼遇下，加之不愿再见那位黑脸"坏人"而尽量答应他提出的要求。

（四）国际商务谈判让步阶段的策略

1. 步步为营

步步为营是一个军事用语，意思是说每前进一步或后退一步都要做好已经占领阵地的加固工作。商场就是战场，在商务谈判中，也要注意到无论是发起攻势还是进行让步，都要循序渐进。例如在让步中，每做出一步让步，应该巩固阵地，每让出一步，都要让对方做出艰辛的努力，做出一定的让步，并且感到你再让步的可能已经不大。

2. 于己无损

商务谈判中，损害己方根本利益的让步是不可取的，但有些不损害己方重大利益又有利于达成协议的让步，还是应当采取的。正如寓言"朝三暮四"中的故事：主人喂猴子，早上给它吃三升橡子，晚上给它吃四升橡子，猴子感到不满意，主人重新安排，早上给它四升橡子，晚上给它吃三升橡子，这只猴子满意了。朝三暮四变成朝四暮三于主人是于己无损的让步。商务谈判时常可以用以下的方式做到于己无损的让步。

（1）帮助对方了解市场行情及本公司产品的特点。

（2）暗示或明示成交后下次交易将做出重大让步。

（3）做出姿态上的让步，注意倾听对方陈述，对对方的要求和处境表示理解等。

3. 先硬后软

双方进行谈判处于僵持阶段，没有让步，谈判就无法进行，所以要打破僵局。谈判中的让步是难免的。但是应当怎样让步，一般来说，让步的最佳策略是，在谈判的开始时，要采取比较强硬的立场，在对方进行交锋的过程中进行一定的妥协，但让步幅度不宜过大，而是采取幅度较小的让步。这样做可以削弱对方的信心，并且借机试探对方的实力，由此来确定己方的立场。

（五）促成阶段及其策略

1. 最后通牒

最后通牒是一种军事用语，含有给对方最后一次机会的意思，有时规定一定的时间，即时间性通牒，借用期限来逼迫对方采取某种含有让步意味的行动。

例如：假如明天下午3点30分仍未收到贵方的定金我们将与别的客户成交。

谈判中的最后通牒，不像战争中的最后通牒那样残酷。谈判中的最后通牒，最坏的结果也就是中止谈判。但作为谈判者一般都不愿意中止谈判，因为中止谈判首先意味着自己无任何收获。对方也可能很快找到新的谈判伙伴。所以一般的"最后通牒"只是一种威胁，即使超过对方提出的条件（如期限）只要你的妥协能给对方带来益处，对方仍有可能接受。

一般说来使用"最后通牒"必须具备一定的条件。

（1）谈判者知道自己处于优于对方的有利位置，其他竞争对手均不具备自己拥有的有利条件。

（2）谈判者已试过其他方法均未奏效。

（3）对方现在所持的立场确已超过自己的最低要求。

（4）你发出的"最后通牒"绝对在对方接受的范围之内。

2. 利益诱导

要想让谈判的对方接受你的建议，促成谈判，首先要让对方知道，如果订立合同，他能从中获得哪些利益，如果不能签订合同，对方将有哪些损失，这些将能促使对方签订合同。但利益诱导如果单方强调对对方有何利益，而不提及对己方的好处，往往引起对方的怀疑和误解。所以运用此策略时，也同样指出己方也将获得的若干利益，即合同的签订将是共同受益的事情，这样更能使对方相信你的"诱导"。

这里的"利益"是一个广义的概念，不仅仅是金钱利益，应当理解为泛指有价值的东西，比如一次机会，扩大知名度，享受某一地位等。

三、国际商务谈判中与不同国家商人沟通的技巧

随着中国加入 WTO，中国与世界各地商人经贸活动更加频繁，不同的人种、不同的语言、不同的民族和风俗习惯使各国的商人拥有不同的性格特征，与不同性格的商人进行沟通所运用的技巧也有所不同，现就一些与主要地区商人沟通技巧做简要的介绍。

（一）与美国商人沟通的技巧

美国的历史不长，是一个年轻的国家。同时美国是一个多民族融合的国家，由来自世界各地特别是欧洲的移民组成，白种人大部分是欧洲各国移民的后裔，分布在全国各地，由于移民国的社会等级变化无常，专制君主制、世袭制导致他们无法生存，因此美国人不受权威与传统观念的支配，形成了独特的商业文化特点：创新意识强、性格外露坦率、自信、注重实际等。所以与美国商人沟通应注意以下几点。

首先，要充分利用其性格豪爽的特点，诚挚热情地与美国商人交往很容易创造和谐气氛，创造成功的机会。

其次，利用美国人的自信和滔滔不绝的个性，在其夸夸其谈时找到有价值的信息，探听对方虚实，谋划对策。

最后，利用美国商人喜欢与"高手"过招的特点，在谈判中宜多采取"以战取胜"的技巧。美国商人更赏识能战胜自己的人，而对弱者的态度则蔑视多于同情。

（二）与日本商人沟通的技巧

日本商人具有典型的东方特点，其特点是注重礼节和身份，注重集体智慧，强调集体决策，说话态度婉转暧昧，力求回避直接的否定语，注重和谐的人际关系，精于讨价还价，勇于进取，刻苦耐劳，不择手段获取情报等。与日本商人沟通的技巧有如下几点。

（1）针对日本商人注重礼节和身份的特点，我方商务活动人员与日方交往时必

须要彬彬有礼。

（2）在商务活动中，注意处理好人际关系，建立和谐的气氛。

（3）针对日本商人精于讨价还价、寸利不让的特点，我方报价及商谈事宜时要留有较大余地，以防日本商人杀价或讨价过狠。

（4）针对日本商人不惜重金获取情报这一特点，我方商务活动人员应持既积极又慎重的态度，介绍情况时要适度。

（三）与犹太商人沟通的技巧

犹太商人具有重信守约、厚利适销、节省时间、和气生财、善找财源等特点，世界各地许多商人都颇受犹太商人的影响。针对犹太商人的特点，与其进行沟通时应注意采用下列技巧。

（1）以诚实的作风和犹太人沟通，自己也要注重长远利益，信守诺言，力争获得犹太人的信任。

（2）与犹太商人建立长期合作关系，在合作中共同受益，不要幻想独家获利，不要与犹太人做"一锤子买卖"。

（3）同犹太人做生意的过程中，注意关心周围的各种人，让他们看得出你在关心他们，能容纳他们。不要伤害对方的自尊心，让对方说出他的意见。以询问的方式向对方提出主张。

（四）与欧洲商人沟通的技巧

欧洲是资本主义经济发展最早的地区，有三十多个国家，这里只介绍与英国、法国商人沟通的技巧。

1. 与英国商人沟通的技巧

第一，英国的北爱尔兰、女王等问题有很多禁忌，涉及此类问题时一定要慎重。第二，要学会与傲慢的人打交道，在级别上要对等，在形象上要注意修养、气质、风度等。第三，注意英国商人讲究绅士风度的特点，可在适当的时候，选派高官出访，满足其虚荣心理。第四，尽量选派能讲流利英语的人与之交谈。

2. 与法国商人沟通的技巧

针对法国商人自尊自强的特点，我们要尊重法国的礼仪，并且注重服装、外表。派熟悉法国礼仪的翻译前往会收到意想不到的效果。法国人注重休闲，去法国进行商务活动最好避开节假日，特别是每年的八月。

针对法国人谈生意注重友情的特点，我们要利用各种场合、机会与法国人交朋友，有计划地安排出访、邀请。

针对法国人谈判风格顽强、有度的特点，我方绝不能因对方坚持而过早放弃自己的立场。

针对法国人特别的爱国热情，有时可以采取贸易与外交相结合的谈判方法。

第四节 合同的签订

一、合同有效成立的条件

合同磋商的过程中，一方的发盘经过对方有效接受，合同即告成立，该合同虽已成立，但要具有法律效力，还需要具备下列条件。

（一）当事人必须在自愿和真实的基础上达成协议

商订合同必须是双方自愿的，不得存在一方把自己的意志强加给对方的行为，任何一方也不得采取欺诈或胁迫手段。我国合同法明确规定："当事人依法享有自愿订立合同的权利，任何单位和个人不得非法干预"，合同法还规定"一方以欺诈、胁迫的手段或者乘人之危，使对方在违背真实意思的情况下订立的合同，受害方有权请求人民法院或者仲裁机构变更或者撤销"。

（二）当事人应具有相应的行为能力

即双方当事人应具有商订国际货物买卖合同的合法资格。具体要求如下：作为自然人应是成年人并且须有固定住所。神志不清、未成年人等不具有签订合同的合法资格。作为法人，应是已经依法设立的企业组织，有关业务应当属于其合法单位的法定经营范围之内，负责磋商及签约者应当是其法人的法定代表人或其合法授权人。

（三）合同的标的和内容必须合法

合同的标的，是指交易双方买卖行为的客体，签订合同时，合同的标的和内容必须符合双方国家法律的规定，才是有效的合同。

（四）必须是互为有偿的

国际货物买卖合同是货币与货物互换的交易。一方提供货物，另一方支付价款。如果一方不按合同的规定提供货物，或另一方违约拒不付款或不按合同规定支付钱款都要以合同为依据负有赔偿对方损失的责任。

（五）合同的形式必须符合法律规定的要求

我国《合同法》第10条规定："当事人订立合同，有书面形式、口头形式和其他形式。法律行政法规规定应采用书面形式的，要采用书面形式。当事人约定采用书面形式的应当采用书面形式。"无论采用书面形式还是口头形式，均不影响合同的效力。

二、书面合同的签订

虽然在交易磋商的过程中，接受发盘之后交易即告成立，双方构成合同关系，双方磋商过程的函电也可作为合同的书面证明，但根据国际贸易惯例，要进一步明确买卖双方的权利和义务，买卖双方还须签订书面合同。

(一) 签订书面合同的意义

各国法律都承认书面合同，而口头合同往往存在许多不明确的因素。尽管有些国家的法律上还承认口头合同，但在国际贸易实践中在当事人双方经过磋商一致、达成交易后一般均须另行签订具有一定格式的书面合同。签订书面合同具有以下意义。

1. 合同成立的证据

通过口头磋商成立的合同，一旦双方出现纠纷，举证将存在许多困难，而书面形式签订的合同是证明双方存在合同关系的一种最有效、最简便的方法，也可作为仲裁员和法官进行仲裁、做出判断的一个有力证据。

2. 作为履行合同的依据

国际货物买卖合同的履行涉及面广、环境复杂，若仅有口头协议，合同履行过程中将会出现许多麻烦和困难。因此，在实际业务中，双方一般都要求将各自的权利与义务用书面形式规定下来，作为合同履行的依据。

3. 作为合同生效的条件

在国际贸易实务中，有时合同的生效是以书面形式签订合同作为条件的，虽然双方达成协议所交换的信件、电报、电传也常常构成书面合同，但只有签订确认书后，合同才告成立，才算存在法律意义上的有效合同。

(二) 书面合同的形式

1. 合同和确认书

实际业务工作中，外贸企业所采用的书面合同的形式，主要是合同（销售合同 sales contract 和购货合同 purchase contract）和确认书（销售确认书或售货确认书 sales confirmation 和购货确认书 purchase confirmation）一般都印有固定格式，成交后经双方核对无误后，由业务人员按双方谈定的条件逐项填写。签字后各执正本一份，副本若干份作为执行的依据。合同和确认书虽然在格式、条款项目的设立和措辞上有所不同，但作为合同主体的双方协议一致的交易条件都应完整明确。经买卖双方签署的合同和确认书，都是法律上有效的文件，对买卖双方具有同样的约束力。

2. 协议

"协议"或"协议书"（agreement），在法律上是"合同"的同义词，合同本身就是当事人为了设立、变更或经过民事关系而达成的协议，如果书面合同冠以"协议"或"协议书"的名称，只要它的内容对买卖双方的权利和义务已做明确、具体和肯定的规定，这就与合同一样对买卖双方具有约束力。

3. 备忘录

备忘录（memorandum）也可作为书面合同的形式之一，一般在外贸实际业务中运用较少，如果双方经洽谈后，就某些事项达成一定的理解和谅解，并将这种"理解"和"谅解"以"备忘录"的形式记录下来，作为双方进一步合作的依据和参考，它在法律上不具约束力。如果双方交易条件明确、具体地在备忘录中一一作了规定，并经双方签字，那么这份备忘录的性质与合同无异，在法律上具有约束力。

4. 意向书

意向书（letter of intent）只是双方当事人为了达成某项协议所做出的一种意愿表示，它不是法律文件，对有关当事人没有约束力。但意向书上载明双方的实现目标设想、意愿可作为进一步谈判的参考和依据。

5. 定单

定单（order）是指由进口商或实际买户拟定的货物定购单。在出口业务中，外贸企业于交易达成后，将合同或确认书缮制一式两份，经签署后寄给国外客户，要求其签署后，将合同退回一份，以备存查。但有些客户将其定单寄来，要求我方签回，以便于我方据以履行交货和交单等合同义务，有的还寄来正本一式两份，要求我方签署后退回一份，这种经洽谈成交后寄来的定单，实际上是国外客户的购货合同或购货确认书。

（三）书面合同的内容

书面合同的内容一般包括下列三个部分。

1. 约首

约首是指合同的序言部分，其中包括合同的名称和编号，订约双方当事人的名称和地址（要求写明全称），除此之外，在合同序言部分常常写明双方订立合同的意愿和执行合同的保证。

2. 正文

正文是合同的主体部分，具体列明各项交易的条件或条款，如品名品质条款、数量条款、价格条款、包装条款、装运条款、支付条款及商检、索赔、仲裁和不可抗力条款等。

3. 约尾

一般列明合同的份数，使用文字及其效力，订约的时间、地点、生效的时间以及双方当事人的签字等内容。合同的缔约地点将涉及合同准据法的问题，因此要慎重对待。我国的出口合同的缔约地点一般都写在我国，有时合同将缔约时间和地点在约首订明。

（四）合同的修改与终止

交易双方合同一经订立，就成为具有法律效力的文件，对订立的双方均有法律约束力，双方应当按照合同的约定履行自己的义务，任何一方不得擅自变更或者解除合同。

但在实际业务中，合同虽经双方确认并签字，有时一方或双方当事人发现需要对合同的某些内容加以修改或补充，在此情况下必须经过双方协商同意才能对合同进行修改。

Export Business Negotiation and Conclusion of Contract

The export business negotiation is one of the most important step in foreign trade since it is the foundation of the contract, while the contract is the result of the business negotiation.

The whole business process i. e. , from the business negotiation to the performance of the contract is quite complicated. The contents of business negotiation shall not only include the basic contractual rights and duties of both parties, but also include the likely arisen disputes and the relative measures to prevent and handle them.

The two parties shall negotiate amicably on the basis of the principles of equality and mutual benefit; and the contract shall be in conformity with the regulations and requirements of relative laws and international practices.

A. Making Preparation for Export Business

An enterprise which decides to go into export and try to canvass orders from abroad will first engage in an exploration of the opportunities which its products have in the markets to which it wishes to export. The exporter may have inhouse experts or he may consult other marketing experts on marketing information, techniques, strategies, etc. He may visit the overseas markets himself or send representatives to make marketing surveys. He may receive direct enquires from importing companies abroad and may also be contacted by overseas customers who may have obtained the name and address from advertisements in the newspapers or by other means.

However, it is very rare that an exporter can sell his products directly to his remote overseas customers. It is impossible for the exporter to go to every country to find out whether his products can sell on a particular market. Therefore, market research is very useful both for the newly established trading companies to build up business relations with overseas customers, and for the early established ones which have regular customers to expand their business.

First of all, the exporter should use various trade statistics and literature published by most countries and world trade organization to narrow down the scope of his research. Important information sources include: national trade statistics which indicate a number of importing houses, wholesalers, retailers and other kinds of marketing intermediaries (information classified according to the types of products trade journals and directories, banks, international organizations such as the International Chamber of Commerce, and the China Council for promotion of International Trade).

After carefully studying the information obtained from the above mentioned sources, the exporters will find out what countries are not importing the specific products and from what sources. He can judge the amount of business and the rate of growth or decline. Then he may choose a number of target markets which merit further study. The market research mainly includes the analysis is of marketing opportunities, investigations as to the needs of customers or end-users for the products and market forecasting.

Secondly, the exporter must bear in mind the cultural and social background of his target markets, such as the language, religion and the local people's aesthetical viewpoints, etc. Since all these factors influence people's consumption patterns, a deep understanding of them will help the exporter to predict the changes in the market and follow the new market trend.

Thirdly, the exporter must know the relevant government policies; what kind of product is limited or restricted in import activities? Are they restricted because of shortage of foreign currency, tendency to protect national industries or safety and sanitation requirements? What kind of goods does the government levy high tax against?

Fourthly, geographical factors may influence profoundly on the distribution of goods and the development of marketing channels in a country. The temperature, altitude and humidity extremes may affect the proper functioning of some equipment. Products which function well in temperate zones do not always perform well in the tropical area. With regard to products like timber, food and paper, the amount of water absorption or evaporation in transit can be very influential.

Finally, the exporter must take into account the political risks (whether there are military clashes), the transportation infrastructure (whether there are ports, railroads, highways, airports, etc. available), and the local legal systems (since no single uniform international commercial law governing exporting transactions exists).

B. General Procedure in Business Negotiation

Under normal circumstances, the business negotiation may be carried out through correspondence, cables and telexes or be conducted orally or both. In international practices, the business negotiation will usually go through 4 steps, i.e., enquiry, offer, counteroffer and acceptance.

1. Enquiry

In International trade, enquiries are usually made by the buyers without engagement to get information about the goods to be ordered, such as quality, quantity, price, delivery date and terms.

The enquiry made by the buyer is also called invitation make an offer. For example, a foreign customer may make an enquiry by cable to our Light Industrial Products Import & Export Corporation.

"BOOKABLE MAXAM BRAND DENTAL CREAM LARGE SIZE MAX 10,000 GROSS PLSCBL LOWEST PRICE EARLIEST DELIVERY TIME".

In some cases the enquiry can also be made by the seller, which is called invitation to make a bid. For example, our Light Industrial Products Import & Export Corporation may send a cable to a foreign customer.

"CAN SUPPLY MAXAM DENTAL CREAM USD 0.50 PERPC MAR SHPMT CBLREP IF INTERESTED".

The points that the buyer should pay attention to when making an enquiry are:

1) Although an enquiry can be made to one or more suppliers simultaneously, the buyer should not give away his real intentions otherwise the suppliers will sense that he is in urgent demand for the goods.

2) When making an enquiry, besides the prices of the goods, the buyer may ask for more information such as the specification, packing, delivery date and other terms.

3) Although making an enquiry is the first step in the business negotiation, it is not an essential one and the enquiry will not bind upon both parties.

4) Enquiries should be brief, specific, courteous and reasonable.

In return, the answers to enquiries should be prompt, definite and helpful.

5) Although an enquiry is not binding upon both parties, if the contract is concluded on the basis of it and in the performance of the contract any disputes arise, the contents of the enquiry can be taken as an integral part of the documents and be used as evidence to handle the disputes.

2. Offer

An offer is a promise conditioned on acceptance which, no matter whether from an exporter or an importer, must be communicated to the offeree and must clearly undertake a performance definite as to all essential terms.

In international trade practices, there are two kinds of offers, i. e., firm offer and non-firm offer.

A firm offer is a promise to sell goods at a stated price, usually within a stated period of time.

In making a firm offer mention should be made of the time of shipment and the mode of payment desired in addition; an exact description of the goods should be given and, if possible, a pattern or sample should be sent to the offeree for examination.

A firm offer, unlike a quotation, once it has been accepted within its stipulated validity it can not be withdrawn.

A non-firm offer is an offer without engagement. In most cases, the contents of a non-firm offer are not clear and definite, the main terms and conditions are not complete. For example, "OFFER NORTHEAST CHINA SOYBEAN 10,000 M/T OUR REFERENCE PRICE USD 300 PER M/T FOB DALIAN SUBJECT TO OUR FINAL CONFIRMATIONS".

The above example is a non-firm offer, because:

1) The contents of the offer is not clear and definite, e. g., "OUR REFERENCE PRICE USD 300 PER M/T".

2) The main terms and conditions are not complete, since this offer has not stipulated the quality, crop year, packing, delivery time of the goods, terms of payment, etc.

3) There is a restrictive condition, i. e., "SUBJECT TO OUR FINAL CONFIRMATION".

The party who makes an offer is called an offerer, the offeror may be the buyer or the seller, in the case of the seller, the offer is called a selling offer, while in the case of the buyer, it is called a buying offer or bidder. In import and export trade, the importer may request the exporter to make an offer or the importer himself may make a bid to the exporter to buy certain goods.

A satisfactory offer will include the following aspects:

1) The goods mentioned in the offer should be described without any ambiguity, including quality, specification, quantity, packing, unit price, origin, etc.

2) Terms of payment should be expressly stated.

3) Terms of delivery, including the mode of transportation, shipment time, place of shipment and destination, partial shipments and transhipment, shipping documents, trans-

port insurance, etc., should be clearly stipulated.

4) The period for which the offer is valid should be indicated.

Clause 1, article 14 of "the United Nations Convention on Contracts for the International Sale of Goods" stipulates: "A proposal for concluding a contract addressed to one or more specific persons constitutes an offer if it is sufficiently definite and indicates the intention of the offerer to be bound in case of acceptance. A proposal is sufficiently definite if it indicates the goods and expressly or implicitly fixes or makes provision for determining the quantity and the price".

According to this stipulation, the formation of an offer shall possess the following 4 basic conditions:

1) The offer shall be made to one or more specific persons. The offer shall be the definite representation in which the offerer expresses that he shall conclude the transaction on the terms and conditions stipulated therein.

2) The offer shall indicate the intention of the offerer to be bound in case of acceptance. This intention may be indicated by terms as "firm" offer "offer with engagement" etc.

3) Contents of the offer shall be definite, i. e., trade terms of the offer shall be complete, clear and final.

In our international trade practice, a complete offer shall include the quality, quantity, packing, price, terms of delivery of the goods and terms of payment.

But in some cases, while some offers are often made without listing all the above-mentioned terms, they are in fact complete.

1) The two parties may arrive at an agreement on "general terms and conditions" in advance, which have already included the main trade terms.

2) In business negotiations, the offerer often quotes the main trade terms from previous letters, cables, telexes, contracts etc. and declares that the major terms in the offer are same as the previous ones.

3) The two parties may have already formed certain trade practices which are known to them.

A definite offer also requires that the terms be clear. For example, if the offerer declares that "the price is only for your reference" or "delivery may be made in August or in September", the offer will be unclear.

A firm offer shall be final, i. e., without any restrictive conditions, such as subject to our final confirmation, subject to prior sale, "without engagement".

4) The offer shall be sent to the offeree and contain the term of validity.

An offer becomes effective when it reaches the offeree. For example, the offerer makes an offer by letter or cable, if the letter or cable loses during the transmission, the offer will not take effect.

An offer becomes effective when it reaches the offeree and is terminated until the date of validity stipulated in the offer. If an offer doesn't clearly stipulate the time of validity, it will be effective within a reasonable time. An oral offer unless otherwise agreed, must be accepted immediately unless the circumstances indicate otherwise.

In our export business, the most commonly used methods to stipulate time of validity are:

(1) Stipulate the latest date for acceptance, for example:

OFFER SUBJECT TO REPLY HERE TENTH;

OFFER SUBJECT TO REPLY HERE ON OR BEFORE TENTH;

OFFER VALID TILL TENTH OUR TIME.

(2) Stipulate a period of time for acceptance, for example:

OFFER VALID FOR THREE DAYS;

OFFER SUBJECT TO REPLY IN TEN DAYS.

As to this method, Article 20 in the United Nations Convention on Contracts for the International Sale of Goods "stipulates" A period of time for acceptance fixed by the offerer in a telegram or a letter begins to run from the moment the telegram is handed in for dispatch or from the date shown on the letter or, if no such date is shown, from the date shown on the envelope. A period of time for acceptance fixed by the offerer by telephone, telex or other means of instantaneous communication, begins to run from the moment the offer reaches the offeree. Official holidays or non-business days occurring during the period for acceptance are included in calculating the period.

However, if a notice of acceptance cannot he delivered at the address of the offerer on the last day of the period because that day alls on an official holiday or a nonbusiness day at the place of business of the offerer, the period is extended until the first business day which follows.

(3) Not stipulate clearly the time of validity, for example:

OFFER ··· REPLY BY TELEX;

OFFER ··· CABLE REPLY IMMEDIATELY;

OFFER ··· REPLY PROMPTLY;

OFFER ··· REPLY IMMEDIATELY;

OFFER ··· REPLY BY URGENT TELEGRAM;

OFFER ··· REPLY AS SOON AS POSSIBLE.

Withdrawal or revocation of the offer is another matter worthy of close attention.

An offer, even if it is irrevocable, may be withdrawn if the withdrawal reaches the offeree before or at the same time as the offer.

As to whether an offer can be revoked or not, different laws have different explanations.

1) The British laws and the American laws stipulate that an offer can be revoked at any time before acceptance, except the offer which is made with a consideration or signed and sealed by the offerer.

2) The law of the Continental countries stipulate that the offer cannot be revoke within the time of validity.

3) Article 16 of "the United Nations Convention on Contracts for the International Sale of Goods" stipulate "Until a contract is concluded, an offer may be revoked if the revocation reaches the offeree before he has dispatched an acceptance. However, an offer cannot be revoked a. if it indicates, whether by setting a fixed time for acceptance or otherwise, that it is irrevocable (or b. if it was reasonable for the offeree to rely on the offer as being irrevocable and the offeree has acted in reliance on the offer."

In the following cases, an offer is terminated:

1) The time validity stipulated in the offer becomes due;

2) The offeree rejects or makes a counter offer;

3) The offerer revokes the offer before acceptance.

3. Counter – Offer

After the offeree has received the firm offer, he may accept it and conclude the business with the offeror, or he may not accept it, or may not accept it wholly and put forward some additions, modifications, limitations, etc. as to the basic terms and conditions contained in the offer. Once a counter-offer is made, the original offer made by the offerer loses its effectiveness.

In Article 19, "the United Nations Convention on Contracts for the International Sale of Goods" stipulates:

1) A reply to an offer which purports to be an acceptance but contains additions limitations or other modifications is a rejection of the offer and constitutes a counter-offer;

2) However, a reply to an offer which purports to be an acceptance but contains additional or different terms which do not materially alter the terms of the offer constitues an acceptance, unless the offerer, without undue delay, objects orally to the discrepancy or dispatches a notice to that effect. If he does not so object, the terms of the contract are the terms of the offer with the modifications contained in the acceptance;

3) Additional or different terms relating among other things, to the price, payment, quality and quantity of the goods, place and time of delivery, extent of one party's liability to

the other or the settlement of disputes are considered to alter the terms of the offer materially.

4. Acceptance

Article 18 of "the United Nations Convention on Contracts for the International Sale of Goods" stipulates: "A statement made by … or other conduct of the offeree indicating assent to an offer is an acceptance. Silence or inactivity does not in itself amount to acceptance."

A valid acceptance shall possess the following 4 conditions:

1) Acceptance shall be made by a specific offeree. The acceptance made by the third party will not be effective.

2) Acceptance shall be declared in certain ways, either orally or in a written form, silence or inactivity does not in itself amount to acceptance.

3) Acceptance shall reach the offerer within the time of validity. If the parties are in each others presence, when the offeree says "I accept", no problem arises. But when they deal with it at a distance from each other, an exception will be created to the rule that acceptance takes effect only when communicated. The exception is as follows: if the offeree in sending his acceptance uses the means authorized by the offerer, the acceptance takes effect at the moment it is placed in the process of communication by that means. On the other hand, if the offeree varies the means the normal rule applies and the acceptance becomes effective and the contract is concluded only when it is actually communicated.

To illustrate, let us suppose the offerer sends an offer to the offeree by mail, awaiting the latter's reply by mail and the offeree accepts by posting his letter of acceptance. At the moment his letter is dropped in the mail box, the contract is formed. Even though the letter may be lost in the mail transmission, and the offerer is without knowledge that his offer has been accepted until it is found out later, he is bound by the acceptance.

But, still in the above case, if the offeree, instead of replying by mail, telegraphs his acceptance, it is in operation until received by the offerer. If the telegram is delayed or lost, a revocation of offer sent by the offerer is received by the offeree before the cable acceptance is delivered to the offerer, it prevents the formation of the contract.

However, an offerer can, by expressly stipulating for receipt of the acceptance, prevent the above exception from operating. All that is necessary is to add in the offer such words as "if I do not hear from you on or before the 20th, I shall assume your answer is negative" or "subject to cable reply here 5th our time". In these cases, acceptance takes effect only at the time the offeree's letter or cable is received by the offerer. Article 18 stipulates: "An acceptance of an offer becomes effective at the moment the indication of assent reaches the offeror. An acceptance is not effective if the indication of assent does not reach the offerer within the time he has fixed or, if no time is fixed, within a reasonable time, due account being taken of the circumstances of the transaction, including the rapidity of the means of communication employed by the offerer."

4) Acceptance shall be in accordance with the offer.

The acceptance shall be unconditional and without any modified clause.

Additional or different terms relating, among other things, to the price, payment, quality and quantity of the goods, place and time of delivery, extent of one party's liability to the other or the settlement of disputes are considered to alter the terms of the offer materially. However, additional or different terms which do not materially alter the terms of the offer constitute an acceptance, unless the offerer objects.

Late acceptance is generally considered invalid. However, a late acceptance is nevertheless effective as an acceptance if without delay the offerer orally so informs the offeree or dispatches a notice to that effect.

If a letter or other writing containing a late acceptance shows that it has been sent in such circumstances, that if it transmission had been normal, it would have reached the offerer in due time, the late acceptance is effective as an acceptance unless, without delay, the offerer orally informs the offeree that he considers his offer as having lapsed or dispatches a notice to that effect.

An acceptance may be withdrawn if the withdrawal reaches the offerer before or at the same time as the acceptance would have become effective.

C. Conclusion of the Contract

In the business negotiation, a contract is concluded after the offeree accepts the offer.

1. Significance of Signing a Written Contract

According to different regulations and laws, the conclusion of a contract depends on the procedure of making an offer by one party and making acceptance by the other, signing a contract in writing is not an essential condition for the effectiveness of the contract.

Article 11 of "the United Nations Convention on Contracts for the International Sale of Goods" stipulates: "A contract of sale need not be concluded in or evidenced by writing and is not subject to any other requirement as to form. It may be proved by any means, including witnesses." But in international trade practices, after the two parties reach an agreement, they usually sign a contract in writing because it is very important.

1) The contract in writing can be used as evidence for the conclusion of the contract.

2) Sometimes the contract in writing is a necessary condition for the effectiveness of the contract.

3) The contract in writing may be used as a foundation for performance of the contract.

2. Forms of the Contract in Writing

In international trade, as to the names and forms of sales contracts, there is no specific limitation. Contracts, confirmation, agreements and memorandums all can be adopted. In our foreign trade business, we mainly adopt the sales contract, sales confirmation, purchase contract and purchase confirmation.

1) **Sales contract.** The contents of a sales contract shall be complete and detailed and shall include the main trade terms and conditions.

2) **Sales confirmation.** A sales confirmation is usually a simplified contract, but it has the same legal effect as a contract. A formal contract embodying all terms of the agreement should be prepared in duplicate, each copy should be signed by both parties, and each party should retain one copy of the contract.

Where a contract is negotiated verbally or by correspondence, and later on one party sends to the other party a contract (or sales confirmation) made in duplicate, one copy of which duly signed has to be returned by the other party.

A contract in writing generally includes 3 parts:

1) **Preamble.** The preamble mainly includes the name, number, date and place of signing the contract, the names and addresses of both parties, etc.

2) **Body.** The body of a contract mainly includes the general and basic terms and conditions, such as the name of the goods, quality, quantity, packing, unit price "total value, date of delivery, port of shipment and port of destination" terms of payment, insurance, inspection, claim, arbitration and force majeure, etc. It may also include the hedging clause, more or less clause, governing law, duration and termination, amendment, etc.

3) **Witness clause.** The witness clause mainly includes the language validity, copies of the contract, signatures, etc.

Import Business Negotiation and Conclusion of Contract

Import business is one of the most important parts in our foreign trade and it plays a great role in our national economy. Through import business, we can buy advanced equipment and technology and some badly-needed materials for the purpose of promoting our modern socialist construction, enlivening our home market as well as enriching our people's life.

A. Preparation for Import Business

Making preparations for import business includes the following steps:

- Work out an import plan;
- File an application with the competent department;
- Fill in an order card;
- Examine and approve of import items by the authorities concerned;
- Make preparations for import business by the appointed import and export company.

As the aggregate amount of foreign exchange available for import is greatly limited to a certain extent by the foreign exchange earning capability, what to import should be based on a reasonable import plan.

1. Work Out an Import Plan

At present, our import goods mainly include the following two kinds:

1) General goods and materials, such as machinery, electronic products, instruments and meters, ore, steel products, textile products, chemical products, grain, oil, etc.;

2) Full set of equipment and assembly lines, including technology.

According to the stipulations of our country, the main import business may be subdivided into two parts: import supported by national foreign exchange and import supported by local foreign exchange. No matter on what scale the import is, how much foreign exchange is involved in and where funds come from, as long as the import items are purchased by using foreign exchange, it shall be based on the national import plans.

We have long-term plans and annual plans.

The long-term plan is worked out by the State Planning Commission together with the relative ministries and commissions and ratified by the State Council.

The annual plan is made out under the instructions of the national long-term plan. The procedure for making out the annual plan is: first, before programming, the provinces, municipalities under the Central Government, autonomous regions, independently planned cities and specific end-users must submit import items to the competent authorities. Then the import items after being examined by the relative competent authorities are submitted to the State Planning Commission and the Ministry of Foreign Economic Relations and Trade for review. Finally, the import items will be submitted to the State Council for ratification. The ratified plan shall be performed strictly.

2. File an Application for Import

In order to make sure that the import goods are really in urgent need, the end-user or import company shall first engage in an exploration of the market abroad and then evaluate the selected items in the light of specific conditions of the enterprise. Finally, in case the import plan is really practical, the end-user or import company may submit a written application to the relative competent authority for approval.

3. Filling in an Order Card

After the import plan is ratified by the competent authority, the import unit will fill in an order card in accordance with the plan and the foreign exchange quota available and then submit it to the competent authority for verification. The Planning Commission together with the competent authority concerned will finally examine and approve the import items.

The main contents of the order card are: the code number of the end-user, card number, total amount, detailed specification, detailed uses of the commodity, time of delivery, mode of transportation, port of destination, name and address of the consignee settling bank, name and account number of the bank with which the end-user opens an account, etc.

4. Examination and Approval by the Authority Concerned

The examination and approval of import items is determined by the scope of foreign exchange used in import business.

In accordance with our foreign trade policy, we handle foreign exchange according to the principle of centralized control and unified management, i. e. Foreign exchange is controlled by the foreign exchange bank and any disbursement involved in foreign trade shall be ratified by the foreign exchange management department.

The foreign exchange to be used in the national import plan is called central foreign exchange; while that to be used in the local import plan is called local foreign exchange which mainly comes from 3 sources:

1) A sum of foreign exchange annually allocated by the Central Government to the local government;

2) The foreign exchange earmarked by the Central Government or the local revolving foreign exchange or short-term foreign exchange loan;

3) The portion of foreign exchange retained by the local government.

The principles of examination and approval by the competent authorities concerned are:

1) The commodity that can be produced at home and can meet the demand of the people shall not be imported.

2) The commodity which can be produced at home, but cannot meet the demand of the people both in quality and in quantity, may be imported properly.

3) The commodity which cannot be produced at home, and is needed urgently shall be imported to the best of our abilities.

4) The advanced technology and equipment which may strengthen our self-reliance abili-

ty and fasten our modern construction shall be given priority to importing.

5) Making preparations for import business by the import and export company:

Before handling import business, the import and export company shall make out a business project based on market research. The main contents should usually include the quantity to be ordered, technological requirements, time arrangement, purchase area, choice of manufacturers, control of procurement prices, trade terms, etc.

B. Import Business Negotiation

The import business negotiation is similar to the export business negotiation, but it is more complicated. It may be carried out through face-to-face negotiations or by correspondence.

1. The Procedure of Import Business Negotiation on General Cargoes

The general procedure of import business negotiation includes five steps: i. e., inquiry, offer, comparison of the prices, counter-offer and acceptance, among which offer and acceptance are essential.

Enquiry: In import business, enquiry is usually made by the buyer for the purpose of inviting the seller to make an offer in the enquiry. In case of having known what goods the seller is managing, we may put forward certain trade terms directly and request the seller to make an offer so as to get information about the goods, such as price, quantity, specification, delivery date, etc. This is generally referred to as specific enquiry. In some other cases, as the case may be, we may make general enquiries.

When making enquiry, we should pay attention to the tactics and strategy. We should make enquiry with a definite object in view. It is inadvisable to make enquiries to many sellers abroad simultaneously without careful consideration. As to goods which are monopolized by a few groups abroad, we may make several enquiries at the same time in order to make the sellers abroad compete with each other, which is quite profitable to us.

2. Comparison of Prices and Counter – Offer

After receiving the offers from abroad, we must analyse the trade terms all-sidedly and make a thorough comparison of the prices.

As to common goods, the comparison of prices is comparatively simple since it only concerns the specific trade terms, such as quality, specification, quantity, delivery date and terms of payment, etc.

But as to technological equipment, the comparison of prices is quite complicated. If it is a single machine, the comparison of prices mainly involves the differences of material prices, of structural prices, and of serial prices. Material price differences refer to the fact that under the same conditions, prices of steel and other materials used in manufacturing the machine are different. Structural price differences refer to the price differences directly resulting from the structure of the machine. Serial price differences refer to the price differences made, in case of the materials and structures being the same, on account of the differences of the specification, performance and efficiency.

As to a full set of equipment, the comparison of prices may be carried out by comparing the single machines which make up the full set of equipment.

Besides the above mentioned points, we should also, under the same conditions, compare the other trade terms, such as delivery date, terms of payment, etc.

After comparison of prices, we may choose a suitable one and make a counter-offer. When making the counter-offer, we must pay attention to the following points:

1) We shall make a counter-offer duly according to our buying intention and proper opportunity. The counter-offer shall be made after careful comparison of prices which absolutely cannot be neglected.

2) We shall put forward different counter-offer conditions according to the result of market investigation. In case supply exceeds demand in the market, we may make counter-offer strict, vice versa.

3) The counter-offer includes not only the price, but also other trade terms. So we must make a comprehensive analysis. We may make a counter-offer in respect to the price directly, and demote the other unessential terms to force the seller to reduce the price.

In case the seller insists on his price, we may put forward other additional terms, for example we may request him to change the L/C at sight to the L/C after sight, or payment under the L/C to collection, or FOB trade terms to FOB stowed, etc.

4) Acceptance: in business negotiations, in case we agree to the contents of a firm offer completely, we may accept the offer within the valid time, or our counter offer is accepted by the other party. As long as the offer is effectively accepted, the transaction is concluded and is binding upon both parties.

3. Negotiation on Technology

When importing technical equipment, in case technology transfer is involved, we usually open face-to-face negotiations with the seller.

The center of technology negotiation is to determine the trade terms concerning technology transfer in the contract, which mainly include the following points:

1) The seller shall guarantee that the transferred technology is valid; technology provided by the seller shall be in conformity with the norm and effect stipulated in the contract. At the same time, the seller shall guarantee that the technology transferred does not infringe upon

the industrial property right of any third party.

2) Price of technology: The price of technology is usually the focus over which the two parties will drive a hard bargain during the negotiation.

The price of technology refers to the fees for use collected by the seller for his transfer of technology which are generally made up of 3 parts, i.e., direct cost, distribution to the expenses resulting from research and development of the technology, losses sustained by the seller resulting from transferring the technology.

3) Mode of payment: There are 3 modes of payment, i.e., lump-sum payment, royalty payment, royalty and initial payment. The mode of payment is determined by the level of the technology availability of the funds financed by the buyer, economic performance brought about by the technology.

4) Restrictive clause: The seller may sometimes take advantage of the technological superiority to impose some unreasonable stipulations upon the buyer. In principle, we usually do not accept such clauses.

5) Governing Law: The Law negotiation mainly concerns the matter that which kind of law shall be adopted to explain and govern the rights and obligations of the two parties or during the performance of the contract, which kind of law shall be used to settle disputes, if any.

In practice, if one party is not willing to accept the law of the other party's country, nor that of a third country as the governing law, the two parties shall stipulate the arbitration clause in the contract. In case of disputes, the arbitration institution will determine a suitable law according to the relative arbitration rule.

C. Conclusion of Import Contract

As long as the offer is accepted, the two parties shall conclude and sign the import contract. The format of the import contract is generally made out by our party.

1. Contents of the Contract

1) Description or specification, and unit prices. If the specifications of the goods are complicated or if they concern the technical order, an attachment shall be used for further explanations, which has the same legal effect as the contract.

Unit prices usually include the unit price of the goods and the fees for use of the technology, which are listed respectively.

2) Total amount: Besides the total amount of the goods listed, we shall also list other charges and expenses, if any.

3) Origin and name of manufacturer: The main purpose in providing this stipulation in

the contract is to determine the rate of customs duties and to make sure where the products come from.

4) Packing: The packing of the goods shall be strong enough to go through the long distance transportation. In case of insufficient packing, the seller shall be responsible for the loss of, or damage to the goods.

5) Shipping mark: The shipping mark of the goods shall catch the eye and shall indicate the number, volume, gross weight, net weight, etc. of the goods as well as handling instructions, such as "this way up" "handle with care" "keep away from heat", etc.

6) Time of shipment: Under FOB trade terms, it is we who shall be responsible for dispatching the ship for carrying the goods. In the contract, we shall stipulate that should the carrying vessel chartered by the buyer arrive at the loading port within the time limit, in the event of the seller's failure in effecting shipment upon arrival of the vessel, all losses, including the dead freight, demurrage, fines, etc. thus incurred shall be for the seller's account; Should the buyer fail to dispatch the vessel within the laydays previously declared by the seller or the shipping agent, all losses, including the storage charges, insurance premium etc. at the port of shipment shall be borne by the buyer.

7) Loading port: Under FOB terms, the port of shipment is the port to which the buyer dispatches the ship. In case the seller requires to change the port of shipment, he shall get the prior agreement on the part of the buyer. In case the contract stipulates two or more ports of shipment, he shall advise the buyer of the name of the port certain days before the month of shipment.

8) Shipping advice: Under FOB terms, the contract shall stipulate that the seller shall advise the buyer by cable, certain days before the contracted time of delivery, of the contract number, name of commodity, quantity, value, number of packages, gross weight, measurements, and date of readiness at the port of shipment in order for the buyer to book shipping space, or charter a vessel, absence of such advice within the time limit specified above shall be considered as the sellers readiness to deliver the goods on any date during the time contracted and the buyer shall arrange for shipping space or dispatching the vessel accordingly. The buyer shall advise the seller by cable, certain days before the expected loading date, of the contract number, estimated laydays, name of vessel, quantity to be loaded, and shipping agent in order for the seller to arrange shipment. In case of necessity for substitution of the vessel or alteration of the shipping schedule, the buyer or the shipping agent shall duly advise the seller to the same effect.

Immediately after the completion of loading of the goods on board the vessel, the seller shall advise the buyer by cable of the contract number, name of goods, quantity or weight loaded, invoice value, name of vessel, port of shipment, sailing date and port of destination.

Should the buyer be made unable to arrange insurance in time owing to the seller failure to give the above mentioned advice of shipment by cable, the seller shall be held responsible for any and all damage and or loss attributable to such failure.

9) Insurance: If under CFR or FOB terms, the contract shall stipulate that insurance on the goods after shipment shall be taken out by the buyer. If under CIF terms, the contract shall stipulate that the seller shall cover insurance on the goods for 110% of the invoice value against all risks, (or FPA, or WPA) and a certain additional risk agreed in the contract, usually with W/W clause as well.

10) Documents: The seller shall provide the following documents to the paying bank:

- Full set of clean on board ocean Bs/L, made out to order and blank endorsed, marked freight prepaid or freight to collect;
- Commercial invoice in triplicate;
- Packing list or weight memo usually in triplicate;
- Quality certificate usually in triplicate;
- Other relative documents.

11) Payment: According to the agreement arrived at in the negotiation, payment may be made by the L/C, collection, remittance or the combination of those terms of payment.

12) Technical documentation: If technology transfer is included in the transaction, all the necessary technical documents agreed on by the both parties shall be provided sufficiently in time.

（资料来源：宋秀峰. 国际贸易（双语版）[M]. 中国发展出版社，2010.）

➤ 本章小结

国际商品市场调研包括市场环境和市场行情调研。企业进入国际市场的渠道多种多样，归纳起来主要有三种，即间接出口、直接出口和国外生产。为了更有效地做好交易前的准备工作，使对外洽商交易有所依据，一般都需要先制订经营方案，并通过相关渠道对交易客户进行必要的资信调查，以保证经营意图的贯彻和实施。中国企业到国外注册商标主要有两条途径：一是直接向所在国逐一申请商标注册，即逐一国家注册；二是办理商标国际注册。

交易磋商是指买卖双方通过一定程序就交易的各项条件进行洽商的全过程。交易磋商在形式上可分为口头和书面两种。交易的一般程序包括邀请发盘、还盘、接受和签约合同等环节，其中发盘和接受是交易成立的基本环节，也是合同成立的必要条件。

国际货物买卖合同成立应具备必要的条件。在我国对外贸易业务中，主要采用的书面合同是正式合同和确认书两种。电子商务与传统交易有很大的不同，属于一种新的交易形式。

➢ 本章名词

国际商品市场调研　商品经营方案　国际货物买卖合同　诚实信用原则　交易磋商　询盘　发盘　还盘　接受

➢ 理论思考

1. 交易磋商前应做哪些准备工作？
2. 交易磋商一般要经过哪些环节？它们的含义是什么？
3. 一项法律上有效的发盘必须具备哪些条件？
4. 国际谈判策略有哪些？
5. 合同有效成立的条件是什么？

➢ 实训习题

交易前的准备

一、模拟业务背景

2016年9月福州闽江纺织品进出口公司（FUZHOU MINJIANG TEXTILS IMPORT & EXPORT CORP. 86，JINSHAND ROAD，MINHOU DISTRICT，FUZHOU，CHINA）收到新加坡一新客户来函，表明对公司在网上发布的"四方"牌漂布感兴趣。

二、模拟训练任务

根据相关背景及资料，以纺织品进出口公司业务员身份，模拟完成：

1. 客户资信调查；
2. 与客户建立业务关系：函件需反映向客户寄送样品、空白合同（带有一般交易条件）、介绍"四方"牌漂布、要求客户确认等内容。

三、模拟训练资料

1. 客户名称、地址：

OVERSEAS TRADING CO. LTD.，

100 JULAN SULTAN # 01－20 SULTAN PLAZA SINGAPORE

2. "四方"漂布资料：

（1）货号：9801－1；

（2）规格：坯布经纬纱-30 支×36 支，每英寸经纬密度 72×69，每匹幅宽 35/36 英寸，长 42 码；

（3）包装捆（布），每捆 20 匹，体积：长 19（英寸）×宽 17（英寸）×高 23（英寸），毛重：71 公斤，净重：69 公斤。

交易磋商与合同的签订

一、模拟业务背景

（接上述任务）新加坡客户接我方去函后，确认了我方样品及交易一般条件于 2016 年 9 月 10 日来函，要求我方报价。经谈判，我方与新加坡客户达成初笔漂布买卖交易。

二、模拟训练任务

根据所给条件及要求，模拟双方谈判及签约过程。

1. 根据客户 9 月 10 日来函，向客户发盘（报价）
2. 回复客户还盘
3. 对客户还盘进行再还盘
4. 根据双方往来函电缮制出口销售确认书
5. 寄送合同，要求客户会签和准时开证

三、模拟训练资料、要求

（一）发盘（报价）资料、要求

1. 客户 9 月 10 日来函

SAMPLES AND GENERAL TERMS AND CONDITIONS CONFIRMED. PLEASE OFFER FIRM 9,801-14,200 YARDS.

2. 报价要求

（1）报价数量—4 200 码；

（2）报价价格—CIF 新加坡每码 1.48 美元；

（3）装运期—2010 年 11 月；

（4）支付方式—不可撤销即期信用证；

（5）报价日期—2010 年 9 月 12 日。

（二）回复客户还盘资料、要求

1. 9 月 14 日客户还盘

YOURS TWELVETH 8,400 YARDS SHIPMENT NOVEMBER USDOLLARS 1.2 CIFC3 D/P SIGHT PLEASE REPLY SIXTEENTH.

2. 还盘要求：根据还盘情况，自行合理确定。

（三）再还盘资料、要求

1. 客户 9 月 17 日还盘

YOURS 16th OTHER SOURCES SIMILAR QUALITY QUOTING 1.25 COMPETITION KEEN HENCE BEST 1.30 6,720 YARDS 60 DAYS SIGHT.

2. 再还盘要求

考虑竞争特别是初次交易，同意将每码价格降低 0.12 美元、见票 30 天信用证付款，限 19 日前复。

注：模拟填制单据—福州闽江纺织品进出口公司销售确认书

福州闽江纺织品进出口公司

FUZHOU MINJIANG TEXTILS IMPORT & EXPORT CORP.

NO 86，JINSHAN ROAD，JINSHAN DISTRICT，FUZHOU，CHINA

销售确认书

SALES CONFIRMATION　　　　　正本：ORIGINAL

　　　　　　　　　　　　　　　合同号 NO.：

　　　　　　　　　　　　　　　日期 Date：

买方
Buyer：

地址
Address：

电话　　　　　　　传真
Tel：　　　　　　　Fax：

兹经买卖双方同意成交下列商品订立条款如下：

The undersigned sellers and buyers have agreed to close the following transaction according to the terms and conditions stipulated below：

货物名称及规格 Name of commodity and specification	数量 Quantity	单价 Unit price	金额 Amount

总值
Total value：

货运
Shipment：

付款条件

Payment:

包装

Packing:

唛头

Marks & nos.:

保险

Insurance:

买方	卖方
The buyer	The seller

CHAPTER 3

第三章 国际贸易术语和商品的价格

➢ 本章指导

通过对本章的学习要求能够了解国际货物买卖合同中价格术语方面的国际惯例，掌握并能够在进出口业务中运用：

1. 《INCOTERMS 2010》中最常用的几种价格术语关于买卖双方的责任、风险、费用的划分；
2. 佣金和折扣的计算方法及价格换算；
3. 主要术语的价格换算及出口报价。

第一节 国际贸易术语概述

一、贸易术语及其国际惯例

贸易术语又称价格术语，是国际贸易中用于商品报价的方式，是国际贸易与国内贸易相比，最具有"国际"特色的贸易条件。贸易术语由国际惯例规定。

（一）贸易术语的概念

国际贸易中，买卖双方所承担的义务，会影响到商品的价格。在长期的国际贸易实践中，某些和价格密切相关的贸易条件逐渐与价格直接联系在一起，形成了若干报价的模式。每一种模式都规定了买卖双方在某些贸易条件中所承担的义务。用来说明这种义务的术语，称为贸易术语。

贸易术语所表示的贸易条件，主要分两个方面：其一，说明商品的价格构成中，是否包括成本以外的主要从属费用，即运费和保险费；其二，确定交货条件，即说明交货方式与交货地点，以及买卖双方在交接货物方面彼此所承担的责任、费用和风险的划分。

贸易术语是国际贸易中表示价格的必不可少的内容。在报价中使用贸易术语，明确了双方在货物交接方面各自应承担的责任、费用和风险，说明了商品的价格构成，从而简化了交易磋商的手续，缩短了成交时间。

另外，由于规定贸易术语的国际惯例对买卖双方应该承担的义务，作了完整而确切的解释，因而避免了由于对合同条款的理解不一致在履约中可能产生的某些争议。

（二）关于贸易术语的国际惯例

有关贸易术语的国际惯例，主要有三种。

1. 《1932年华沙—牛津规则》（W. O. Rules）

由国际法协会制定，本规则共21条，主要说明CIF买卖合同的性质。具体规定了买卖双方所承担的费用、风险和责任以及所有权转移的方式。

2. 《1941年美国对外贸易定义修正本》

由美国九大商业团体制定，对以下六种术语作了解释：

（1）EX（point of origin）—产地交货价。

（2）FOB—运输工具上交货价。

FOB又分为六种，其中第五种为装运港船上交货价FOB vessel（…named port of shipment）。

（3）FAS—船边交货价。

（4）CFR—成本加保险费、运费。

（5）EX DOCK—目的港码头交货价。

该惯例在美洲国家中影响较大。在与采用该惯例的国家贸易时，要特别注意与其他惯例的差别，双方应在合同中明确规定贸易术语所依据的惯例。

3. 《国际贸易术语解释通则》

《2010年国际贸易术语解释通则》（International Rules for Interpretation of Trade Terms 2010）（以下简称《2010年通则》），缩写形式为《Incoterms 2010》。它是国际商会为了统一对各种贸易术语的解释而制定的。最早的通则产生于1936年，后来为适应国际贸易业务发展的需要，先后进行过多次的修改和补充。现行的《2010年国际贸易术语解释通则》是国际商会根据国际贸易实践发展的需要，在《2000年国际贸易术语解释通则》的基础上修订产生的，并于2011年1月1日生效。

《2010年国际贸易术语解释通则》（见表3-1）考虑了无关税区的不断扩大，商业交易中电子信息使用的增加，货物运输中对安全问题的进一步关注以及运输方式的变化。《2010年国际贸易术语解释通则》更新并整合与"交货"相关的规则，将术语总数由原来的13条减至11条，并对所有规则做出更加简洁、明确的陈述。值得注意的是，新版本出版后，《2000年国际贸易术语解释通则》仍然有效。合同各方可选择任意一版《国际贸易术语解释通则》使用,但必须在合同中注明所使用的版本。

表 3-1　　　　　　　　　　　《2010 年通则》的贸易术语分类

组别	术语	术语中文
适用于任一或多种运输方式	EXW Ex Works (… Named Place)	工厂交货(……指定地)
	FCA Free Carrier (… Named Place)	货交承运人(……指定地)
	CPT Carriage Paid to (… Named Place of Destination)	运费付至(……指定目的地)
	CIP Carriage, Insurance Paid to (… Named Place of Destination)	运费、保险费付至(……指定目的地)
	DAT Delivered at Terminal (… Named Terminal at Port or Place of Destination)	运输终端交货(……指定目的港或目的地)
	DAP Delivered at Place (… Named Place of Destination)	目的地交货(……指定目的地)
	DDP Delivered Duty Paid (… Named Place of Destination)	完税后交货(……指定目的地)
只适用于海运及内河运输	FAS Free Alongside Ship (… Named Port of Shipment)	装运港船边交货(……指定装运港)
	FOB Free on Board (… Named Port of Shipment)	装运港船上交货(……指定装运港)
	CFR Cost and Freight (… Named Port of Destination)	成本加运费(……指定目的港)
	CIF Cost, Insurance and Freight (… Named Port of Destination)	成本加保险费、运费(……指定目的港)

若沿袭《2000 年通则》的分组法,《2010 年通则》中的贸易术语包括以下几个方面。

E 组:EXW。当卖方在其所在地或其他指定地点将货物交给买方处置时,即完成交货,卖方不办理出口清关手续或将货物装上运输工具。

F 组:FCA、FAS、FOB。要求卖方在装运地或装运港将货物交至买方指定的承运人而不支持主要运费。F 组术语属于交运合同术语。

C 组:CFR、CIF、CPT、CIP。要求卖方按照通常条件自付费用订立运输合同,卖方要支付货物按照惯常航线和习惯方式运至约定地点所需的通常费用,在货物以适当方式交付运输后,货物灭失或损坏的风险及发生意外而发生的额外费用由买方承担。C 组术语属于交运合同术语。

D 组:DAP – Delivered At Place,DAT – Delivered At Terminal,DDP – Delivered Duty Paid。卖方负责将货物运至约定目的地,卖方必须承担货物运至该地前的全部风险和费用。D 组术语属于到货合同术语。

《2010年通则》实际上是把术语分为两类：适用于各种运输方式和水运。11种术语中，只适用于海运及内河运输的有FAS、FOB、CFR、CIF四种，其他7种适用于任何运输方式。

第二节　六种主要贸易术语

《2010年通则》中共有11个贸易术语，其中使用较多的贸易术语：FOB、CFR、CIF、FCA、CPT和CIF。

因此，熟悉这6种贸易术语的含义、买卖双方的义务，以及在使用中应注意的问题，特别重要。

一、FOB

1. FOB术语的基本含义

FOB全称为free on board（…Named Port of Shipment）即船上交货（……指定装运港），习惯上称为装运港船上交货。其含义为：卖方必须在指定装运港、在买方指定的船上交货，或者取得被如此交付后的货物。自货物装上船起，货物灭失或损坏的风险即告转移，自此时起买方承担一切费用。卖方还负责办理货物出口清关手续。本术语只能用于海运或内河运输。

这里的"取得被如此交付后的货物"是《2010年通则》的新规定，针对的是国际贸易中的连环销售（string trade）现象。在农矿产品销售中，相对于工业品的销售，货物经常在运输过程中被频繁转售多次。这种情况发生时，在链条中间环节的卖方并不"装运"这些货物，因为这些货物已经由最开始的卖方装运了。连环运转中间环节的卖方因而履行其对买方的义务，并不是通过装运货物，而是通过"取得"已经被装运的货物。

例：USD 200 PER M/T FOB Shanghai Incoterms 2010。

2. 买卖双方基本义务

采用FOB术语，买卖双方各自承担的基本义务概括如下。

（1）卖方义务。

①提供符合合同的货物，在合同规定的日期或期间内，在指定装运港，将货物按港口惯常方式交至买方指派的船上，或者取得被如此交付的货物，并给予买方充分通知。

②负责取得出口许可证或其他官方文件，办理货物出口清关。

③承担货物在指定装运港装上船为止的一切费用和风险。

④负责提交商业发票和证明货已交至船上的通常单据,或具有同等效力的电子信息。

(2)买方义务。

①负责租船订舱,支付运费,并给予卖方关于船名、装船地点和要求交货时间的充分通知。

②负责取得进口许可证或其他官方文件,办理货物进口清关以及必要时的过境手续。

③承担货物在指定装运港装上船后的一切费用和风险。

④接受卖方提交的与合同相符的单据,受领符合合同的货物,按合同规定支付货款。

3. 使用 FOB 术语需注意的问题

(1) 风险的转移。

在《2000 年通则》中,FOB 风险转移点为装运港船舷。在装船货物跌落码头或海中所造成的损失,均由卖方承担;货物装上船之后,包括在启航前和在运输过程中所发生的损坏或灭失,则由买方承担。

在《2010 年通则》中,风险转移点修改为货物装上船为止。增加了卖方装运港义务,风险也在货物装船后转移。

但要注意,风险有时会提前转移。若在交货期限届满时,买方所派船只未能过来正常接货,而又未曾给予卖方充分的通知,则风险自动转移给买方。

但无论是风险的正常转移还是风险的提前转移都有前提条件,即货物需特定化(Specialization)。即货物已经适当地划归本合同,即已清楚地分开或以其他方式特定为该合同项下的货物。

(2) 关于船货衔接问题(link-up of vessel and goods)。

在 FOB 合同中,由于租船或订舱是由买方负责办理的,因此,买方必须给予卖方关于船名、装船地点及所要求的交货时间的充分通知。若买方没给予卖方上述通知,有可能导致货物灭失或损坏的风险在货物交付前转移,且买方还需承担因此而产生的卖方仓储、保险等一切额外费用。

卖方则必须负责在合同规定的装船期和装运港,将货物装上买方指定的船只。如卖方因货未备妥而不能及时装运,则卖方应承担由此而造成的空舱费(dead freight)或滞期费(demurrage)。

船货衔接问题包括:卖方按时备货,但买方所派船只未能按时到港、提前到港且要提前离开、按时到港但不能完成装货(如舱容不足),则为买方责任;买方所派船只按时到港,但卖方不能按时备货。通常来说,卖方备货好控制,多为买方船只不能按时接货。

在 FOB 合同下,如成交货物的数量不大,只需部分舱位而用班轮装运时,卖方往往按照买卖双方之间明示或默示的协议,代买方办理各项装运手续,包括以卖方自己的名义订舱和取得提单。除非另有协议或根据行业习惯,买方应负责偿付卖方由于代办上述手续而产生的任何费用;同时,卖方订不到舱位的风险由买方承担。

(3)《1941年美国对外贸易定义修订本》和《2010年通则》对FOB术语解释的区别。

《1941年美国对外贸易定义修订本》将FOB概括为六种,其中前三种在出口国指定内陆发货地点的指定内陆运输工具上交货,而第四种是出口国指定出口地点的指定内陆运输工具上交货,第五种是装运港船上交货,第六种是在进口国指定内陆地点交货。第四种和第五种使用时应加以注意。如都是在旧金山交货,如果买方要求在装运港的船上交货,则应在FOB和港口名称之间加"VESSEL"(轮船)变成"FOB轮船旧金山",否则卖方可能按第四种情况在旧金山市的内陆运输工具上交货。

即使都是在装运港船上交货,《2010年通则》中的FOB和《修订本》中的FOB VESSEL对于办理出口手续的规定存在差异。按照《2010通则》上解释,"卖方有义务自负风险和费用,取得出口许可证或其他官方批准的证件,并办理出口必需的海关手续"。但是按照《1941年美国对外贸易定义修订本》的解释,卖方只是"在买方请求并由其负担费用的情况下,协助买方取得由原产地及装运地国家签发的,为货物出口或在目的地进口所必需的各种证件"。

在同美国、加拿大等国家进行的进出口贸易业务中,采用FOB成交时,应对有关问题在协议中定明,以免因解释上的分歧引起争议。

(4)装运通知。

货物装船后,卖方应及时通知买方,以便买方能够及时办理货运保险。所谓"及时",按照惯例,一般可以理解为"在货物装上指定远洋货轮以后的24小时以内"。

关于"装运通知",无论是买方发给卖方的,还是卖方发给买方的,一般专业教科书都不予区别,一律都笼统地叫做"装运通知",而实际上这二者是有区别的,买方发给卖方的,是在货物装运之前,买方把有关预订的船名以及装船时间、地点和有关注意事项告知卖方,叫"装运需知";卖方发给买方的,是货运装运之后,卖方把有关装船的详细信息通知给买方,这才叫"装运通知"。

二、CIF

1. CIF术语的基本含义

CIF的全称是Cost, Insurance and Freight(… named port of destination),即成本加保险费、运费(……指定目的港)。CIF是指卖方将货物装上船或者设法获取这样交付的商品时,即完成交货。卖方必须支付将货物运至指定目的港所必需的费用和运费,但交货后货物灭失或损坏的风险,以至于发生事件而引起的任何额外费用,自卖方转移至买方。在 CIF 术语中卖方还必须为货物在运输灭失或损坏的买方风险取得海上保险。

CIF 术语要求卖方办理货物出口清关。该术语只能用于海运和内河运输。

例：USD 200 PER M/T CIF BANGKOK PORT Incoterms 2010。

2. 买卖双方的基本义务

采用 CIF 术语，买卖双方各自承担的基本义务概括如下。

（1）卖方义务。

①提供符合合同的货物；负责租船订舱，支付至目的港的运费；在合同规定的日期或期间内，在装运港将货物装上船；或者设法获取已按上述方式交付的商品，并给予买方充分的通知。

②承担货物装上船为止的一切费用和风险。

③负责办理货物运输保险，支付保险费。

④负责取得出口许可证或其他官方文件，办理货物出口清关。

（2）买方义务。

①接受卖方提供的与合同相符的单据，受领符合合同的货物，并按照合同规定支付货款。

②承担货物装上船之后的一切费用和风险。

③负责取得进口许可证或其他官方文件，办理货物进口清关及必要时的过境手续。

3. 使用 CIF 术语需注意的问题

（1）保险险别问题。

按照 CIF 术语成交，卖方要办理货运保险，办理保险必须明确险别，因为保险人承担的责任范围不同收取的保险费也不同。在实际操作中，应该明确险别、保险金额等内容。如果没有写清楚，那么就按照惯例操作。根据《2010 年通则》规定，卖方只需要投保最低的险别。但是如果买方要求并由买方承担费用的情况下，可加保战争、罢工和民变险，可以在信用证里注明，实际上可以变通。如果买方特别要求加特殊附加险别，则费用由买方承担。

（2）卖方办理租船订舱问题。

在 CIF 贸易术语下，卖方必须自担费用，按照通常条件订立运输合同，将合同规定的货物，按通常用于运输此类货物的船舶的惯常航线，运至指定目的港。

除非双方另有约定，对于买方提出的关于限制载运船舶的国籍、船龄、船型、船级以及指定装载某班轮工会的船只等项要求，卖方均有权拒绝接受。

（3）象征性交货。

从交货方式来看，CIF 是典型的象征性交货（symbolic delivery）。所谓象征性交货是相对于实际交货（physical delivery）来说的（见表 3-2）。前者指卖方只要按照约定地点完成装运，并向买方提交合同规定的包括物权凭证在内的有关单据，就算完成了交货义务，无须保证到货。后者则是指要在规定的时间、地点，将符合合同规定的货物提交给买方或其指定人，而不能以交单代替交货，在 CIF 条件下交货，卖方凭单交货，买方凭单付款。只要卖方如期向买方提交了合同规定的全套合格单据，即使货物在运输途中损坏或灭失，买方也必须履行付款义务。反之，如果卖方提交的单据不符合要求，即使货物完好无损地运达目的地，买方仍然有权拒绝付款。

表 3-2　　　　　　　　　　象征性交货和实际交货的区别

	象征性交货	实际交货
交货和收货是否同时发生	交货和收货不同时发生	交货和收货同时发生
货交对象	货交承运人或其代理人	货物直接交给买方或卖方指定的人
交单能否代替交货	交单代替交货	交单不能代替交货
是否规定装运期和到货期	只规定装运期限，不规定到货期限	规定装运期限，也规定到货期限
风险转移和买方接受货物是否同时发生	风险转移和买方接受货物不同时发生	风险转移和买方接受货物同时发生

CIF 合同中，要防止出现"要求卖方保证到货或以到货作为付款条件"的陷阱条款。

（4）卖方应该向买方发装运通知。

在 CIF 条件下，虽然买方不急需船名、船期等信息去办理货物保险，但卖方还是应该在适当时候将有关的装运信息通知给买方，以便买方及时办理销售、进口通关以及提货等事宜。

三、CFR

1. CFR 术语的基本含义

CFR 的全称是 Cost and Freight（… named port of destination），即成本加运费（……指定目的港）。CFR 是指卖方在装运港把货物装上船或者卖方获取被如此交付后的货物，即完成交货。卖方必须支付将货物运至指定目的港所必需的费用和运费，但交货后货物灭失或损坏的风险，以及由于交货后发生的事件而引起的任何额外费用，自卖方转移至买方。

CFR 术语要求卖方办理货物出口清关。本术语只能用于海运和内河运输。

例：USD 200 PER M/T CFR BANGKOK PORT Incoterms 2010。

2. 买卖双方的基本义务

采用 CFR 术语，买卖双方各自承担的基本义务概括如下。

（1）卖方义务。

①提供符合合同的货物；租船订舱，支付货物运至目的地的运费；在合同规定的时间和港口，将货物装上船；或者设法获取已按上述方式交付的商品，并给予买方充分的通知。

②承担货物装上船为止的一切费用和风险。

③负责取得出口许可证或其他官方文件，办理货物出口清关。

④负责提供商业发票以及证明货物运至约定目的港的通常的运输单据，或具有同等效力的电子信息。

（2）买方义务。

①接受卖方提供的与合同相符的单据，受领符合合同的货物，按合同规定支付货款。

②承担货物装上船后的一切风险。

③负责取得进口许可证或其他官方文件，办理货物进口清关以及必要时的过境手续。使用 CFR 术语时，买方需自费办理投保事宜，但这是为了其自身利益，并非买方的义务。

3. 使用 CFR 术语需注意的问题

（1）装船通知的重要作用。

卖方需要特别注意的问题是，货物装船后必须及时向买方发出装船的通知，以便买方办理投保手续。因为一般国际贸易惯例以及有些国家的法律，如英国《1839 年货物买卖法》（1979 年修订）规定：如果卖方未向买方发出装船通知，致使买方未能办理货物保险，货物在海运途中的风险由卖方负担。尽管在 FOB 和 CIF 条件下卖方装船后应向买方发出通知，但是 CFR 条件下装船通知，具有更为重要的意义。

（2）注意避免使用买方指定船舶。

在 CFR 条件下卖方支付运费，而如果买方指定船舶可能会增高成本。

四、FCA

1. FCA 术语的基本含义

FCA 的全称是 Free Carrier（... named place），即"货交承运人（……指定地点）"，是指卖方在指定地将经出口清关的货物交给由买方指定的承运人。应该注意，选定的交货地点对在该地装货和卸货义务有影响。如在卖方所在处所交货，卖方负责装货。如在其他任何地方交货，卖方不负责装卸货。本术语适用于任何运输方式，包括多式联运。

《2010 年通则》规定："承运人"是指任何人在运输合同中，承诺通过铁路、公路、海运、空运、内河运输或上述运输的联合方式履行运输或由他人履行运输。如买方指定承运人以外的人收取货物，当卖方将货物交给该人时，即视为已履行了交货义务。

例：USD 200 PER M/T FCA Changsha Incoterms 2010。

2. 买卖双方的基本义务

采用 FCA 术语，买卖双方各自承担的基本义务概括如下。

（1）卖方义务。

①提供符合合同的货物。在合同规定的时间、地点，将货物交给买方指定的承运人，并及时通知买方。

②负责取得出口许可证或其他官方文件，办理货物出口清关。

③承担货交承运人之前的一切费用和风险。

④负责提供商业发票和证明货物已被交付的通常单据，或具有同等效力的电子信息。

（2）买方义务。

①订立自指定地点将货物运至目的地的合同，支付运费，将承运人名称及有关情况及时通知卖方。

②承担货交承运人后的一切费用及风险。

③负责取得进口许可证或其他官方文件，办理货物进口清关及必要时的过境手续。

④接受卖方提交的与合同相符的单据，受领符合合同的货物，按合同规定支付货款。

3. 使用 FCA 术语需注意的问题

（1）交货地点。

采用 FCA 术语，合同中交货地点的规定影响装卸货义务的承担。如在卖方所在处所交货，卖方负责装货。即当卖方将货物装上由买方指定的承运人或代表他行事的另一人提供的运输工具上时，完成交货义务。如在卖方所在地以外的其他地方交货，卖方不负责卸货。即当卖方将装载于运输工具上未卸下的货物交由买方指定的承运人或另一人处置之下时，完成交货义务。如果没有约定特定的交货地点，或者有几个地点可利用，卖方可在交货地选择一个最适合其意图的地点交货。

（2）风险转移。

在采用 FCA 术语成交时，买卖双方的风险是以货交承运人为界，但可能存在风险提前转移的情形。由于在 FCA 术语下，由买方负责订立运输契约，并将承运人名称及有关事项及时通知卖方，如果买方未能及时给予卖方上述通知，或者他所指定的承运人在约定的时间未能接受货物，则自规定的交付货物的约定日期或期限届满之日起，由买方承担货物灭失或损坏的一切风险，但以货物已被划归本合同下为前提条件。

（3）安排运输。

FCA 术语适用于任何运输方式，包括多式联运。由买方负责指定承运人，订立自装运地至目的地的运输合同。但《2010 年通则》同时又规定，如果买方请求，或如果这是一种商业惯例以及买方未在合适的时间内给予相反的指示，只要买方承担风险和费用，卖方可按通常条件订立运输合同。但这并非是卖方的义务，在任何一种情况下，卖方可以拒绝订立运输合同，如果拒绝，必须立即通知买方，以便买方另做安排。

（4）FCA 与 FOB。

FCA 是在 FOB 术语的基础上发展起来的适用于各种运输方式的贸易术语，买卖双方义务划分的原则是完全相同的，卖方都以将经出口清关的货物交给买方指定的承运人（在 FOB 术语下是海运承运人）完成交货义务。因此，FOB 术语可以视作 FCA 术语的一个特例。

由于 FOB 术语仅适用于海运和内河航运，并以货物装上船划分买卖双方承担的风险，其适用范围非常有限。采用非海运或内河航运的贸易，或虽采用海运但不适宜以货物装上船划分风险的运输方式（如集装箱运输、多式联运等）的贸易，均不适宜使用 FOB 术语，应采用 FCA 术语。

五、CPT

1. CPT 术语的基本含义

CPT 的全称是 Carriage Paid to（… named place of destination），即运费付至（……指定目的地）。CPT 是指卖方将货物交给由他指定的承运人，但卖方还必须支付将货物运至指定目的地的运费。买方负担在货物被如此交付后发生的一切风险和任何其他费用。

CPT 术语要求卖方办理货物出口清关手卖。本术语适用于任何运输方式，包括多式联运。

例：USD 30 PER JAR CPT NINGBO AIRPORT Incoterms 2010。

2. 买卖双方的基本义务

采用 CPT 术语，买卖双方各自承担的基本义务概括如下。

（1）卖方义务。

①提供符合合同的货物；订立将货物运至目的地的合同并支付运费；在合同规定的时间、地点将货物交给承运人；及时通知买方。

②负责取得出口许可证或其他官方文件，办理货物出口清关。

③承担货交承运人前的一切风险。

④向买方提供商业发票、通常的运输单据，或具有同等效力的电子信息。

（2）买方义务。

①负责取得进口许可证或其他官方文件，办理货物进口清关及必要时的过境手续。

②承担货交承运人后的一切风险和费用。

③接受卖方提交的与合同相符的单据，受领符合合同的货物，按合同规定支付货款。

从以上买卖双方义务划分可知，CPT 术语下的卖方义务仅比 FCA 下多了办理运输，因此 CPT 的价格构成中含有出口运费，即 CPT 价 = FCA 价 + 运费。其余在交货地点、风险划分上，都是相同的。

3. 使用 CPT 术语时应注意的问题

（1）风险划分。

CPT 术语虽然要求卖方负责办理货物的运输并支付运费，但并不要求卖方负担运输途中的风险和由此产生的额外费用。卖方只承担货物交给承运人控制之前的风险，在多式联运情况下，承担货物交给第一承运人之前的风险。

（2）装运通知。

采用 CPT 术语时，买卖双方要在合同中规定装运期和目的地，以便于卖方选定承运人，订立将货物运至目的地的运输合同。卖方将货物交给承运人后，应及时向买方发出货已交付的通知，便于买方及时为货物投保，以及在目的地受领货物。

（3）CPT 与 CFR。

CPT 是在 CFR 术语的基础上发展起来的适用于各种运输方式的贸易术语，在买卖双方义务划分的原则上，两者是完全相同的；卖方都要负责安排货物自交货地至目的地的运输并负担费用；卖方承担的风险都在交货地点随交货义务的完成而转移至买方；两种术语达成的合同都属于装运合同，卖方只负责按时交货，而不保证到货。在使用上，CFR 术语仅适用于海运和内河航运，且以货物装上船为界划分风险，而 CPT 术语适用于各种运输方式，包括多式联运，以货物交付给承运人为界划分风险。因此，CPT 术语的适用范围比 CFR 术语大得多，不仅适用于航空、铁路、公路等非水上运输方式，也适用于不宜以装上船划分风险的海运集装箱运输及多式联运。

六、CIP

1. CIP 术语的基本含义

CIP 的全文是 Carriage, Insurance Paid to（… named place of destination），即运费、保险费付至（……指定目的地）。CIP 是指卖方将货物交给由他指定的承运人，同时还必须支付将货物运至指定目的地的运费，买方负担在货物被如此交付后发生的一切风险和任何其他费用。在 CIP 术语下卖方还需对货物在运输途中灭失或损坏的风险取得货物保险。

买方应注意到，按 CIP 术语，卖方只需按最低责任的保险险别取得保险。如果买方要得到更大责任保险险别的保障，他需明示地与卖方达成协议，或者自行做额外保险的安排。

CIP 术语要求卖方办理货物出口清关手续。本术语适用于任何运输方式，包括多式联运。

例：USD 30 PER JAR CIP NINGBO AIRPORT Incoterms 2010。

2. 买卖双方的基本义务

采用 CIP 术语，买卖双方各自承担的基本义务概括如下。

（1）卖方义务。

①提供符合合同的货物；订立将货物运往指定目的地的合同并支付运费；在合同规定的时间、地点，将货物交给承运人；及时通知买方。

②承担货交承运人前的风险。

③按照合同的约定投保货物运输险并支付保险费。

④负责取得出口许可证或其他官方文件，办理货物出口清关。

⑤提交商业发票和通常的运输单据，或具有同等效力的电子信息。

（2）买方义务。

①负责取得进口许可证或其他官方文件，办理货物进口清关及必要时的过境手续，承担货交承运人后的一切风险。

②接受卖方提交的与合同相符的单据，受领符合合同的货物，按合同规定支付货款。

3. 使用 CIP 术语时需注意的问题

（1）保险险别。

按 CIP 术语成交的合同，卖方要办理货运保险并支付保险费，但货物从交货地点运往目的地的运输途中的风险由买方承担，所以卖方的投保属于代办性质。根据《2010 年通则》规定，卖方要按双方协商确定的险别投保，如买卖双方未约定具体投保险别，则按惯例卖方投保最低险别即可，保险金额为 CIP 价格基础上加成 10%。

（2）价格的确定。

按价格构成看，CIP 价 = CPT 价 + 保险费 = FCA 价 + 运费 + 保险费。因此，卖方对外报价时，要认真核算运费和保险费，并要预计运价和保险费的变动趋势等情况，以免价格报低，造成损失。

（3）CIP 与 CIF。

CIP 是在 CIF 术语基础上发展起来的适用于各种运输方式的贸易术语，两者在买卖双方义务划分的原则上是相同的：卖方都要负责安排货物自交货地至目的地的运输、保险并支付运费、保险费,卖方承担的风险均在交货地随交货义务的完成而转移至买方,两种术语达成的合同均属装运合同,卖方只负责按时交货,而不保证到货。

在使用上,CIF 术语仅适用于海运和内河航运,且以货物装上船为界划分风险,而 CIP 术语适用于任何运输方式,以货物交付给承运人为界划分风险。因此,CIP 术语的适用范围远大于 CIF 术语,不仅适用于铁路、公路、航空等非水上运输方式,也适用于不宜以装上船划分风险的海运集装箱运输及多式联运。

第三节 其他贸易术语

《2010 年通则》包含了 11 种贸易术语,介绍完常用的 6 种贸易术语,现将余下 5 种贸易术语简介如下:

一、EXW

EXW:Ex Works(... named place),工厂交货(……指定地点)。

1. EXW 术语的基本含义

卖方在规定的时间和地点将合同规定的货物交给买方;买方自己到交货地点接收货物,自己承担风险、责任和费用将货物从交货地点运到目的地。

EXW 术语适用于任何运输方式,而且,它属于实际交货方式。

在《2010 年通则》的全部 11 种贸易术语中,EXW 是卖方义务最少、买方义务最大的一种术语。货物在出口国的出口国证件,出口通关手续、费用和风险,买卖货物的运输、保险等手续、费用和风险都要由买方办理和承担。

2. 卖方义务

(1)在合同规定的时间和地点将合同规定的货物置于买方的处置之下;

(2)承担货物交给买方以前的一切风险和费用;

(3)提交商业发票或同等的电子信息。

3. 买方义务

(1)按合同规定受领货物并支付货款;

(2)承担受领货物以后的一切风险和费用;

(3)自负风险和费用,取得出口和进口许可证或其他官方证件,并办理货物的出口和进口海关手续。

4. 采用 EXW 术语需注意的问题

(1)关于货物的交接问题。

当买方有权决定交付货物的具体时间和具体地点时,买方应当通知卖方。若买方未能及时通知卖方上述事项，则在货物交付前就可能发生货物灭失或损坏所造成的风险转移给买方。卖方必须给予买方充分的通知，以告知货物何时可按双方规定的交货地点置于买方处置下，以便于买方能及时接货。

（2）关于货物的包装和装运问题。

为保留 EXW 下卖方义务最小的原则，一般卖方不承担将货物装上运输工具的责任和费用。

（3）关于办理出口手续问题。

货物出口的所有手续由买方负责办理，若买方需要得到卖方的协助，卖方可予以接受，但风险和费用均由买方承担。

（4）关于检验费用问题。

EXW 下，装船前检验费用（pre-shipment inspection，PSI），包括出口国当局强制要求检验的费用皆由买方承担。

二、FAS

FAS：Free Alongside Ship（…named port of shipment），装运港船边交货（……指定装运港）。

1. FAS 术语的基本含义

卖方在约定的时间和装运港口，将合同规定的货物交到买方所派的船只旁边，并及时通知买方；货运风险和费用均以装运港船边为界。

FAS 术语适用于水上运输方式。

2. 两点说明

（1）"船边"指载货船舶的吊钩所及之处；

（2）如果载货船舶因为码头原因不能靠岸，则卖方应负担装运港转运的驳船费用。

3. 买卖双方的义务

FAS 与 FOB 基本相似，其区别主要有以下几点：

（1）卖方只须将货物交到船边，而无须装上载货船舶；

（2）风险划分以"船边"为界，而不以装运港货物装上船为界；

（3）交货凭证是"承运货物收据"（Cargo Receipt），而不是"已装船提单"（On Board Bill of Lading）。

4. 注意事项

美国也有一种贸易术语叫"FAS"，但那里面的 FAS 却是"Free Along Side"的缩写，其含义是"卖方只要将货物交到任何运输工具旁边即可"，这与我们讨论的《通则》中"FAS"术语的含义相去甚远。因此，每当我们与美洲国家贸易使用 FAS 术语时，也一定要在"FAS"术语后面加上"Vessel"字样，如："FAS Vessel New Orleans（新奥尔良）""FAS Vessel Philadelphia（费城）"等。

三、DAP

DAP：Delivered at Place（... named place of destination），指定地交货（……指定目的地）。

"指定目的地交货"是指卖方已经用运输工具把货物运送到达买方指定的目的地后，将装在运输工具上的货物（不用卸载）交由买方处置，即完成交货。

类似于所取代的 DAF、DES 和 DDU 三个术语，卖方在指定目的地交货，只须做好卸货准备无须卸货即完成交货。术语所指的运输工具包括船舶，目的地包括港口。卖方应承担将货物运至指定的目的地的一切风险和费用（除进口费用外）。本术语适用于任何运输方式、多式联运方式及海运。

四、DAT

DAT：Delivered at Terminal（named terminal at port or place of destination），指定终端交货（……指定终端）。

指定终端交货意为，卖方在便于买方处置的终点港或终点地将货物从运输工具中卸下，完成交货。

类似于所取代的 DEQ 术语，卖方在指定终端货站卸货后将货物交给买方处置即完成交货，术语所指终端包括港口码头、仓库、集装箱堆场或者铁路、公路或航空货运站等。卖方应承担将货物运至指定终端集散站的一切风险和费用（除进口费用外）。本术语适用于任何运输方式或多式联运。

五、DDP

DDP：Delivered Duty Paid（... named place of destination），完税后交货（……指定目的地）。

1. DDP 术语的基本含义

完税后交货是指卖方将货物运至进口国的指定地点，将在运输工具上尚未卸下的货物交付给买方，并负责办理进口报关手续、支付在需要办理海关手续时在目的地应缴纳的任何进口"税费"，即履行了交货义务。卖方必须负担将货物运至该地点为止的一切费用和风险。本术语适用于任何运输方式。

2. 使用DDP术语应注意的问题

（1）DDP术语是卖方承担责任、费用及风险最大的贸易术语。

（2）DDP术语是唯一一个需卖方办理进口清关手续的术语。

（3）如果卖方不能直接或间接地取得进口许可证，则不应使用本术语。

第四节 商品的价格

一、进出口商品价格核算

（一）出口企业经济效益核算

出口企业的经济效益一般是通过成本和收入的比较来衡量的，主要的核算指标有：出口商品换汇成本、出口商品盈亏率和外汇增值率三项。在成本计算方面把成本算到"出口"启运前为止，称为"出口总成本"，而不把出口后的国外费用包括在内；在收入计算方面，把各种不同的成交价格条件统一以FOB价作为净收入，并称为"出口外汇净收入"，而把可能发生在运输、保险方面的外汇收入给予扣除，这是因为运费、保费实际上已归运输公司和保险公司，并不能算作是出口企业的收入。

（二）出口商品换汇成本的核算

出口商品换汇成本是指出口商品用多少元人民币换回一单位外汇（美元）。外汇统一以美元表示其他货币的外汇收入也都按当日汇率折算成美元。其计算公式是：

出口商品换汇成本＝出口总成本（人民币）/出口销售外汇净收入（美元）

一般将换汇成本同美元与人民币的汇率比较来决定盈亏，出口商品换汇成本小于外汇汇率则为盈利，反之为亏损，并且换汇成本越高，盈利越小或亏损越大；换汇成本越低，亏损越小或盈利越大。

我们有时也用换汇率来比较盈亏，换汇率也可称为换汇能力，是指用一元人民币能换回多少美元。因此，换汇率是换汇成本的倒数，我们决不可混淆。

例1：

某出口商品每吨进货成本7 000元人民币，商品流通费2 000元人民币，成交价为CIFC3每吨1 200美元，其中含运费42.37美元，保险费8.58美元，佣金36美元/吨。求该商品的换汇成本？

解：根据公式

换汇成本＝出口总成本/出口外汇净收入

其中：出口总成本 = 7 000 + 2 000 = 9 000（元）
FOB = CIFC – C – I – F = 1 200 – 36 – 8.58 – 42.37 = 1 113.05（美元）
所以：换汇成本 = 9 000/1 113.05 = 8.09（RMB/USD）
答：该商品的换汇成本为 8.09 元人民币。

（三）出口商品盈亏率的计算

出口商品盈亏率是指该商品按人民币核算的出口盈亏额与出口总成本的百分比率。盈亏额是指出口销售人民币净收入与出口总成本相比的差额。出口商品盈亏率的计算公式为：

出口商品盈亏率 =（盈亏额/出口总成本）×100%
= （出口销售人民币净收入出口总成本/出口总成本）×100%

计算结果是正数则为盈利率，负数为亏损率。

根据上述盈亏率和换汇成本的计算公式，可以推导出下列公式：

盈亏率 =（汇率 – 换汇成本）/换汇成本 ×100%

例 2：

仍以例 1 的条件为基础，假设出口商品 200 吨，求该商品的盈亏额及盈亏率各为多少？（美元对人民币的比价为 1∶8.3）

解：根据公式

盈亏额 = 出口销售人民币净收入 – 出口总成本

盈亏率 = 盈亏额/出口总成本 ×100%

其中：出口销售人民币净收入（FOB）=（CIFC – C – I – F）×8.3 =（1 200 – 36 – 8.58 – 42.37）×8.3 = 9 238.32（元）

因此：盈亏额 = 9 238.32 –（7 000 + 2 000）= 238.32（元）
盈亏率 = 238.32/9 000 ×100% = 2.6%

或： 盈亏率 =（汇率 – 换汇成本）/换汇成本 ×100%
=（8.3 – 8.09）/8.09 ×100% = 2.6%

答：该商品盈利 238.32 元人民币，盈利率为 2.6%。

（四）折扣和佣金的计算

1. 折扣

折扣（DISCOUNT）是指卖方按原价给予买方一定百分比的减让，一般由卖方在付款时预先扣除。在合同中，通常用文字说明的方法表示折扣，例如：

CIF 香港每吨 2 500 港元减 2% 折扣

HK $2,500 PER M/T CIF HONGKONG LESS 2% DISCOUNT

国际贸易中常用的折扣形式有品质折扣、数量折扣、季节折扣、现金折扣、特别

折扣等。折扣的表示方法及计算方式有很多种,但最主要的计算方法是:

$$折扣 = 金额 \times 折扣率$$

$$折实售价 = 原价(1-折扣率)$$

例4:

某出口商品对外报价为FOB上海价每打50美元,含3%折扣,如出口该商品1 000打,试计算其折扣额和实收外汇各为多少?

解:因为:折扣 = 金额 × 折扣率

　　　　折实售价 = 原价(1 − 折扣率)

所以:　折扣额 = 1 000 × 50 × 3% = 1 500(美元)

　　　　折实售价 = 50(1 − 3%) = 48.5(美元)

　　　　实收外汇 = 48.5 × 1 000 = 48 500(美元)

或:　　实收外汇 = 50 000 − 1 500 = 48 500(美元)

答:折扣额为1 500美元;实收外汇为48 500美元。

2. 佣金

佣金(commission)又称手续费(brokerage),是买方(如由他委托第三者采购)或卖方(由他委托第三者推销)付给"第三者"的报酬。佣金分"明佣"和"暗佣"两种,在价格中体现佣金的为明佣,在价格中看不出含佣,但实际上含佣的为暗佣,两者通称为含佣价。暗佣表面上与净价没有区别,为了明确起见,一般在净价的贸易术语后加"Net"字样。如:

USD25 per case CFR Rotterdam including 2% commission

或 USD25 per case CFRC2 Rotterdam

在实际业务中,一般按成交额为计算佣金的基数,用公式表示:

$$佣金 = 含佣价 \times 佣金率$$

由此可得出两个公式:

$$净价 = 含佣价/(1-佣金率)$$

$$含佣价 = 净价/(1-佣金率)$$

具体到某一贸易术语:

$$FOB\ 含佣价 = FOB\ 净价/(1-佣金率)$$

$$CFR\ 含佣价 = CFR\ 净价/(1-佣金率)$$

$$CIF\ 含佣价 = CIF\ 净价/(1-佣金率)$$

但CIF有其特殊性,所以上述CIF含佣价的公式也可以表示如下:

$$CIF\ 含佣价 = CFR\ 净价\{1-[佣金率-(1+投保加成率)\times 保险费率]\}$$

实际业务中,有时外商因情况变化,要求将一种贸易术语改报成另一种贸易术语,或将净价改报成含佣价,或调整含佣价的佣金率,只要不影响我方净收入,都可以接受。至于调整或改报的结果均可通过以上公式计算并获得。

(1) 改报 CFR 价为 CIF 价。

例 5：

设 CFR 为 840 美元，加成 10% 投保，保险费率为 1.2%，求：CIFC5 价。

第一种方法：$\text{CIF} = \dfrac{\text{CFR}}{1-(1+10\%)\text{保险费率}} = 851.24$（美元）

$\text{CIFC5} = 851.24/(1-5\%) = 896.04$（美元）

第二种方法：$\text{CIFC5} = \dfrac{\text{CFR}}{1-(1+10\%)\text{保险费率}-\text{佣金率}} = 896.67$（美元）

如保险时以 CIFC 价投报，则用第二种方法计算较准。

答：CIFC5 应为 896.04 或 896.67 美元。

(2) 净价改报含佣价。

例 6：

设某商品 CFR 价 2 000 美元，试改为 CFRC4% 价，并保持卖方的净收入不变。

解：含佣价 $= \dfrac{\text{净价}}{1-4\%} = 2\,083.33$（美元）

答：改报后的 CFRC4 价为 2 083.33 美元。

(3) 调整含佣价的佣金率。

例 7：

已知 CFRC3 为 1 200 美元，保持卖方净收入不变。试改报为 CFRC5% 价。

解：先把 CFRC3 价改为 CFR 价。

$\text{CFR} = \text{CFRC3}(1-\text{佣金率}) = 1\,200(1-3\%) = 1\,164$（美元）

再把 CFRC 改为 CFRC5。

$\text{CFRC5} = \text{CFR}/(1-C5) = 1\,164/(1-5\%) = 1\,225.26$（美元）

或：

$\text{CFRC5} = [\text{CFRC3}(1-3\%)]/(1-5\%) = 1\,225.26$（美元）

答：改报后的 CFRC5 价为 1 225.26 美元。

（五）出口价格核算

价格核算是进出口业务的关键环节，它直接关系到交易磋商的成败和买卖双方的利益，因此，只有了解并掌握出口价格的核算方法，才能保证其所报价格的准确与合理。

1. 出口价格构成

国际贸易中的价格主要由成本、费用和利润构成。

(1) 成本。

成本是整个价格的核心，它不同于我们前面所述的出口总成本，它只是出口企业或外贸单位为出口其产品进行生产、加工或采购所产生的生产成本、加工成本或采购成本,为计算方便,我们统一购货成本为含税成本。但是,对外出口报价时应将出口退税因素考虑进去,将退税收入扣除,最终以实际采购成本来核算价格。

(2) 费用。

出口价格核算中的费用主要有国内费用和国外费用两部分,如包装费、仓储费、国内运费、港口费、商检报关费、经营管理费等均属国内费用,而国外费用主要指的是出口运费和出口保险费,且只有对外报 CFR 或 CIF 价时才会用到国外费用。

(3) 利润。

利润指的是卖方的预期利润,一般以成交额为基数计算。

2. 出口报价核算

我们以 FOB、CIF、CFR 为例来说明出口报价步骤及使用的公式。

$$出口报价 = 成本 + 费用 + 预期利润 \tag{3.1}$$

式(3.1)中的成本应该是不含税成本,即退税后的实际采购成本,可用以下公式计算:

$$实际采购成本 = 含税成本 - 退税收入$$

$$退税收入 = 含税成本 \times 出口退税率/(1+17\%)$$

故

$$实际采购成本 = 含税成本 \times (1-出口退税率)/1+17\% \tag{3.2}$$

式(3.1)中的费用根据价格不同来确定,可以是国内费用或国外费用加国内费用。如报 FOB 价,只包括国内费用,报 CFR 价则要加上国外费用,报 CIF 价还要加上国外保险费。

式(3.1)中的预期利润是指按成交价的一定百分比算出的卖方收益。

下面我们以 FOB 为例来推导其报价公式:

$$FOB = C + ZF + FOB \times P$$

其中

FOB = 出口报价

C = 实际采购成本

ZF = 国内费用之和

P = 预期利润率

$$FOB - FOB \times P = C + ZF$$

$$FOB = \frac{C + ZF}{1 - P}$$

即

$$FOB 报价 = \frac{实际采购成本 + 各项国内费用之和}{1 - 预期利润率} \tag{3.3}$$

同理

$$FOBC = \frac{实际采购成本 + 各项国内费用之和}{1 - 佣金率 - 预期利润率} \quad (3.4)$$

如果对外报 CFR 或 CIF 价也可以通过推导得出下例公式：

$$CFR = \frac{实际采购成本 + 各项国内费用之和 + 国外费用}{1 - 预期利润率} \quad (3.5)$$

$$CFRC = \frac{实际采购成本 + 各项国内费用之和 + 国外费用}{1 - 佣金率 - 预期利润率} \quad (3.6)$$

$$CIF = \frac{实际采购成本 + 各项国内费用之和 + 国外费用}{1 - 预期利润率 - (1 + 投报加成率) \times 保费率} \quad (3.7)$$

$$CIFC = \frac{实际采购成本 + 各项国内费用之和 + 国外费用}{1 - 佣金率 - 预期利润率 - (1 + 投报加成率) \times 保费率} \quad (3.8)$$

例8：

我国某工艺品进出口公司拟向客户出口某种工艺品100箱，该产品国内采购价为每件28元人民币，按每50件装一纸箱，包装费用每箱100元，国内运杂费共1 500元，商检报关费500元，港口各种费用400元，公司各种相关的管理费用1 000元，经核实，该批货物出口需运费800美元，如由我方保险，其保险按 CIF 成交价加一成投报一切险，费率为0.5%，另外，这种产品出口有13%的退税，现假设该公司欲获得10%的预期利润，且国外客户要求价格中含5%佣金，试报该产品的 FOBC5 及 CIFC5 美元价格（美元对人民币的汇率为1:8.30，计算过程保留4位小数，计算结果保留2位小数）。

解：出口总数 = $100 \times 50 = 5\,000$（件）

实际采购成本 = 含税成本 $\times \left(1 - \dfrac{出口退税率}{1 + 17\%}\right)$

$= 28 \times \left(1 - \dfrac{13\%}{1 + 17\%}\right) = 24.89$（元/件）

国内费用 = $100/50 + (1\,500 + 500 + 400 + 1\,000)/5\,000 = 2.68$（元/件）

出口运费 = $800/5\,000 = 0.16$（美元/件）

$FOBC5 = \dfrac{实际采购成本 + 各项国内费用之和}{1 - 佣金率 - 预期利润率}$

$= \dfrac{(24.89 + 2.68)}{(1 - 5\% - 10\%) \times 8.3} = 3.91$（美元/件）

$CIFC5 = \dfrac{实际采购成本 + 各项国内费用之和 + 国外费用}{1 - 佣金率 - 利润率 - (1 + 投报加成率) \times 保费率}$

$= \dfrac{(24.89 + 2.68)/8.3 + 0.16}{1 - 5\% - 10\% - (1 + 10\%) \times 0.5\%}$

$= 4.12$（美元/件）

答：我国对外所报 FOBC5 和 CIFC5 价分别为每件3.91美元和4.12美元。

第五节　买卖合同中的价格条款

国际货物买卖合同中的价格条款，一般包括单价和总值两部分。

一、国际货物买卖合同中的价格条款举例

（1）净价条款举例。

单价：每吨97英镑CIF哥本哈根

总值：14 550英镑

Unit Price：at GBP 97 per metric ton CIF Copenhagen

Total Value：GBP 14,550（Say Pounds Sterling Fourteen Thousand Five Hundred And Fifty Only）

（2）佣价条款举例。

单价：每箱0.70美元FOB天津含2%佣金

总值：14 850美元

Unit Price：at USD 0.70 per box FOB Tianjin including 2% commission

Total Value：USD 14,850（Say US Dollars Fourteen Thousand Eight Hundred And Fifty Only）

单价：每吨1 000人民币元CIFC3%新加坡

总值：50 000元人民币

Unit Price：at RMB×(CNY) 1,000 per M/T CIFC3% Singapore

Total Value：RMB×(CNY) 50,000

（3）含折扣条款举例。

单价：每件45美元CIF汉堡折扣2%

总值：45 000美元

Unit Price：at USD 45 per piece CIF Hamburg less 2% discount

Total Value：USD 45,000（Say US dollars Forty-five Thousand Only）

二、规定价格条款时应注意的问题

（1）合理确定商品的单价，防止偏高或偏低。

（2）根据经济意图和实际情况，在权衡利弊的基础上选用适当的贸易术语。

（3）争取选择有利的计价货币，以免遭受币值变动带来的风险。如采用了对我

不利的计价货币，应争取订立外汇保值条款。

（4）灵活运用各种不同的作价方法，以避免价格变动的风险。

（5）参照国际贸易的习惯做法，注意佣金和折扣的运用。

（6）如果货物品质和数量约定有一定的机动幅度，则对机动部分的作价也应一并规定。

（7）如果包装材料和包装费用另行计算，对其计价方法也应一并规定。

单价中涉及的计价数量单位、计价货币、装卸地名称等必须书写正确、清楚、以利合同的履行。

International Trade Terms And Price of Goods

In international trade, the price is the maim content involved in the business negotiation.

The price of commodity usually refers to the unit price, which is made up of a measuring unit, a unit price, a name of currency, trade term, and a name of destination or shipping place. For example,

USD 500 per M/T CIF Boston;

HKD 30 per Carton FOB Dalian.

The two parties in international trade are usually far away from each other and are separated by vast oceans. The cargoes carried from the export country to the import country will usually go through a long distance of transportation and sometimes, several transshipments during the process of transit of the goods. The seller or the buyer shall handle a series of complicated formalities, which include carrying out customs formalities for the goods, obtaining the import or export licence, chartering a ship or booking shipping space, taking out insurance, asking for inspection, etc., and pay all kinds of charges and expenses, such as freight, loading and unloading expenses, insurance premium, warehouse charges, duties and taxes, and other miscellaneous expenses. Who shall be responsible for the above mentioned duties and bear the relative expenses? All these problems resulting from international trade shall be solved. Therefore, after a long-term process of business practice, a set of special trade terms have taken shape in international trade which are not customary practices in domestic trade. These terms have developed into the international merchantile customs and have been simplified to a certain extent. They are in universal use in foreign trade transactions. They are, however, sometimes interpreted differently in different countries and their meanings may be modified by the agreement of the parties, by the customs of a particular trade or the usage prevailing at a particular port.

When the two parties determine to adopt certain trade terms, all other clauses in the contract shall be in conformity with them. Therefore, in international trade, we usually make use of certain trade terms to define the nature of the contract, such as FOB contract or CIF contract, to determine expenses and risks as well as their rights and obligations accordingly.

The trade terms refer to using a brief English concept or abbreviation to indicate the formation of the unit price and determine the responsibilities, expenses and risks borne by two parties as well as the time of the passing of the property in the goods.

International Trade Usages

There are 3 influential international trade practices.

1. Warsaw – Oxford Rules 1932

In 1928, the International Law Association held a meeting in Warsaw, and worked out the Uniform Rules for CIF Sales Contracts, which was called "Warsaw Rules 1928", and renamed "Warsaw – Oxford Rules 1932" at the Oxford Convention and includes 21 clauses. It is mainly used to indicate the nature and characteristic of the CIF contract and also to stipulate the responsibilities of the two parties under CIF terms.

2. Revised American Foreign Trade Definitions 1941

In 1919, nine American commercial groups drew up "The U. S. Export Quotations and Abbreviations," which was revised in 1941 and was renamed "Revised American Foreign Trade Definitions 1941". It was adopted by the American Chamber of Commerce, the National Importers Association and the American Foreign Trade Association in the same year. It defines six trade terms, i. e., Ex-point of origin, FOB, FAS, C&F, CIF and Ex – Dock. Except Ex-point of origin and Ex-dock, the other four trade terms are explained quite differently from those in INCOTERMS. These trade terms are often adopted in the United States of America, Canada and some other countries in America.

3. International Rules for the Interpretation of Trade Terms

International Rules for Interpretation of Trade Terms (hereinafter referred to as the general principles of 2010) is abbreviated as Incoterms 2010. It is established by the international chamber of commerce in order to unify the interpretation of various trade terms. The earliest generality was produced in 1936, and then it was amended and supplemented many times to meet the needs of the development of international trade business. The current "Incoterms 2010" is according to the needs of the development of international trade practice, international chamber of commerce in the "incoterms 2000" on the basis of the revised, and take effect on January 1, 2011.

"Incoterms 2010" (see table 3 – 1) consideration of customs has been growing, business transactions of increased use of electronic information, transport of goods in the further attention to security issues, as well as the change of the mode of transportation. The Incoterms 2010 update and integration with relevant rules "delivery", the total number of terms from 13 to 11, and more concise, clear statements on all the rules. It is important to note that after the new version of the publication, "Incoterms 2000" is still valid. The contract the parties may choose any version "incoterms" is used, but must indicate the version used in the contract.

The 2010 general rules actually divides the term into two categories: applicable to various modes of transport and water transport. Of the 11 terms, only FAS, FOB, CFR and CIF are applicable to sea and inland waterway transport, and the other seven are applicable to any mode of transportation.

SECTION ONE

There are 11 trade terms in the 2010 general rules, which use more trade terms: FOB, CIF, CFR, FCA, CPT and CIP.

Therefore, it is particularly important to familiarize yourself with the meanings of these six trade terms, the obligations of the buyers and sellers, and the issues to be noted in their use.

一、FOB

1. Basic meanings of FOB terms

FOB is called free on board (… Named Port of Shipment) It is customary to say that shipment is effected on board the port of shipment. It means that the seller must deliver the goods on the designated port of shipment, on the vessel designated by the buyer, or obtain the goods after such delivery. The risk of loss or damage of the goods from the loading of the goods shall be transferred, and the buyer shall bear all expenses from this time. The seller is also responsible for customs clearance of the goods. This term can only be used for sea or inland waterway transport.

The new provisions of the 2010 general rules, "the acquisition of goods so delivered", are aimed at the phenomenon of String Trade in international Trade. In the sale of agricultural and mineral products, the goods are frequently resold frequently during transportation, relative to the sales of industrial products. When this happens, the seller in the middle of the chain does not "ship" the goods because the goods have been shipped from the original seller. The seller, in the middle of the chain operation, thus fulfils its obligations to the buyer, not by loading the goods, but by "getting" the goods that have been shipped.

Example: USD 200 PER M/T FOB Shanghai Incoterms 2010.

2. Basic obligations of both parties

Using FOB terms, the basic obligations of the buyer and seller are summarized as follows.

1) seller's obligations

To provide goods in conformity with the contract, on the date or within the period stipulated in the contract, at the named port of shipment, the goods according to the usual way to pay to the buyer's appointed port ship, or receive a delivery of the goods, and give the buyer sufficient notice.

In charge of obtaining export licenses or other official documents for customs clearance of goods.

To bear all costs and risks of loading the goods at the designated loading port.

It is responsible for submitting the commercial invoice and certifying that the goods have been delivered to the ship's usual documents or with the same electronic information.

2) buyer's obligations

To be responsible for chartering the shipping space, paying the freight, and giving the seller full notice of the name of the vessel, the place of loading and the time required for delivery.

It is responsible for obtaining import license or other official documents for customs clearance of goods and transit formalities when necessary.

All costs and risks of loading the goods at the designated loading port.

The seller shall accept the documents submitted by the seller in accordance with the contract and shall be subject to the goods in conformity with the contract and shall pay the goods in accordance with the contract.

3. Use FOB terms to pay attention to problems

1) transfer of risk

In the general principles of 2000, the FOB risk transfer point is the port of shipment. The seller shall bear the losses caused by the fall of the goods on board or in the sea. The buyer shall bear the goods loaded on board, including the damage or loss incurred before and during the voyage.

In the general principles of 2010, the risk transfer point is modified to be loaded onto the ship. Increases the seller's loading port obligation, and the risk is also transferred after shipment.

But be aware that risks can sometimes be moved ahead of time. The risk is automatically transferred to the buyer if the buyer sends a vessel that fails to receive the goods and has not given full notice to the seller at the expiration of the delivery term.

However, both the normal transfer of risk and the early transfer of risk have the precondition that the goods should be specific. That is, the goods have been duly assigned to this contract, that is, clearly separated or otherwise specified as the goods under the contract.

2) on the issue of cargo connection

In the FOB contract, the buyer shall give full notice to the seller about the name of the vessel, the place of shipment and the required delivery time, as the buyer is responsible for the chartering or booking. If the buyer did not give the seller the above notice, may cause the risk of loss of or damage to the goods before delivery of the goods transfer, the seller and the buyer shall bear the resulting storage, insurance, etc., all additional costs.

The seller shall be responsible for loading the goods on the vessel designated by the buyer at the time of shipment and the port of shipment as stipulated in the contract. If the seller fails to ship the goods due to the goods, the seller shall bear the Dead Freight or Demurrage. Cargo cohesion problems include: the seller the goods on time, but the buyer port of ships failed to arrive on time, in advance to the port and want to leave early, on time but can not be completed at the port of loading, such as inadequate capacity, is for the buyer's responsibility; The buyer sent the ship to the port on time, but the seller could not prepare the goods on time. Generally speaking, the seller is in good control of the goods and cannot receive the goods on time.

Under the FOB contract, such as clinch a deal the quantity of the goods is not big, only part of the shipping space with liner, at the time of shipment, the seller usually in accordance with the express or implied agreement between the buyer and the seller, all the shipping formalities on behalf of the buyer, including in the name of the seller's own booking and bill of lading. The buyer shall be liable for any expenses incurred by the seller in connection with the above formalities unless otherwise agreed or in accordance with the trade practices. At the same time, the seller's risk of booking the shipping space shall be borne by the buyer.

3) the difference between the definition of American foreign trade in 1941 and the 2010 general principles on FOB terms. The 1941 revised American foreign trade definitions will FOB summarized into six kinds, one of the top three in the exporter inland delivery location specified inland transport vehicle delivery, and the fourth is the exporter of export location specified inland transport vehicle delivery, the fifth kind is the port of shipment on FOB, 6 kinds of inland place of delivery specified in the importing country. The fourth and fifth USES should be noted. If the shipment is in San Francisco, if the buyer asks for free on board at the

port of shipment, should be in between FOB and port name "VESSEL" (the ship) become "FOB ship San Francisco", otherwise the seller may according to the fourth situation inland transportation in the city of San Francisco on delivery of the goods.

Even if all the goods are delivered on board the shipping port, the FOB VESSEL in the general rules of 2010 and the FOB VESSEL in the revised edition are different from the stipulations in the export procedures. According to the 2010 general rules, "the seller has the obligation to take risks and expenses, obtain export licenses or other official documents, and handle the customs formalities necessary for export". But according to the 1941 revised American foreign trade definitions, the seller is only "in the buyer's request and by its expense, to assist the buyer has issued by the countries of origin and loading, as exports or imports at the destination required for various certificates".

In the import and export trade with the United States, Canada and other countries, the relevant issues shall be determined in the agreement when the agreement is made on FOB basis, so as to avoid disputes arising out of the differences in interpretation.

4) shipping notice

After the goods are shipped, the seller shall inform the buyer in time so that the buyer can handle the cargo insurance in time. The so-called "just-in-time", as usual, is generally understood to be "within 24 hours after the shipment of an ocean-going cargo ship".

About the "shipping advice", whether the buyer to the seller, or the seller to the buyer, usually not have the difference between professional textbooks, all are generally called "shipping advice", but in fact there is a difference between the two, the buyer to the seller, is in before shipment, the buyer the relevant booking as well as the time and place of shipment and the name of the ship to inform the seller about the idea items, called "shipment need to know"; The seller shall send to the buyer the detailed information about the shipment to the buyer after the shipment is made by the seller, which is called "shipping notice".

二、CIF

1. Basic meaning of CIF terms

The full name of CIF is Cost + Insurance and Freight. Named Port of Destination, i.e., cost plus insurance, freight (... Designated port of destination). CIF means that the seller will complete the delivery of the goods by loading the goods on the ship or trying to obtain such delivery. The seller must pay the goods shipped to the costs and freight necessary to specify the port of destination, but the risk of loss of or damage to the goods after delivery, as well as in events and cause any extra charge, from the seller to the buyer. In CIF terms, the seller must also obtain marine insurance for the loss or damage of the goods to the buyer.

The CIF term requires the seller to clear the goods for export. The term can only be used for sea and inland waterway transport.

Example: USD 200 PER M/T CIF BANGKOK PORT Incoterms 2010.

2. Basic obligations of both parties

Using CIF terms, the basic obligations of the buyer and seller are summarized as follows.

1) seller's obligations

To provide the goods in conformity with the same goods: responsible for the booking of the vessel and the freight payable to the destination port; to ship the goods at the port of shipment during the date or period specified in the contract; or try to obtain the goods delivered in the above manner and give the buyer full notice.

To bear all the costs and risks of loading the goods on board.

In charge of cargo transportation insurance, pay insurance premium.

It is responsible for obtaining export licenses or other official documents for customs clearance of goods.

2) buyer's obligations

The seller shall accept the documents provided by the seller in accordance with the contract, accept the goods in conformity with the contract and pay the goods according to the contract stipulations.

All expenses and risks after loading the goods on board.

It is responsible for obtaining import license or other official documents to handle the customs clearance of goods and the transit formalities when necessary.

3. Use CIF terms to pay attention to problems

1) insurance coverage

According to CIF terms, the seller should handle the cargo insurance, and the insurance must be clear and clear, because the insurance premium of the insurer is different. In practice, it should be clear about risks, insurance amount and other contents. If it's not clear, then follow the usual practice. According to the 2010 general rules, the seller only needs the lowest risk. However, if the buyer requires and is charged by the buyer, the insurable war, strike and civil risks may be indicated in the credit, in fact, flexible. If the buyer specifically asks for special additional risks, the cost shall be borne by the buyer.

2) the seller shall handle the booking of the chartered ship

Under CIF terms, the seller must bear the cost, according to the condition to enter into a contract of carriage, usually the goods will be stipulated in the contract, according to the commonly used to transport the goods of the usual route of the vessel, shipped to the designated port of destination.

Unless otherwise agreed by the parties, for the buyer to limit the carrying vessel nationality, age, type, class, and specified requirement for loading a liner the ships of the trade union, etc, the seller shall have the right to refuse to accept.

3) symbolic delivery

In terms of delivery, CIF is a typical Symbolic Delivery. The so-called symbolic delivery is relative to Physical Delivery (see table 3-2). The former means that the seller shall complete the shipment in accordance with the agreed place and shall submit the relevant documents, including the property right certificate, to the buyer, even if the delivery obligation is completed, there is no need to guarantee the arrival of the goods. The latter refers to all want to be in the stipulated time, place, the goods will conform to the provisions of the contract submitted to the buyer or its designated person, and not to be in place of delivery, under the condition of CIF delivery, the seller is against documents delivery, the buyer is the payment voucher. As long as the seller has submitted the full set of qualified documents to the buyer as scheduled, the buyer must perform the payment obligation even if the goods are damaged or lost in transit. On the contrary, if the seller's documents do not meet the requirements, the buyer shall have the right to refuse to pay even if the goods are delivered to the destination in good condition.

In a CIF contract, it is necessary to avoid the trap clause "requiring the seller to guarantee the arrival of the goods or the payment terms".

4) the seller shall send the shipping advice to the buyer

Under CIF terms, although the buyer do not need to be dealt with to the information such as name of vessel, shipment cargo insurance, but the seller should in due time shall notify to the buyer about shipment information, so that the buyer in a timely manner to deal with matters such as sales, import customs clearance and pick up the goods.

三、CFR

1. The basic meaning of CFR terminology

The full name of CFR is Cost and Freight. Named port of destination, i.e., cost plus freight (… Designated port of destination). CFR refers to the seller's loading of the goods at the port of loading or the seller obtaining the goods delivered so delivered. The seller must pay the goods shipped to the costs and freight necessary to specify the port of destination, but the risk of loss of or damage to the goods after delivery, and caused by events that occurred after the delivery of any additional fees, from the seller to the buyer.

The CFR term requires the seller to clear the goods for export. This term can only be shipped per month by sea and inland.

Example: USD 200 PER M/T CFR BANGKOK PORT Incoterms 2010.

2. Basic obligations of both parties

In CFR terms, the basic obligations of the buyer and seller are summarized as follows.

1) seller's obligations

To provide goods in conformity with the contract; to charter a shipping space and pay for the delivery of goods to the destination; loading the goods into the ship at the time and port specified in the contract; or try to obtain the goods delivered in the above manner and give the buyer full notice.

To bear all the costs and risks of loading the goods on board.

In charge of obtaining export licenses or other official documents for customs clearance of goods.

It is responsible for providing commercial invoices and the usual transport documents evidencing the shipment of goods to the port of destination, or electronic information with the same effect.

2) buyer's obligations

The seller shall accept the documents provided by the seller in accordance with the contract and shall be subject to the goods in conformity with the contract and shall pay the goods in accordance with the contract.

To undertake all risks after loading the cargo. It is responsible for obtaining import license or other official documents for customs clearance of goods and transit formalities when necessary. When using CFR terminology, the buyer shall apply for the insurance at his own expense, but this is for his own benefit, not the buyer's obligation.

3. The use of CFR terminology

1) the important role of shipping advice

The seller needs to pay special attention to the issue that the goods must be sent to the buyer in time after shipment so that the buyer can go through the insurance formalities. Because the general international trade practice and the laws of some countries, such as Britain, the sale of goods act 1839 (revised in 1979) regulation, if the seller does not give notice of shipment to the buyer, the buyer fails to do the insurance of the goods, goods in shipping on the way of risk borne by the seller. Although the seller shall issue a notice to the buyer after shipment on FOB and CIF terms, the shipping notice under CFR condition is provided. It's more important.

2) avoid using the buyer's designated vessel

Under CFR, the seller pays the freight, and the buyer may raise the cost if the ship is named.

四、FCA

1. Basic meaning of FCA terminology

The full name of FCA is Free Carrier "delivery of goods to the carrier" "place of designation" means that the seller shall hand over the goods to be designated by the buyer to the carrier specified by the buyer. It should be noted that the selected delivery location has an effect on the loading and unloading obligations of the site. If the goods are delivered at the seller's premises, the seller shall be responsible for loading. If the goods are delivered elsewhere, the seller is not responsible for unloading the goods. This term is applicable to any means of transport, including multimodal transport.

The general principles of the "2010" regulation: "carrier" means anyone who, in a contract of carriage commitment by rail, road, sea, air, inland waterway or by a combination of the above transport performance of the transportation or performed by others. If a person other than the carrier is appointed by the buyer to collect the goods, the seller shall be deemed to have fulfilled the delivery obligation when the goods are sold to the person.

Example: USD 200 PER M/T FCA Changsha Incoterms 2010.

2. Basic obligations of both parties

Using FCA terminology, the basic obligations of the buyer and seller are summarized as follows.

1) seller's obligations

To provide the goods in conformity with the contract. In the time and place specified in the contract, the goods shall be delivered to the carrier designated by the buyer and promptly notified to the buyer. In charge of obtaining export licenses or other official documents for customs clearance of goods.

All expenses and risks prior to the delivery of the goods to the carrier.

It is responsible for providing commercial invoices and documents certifying that goods have been delivered, or electronic information with the same effect.

2) buyer's obligations

To enter into a contract to transport the goods to the destination from the designated place, pay the freight, and promptly notify the seller of the name of the carrier and the relevant information.

To bear all expenses and risks after delivery of the goods.

It is responsible for obtaining import license or other official documents to handle the customs clearance of goods and the transit formalities when necessary.

The seller shall accept the documents submitted by the seller in accordance with the contract, and shall be subject to the loan in conformity with the contract, and shall pay the payment in accordance with the contract.

3. Use FCA terminology for attention

1) place of delivery

Using FCA terminology, the provisions of the delivery place in the contract will affect the loading and unloading obligations. If the goods are delivered at the seller's premises, the seller shall be responsible for loading. The delivery obligation shall be completed when an effort is made to load the goods on the means of transport provided by the carrier or the other person acting on behalf of him. If the goods are delivered in other places other than the place where the seller is located, they are not responsible for discharging the goods. When the seller shall deliver the undischarged goods to the carrier or another person designated by the buyer, the seller shall fulfill the obligation to pay the loan. If no specific place of delivery is agreed upon, or if there are several locations available, the seller may choose a place of delivery which is best suited to its intent.

2) risk transfer

When FCA terms are used, the risk of both buyers and sellers is that the carrier is bound to the carrier, but there may be a risk of early transfer. Because under the FCA terms, the buyer is responsible for the transport contract is concluded, and the carrier name and relevant matters promptly notify the seller, if the buyer failed to give the seller the above notice, or he specified by the carrier at the appointed time failed to accept the goods, the delivery of the goods from the agreed date or the date of expiration, bear all risks of loss of or damage to the goods by the buyer, but as the goods have been classified as the prerequisite conditions under this contract.

3) arrange transportation

FCA terms are applicable to any mode of transport, including multimodal transport. The buyer shall be responsible for the designation of the carrier and the contract of carriage of the goods from the place of shipment to the destination. But the general principles of the "2010" at the same time regulation, if the buyer request, or if this is a kind of business practices and the buyer is not at the right time to give contrary instructions, as long as the buyer's risk and expense, the seller can press usually condition to enter into a contract of carriage. However, this is not a seller's obligation. In either case, the seller may refuse to enter into a contract of carriage. If the seller refuses, the buyer must be notified immediately so that the buyer can make another arrangement.

4) the FCA with FOB

FCA is developed on the basis of FOB term is suitable for various mode of transportation of trade terms, the buyer and the seller obligation classification principles are the same, the seller has to the export customs clearance of goods to the carrier named by the buyer (under FOB terms, ocean carrier, the vessel) to complete the delivery obligations. Therefore, FOB terms can be regarded as a special case of FCA terminology.

Since FOB term is only applicable to sea and inland waterway transport, and the risks of the buyer and seller are divided by cargo loading, the scope of application is very limited. By the sea or inland waterway transport trade, or for the goods shipped by sea but not suitable for mode of transportation of the division of risk (e.g., container transport, multimodal transport, etc.) trade, are not appropriate to use FOB terms, the FCA terms should be adopted.

五、CPT

1. The basic meaning of CPT terminology

The full name of CPT is Carriage Paid to. Named Place of Destination. Specify the destination. CPT means that the seller gives the goods to the carrier specified by him, but the seller must also pay the freight to the designated destination. The buyer shall bear all risks and any other expenses incurred after the goods have been delivered so.

The CPT term requires the seller to clear the goods for export. This term is applicable to any means of transport, including multimodal transport.

Example: USD 30 PER JAR CPT NINGBO AIRPORT Incoterms 2010.

2. Basic obligations of both parties

In CPT terms, the basic obligations of the buyer and seller are summarized as follows.

1) seller's obligations

To provide goods in conformity with the contract; to conclude and pay the freight for the goods to be shipped to the destination; deliver the goods to the carrier at the time and place specified in the contract; inform the buyer in time.

In charge of obtaining export licenses or other official documents for customs clearance of goods.

All risks prior to the delivery of the goods to the carrier.

To provide the buyer with commercial invoice, usual transport document, or electronic information with the same effect.

2) buyer's obligations

It is responsible for obtaining import license or other official documents for customs clearance of goods and transit formalities when necessary.

To bear all risks and expenses after delivery of the goods.

The seller shall accept the documents submitted by the seller in accordance with the contract and shall be subject to the goods in conformity with the contract and shall pay the goods in accordance with the contract.

From the above, the seller's obligation under CPT is only more than that under FCA. Therefore, the price of CPT contains the export freight, namely CPT price = FCA 10 freight. The rest is the same at the place of delivery and risk division.

3. Problems should be noted when using CPT terminology

1) risk division

The CPT term requires the seller to be responsible for the carriage of the goods and to pay the freight, but does not require the seller to bear the risks and the additional costs arising therefrom. The seller shall bear the risk of the goods being delivered to the carrier prior to the delivery of the goods to the carrier prior to the delivery of the goods.

2) shipping advice

In CPT terms, the buyer and seller shall specify the time of shipment and destination in the contract so that the seller chooses the carrier and the contract of carriage of the goods to the destination. Upon delivery of the goods to the carrier, the seller shall promptly issue a notice of delivery to the buyer, so that the buyer can insure the goods in time and receive the goods at the destination.

3) the CPT and CFR

CPT is a trade term developed on the basis of CFR terminology. In principle, the two are identical in principle. The seller shall be responsible for arranging the delivery of the goods to the destination and the cost of the goods. The risks borne by the seller shall be transferred to the buyer upon completion of the delivery duty. The contract between the two terms is the shipping contract, and the seller is only responsible for the delivery on time, not the delivery. In use, CFR term can only be used for sea and inland waterway transport, and demarcated risks for the goods shipped, the CPT term is suitable for any mode of transport, including multimodal transport, based on the industry to deliver the goods to the carrier. Therefore, the applicable scope of the CPT term is much bigger than the CFR term, applies not only to aviation, railways, highways and other non water transport mode, applies to the unfavorable to shipped divide the risk of shipping container transportation and multimodal transport.

六、CIP

1. The basic meaning of CIP terminology

The full text of CIP is Carriage, Insurance Paid to (… Named Place of Destination, i.e., freight, insurance, etc. Specify the destination. CIP means the seller deliver the cargo to the designated carrier, at the same time, you have to pay the freight on the goods shipped to the specified destination, buyers bear the risk of what happened after the goods are delivered and any other fees. In CIP terms, the seller shall also obtain cargo insurance for the buyer's risk of loss or damage to the goods in transit.

The buyer shall note that, in CIP terms, the seller shall only obtain insurance against the minimum liability insurance. If the buyer is to be covered by a greater liability insurance, he will have to make a clear agreement with the seller or arrange for additional insurance on his own. The CIP term requires the seller to clear the goods for export. This term is applicable to any means of transport, including multimodal transport.

Example: USD 30 PER JAR CIP NINGBO AIRPORT Incoterms 2010.

2. Basic obligations of both parties

In CIP terms, the basic obligations of the buyer and seller are summarized as follows.

1) seller's obligations

To provide goods in conformity with the contract;

To conclude a contract to transport the goods to a designated destination and to pay the freight;

Deliver the goods to the carrier at the time and place specified in the contract; inform the buyer in time;

The risk of delivery to the carrier before delivery;

The insurance shall be covered by the contract and the insurance premium will be paid;

It is responsible for obtaining export licenses or other official documents for customs clearance of goods;

To submit commercial invoices and ordinary transport documents, or electronic information with the same effect.

2) buyer's obligations

It is responsible for obtaining import license or other official documents, handling the customs clearance of goods and the necessary transit formalities, and taking all risks after the delivery of the goods. The seller shall accept the documents submitted by the seller in accordance with the contract and shall be subject to the goods in conformity with the contract and shall pay the goods in accordance with the contract.

3. Problems to be noted when using CIP terminology

1) insurance coverage

Clinch a deal on CIP term of contract, the seller should deal with freight insurance and pay insurance premium, but the cargo from the place of delivery to destination risk borne by the buyer in transit, so the seller's insurance belongs to nature. In accordance with the general principles for 2010, the seller according to mutual agreement, to determine the risks insured, as buyers and sellers don't have no agreement on the specific insurance, minimum coverage is traditionally the seller take can, insurance amount for 10% bonus on CIP price.

2) price determination

According to the price structure, CIP price = CPT price + insurance premium = FCA + freight 10 premium. Therefore, when the seller makes an external offer, the freight and insurance should be calculated carefully, and the change trend of freight rate and insurance premium should be expected, so as to avoid the low price and cause the loss.

3) the CIP and CIF

CIP is developed on the basis of CIF term trade terms are suitable for all kinds of transportation means, between buyers and sellers of obligation in principle is the same: the seller should be responsible for security on the delivery of goods to the destination of the transportation, insurance and pay the freight, insurance premium, the seller's risks are completed in the delivery of the goods with the obligation of delivery and transferred to the buyer, the two terms of contract of shipment, the seller is responsible for on time delivery of the goods only, and does not guarantee that the arrival of the goods.

In use, CIF term can only be used for sea and inland waterway transport, and demarcated risks for the goods shipped, the CIP term is applicable to any mode of transportation, based on the industry to deliver the goods to the carrier.

SECTION TWO

The general rule 2010 contains 11 trade terms, which cover six commonly used trade terms. The remaining five trade terms are summarized as follows:

一、EXW

EXW: Ex Works (... The factory delivered the goods (... Designated location).)

1. The basic meaning of EXW terminology

The seller shall deliver the contracted goods to the buyer at the specified time and place; The buyer shall accept the goods at the place of delivery and bear the risks, responsibilities and expenses to transport the goods from the place of delivery to the destination.

The EXW term is applicable to any mode of transportation, and it belongs to the actual mode of delivery.

Of all Ⅱ trade terms in INCOTERMS 2010, EXW is a term that is the least obligation of the seller and the buyer's obligation. The formalities, costs and risks of the goods, such as transportation and insurance, shall be handled and assumed by the buyer.

2. Seller's obligations

1) place the contracted goods under the buyer's disposal at the time and place specified

in the contract;

2) all risks and expenses before the goods are delivered to the buyer;

3) submit commercial invoice or equivalent electronic information.

3. Buyer's obligations

1) to receive and pay the goods in accordance with the contract;

2) all risks and expenses incurred after receiving the goods;

3) to obtain export and import licenses or other official documents and to handle the export and import customs formalities of the goods at their own risk and expense.

4. Problems requiring attention in EXW terminology

1) About the delivery of goods

When the buyer has the right to determine the specific time and place of delivery of the goods, the buyer shall notify the seller. If the buyer fails to notify the seller in time, the risk of loss or damage of the goods may be transferred to the buyer prior to the delivery of the goods. The seller shall give full notice to the buyer to advise when the goods may be placed at the disposal of the buyer in accordance with the terms of delivery, so that the buyer can pick up the goods in time.

2) Packing and shipping of the goods

In order to keep the principle of minimum seller's obligation under EXW, the seller shall not bear the responsibility and expense of loading the goods into the transportation vehicle.

3) about handling the export formalities

All procedures for the export of goods shall be handled by the buyer. If the buyer needs the assistance of the seller, the seller may accept the goods, but the risks and expenses shall be borne by the buyer.

4) on inspection fee

Under EXW, the pre-shipment inspection fee (PSI) shall be borne by the buyer, including the compulsory inspection by the exporting country authorities.

二、FAS

FAS: Free rider Ship (... Delivery by the Port of Shipment, ... Designated port of shipment).

1. The basic meaning of FAS terms

The seller shall, at the appointed time and the port of shipment, deliver the contracted goods to the vessel assigned by the buyer and notify the buyer in time; shipping risks and charges are bound by the loading port.

FAS terms apply to water transport.

2. Two points

1) "side" means the place where the hook of the carrying vessel is;

2) if the carrying vessel is unable to reach the shore for the reason of the wharf, the seller shall bear the cost of the lighters transferred at the port of shipment.

3. Obligations of both parties

FAS and FOB are basically similar, the differences are as follows:

1) the seller shall deliver the goods to the side of the ship without loading the vessel;

2) the risk division is bound by "ship side" and not bound by loading port;

3) the delivery voucher is "carrying goods receipt" (Cargo Receipt), rather than of bills of Lading (On Board Bill of Lading).

4. Precautions

The United States also has a trade term called "FAS," but where the FAS is "Free Along Side", its meaning is "next to the seller as long as the goods have any transportation", it has to do with our discussion of the meaning of the term "FAS" in "general principles". Therefore, whenever we use FAS terms in trade with the Americas, we must add "Vessel" to the term "FAS", such as "FAS Vessel New Orleans" "FAS Vessel Philadelphia", etc.

三、DAT

Delivered at Terminal (Named Terminal at Port or Place of Destination), Delivered to the Terminal (…Specify a terminal).

"Designated terminal delivery" means that the seller removes the goods from the means of transport at the end of the port or terminal where the buyer can dispose of the goods.

Similar to replaced the DEQ term, the seller in the specified terminal station after unloading the goods to the disposal of the buyer to complete delivery, term referring to the terminal including port wharf, warehouse, container yard or railway, highway and air cargo terminal, etc. The seller shall bear all risks and expenses (except the import costs) of transporting the goods to the terminal. This term is applicable to any mode of transport or multimodal transport.

四、DAP

DAP: Delivered at Place (…Named Place of Destination). Specify the destination.

"Designated destination delivery" means the seller has used to transport the goods arrived at the destination specified by the buyer, will be installed on the transport of goods (without unloading) to the disposal of the buyer, or to complete the delivery of the goods.

Similar to the three terms of DAF, DES and DDU, the seller will deliver the goods at the specified destination, and the delivery will be completed only if the goods are ready to be unloaded. The term refers to the means of transport including the ship and the destination including the port. The seller shall bear all risks and expenses (except the import costs) of transporting the goods to the designated destination. This term is applicable to any mode of transport, multimodal transport and sea transport.

五、DDP

DDP: Delivered Duty Paid (… Named Place of Destination). Specify the destination.

1. The basic meaning of DDP terminology

Payment after delivery of the goods refers to the seller the goods shipped to the importer's designated locations, will be in delivery transport has not yet been unloaded the goods delivered to the buyer, and is responsible for the import customs clearance formalities, pay to the customs formalities in the should pay any "duty is expended", fulfils his obligation to deliver. The seller must bear all costs and risks of transporting the goods to the site. This term is applicable to any mode of transportation.

2. Use of DDP terminology

1) DDP term is the trade term that the seller bears the most responsibility, expense and risk.

2) DDP term is the only term that requires the seller to import customs clearance procedures.

3) if the seller cannot obtain the import license directly or indirectly, the term shall not be used.

(资料来源：丁溪，唐赛. 国际贸易理论与实务 [M]. 中国商务出版社，2013.)

➢ 本章小结

贸易术语来源于国际贸易惯例，它是在长期贸易时间的基础上发展起来的。目前国际上较为权威性的惯例主要有《1932年华沙——牛津规则》《1941年美国对外贸易定义修订本》以及《2010国际贸易术语解释通则》。其中，《2010年通则》是世界上影响最为深远、使用最为广泛的惯例之一。

《2010年通则》将贸易术语分两组，共11种术语。其中EXW卖方责任和义务最小的贸易术语，DDP是卖方责任和义务最大的贸易术语。

由于价格构成因素不同，影响价格变化的因素也多种多样。因此，在确定进出口商品价格时，必须充分考虑影响价格的因素，并注意同一商品在不同情况应有合理的差价。合同中的价格条款一般包括商品的单价和总值两项基本内容。对外贸易效益或成本核算通常包括出口商品盈亏率、出口商品换汇成本和出口创汇率等。佣金是代理人为委托人进行交易而收取的报酬。折扣是指卖方按原价给予买方一定比例的减让。根据国际贸易的特点，用来计价的货币，可以是出口国货币，也可以是进口国货币或双方同意的第三国货币，由买卖双方协商确定。

➢ 本章名词

贸易术语　国际贸易惯例　《2010年通则》　FOB　CFR　CIF　FCA　CPT　CIP　EXW　FAS　DAT　DAP　DDP　出口商品盈亏率　出口商品换汇成本　出口销售外汇净收入　计价货币　佣金　折扣

➢ 理论思考

1. 何谓贸易术语？其对国际贸易的作用是什么？有关贸易术语的国际惯例有哪些？
2. 装运港完成交货的常用贸易术语有哪三种？它们的异同点是什么？
3. 试分析FOB、CFR、CIF术语与FCA、CPT、CIP术语的异同。

➢ 实训习题

1. 我国A公司向德国B公司订购冰箱800台。合同规定，冰箱价格为每台600美元CIF大连，2017年6月30日汉堡港装货。货物于2017年6月30日装船，B公司向船公司出具了货物品质的保函。船长应B公司的请求，出具了清洁提单。B公司据此从银行取得了货款。货物到达大连港后，A公司发现，该批货物外包装箱有严重破损，机器亦受到严重损坏，遂向船方提出索赔。船公司出示了B公司提供的保函，认为该事应由B公司负责，并建议A公司凭手中的保单向保险公司索赔。请问：

（1）关于船公司的责任问题，说法错误的是（　　）。

A. 船公司不应承担责任

B. 船公司应承担责任

C. 船公司有义务将表面状况良好的货物交给收货人

D. 以上说法都正确

（2）关于B公司的责任问题，说法正确的是（　　）。

A. B公司不应承担责任

B. B公司应承担责任

C. 本题目中说"装船时外包装有严重破损"没有交代是在越过船舷之前还是之后，无法判断B公司是否应担责

D. 以上说法都不对

（3）关于保险公司如何对待 A 公司的索赔，正确的说法的是（   ）。

A. 如无约定，保险公司可以不赔

B. 如有约定，保险公司应在承保范围内向 A 公司赔偿

C. 如有约定，保险公司可代位取得向船公司索赔的权利

D. 以上说法都不对

（4）对于 A 公司的损失如何得到补偿问题，说法错误的是（   ）。

A. A 公司可向保险公司索赔　　　B. A 公司可向船公司索赔

C. A 公司可向 B 公司索赔　　　　D. 以上说法都不对

（5）下列说法正确的是（   ）。

A. 银行不应将货款给 B 公司

B. 银行有权将货款给 B 公司

C. A 公司德国 B 公司的合同应无效

D. 以上说法都不对

2. 我国 A 公司与某国 B 公司于 2015 年 10 月 20 日签订购买 52 500 吨化肥的 CFR 合同。A 公司开出信用证规定，装船期规定 2016 年 1 月 1 日至 1 月 10 日，由于 B 公司租来货船"大丰号"在开往某外国港口途中遇到飓风，该船于 1 月 21 日抵达装运港，2016 年 1 月 27 日才装货完毕。承运人取得 B 公司出具的保函的情况下签发了与信用证条款一致的提单。A 公司为这批货物投保了水渍险。2016 年 1 月 30 日"大丰号"途经达尼尔海峡时起火，造成部分化肥烧毁。船长在命令救火过程中又造成部分化肥湿毁。由于船在装货港口的延迟，使该船到达目的地时赶上了化肥价格下跌，A 公司在出售余下的化肥时价格不得不大幅度下降，给 A 公司造成很大损失。

请根据上述事例，回答以下问题：

（1）途中烧毁的化肥损失应由（   ）承担。

A. A 公司　　　B. B 公司　　　C. 船公司　　　D. 保险公司

（2）途中湿毁的化肥损失应由（   ）承担。

A. A 公司　　　　　　　　　　B. 保险公司

C. 船公司　　　　　　　　　　D. A 公司与船公司共同承担

（3）下列说法错误的是（   ）。

A. A 公司不可向承运人追偿由于化肥价格下跌造成的损失

B. A 公司可以向承运人追偿由于化肥价格下跌造成的损失

C. 承运人可以向托运人 B 公司追偿责任

D. 承运人可以向 A 公司追偿责任

3. 内地外贸 E 公司以 FOB 中国口岸价与中国香港 W 公司成交钢材一批，港商即转手以 CFR 釜山价售给韩国 H 公司。港商来证价格为 FOB 中国口岸，要求货运釜山，并在提单上表明"Freight Prepaid"（运费预付），试分析港商为什么这样做？内

地方应如何处理。

4. 我国"长远"公司向德国"卡尔"公司出口瓷器一批，采用 FCA 方式成交。德方要求中方协助联系运输公司，中方同意协助联系，并最终促使德方与船公司签订了海运合同，与国际货物运输公司签订了铁路运输合同。同时，买方办理了相关的保险。买方在信用证规定的日期内及时交货，并取得了相应的单据。但是货到柏林后买方发现瓷器有部分破损现象，损失较严重。于是找到了负责铁路运输的国际货物运输公司，但被告知，铁运途中并无任何违规操作，货物也未发生异常现象，运输平稳、安全，货物破损应为海上运输所致，于是找到船方，船方声称，海上运输亦严格遵守国际货物海运有关的国际惯例，货物损失应为厂家交货时，中途换货所致。于是买方提出向卖方索赔。

请问：

（1）卖方应否索赔？为什么？

（2）谁来承担损失？

（3）承担损失的一方应如何处理，才能合理转嫁自己的损失？

5. 中国"新达"贸易公司与荷兰一家公司签订了 FCA 出口合同，信用证交货期限为 7 月前。但交货期将近，买方仍迟迟没有通知承运人的名称及情况，后来，在发来的传真中得知：与买方一直有合作关系的丹麦联合运输公司日前经营不善而倒闭。为了不影响及时装货及收汇，我公司及时联系了运输公司、订立运输合同，并准备好运输工具，一切准备就绪后，卖方电告通知买方，卖方在复函中对于中方的帮助表示了感谢，并说明对于卖方垫付的运费买方将给予补偿。

请回答：

（1）卖方和买方各自的失误之处是？

（2）卖方能否顺利结汇，请说明原因。

6. 我出口新野公司与德国进口商签订 CPT 出口大豆 30 万吨的合同，合同中约定货到汉堡。不久，对方开来了目的地为汉堡的信用证，卖方遂将已备好的货物包装完毕，与铁运公司签订了运输契约，并及时通知了买方。但在铁路运输途中，由于这家铁路公司所派的集装箱年久欠修，箱顶因锈蚀而不防雨，恰正值连阴雨天气，致使大部分大豆被泡，已无利用价值。买方提出，运输公司是卖方联系的，合同中又约定是货到汉堡，现今，卖方所交货物已无价值，全部责任应有卖方承担并向提出索赔。卖方以出现此种情况皆是由于铁运公司的过失所导致，理应由铁路公司赔偿为由拒绝向买方赔偿。

判断并回答：

（1）买方的过失在于。

（2）卖方有过失在于。

（3）铁路公司有过失在于。

（4）此项损失应由谁来承担？理由是？

7. 我国某出口公司与伊朗外商以 CIP 方式订立了一份出口合同，签订合同后，我方积极备货并包装，同时，与中远国际运输公司签订了运输契约。中远公司承诺为我方提供"门到门"的全程运输服务，并对此次运输上了保险。外商也及时开出了信用证。我方在规定的交货日期前，将包装好的货物装上了中远公司派来的运输车。但后来从买方得知，货物并没有在预计的日期抵达伊朗，后经我方向中远公司核查了解到：货物的确是在起运地点我方装货的运输车上丢失的。于是，买方以运输合同系我方订立，并运输工具也是我方提供而造成货物的丢失为由，向我方提出索赔。我方找到中远公司，希望能够协商解决，中远公司声称自己并无责任。因为当日的载货司机是由于公司临时急需用人而招聘的临时工。就连卡车现在也不知去向，此种行为已经构成刑事犯罪，此事正通过公安机关寻找此人。请问，我方该如何处理此事？

CHAPTER 4

第四章 商品的描述

> **本章指导**

通过对本章的学习要求能够了解国际货物买卖合同中关于商品的品名、品质、数量、包装的基本内容及其在订立合同时应注意的问题,掌握并能够在进出口业务中运用:

1. 表示商品品质的方法;
2. 重量和数量的表示方法及数量的机动幅度;
3. 包装的标志、种类、包装条款。

第一节 商品的品名、品质

一、商品的品名

商品品名,是合同中不可缺少的主要交易条件。品名也代表了商品通常应具有的品质。在合同中,应尽可能使用国际上通用的名称。

新商品的定名,应力求准确、符合国际的习惯称呼。对某些商品还应该注意选择合适的品名,以利降低关税,方便进行出口和节省运费开支。

国际上为了便于统计征税,对商品有共同的分类标准,海关合作理事会于1988年1月1日起正式实施了《商品名称及编码协调制度》(HS)。我国于1992年1月1日起采用该制度。目前,各国的海关统计、普惠制待遇等都按HS进行。所以,我国在采用商品名称,特别是通用名称时,应该与HS规定的品名相符合。

二、商品的品质 (quality of goods)

商品的品质,是商品的内在品质和外观形态的综合。商品的品质好坏直接关系到商品的市场价格、销售、企业的信誉、国家的形象，影响到进出口双方的经济利益，品质已经成为各国发展贸易的一项必要条件。

三、对商品品质的要求

1. 对出口商品的品质要求

（1）世界各国（地区）经济水平的不均衡，消费者的消费习惯、风俗习惯有差异，从世界市场的各种要求出发，生产出适销对路的出口商品，使其在品质等方面满足不同档次的消费水平。

（2）必须充分全面了解和熟悉各国对进口商品的相关法律、法规、贸易惯例等，扩大我国商品的出口，促进贸易的发展。

（3）以商品的质量为核心，建立健全企业及商品的质量、环境管理体系。如国际标准化组织（ISO）系列标准，促进商品的市场竞争力。

2. 对进口商品的品质要求

（1）在选购进口商品时，应了解各国对商品的具体质量要求及其规定。

（2）在订立买卖合同时，符合有关标准、规定的进口商品可购买，减少贸易纠纷，保护人民的生命财产健康安全。

四、表示商品品质的方法

国际贸易中，表示商品品质的方法为两类：

1. 实物样品表示法

这种方法称"凭样品买卖"（sale by sample）。它分为：

凭卖方样品买卖（sale by seller's sample）；

凭买方样品买卖（sale by buyer's sample）；

凭对等样品买卖：卖方按买方提供的样品，复制出经买方确认的样品，这个样品称"对等样品"（counter sample）。

2. 文字说明表示法

国际贸易中，用文字说明表示商品品质的方法。

凭规格（sale by specification）买卖：指一些足以反映商品品质的主要指标，如化学成分、含量、纯度、性能、容量、长短、粗细等；

凭等级（sale by grade）买卖：分为很多等级，用大、中、小等文字或符号表示，如茶叶、鸡蛋、生丝等；

凭标准（sale by standard）买卖：对商品的规格采用标准化，用文字说明。它分为国际标准、国家标准、行业标准及企业标准等；

凭牌号（sale by brand）或商标（sale by trade mark）买卖：浙江的"龙井"茶叶，瑞士的"罗马表"等；

凭产地名称（sale by name of origin）买卖：以某国某一地区的某地方为标志的，如"绍兴花雕酒"；

凭说明书（sale by description and illustration）买卖：有些商品如仪器、电器等。

对于某些农副产品，采用良好平均品质"F. A. Q."（fair average quality），如用于大米、棉花等。

五、合同中的品质条款（quality clause）

1. 品质条款的基本内容

基本内容要求清楚、具体、详细，包括表示商品品质的方法、等级等。如采用说明书表示品质时，合同中应标明该说明书的名称和份数。若商品是农副产品时，合同中应注明生产时间、采用的标准等。

例：柠檬酸钠，规格：①符合1980年版英国药典标准；②纯度：不低于99%。

2. 品质机动幅度和品质公差

品质机动幅度：卖方所交商品品质指标可以在一定幅度内浮动，适用于初级产品。如：山东花生，含油量最低为44%，杂质不超过1%。

品质公差：适用于工业制成品，即品质指标允许一定的误差，即品质公差。如手表每天误差若干秒，在合同里需明确认定品质公差的内容。

卖方交货品质在机动幅度或品质公差允许的范围内，货物价格一般按合同计算，不再另作调整。需要调整价格，按买卖双方的约定。

六、订立品质条款注意

1. 正确使用表示商品品质的方法，按具体的商品，采用合理的方法。

2. 订立合同中的品质条款时，语言应恰当。一般可写为"交货品质与样品大体相符"，不用绝对词语。

3. 科学、实事求是地订立品质条款，避免太高或太低，减少履行合同的纠纷。

《联合国国际货物销售合同公约》规定："卖方交付的货物必须与合同规定的数量、质量和规格相符，否则买方有权要求损害赔偿，也可要求修理或交付替代货物，甚至拒收货物或撤销合同。卖方所交货物的实际品质不能低于合同规定，低于合同规定就是违约行为，货物实际品质也不宜高于合同规定，高于合同规定，有时也会构成违约。"

第二节 商品的数量

合同中的数量条款，是合同中的重要条款之一，是买卖双方交接货物的重要依据。

一、商品的计量单位

国际货物买卖中常用的计量单位：

1. 重量单位（weight）

吨（metric ton，M/T）、长吨（long ton，L/T）、短吨（short ton，S/T）、千克（kilogram，kg）、磅（pound，Lb）、盎司（ounce）等。适用于农副产品等。

2. 数量单位（number）

只（piece）、双（pair）、套（set）、箱（bag）、打（dozen）、件（package）、令（ream）等。适用于工业制成品、土特产品等，例如电视机、纸张、服装等。

3. 长度单位（length）

米（meter）、英尺（foot）、厘米（centimetre）、码（yard）等。适用于布料、绳索、丝绸等。

4. 面积单位（area）

平方米（square meter）、平方英尺（square foot）、平方码（square yard）等。适用于玻璃等。

5. 体积单位（volume）

立方米（cubic meter）、立方英尺（cubic foot）、立方码（cubic yard）等。适用于木材、天然气等。

6. 容积单位（capacity）

升（litre）、加仑（gallon）、蒲式耳（bushel）等。适用于谷物、酒类、油类等。

二、商品的计算方法

1. 按毛重计算

毛重（gross weight）指商品本身重量加上包装的重量，如在合同中规定为："中国大米，50公吨，单层新麻袋装，每袋100千克，以毛作净。"

2. 按净重计算

净重（net weight）是商品本身的重量，不含包装物的重量，计算包装物的重量有4种方法：

（1）实际皮重（actual tare），将商品的包装物逐一过秤后的实际重量。

（2）平均皮重（average tare），在重量大致相同的情况下，取若干件的实际重量，计算包装的平均重量。

（3）习惯皮重（customary tare），有些较规格化的包装，市场公认其重量，即习惯皮重。

（4）约定皮重（computed tare），按买卖双方约定的包装重量为准。

3. 按公量计算

公量（conditioned weight）是采用科学方法抽去商品的水分，再加上标准水分计算重量。有些商品，如羊毛、生丝等价值较高、含水量不稳定，通常采用公量来计算这类商品的重量。

4. 按理论重量计算

理论重量（theoretical weight），一些商品重量大致相等，可通过件数计算重量。如马口铁、钢板等。

三、合同中的数量条款（quantity clause）

1. 基本内容包括买卖双方成交商品的数量、计量单位、计量方法、毛重、净重等。

2. 订立数量条款需要注意：

（1）溢短装条款（more or less clause），是指在买卖合同的数量条款中，明确规定卖方允许多装或少装的百分比。如1 000吨，卖方可溢短装5%（100M/T, with 5% more or less at seller's option），即卖方交货量可在95M/T～105M/T之间。具体来讲，A. 可溢短装的百分比，应视商品的特点、数量、交易习惯、运输工具等情况确定。B. 溢短装的选择权可由买方、卖方或船方决定。C. 溢短装的计价，一般按合同价格计算。

（2）进出口双方应考虑货物的具体数量、市场的动态、客户的资信等因素。在数量条款中，商品的数量应明确、具体，商品采用的计量单位应准确；如货物用重量计算，注明采用的计量方法。如用"吨"单位时，应明确、具体的规定是长吨、短吨、还是吨，一般不采用"约、大概"等模棱两可、含糊不清的用语。

（3）跟单信用证业务中，按国际商会《跟单信用证统一惯例》（简称UCP500）中第39条a款规定："大约""近似"或类似意义的词语用于涉及信用证规定的数量时，应解释为允许有关数量有10%的增减。b款规定：除非信用证规定数量不得增减，只要支取金额不超过信用证金额，可有5%增减幅度。

第三节 商品的包装

商品总是和一定的包装联系在一起，有些包装已成为商品的必要组成部分。在国际货物买卖中，商品的包装成为交易达成的重要环节，是交易双方订立合同的一项主要内容。

国际贸易较复杂，交易双方涉及的地域较广，关系到多种运输方式，许多商品进入世界市场需要经过长途运输，通过多次装运、转存，才能到达目的地，商品的包装因此十分重要，对出口货物的包装要求更为严格。交易方的消费习惯、区域差异对商品的包装提出要求，要求买卖双方签订买卖合同时，对商品的包装进行洽谈协商，列出有关包装的规定。包装条款是买卖合同的重要条款之一。

国际贸易中，按流通过程中作用不同，包装分类如下：

运输包装和销售包装。商品的包装可保护商品，可用于宣传、展销、提高商品的市场竞争力。

一、运输包装

运输包装（transport package）（又称外包装、大包装）是指将货物装入特定容器内，以特定方式成件成箱包装。可以在长途运输过程中，有效保护商品不被损坏，便于运输，节省费用，避免因气候条件对商品产生影响。

（一）运输包装的种类

1. 单件运输包装

箱装：按包装材料分木箱、纸箱、铁箱、塑料箱等，适用于服装等。

袋装：分纸袋、塑料袋、布袋、麻袋等。适用于颗粒状农产品等货物。

桶装：分木桶、铁桶、塑料桶等。适用于液体、粉状等货物的包装。

捆装：将货物用棉布、麻袋包装，在外面加箍铁和塑料袋的包装方式，适用于羊毛、棉花等可压紧的货物。

2. 集合运输包装

将单件运输包装组成一个大的包装，有集装袋、集装包、集装箱、托盘。

（二）运输包装的标志

按用途分运输标志、指示性标志和警告性标志。

1. 运输标志（shipping mark）

常用一个简单的几何图形和一些字母、数字、简单文字组成。便于运输、辨认货物、顺利完成交易，防止错发错运。

运输标志分三部分：

（1）收货人的名称，合同号码、发票号，在简单的几何图形中标明，用于识别货物。

（2）目的地名称（或目的港名称），需经过其他（港口）转运，在目的地（目的港）下面加上转运地名称，便于运输部门正确装运。

（3）件号，包装货物的总件数和每件货物大小顺序号。如"No. 1~100"。

ABC	收货人名称缩写
LC-5	参考号
SAN FRANCISCO	目的地（目的港）
No. 1~100	件数及箱号

包装上采用运输标志，按合同规定或由交易方决定。

2. 指示性标志（indicative mark）

对一些易碎、易损、易变质的商品，在商品包装上标注醒目的标志，引起装运人员的注意，便于运输、仓储，保护人员、货物的安全，如"防湿""小心轻放""向上"等。

3. 警告性标志（warning mark）

又称危险品标志，是对装有危险品、易燃品、有毒气体、腐蚀性物品和放射性物品等的运输包装上用文字或图形表示各种危险品的标志，提示工作人员警惕、采取保护措施、安全措施，保护工作人员及货物的安全。

（三）运输包装的要求

国际贸易商品采用的运输包装要求严格。应符合商品的特点，满足运输方式的要求，符合交易方的贸易规则，便于货物装运、操作人员的工作。

二、销售包装（selling packing）

1. 它是指商品制造出来以后采用适当的材料、容器进行的初次包装

条形码标志用于销售包装上。条形码（product code），是由一组粗细间隔不等的平行线条及其相应的数字组成的标记。商品包装上使用条形码标志，便于销售，可以识别商品的信息。

国际上通用的条形码主要有两种：一种是美国统一代码委员会编制的 UPC 码（Univeral Product Code）。另一种是由国际物品编码协会编制的 EAN 码（European Article Number)。为扩大商品出口,我国 1988 年成立中国物品编码中心,1991 年 4 月,中心代表中国加入国际物品编码协会。该协会分配给我国的国别号为"690""691""692"。凡标有"690""691""692"条形码的商品,表示中国生产的商品。

2. 销售包装的要求

商品的销售包装应满足市场需求,符合包装要求,易于货物的运送、销售、使用,符合推广宣传的要求。

三、定牌、无牌和中性包装

定牌:是卖方按买方要求在其出售的商品或包装上标明买方指定的商品或牌名。为了扩大商标、牌名的知名度,扩大商品的销售市场,用于国外长期、数量较大的订货。

无牌:在出口商品上或包装上不用任何商标和牌号,用于半制成品或低值易耗品。为了降低成本,节省费用。

中性包装:在商品上和内包装、外包装上不注明生产国别的包装。主要为了打破一些进口国和地区的关税、非关税壁垒,扩大商品出口。中性包装分无牌中性包装和定牌中性包装。中性包装的做法在贸易中容易引起非议,应慎用。

在一般定牌、无牌商品中,在我国出口商品或包装上均需注明中国制造字样。

四、合同中的包装条款 (packing clause)

1. 基本内容

一般由包装材料、包装方式、包装商品的数量或重量构成。

例如,木箱装每箱 100 千克净重。

In wooden cases of 100 kilos net each.

2. 订立包装条款

(1) 规定的包装应明确、具体,不宜采用"海运包装""习惯包装"等含糊其词的词语,缺乏统一的解释,易引起贸易纠纷。

(2) 为履行合同,应考虑世界各国对包装的特殊要求,考虑交易方的风俗习惯、贸易惯例等。

(3) 按《联合国国际货物销售合同公约》规定:卖方交付的货物,需按照合同规定的方式装箱或包装。

(4) 在包装条款中明确使用包装方式和包装材料。

(5) 包装条款中应规定所用的运输标志。

(6) 包装条款中对包装费用应规定清楚。

Quality of Goods

The quality of the goods refers to the outward appearance and the essential quality of the goods, such as shape, structure, colour, flavour as well as chemical composition, physical and mechanical property, biological feature, etc.

In international trade, the quality of the goods not only concerns the value in use and the price of the goods, but also concerns the sales of the goods and credit standing of the manufacturer.

In international trade, the quality clause in the sales contract is the basis for delivery of the goods. In case the quality of the goods is not in conformity with the stipulation of the contract, the seller shall undertake the relevant legal responsibility, the buyer is entitled to file a claim against the seller or even cancel the contract.

Therefore in business negotiation and conclusion of the contract, the quality clause shall be stipulated clearly.

A. Methods of Stipulating Quality of the Goods

In international trade, there are 2 ways to indicate the quality of the goods either by description or by sample.

1. Sale by Description

In international business, most commodities are suitable to sale by description which can be subdivided into 4 kinds.

1) **Sale by specification, grade or standard.** The specification of the goods refers to certain main indicators which indicate the quality of the goods, such as composition, content, purity, size, length, etc.

The way of determining the quality of the goods by specification is called sale by specification. Sale by specification is comparatively convenient and accurate, so it is the most widely used method in international trade.

The grade of the goods refers to the classifications of the commodity of one kind which is indicated by words, numbers or symbols. The classifications are usually decided by different qualities, weights, compositions, appearances, properties, etc.

The standard refers to the specifications or grades which are stipulated and announced by the government or the chamber of commerce, etc.

In the international agricultural and by-product market, there is a commonly adopted standard, i. e., fair average quality (F. A. Q.). According to the explanation of some countries, F. A. Q. refers to the average quality level of the export commodity within a certain period of time. This kind of standard is quite ambiguous. In fact, it does not represent any fixed, accurate specification. At present, we adopt F. A. Q. to indicate the qualities of some of our agricultural products and by-products which are usually determined by the average quality level. When adopting this kind of method, we shall stipulate the main specification indexes as well in the contract.

For example,

Chinese Groundnut, 1994 crop, F. A. Q.,

Moisture (max.) 13%,

Admixture (max.) 5%,

Oil content (min.) 44%.

Sometimes G. M. Q., i. e., good merchantable quality, is adopted to indicate the quality of the goods, which is even more unclear than F. A. Q.

2) **Sale by brand name or trade mark.** As to the goods whose quality is stable, reputation is sound and with which the customers are quite familiar, we may sell it by brand name or trade mark.

3) **Sale by name of origin.** There are some agricultural products and by-products whose origins are well known all over the world. As to these products, the origins may well indicate their qualities.

The quality of some commodities, such as technological instruments, electric machines, etc. can not be simply indicated by quality indexes, instead it is quite necessary to explain in detail the structure, material, performance as well as method of operation. Thus, the specific descriptions of products are required to indicate the quality of the goods. If necessary, pictures, photos, etc. must also be provided.

2. Sale by Sample

In our export business, owing to the feature of some commodities themselves, it is quite difficult to indicate the quality of those goods only by words, thus, sale by sample comes into being. For example, handicraft articles, clothes or native products etc. are usually sold by sample. The sample refers to the article which can be used to represent the quality of the whole lot.

Sale by sample includes two cases, i. e., sale by the seller's sample and sale by the buyer's sample.

1) Sale by the seller's sample: In this case, the seller shall supply a representative

sample which will possess the moderate quality among a large quantity of the physical goods, and at the same time keep a duplicate sample, which shall be in quality as or on the whole as the same as the standard sample. The sample dispatched and the duplicate sample kept shall have the same article number so as to make it convenient for delivery, verification when handling quality disputes or future transactions.

2) Sale by the buyer's sample.

a) In this case, the seller shall first take into consideration the availability of the new material and the possibility of providing the processing technology.

b) In order to take the initiative, the seller may reproduce the buyer's sample i.e., counter sample, and send it back to the buyer as a type sample. After the buyer confirms the counter sample, sale by the buyer's sample is changed into sale by the seller's counter sample.

c) The two parties shall stipulate that in case the buyer's sample results in any disputes of infringement of industrial property, the seller will have nothing to do with it.

B. Quality Clause in the Sales Contract

The quality clause usually includes the specification, grade, standard or brand, etc. of the goods. In the case of sale by sample, it is necessary to indicate the number of the sample and the date of despatch.

For example,

1) 9371 China Green Tea Special Chunmee;
2) Sample No. 612 Cloth Doll;
3) White Rice, Long – Shaped,

Broken Grains (max.) 25%,

Admixture (max.) 0.25%,

Moisture (max.) 15%.

As to the goods whose specifications and properties or performances are complicated, we shall adopt the following clauses:

1) Quality as per sample No ... and the technical features indicated in the illustrations submitted by the seller.

2) Quality and technical data as per the seller's catalogue No ...

3) Quality and technical data to be in conformity with the attached technical agreement which forms an integral part of the contract.

In many cases, the quality indexes shall be stipulated flexibly and scientifically. We usually adopt the quality latitude which means that the quality indexes of the goods delivered by the seller may be controlled flexibly within a certain latitude.

There are 3 ways to stipulate the quality latitude.

1) To stipulate a certain scope, for example, the width of the cotton cloth is 47/48 inches.

2) To stipulate more or less clause, for example, as to grey duck's down, we may stipulate "duck's down content 18% (1% more or less)".

3) To stipulate "max" or "min",

For example,

Rice Broken Grains (max.) 25%,

Admixture (max.) 1%.

Moisture (max.) 15%.

The quality tolerance is used in the trade of industrial products, which means that the quality of the goods delivered by the seller is allowed to have certain differences within a certain range since such differences are usually unavoidable and commonly accepted as the usage of the same special trade.

C. Importance of Quality

The quality of the goods is not only the focus of attention which the both parties to the transaction always concern themselves with in their business negotiation, but also the major point which the distributing or operating enterprises, trading corporations or commercial firms, end-users or consumers follow with great interest on the market.

It is self-evident that the importance of quality can not be over-emphasized:

1) It involves the fundamental rights and obligations of both parties.

2) It determines the price value of the goods.

3) It is the most important one of the many factors that exerts a tremendous influence over the sales and prestige of the goods.

4) The fine-quality goods always find themselves in an advantageous position in the intense competition.

5) The well-known goods of high quality are always welcomed by the end-users or consumers.

6) If the quality of the goods is not in conformity with the contractual description, it is regarded as a breach of the contract and thus leads to disputes.

Therefore, the quality of the goods has a great and close bearing upon the sales volume. Constantly improving the quality of the goods and maintaining the high quality standard is no doubt a powerful means to secure, keep and expand big marketing shares in the competitive world market.

Quantity of Goods

In international trade, both parties to the transaction must take the agreed quantity of the goods as the foundation for performance of the contract. The quantity of the goods refers to the weight, number, length, volume, area, capacity, etc. which are indicated by different measuring units. The goods not only find expression in a certain quality, but also in a certain quantity. The quantity of the goods not only concerns the volume of the specific transaction, but also influences the changes of the market. According to the legal stipulations of some countries, the quantity of the goods delivered by the seller must be in conformity with that stipulated in the contract. Article 52, Item 2 in "the United Nations Convention on Contracts for the International Sale of Goods" stipulates "If the seller delivers a quantity of the goods greater than that provided for in the contract, the buyer may take delivery or refuse to take delivery of the excess quantity. If the buyer takes delivery of all or part of the excess quantity, he must pay for it at the contract rate." So the quantity of the goods is very important to both parties to the transaction. Trade without quantity of the goods is not trade at all. Therefore, in any trade the volume must be indicated by a certain quantity of the goods.

A. Calculating Methods of Quantity of the Goods

1. Calculating Units of Quantity of the Goods

In international trade, when determining the quantity of the goods, we have to be clear about the measuring units at first.

The adoption of measuring units is decided by the nature of the goods. Owing to the fact that the measuring systems in different countries are not the same, the measuring units and measuring methods are accordingly different. Usually the following measuring units are adopted in China.

1) Weight: Usually used for mineral products, agricultural and by-products, it includes gram, kilogram, ounce, metric ton, long ton, short ton, etc.

2) Number: Constantly used for measurement of industrial products and general products, it includes piece, pair, set, dozen, gross, ream, etc.

3) Length: Mostly used for textile products, metal cords, etc., it includes meter, foot, yard, etc.

4) Area: Often used for glass, textile products, etc., it includes square meter, square foot, etc..

5) Volume: Generally used for timber, chemical gases, etc., it includes cubic meter, cubic foot, cubic yard, etc..

6) Capacity: Mostly used for grain, petroleum, etc., it includes litre, gallon, bushel, etc..

Since different countries adopt different measuring systems, the same name of the measuring unit does not always refer to the same quantity.

Currently, the commonly used measuring systems in international trade are "SI" (International System of Units), the Metric System, the U. S. system and the British System.

The basic measuring system adopted in our country is the Metric System, and we are adopting SI gradually. According to Article 3 in the Measurement Act of the People's Republic of China, our country adopts SI. SI and the other measuring units selected by our country are legal measuring units of the nation. Beginning in January, 1991, except in a few special fields, nonlegal measuring units are not allowed to be used in China. In foreign trade, we shall also adopt legal measuring units, if the metric system or the British system or the U. S. system is not stipulated in the contract. We usually do not import non-legally measured machines and equipment. In case of some special needs, they shall be used subject to the authorization by the relative standard measurement administrations.

2. Methods of Calculating Weight

In international trade, there are many goods which are calculated by weight.

The following calculating methods are often used.

1) Gross weight. The gross weight refers to the weight of the cargo itself plus the tare, i. e., the weight of the cargo plus the weight of the packing material.

2) Net weight. The net weight is the actual weight of the goods. The tare is not included. In international trade, the goods which are calculated by weight, in most cases, are calculated by net weight so as to figure out the price value.

Some cargoes, such as tobacco flakes, news reels whose packings are not convenient to be calculated by net weight, or those, the values of the packing materials are almost the same as the values of the cargoes themselves, such as grain, fodder, etc., are often calculated by gross weight, which is called "Gross for Net" in international trade. For example, "Northeast China soybean, 1,000 M/T, packed in single new gunny bags, 100 kilograms per bag, gross for net."

The method of calculating the net weight is pursued by means of the gross weight minus the tare. The methods of calculating the tare are as follows:

a) **Actual tare**: In order to get the actual tare of the goods, we shall calculate the weight of each packing of the goods one by one for the whole lot.

b) **Average tare**: As the packing materials and specifications of some cargoes are uniform, we can get the average tare by weighing a part of the cargo packings.

c) **Customary tare**: As for more unified packings, we can take the weights of them commonly accepted by the market as the customary tares.

d) **Computed tare**: We may take the agreed packing weight as a standard, so that it is unnecessary to weigh any more.

In international trade, sometimes, the net weight also includes the marketing packing weight. For instance, the weight of fruit sweets usually includes the weight of the sugar coating. However, some noble metals and chemical materials are usually weighed in the light of the net weight. The so-called net refers to the weight of the cargo itself, which does not include any packing weight.

3) **Conditioned weight.** In order to get the conditioned weight, we shall first of all by a scientific method abstract water from the cargo then put the standard water content in it. This kind of calculating method is suitable to those cargoes whose water contents are not stable, such as wool, raw silk, etc. The conditioned weight is calculated by a standard regaining rate of water. The regaining rate of water is the ratio between the water content and the dry weight of the cargo. The standard regaining rate of water is the ratio between the water content and the dry weight of the cargo which is accepted on the world market. The actual regaining rate of water is the ratio between the actual regaining water content in the cargo and the actual dry weight.

The formula of calculating the conditioned weight is:

$$\text{conditioned weight} = \frac{\text{actual weight} \times (1 + \text{standard regaining rate of water})}{1 + \text{actual regaining rate of water}}$$

The accepted international standard regaining water content of wool and raw silk is 11%.

4) **Theoretical weight**: Some fixed cargoes, such as tin plate, steel plate, etc. have unified shapes and measurements, as long as the specification is identical, the size is conformable, the weight will be about the same, we can calculate the weight according to the number of pieces.

B. Quantity Clause in the Contract

The quantity clause in the contract is very important, it is the foundation for effecting shipment and taking delivery of the goods.

The basic contents of the quantity clause are the quantity to be delivered and the measuring unit to be used.

As to the goods, calculated by weight, we should clearly stipulate the specific calculating method, such as the gross weight, net weight, conditioned weight, etc. in the contract. For example, "Chinese rice, 500 M/T packed in gunny bags, 50kg. each, net weight." The weights of some goods are not easy to be accurate. Owing to the influence of natural conditions, limitations of packing or transportation conditions, the actual quantity of the goods tends to be not in conformity with that stipulated in the contract. In order to avoid disputes during the fulfillment of the contract, both parties shall determine the delivery quantity reasonably and flexibly beforehand by setting a more or less clause, plus or minus clause or allowance clause in the contract. There are 2 ways to stipulate the quantity latitude:

1. More or Less

In the contract, we can stipulate that the seller may deliver the goods with a certain percentage more or less in quantity according to the agreed quantity latitude. This kind of stipulation is usually called "more or less clause."

The more or less clause is usually at the seller's option. For example, we may stipulate in the contract "Datong steam coal, shipment 5% more or less at the sellers option, value of the excess or shortage quantity to be calculated at the contract rate." Shandong Peanut, 800,000 M/T, 1995 Crop. F. A. Q. with 5% more or less both in quantity and amount to be allowed at the seller's option. But it may also be at the buyer's option.

As to the purchase price of the goods more or less delivered, there are 2 ways to calculate:

1) According to the unit price stipulated in the contract;
2) According to the market price when the cargo is shipped.

The purpose of adopting the latter method is to prevent the party who enjoys more or less rights from loading more or less deliberately owing to the fluctuation of the market price. If the contract does not stipulate the method for pricing of the goods more or less delivered, we usually assign the price to them according to the stipulation in the contract.

2. About or Circa or Approximate

If we put "about" before the quantity of the goods it indicates that the quantity of the good is not exact. For example, "heavy magnesium about 7,000 M/T.". As to the word "about", the implications are different in different countries. Some interpret it as 2.5, some 5%. The Uniform customs and Practice for Documentary Credits of International Chamber of Commerce (revised edition 1983, No. 400) stipulates that "about" should be interpreted as not exceeding 10% of the total quantity.

Packing of Goods

In international trade, most goods need packing. Packing is one of the essential component parts of commodity production. Generally speaking only packed commodities can enter into the circulation field, and attain the commercial value and use value of the goods. Packing can protect the commodity and keep it good in quality and intact in quantity in the circulation process. At the same time, it can increase the marketing value of the goods. As to the goods that need to be packed, both parties shall stipulate a clear packing clause in the contract on account of its great importance.

A. The Function of Packing

The function of packing mainly shows as follows: packing can be used to protect the goods and keep them as good and complete as they are shipped in the circulation field; it makes it convenient for storing, taking care of, transporting, loading, unloading, and calculating them; strong packing can prevent the goods from being stolen and damaged; reasonable packing can lessen shipping space and save freight. Marketing packing makes it convenient for consumers to select, carry, or use the goods; marketing packing can also beautify the commodity, attract consumers, expand sales and increase the gains on foreign, exchange. In addition to all those mentioned above, packing of the goods, in a sense, incarnate the level of a country's economic construction, science and technology, culture and art, etc..

In order to satisfy the rapid development of our foreign trade, we should grasp the latest achievement of packing science. do well in our export trade conscientiously, and try to make our packing more scientific, economical, strong, merchantable, and pleasing to the eye, and do our utmost to increase the foreign exchange earnings. So the following points should be complied with:

1) We should greatly strengthen the research into packing materials, packing containers and packing methods, in which we should not only attach importance to many years' experience in our packing work but also earnestly study the advanced experience of foreign countries, and starting from the reality of our country, continuously improve our commodity packing work.

2) We should carefully study the packing characteristics, developing tendency and rela-

tive packing regulations and decrees in international markets so as to make the packing of our export commodity adaptable to marketing requirements and consumption habits. Especially we should pay close attention to meeting the needs for our packaging decorations of the goods in foreign super-markets, and the reasonable stipulations on packing of import countries, thus increasing our commodity sales.

3) We should strengthen the study on and the design for packaging decorations, improve packing techniques, blaze new trails, and continuously increase the artistic level of packing.

4) We should fasten the realization of mechanization of our exporting commodity packing. Only in this way can we effectively boost our labour productivity, save labour power, better packing quality, cut down cost, economize materials. We should realize the standardization of packing and the unification of materials, specifications, capacities, standards and sealing methods, only in this way can it be easy to measure, identify, load, unload and transport the goods, so as to promote the smooth fulfillment of business.

5) On possible conditions, we should properly make acquisition of advanced technology from abroad, to help produce the high level and advanced packing materials which we cannot make by our own technology process, in order to meet the requirements of the international market for high level packing materials.

B. Kinds of Packing

The kinds of cargoes are various in international trade, from the view point of whether they need packing, they fall into 3 kinds:

1. Nude Cargo

Nude cargoes refer to those kinds of cargoes whose qualities are more stable. They are not easy to be influenced by outside circumstances and they become single pieces of their own. They are difficult to be packed or do not need any packing, such as steel products, lead ingot, timber, rubber, etc.

2. Cargo in Bulk

Cargoes in bulk refer to those goods which are shipped on the conveyance in bulk, such as oil, ore, grain, coal, etc. Cargoes in bulk can be transported, loaded and unloaded by conveyance and loading and unloading equipment designed particularly.

3. Packed Cargo

Packed cargoes refer to those which need shipping packing, marketing packing or both.

1) Shipping packing: Shipping packing is also called big packing or outside packing. The methods of shipping packing usually fall into 2 kinds:

a) Single piece packing: The cargoes are packed as a single unit, i. e. , a measuring unit, in the transportation process. Single piece packing can be sub-divided into the following two kinds:

- According to style: Cases, drums, bags, bales, bundles, etc. .
- According to material: Cartons, wooden cases, iron drums, wooden cases, plastic cases, paper bags, gunny bags, plastic bags, etc. .

b) Collective packing: Collective packing is also called group shipping packing by which a certain number of single pieces are grouped together to form a big packing or are packed in a big container.

Collective packing can be classified into:

- Container: The Container is a kind of tool used for transportation which can be thought of as a particular shipping packing of the cargo, and can be regarded as a component part of the conveyance as well, usually provided by the ship company to go around.

At present, the specifications of containers in common use in the world are: those of the first series, including 1A, 1AA, IB. 1C, 1D, 1E and 1F.

Of the above-mentioned specifications of containers, the most commonly used are $8 \times 8 \times 20$ feet (1C) and $8 \times 8 \times 40$ feet (1A). As to the 20-foot container, the loading capacity can reach as high as 18 M/T, the volume is usually 31-35 cubic meters.

When calculating the circulating quantity of container, we often take the 20-foot container as a measuring unit, 1. e. , TEU (Twenty-foot Equivalent Unit) to indicate it, it means "being equal to a 20-foot unit".

The kinds of containers are various. As per the purpose of use, we have:

☐ Dry container: The dry container is used for carrying general cargoes.

☐ Refrigerator container: There is freezing equipment in the container. The temperature can be adjusted from $+26℃ \sim 28℃$.

☐ Frame container: There is no top part and two flank walls on the container. Cargoes can be loaded into or lifted out of the container through the two side-frames.

☐ Open top container: The open top container does not have the top part. Cargoes can be loaded or unloaded through the top of the container by-elevating equipment. It is suitable for carrying extra big cargoes.

☐ Pen container: The two sides of this kind of container are covered by metal nets, which makes it convenient to feed the live-stock and ventilate the container.

☐ Tank container: The tank container is suitable for carrying liquid cargoes such as oil, etc.

☐ Platform container: The platform container is suitable for carrying extra-long and extra-heavy cargoes. The length can reach more than 6 meters and the weight more than 40 M/T.

☐ Bulk container: There are two or three openings on the top of this kind of container, which makes it convenient to load the cargo. There are elevating frames at the bottom of the container that can elevate at a sloping angle of 40 degrees, which makes it convenient to unload the cargo.

☐ Pallet: The pallet is a kind of single-layer or double-layer flat carrier which is made according to a certain specification. Certain quantities of single pieces are packed collectively on the flat carrier and tied up in the light of the requirements to form a shipping unit, which makes it convenient to load, unload, lift and pile the goods by using machinery in the shipping process.

The pallet is usually made of wood, but it may also be made of plastic, or metal. Sometimes an upper device may be added to the pallet. The commonly used pallets are flat pallets, box pallets, post pallets, etc.

For the convenience of international cargo transportation, ISO (International Standard Organization) recommends several standard sizes of double-layer pallets and larger pallets.

• Flexible container: The flexible container is a kind of round-shaped or square-shaped bag woven with synthetic fibre or compound material. The capacity varies with the material and production techniques used usually from 1 – 4 M/T. The maximum capacity can reach about 13 M/T. The flexible container is suitable for powder or grain cargoes such as fertilizer, ore, flour, sugar, cement, etc. Collective packing can fasten loading and unloading operations and better protect the cargoes. At present, in order to accelerate the speed of loading and unloading and raise utility of ports and docks, letters of credit from some countries stipulate that cargoes shall be transported in collective packings. Some even provide that cargoes without collective packings are not allowed to be unloaded.

2) Marketing packing: Marketing packing is also called small packing or inner packing. The function of marketing packing is to protect the goods as well as to beautify, propagate and introduce them. Therefore, in international trade marketing packing is required not only to be provided with different qualities, which makes it suitable for commodity marketing, but also to be up to a high level in packing material, model structure, packing design and word description. Especially in the face of keen competition at the current international market and the rapid development of the super-market, marketing packing of exporting goods is getting more and more important, requirements for which are getting more and more strict and diversified, and it is acting as "a silent salesman".

1) Types of marketing packing: At present, according to the popular style and function of marketing packing in the international market, marketing packing can be classified into the

following types:

- Patterns for display and sale

□ Piling-up pattern: There is a coinciding part at the top or bottom of the commodity packing. If one commodity is put on the top of the other, the two can tally with each other. This type can keep the commodities firm, and is suitable for super-markets to pile commodities up, such as cans, bottles, boxes, etc.

□ Hanging-up pattern: The packing has a hanging hook or hole, or a pendent band. Usually we have close-to-body packing, case-shaped packing, box-shaped packing, bag-shaped packing, etc. This kind of packing can fully make use of space of shelves and greatly increase areas of display and sale.

□ Spreading-up pattern: The goods have a special-structured cover. When the cover is opened, the picture on the other side of it sets off well with the commodity.

- Patterns for identification of the goods:

□ Transparent pattern and windowed pattern: The cargo is packed wholly or partly with transparent packing material or a windowed paper box which can make the consumers see the shape and quality of the goods directly.

□ Customary packing pattern: Using customary packing and modeling makes the buyers identify the quality of the commodity as soon as they see the packing.

- Patterns with the function of use:

□ Pattern for carrying about: The modeling of this type is suitable for carrying the goods.

□ Pattern for easily opening: This type has the characteristic of being easily opened. The commonly used are easily-opened cans, boxes, bottles, etc.

□ Pattern for spraying out: This packing is a liquid sprayer. When we press the button, the liquid will spray out automatically. This style is suitable for everyday consumer goods and medicines.

□ Pattern for forming a complete set: The goods of different kinds and specifications, which are usually used simultaneously, are arranged into a group to form a complete set and unified packing.

□ Pattern for showing off a gift: The packing is specially designed for a certain gift.

2) Packaging: According to the different characteristics, shapes, quantities, marketing intentions and relative decrees of different countries, we design reasonable packing models, pictures and word descriptions. Word descriptions include marks, brands, origins, qualities, specifications, compositions, uses, methods of use, etc.

Packaging is the main component of marketing packing. It plays a great role in beautifying the goods, attracting consumers, expanding sales, and raising selling prices. Therefore, when we design packaging, we should pay attention to the following points:

- Marketing packing should be beautiful, novel, scientific, reasonable, colourful, and show the unique style of Chinese art.

- The picture designed for packaging should highlight the characteristic of the commodity. For example, the packaging of foodstuffs should make people want to taste them very much; the packaging of light industrial products should make people fondle them admiringly.

- The word description of packaging and the picture should be well co-ordinated. The word description can only be the complement to the picture and should be harmonious with the picture. Especially when we use a foreign language, the words chosen should be accurate.

- Marks and brands should be used properly. Packing designs should highlight the propaganda in favour of the trade mark. The packing material should be suitable, its implication should be proper, the modeling should be bright so as to give consumers a deep impression.

- We should pay attention to the stipulations and different habits and tastes towards packaging. In recent years, most countries have made out label control regulations for foodstuffs, garments and medicines, etc. These regulations are usually used as a means for import restrictions or limitations. If we want to break through these limitations, we should attach importance to the relative regulations or decrees of importing countries. In addition, people in different nations have different habits and tastes towards pictures and colours, all these concern a great deal to the packaging design. Therefore, we should keep on investigating, do well in the packaging work, try our best to cope with the habits and customs of importing countries.

C. Packing Mark

Packing marks refer to different diagrams, words and figures which are written, printed, or brushed on the outside of the shipping packings. According to the uses of the packing mark, it can be divided into:

1. Shipping Mark

Types of shipping marks are various, but they are usually made up of geometrical diagrams, letters, figures and simple words.

Shipping marks make it convenient for identifying and transporting the goods and make it easy to count them out and check them out, so as to make the documents and the corresponding goods be in accordance with each other, and avoid any shipping errors.

It is not advisable that shipping marks be designed to be too complicated. They should be simple and clear and easy to be identified. The position should be proper, the colour should be durable. No advertising propaganda words and pictures are allowed to be inserted into the marks.

Simple shipping marks are generally made up of four parts:

1) Consignee's code: The consignees' codes are usually indicated by different geometrical diagrams, such as triangles, diamonds, circles, etc. with letters inside them as the main marks.

2) Consignor's code: Letters are usually printed inside or outside the diagrams to represent the consignors' codes.

3) Destination;

4) Package number.

C T	C T
ABC	ABC
Singapore	Tokyo
Nos 1up – 100	Nos 1up – 100
No. 5	No. 2

Besides the above-mentioned four parts, the shipping mark may also include the contract number, gross and net weight, origin, etc.. If the cargo is shipped by container, the above-mentioned contents can be simplified. Adopting standard shipping marks can not only make it easy to identify and transport the goods, but also simplify the process of working out relative documents and certificates, save expenses for brushing shipping marks and time for checking out documents and certificates.

2. Indicative Mark

We usually make use of remarkable diagrams and simple words to remind the relative workers of the items for attention when they load, unload, carry and store the goods, such as "handle with care" "this way up" "fragile" "keep dry" "keep away from heat" "prevent freeze" "sling here" "use no hook" "open here" "centre of gravity", etc..

3. Warning Mark

The warning mark is also called dangerous cargo mark, which is brushed clearly and definitely on the shipping packings of the inflammable, explosive, poisonous, corrosive or radioactive goods, so as to give warnings to the workers. Warning marks are usually made up of simple geometrical diagrams, word descriptions and particular pictures, as to which, every country usually has its own stipulations. For example, our country has promulgated "Indicative Marks for Packing, Storage and Transportation", and "Warning Marks for Packing Dangerous Cargoes". The United Nations Ocean Transportation Consultation Organization has also promulgated "Warning Marks for International Ocean Transportation of Dangerous Cargoes".

In order to make it convenient for transportation of our cargoes, when exporting dangerous cargoes, we should brush both the warning marks of our country and those of international ocean transportation.

4. Additional Mark

Sometimes, in accordance with the agreement entered into by the both parties or the regulations laid down by their countries respectively some additional marks are needed.

D. Neutral Packing and Brand Designated by the Buyer

The Neutral packing means that there is neither a name of the origin, nor a name of the factory, nor a trade mark, a brand, or even any words on the packing of the commodity and the commodity itself. In international trade, the neutral packing is used mainly to break through different limitations and political discriminations of importing countries and areas and is used as a struggling means to expand sales. At present, using the neutral packing for the marketing packing of some exporting commodities has become somewhat of a practice in international trade.

1) As to the goods to be ordered regularly in large quantities for a long time by foreign customers, in order to expand sales, we can accept trade marks designated by buyers without indicating the mark of the manufacturing country, that is, the neutral packing with brands designated by the buyers.

2) Sometimes we may accept trade marks or brands designated by buyers from foreign countries, but under the trade marks and brands we indicate "Made in the People's Republic of China" or "Made in China".

3) In some other cases, we may accept the designated trade marks or brands and at the same time, under the trade marks or brands we indicate that the goods are made by a factory in the buyers country, i.e., trade marks or brands and origins designated by the buyers.

In business, if trade marks or brands are designated by the buyer; we should pay close attention to whether there exists the infringement of the named trade marks or brands. In order to avoid the situation in which we are pushed into a passive position, we may stipulate in the contract "As to the trade marks designated by the buyer, if the seller is charged with the infringement by any third party, the buyer shall take up the matter with the plaintiff and it has nothing to do with the seller. Any losses thus sustained shall be compensated by the buyer".

E. Packing Clause in the Contract

The packing clause mainly stipulates the packing manner, packing material, packing expenses to be borne and the shipping mark. On the basis of the practices in international trade and the regulations of some capitalist countries, packing is one of the main trading conditions and is the main component part of the cargo description. If the packing of the cargo is not in conformity with the stipulation of the contract and/or the particular trade practices seriously, the buyer shall have the right to file a claim on account of losses or even to reject the goods.

1. Packing Manner and Packing Material

In the contract we should expressly determine the packing manner and packing material used, such as the material, dimension. weight of every single piece, filling material used and reinforcement conditions, etc.

For example:

Packing: In new galvanized iron drums of 175 kg each, net.

Packing: Each piece in a polybag, half dozen in a box and 10 dozen in a carton.

Packing: In new single jute bags, each 100 kg. net.

In international trade contracts, sometimes we use "Seaworthy packing" "customary packing", etc., but these terms are not clear and are liable to lead to disputes, so we should try to avoid using them. But in some cases, as to cargoes packed in a manner normally accepted in a particular trade, we may use "packed in the usual way" "at sellers option" "in bulk", etc. as packing clauses in the contract.

When the two parties agree that the buyer shall supply the packing material wholly or partly, we should stipulate in the contract the time limitation within which the packing material shall arrive.

2. Packing Expenses to Be Borne

Who shall bear packing expenses? It must be stipulated clearly in the packing clause or in the unit price. Generally speaking, there are 3 ways:

1) The packing expense is included in the price of the cargo.

2) The packing expense is not included in the price of the cargo or partly included. If the buyer has any special requirements for packing, the additional-packing expense should be borne by the buyer. The seller should specify in the contract the expense to be borne and the method of payment definitely. If the pallet is to be used we should add the pallet cost to the price.

3) Gross for net: In this case, the packing material is charged for as much as the price of the goods.

In the contract, especially for the goods packed by using high level technology, we usually indicate that "packing charges are included" in the unit price, in order to prevent disputes from happening.

3. Shipping Marks

Shipping marks are usually to be for determination by the buyer in accordance with the settled custom in the particular trade which the both parties should be held to know of the existence of it and to have contracted with reference thereto.

(资料来源：丁溪，唐赛. 国际贸易理论与实务［M］. 中国商务出版社，2013.)

▶本章小结

品名是买卖双方交接货物的重要依据。品质是决定商品价格高低的重要因素。在国际贸易中，表示品质的方法有两大类：以实物表示品质和以文字说明表示品质。为了便于交货，可加列公差条款或品质机动幅度条款。

数量条款是买卖双方交接货物的依据。统一度量衡制度对买卖双方非常重要。为了便于交货，对于某些商品，在合同中应加订溢短装条款。

商品包装是商品生产的继续。包装依据其流通作用可分为运输包装和销售包装。运输包装上的标志可分为运输标志、指示性标志和警告性标志。

▶本章名词

品质　凭样品买卖　公量　溢短装条款　运输包装　销售包装　中性包装　定牌　条形码　运输标志

▶理论思考

1. 表示商品品质的方法有哪些？在使用时应注意哪些问题？
2. 试分析在买方来样时，使用"对等样品"的意义。
3. 试分析"品质机动幅度"与"品质公差"的含义及其作用。
4. 为什么要在国际货物买卖合同中规定数量机动幅度？订立数量条款时应注意哪些问题？
5. 什么是运输标志？它一般由哪些内容组成？试按一般要求设计一个运输标志。

▶实训习题

训练目的与要求

1. 熟悉、掌握品名、品质、数量、包装条款的内容、表示、规定方法
2. 运用所学知识和法律解决品质、数量、包装方面业务问题

一、阅读合同条款示例，熟悉和掌握品质、数量、包装条款的内容与表示方法

1. 品质条款（quality clause）

国际货物品质条款有多种制定或表示方法，常见的有：

（1）凭等级。如："9371中国绿茶，特珍一级"

9371 CHINA GREEN TEA SPECIAL CHUMMY GRADE 1

（2）凭规格。如：芝麻水分（最高）8%　杂质（最高）2%　含油量（最低）52%

Sesames Moisture（max.）8%

ADMIXTURE（MAX.）2%

OIL CONTENT（MIN.）52%

"跳鲤"花布

纱织　　　寸密　　　幅阔

　　　　（每英寸）　（英寸）

30×36　　72×69　　35/36

PRINTED SHIRTING 'JUMPING FISH'

YARN COUNTS　NO. OF THREADS　WIDTH

　　　　　　　PER INCH　　　　INCH

30×36　　　　72×69　　　　　35/36

（3）凭标准。如：柠檬酸钠

规格：①符合1980年版英国药典标准

②纯度：不低于99%

SODIUM CITRATE SPECIFICATIONS：

①IN CONFIRMITY WITH B. P. 1980

②PURITY：NOT LESS THAN 99%

巴西大豆2001年产，大陆货

BRAZILIAN SOYBEAN, 2001 NEW CROP, F. A. Q.

（4）凭商标、牌号。如：

"张裕干红葡萄酒，糖分12度"

CHANGYU DRY RED WINE, TWELVE DEGREE OF SUGAR

"C708中国灰鸭绒，含绒量为90%，允许1%上下"

C708 CHINESE GREY DUCK'S DOWN WITH 90% DOWN CONTENT, 1% MORE OR LESS ALLOWED

梅林牌辣椒油

MALING BRAND WORCESTERSHIRE SAUCE

佛手牌味精

FINGER CITRON BRAND VE TSIN

（5）品质和技术数据必须与卖方所提供的产品说明书严格相符。

QUALIT AND TECHNICAL DATA TO BE STRICTLY IN CONFIRMITY WITH THE DESCRIPTION SUBMITTED BY THE SELLER

(6) 质量严格符合卖方 2003 年 3 月 10 日提供的样品。样品号 NT003 长毛绒玩具熊，尺码 23 英寸。

QUALITY TO BE STRICTLY AS PER SAMPLE SUBMITTED BY SELLER ON 10TH MARCH 2003.

SAMPLE NUMBER：NT003 PLUS TOY BEAR SIZE23.

2. 数量条款（quantity clause）

数量条款主要由数字和计量单位构成，常见的数量条款示例如下：

(1) "大米，5 000 公吨，5%上下，由卖方决定"。

RICE 5,000 METRIC TONS, 5% MORE OR LESS AT SELLER'S OPTION.

(2) "蚕豆，60 000 公吨，以毛作净，卖方可溢短装5%，增减部分按合同价格计"。

60,000M/T, GROSS FOR NET, 5% MORE OR LESS AT SELLER'S OPTION AT CONTRACT PRICES.

3. 包装条款（packing clause）

包装条款一般包括包装材料和包装方式，常见的包装条款示例如下：

(1) "木箱装，每箱 50 公斤，净重"。

IN WOODEN CASES OF 50 KILOS NET EACH.

(2) "纸箱装，每箱净重 40 公斤，然后装托盘"。

IN CARTONS OF 40KGS NET EACH, THEN ON PALLETS.

(3) "国际标准茶叶，纸箱装，20 纸箱一托盘，10 托盘一集装箱"。

IN INTERNATIONAL STANDARD TEA BOXES, 20 BOXES ON A PALLET, 10 PALLETS IN A FCL CONTAINER.

(4) "双层牛皮纸袋装，每袋 50 公斤"。

PACKED IN DOUBLE BAGS WITH CRAFT PAPER, EACH CONTAINING 50 KGS。

(5) 按买方的包装设计，中性包装，并用铁皮带加固，费用由卖方负担。

THE PACKING IS AT BUYER'S DESIGN WITH NEUTRAL PACKING, EACH REINFORCES WITH IRON STRAPS, THE CHARGES OF PACKING SHALL BE BORNE BY THE BUYER.

二、翻译、改错，锻炼合同条款翻译、拟定能力

1. 合同条款翻译

(1) 东北大豆（Northeast soybean）

中国桐油（Chinese tung oil）

(2) 严格符合卖方 2013 年 2 月 15 日提供的样品。样品号：NT210 长毛绒玩具熊，尺码：24 英寸。

(quality to be strictly as per sample submitted by seller on 15th, February, 2013. sample No. NT210 plus toy bear size 24)

（3）饲料蚕豆：水分［最高］15%，杂质［最高］2%。

(Feeding Broad Beans: moisture [max] 15%, admixture [max] 2%)

（4）数量：1 000吨，3%增减，由买方选择，增减部分按合同价格计算。

(quantity: 1,000 M/T, more or less 3%, at buyer' option such excess or deficiency to be settled of contracted price)

（5）包装：每件装一塑料袋，半打为一盒，十打装一木箱。

(packing: each piece in a polybag, half dozen in a box and 10 dozens in a wooden case)

2. 将下列条款译成中文、修改其中错误

（1）name of commodity: garments (men's shirt/ladies' waistcoat …)

（2）quality as per buyer's sample (+ no ……dated …)

（3）quantity: about 200 tons (200 metric/tons … % more or less allowed)

（4）packing: in new gunny bags (of about … each)

3. 下面所使用的是哪种表示品质的方法？以中英文两种形式拟定合同的品名、品质、数量条款

呈启者：

6月3日传真报第33号毛毯盘，现确认6月6日传真不受约束盘如下：

品质；"天鹅"牌第33号毛毯。

尺寸：72英寸×84英寸。

重量：四磅。

颜色：黄。

数量：500条。

价格：成本加保险费、运费到蒙特利尔价每条40美元。

装运期；7月、8月间。

付款：不可撤销信用证60天期票。

请接受此难得再有的报盘。最近可望有大笔订单从美国方面来，届时，将导致价格猛涨。

想必已从5月所寄目录了解，我们的毛毯经久耐用，柔软暖和，使用方便。相信你们会做这赚钱的买卖的，如可能，盼即日传真。

三、阅读、分析案例，提高解决问题能力

（一）阅读案例

1. 既凭样品又凭规格买卖争议案

我国某公司出口纺织原料一批，合同品质条款规定水分最高不超过15%，杂质最高为3%（文字规格表示法）。德国买方据此合同开来信用证，我方据此合同和信用证装运，交单议付，似乎一切顺利。货到买方港口后，买方对货物进行复验，并

来电指出货物的质量与样品不符,即样品的含水量为8%。并随电附上德方商检证书副本。这时我忽然想起,在签约时我方曾向买方寄过样品,并未曾电告对方成交货物与样品相似。我方急忙发电,告知对方品质以合同中的文字规格为依据,但为时已晚,买方提出索赔,并威胁说,如不赔偿,将在有影响的刊物中披露此事。此争议最终提交仲裁解决,在仲裁庭的调解下,我方同意在下一批货物中减价10%而告终结。

评析

(1) 在此争议中,我方样品含水量8%,合同规定为15%,最终交货也是15%,从合同条款上看,应该是凭规格买卖。遗憾的是我方曾向买方寄过样品,但未声明是"参考样品",也未电告对方,交货与样品相似,这样对方完全可以以《联合国国际货物买卖合同公约》为依据,认为这单业务是既凭规格,又凭样品的。

(2) 更为遗憾的是,我方甚至没有留存复样,导致我方无法证明所交货物与样品并无不符。此案我方损失惨重,教训颇为深刻。

2. 手套交易凭样品买卖品质争议案

我某公司(卖方)与国外买方签订一份买卖工作手套(库存货)1万打的合同。品质条款规定凭卖方样品成交。样品为单只手套。货到目的港后,买方认为手套品质有缺陷,要求换货并赔偿损失。卖方认为所交货物不存在缺陷,拒绝换货和赔偿。买方遂根据合同中的仲裁条款提请仲裁。仲裁庭认为:卖方所交付货物确实与样品不完全相符。样品是单只手套,所交付的手套则是有连线的成副的手套。样品的缝口没有打结,但有足够牢固的回针。而交付的整批货手套的缝口虽有回针,但回针不够,有的甚至仅回一针,不够牢固,而且是把缝线头作为两只手套的连接带,把两只手套连在一起的。一旦把连接带剪断,缝口很容易开线。仲裁庭经咨询专家意见后裁定,所交付的手套的价值比样品低12%。对此卖方应承担全部责任,根据"直接的、合理的和实际的损失"的赔偿原则,卖方(被诉人)赔偿货物贬值12%的价款,并负担检查费、银行手续费和利息损失等。

评析

(1) 本案例是一个品质争议案。争议焦点是所交货物是否与样品相符。《公约》第35条第1款(C)规定:货物的质量与卖方向买方提供的货物样品或样式相符。在凭样品买卖中,无论样品质量好坏,所交货物必须符合样品,否则视为违约。

(2) 在服装和衣着类商品买卖中,对品质问题的考虑应尽量周到。本案中,因手套连线问题导致贬值12%,另外还有各种费用,造成巨大经济损失,应引以为戒。

3. 出口纯毛面料索赔案

北京某纺织厂先后向美国出口纯毛哔叽面料数批,货物到达买方后,从未提出任何异议,但月后,买方寄来用此面料制成的服装一套,提出用我国毛料制成的成衣色差严重,难以销售,要求减价25%,共计约6万美元。问我方应否赔偿?

评析

我方不能接受赔偿要求，理由如下：出口商品的品质以出口方检验机构（中国商检局）出具的商检证书为依据。同时，允许买方有"复验权"，即买方有权在索赔期限内复验，并提出索赔。纺织品的索赔期一般为30、60天。而此案中，买方在数月后才提出索赔，显然已经超过索赔时效。

（二）案例讨论、分析

（1）A公司从国外进口一批青霉素油剂，合同规定该商品品质"以英国药局1953年标准为准"，货到目的港后，发现商品有异样，于是请检疫部门进行检验。经反复查明，在英国药局2013年版本内没有青霉素油剂的规格标准，检疫人员无法检验，A公司失去索赔根据。此案带来的经验教训是什么？

（2）某出口公司与国外成交核桃一批，合同上以及买方开来的信用证上均写的是三级品。但到发货装船时才发现三级核桃库存已完，于是改用二级品交货，并在发票上加注："二级核桃仍按三级计价"。试问这样做是否可行？

（3）我方向科威特出口冻羊肉20公吨，每公吨FOB价400美元，合同规定数量可增减10%，买方按时开来信用证，证中规定金额为8 000美元，数量约20吨。于是我方按22吨发货装运，持单到银行办理议付，我方能顺利收回货款吗？为什么？

（4）某出口公司与日本一商人按每公吨500美元CIF东京条件成交某农产品200吨，合同规定采用双线新麻袋包装，每袋25公斤，信用证付款方式。公司凭证装运出口并办妥结汇手续。事后对方来电称：我公司所交货物扣除皮重后实际到货不足200吨，因此日商要求退回多收的货款，但我出口公司以合同中未规定按净重计价为由拒绝退款。我公司的做法是否可行？

（5）合同规定：红小豆500吨，3%增减，由卖方选择，增减部分按合同价格计算。如果交货时红小豆市场价格上涨，卖方交多少有利？

（6）某外贸公司出口销售果脯2吨，合同规定纸箱装，每箱20千克（内装20小盒每小盒1千克），交货时发现此种包装暂时无货，于是将小包装（每箱仍为20千克，但内装40小盒，每小盒0.5千克）货物发出。这样处理是否妥当？

（7）某公司出口东北大豆，品质条款规定：含油量18%，含水量14%，杂质1%，不完善粒7%，如此规定有无问题？

（8）中国某公司从美国进口小麦，数量为300万吨，允许溢短装10%。美方装船时，共装运400万吨，对多装的70万吨，中方可以如何处理？

四、知识/能力训练、测试与提高

1. 根据所给资料，设计计算商品包装尺寸、装箱数量及方法

（1）根据以下资料设计运输标志上的件号

Commodity：100% cotton men's shirts

Packing：each piece in a polybag 60pc to a carton

| Design No. | Quantity | Carton No. | Nos of Packages |

93 – 13   1 260 pc
93 – 14   1 260 pc
93 – 15   1 200 pc
93 – 16   1 680 pc

出口商品的总数量是　　　　件

包装总件数是　　　　　　　箱

（2）一中东客户向我询购安全皮鞋，要求 5 层瓦楞纸箱包装，每箱装 12 双，每双装一纸盒，纸盒尺寸为 380×240×103 立方毫米，计算纸箱外径尺寸（件数排列规则 2 排×2 行×3 层，长宽和高分别伸放 20 毫米和 40 毫米）。

（3）根据上例算出的外箱尺寸，计算一个 20 英尺集装箱可装的箱数（20 英尺集装箱内径尺寸为：5.9 米×2.35 米×2.38 米）。

（4）我国北方某公司与丹麦客商 Codan Co. 签订一份布鞋合同，共计 2 500 件，合同号为 03BG1038，价格条件 CIF 哥本哈根。根据以上资料制作一个标准头。

2. 利用网上或其他资源，查出常用规格（20'/40'）集装箱装载能力（载重、容积）（用关键字"集装箱技术规范"查找）

3. 利用网上或其他资源，查出下列商品 HS 编码（http://cx.nbnets.com）

（1）自行车　（2）摩托车　（3）电视机　（4）新闻纸

4. 从网查出：（用关键字"各国对进口商品包装的规定"搜索）

（1）阿拉伯国家对进口商品包装禁用的标志图案

（2）欧洲共同体（现在的欧盟）对接触食物的氯乙烯容器及材料要求

（3）加拿大政府对进口商品包装文种规定

（4）澳大利亚对用木箱包装（包括托盘木料）规定

（5）沙特阿拉伯港口对运往该港的袋装货物包装规定

5. 本章英文词语集萃（请自行查阅）

6. 托盘、集装箱、集装袋图片知识（请自行查阅）

CHAPTER 5

第五章 国际货物运输

> **本章指导**

通过本章相关知识的学习,了解国际货物运输的基本知识,掌握各种运输方式的特点,学会:

1. 签订买卖合同中的运输条款;
2. 运费的计算;
3. 制作提单等货运单据。

第一节 国际海上货物运输

海洋运输(ocean transport)简称海运,是指利用海洋通道,使用船舶在国内外港口之间,通过一定的航区和航线运送货物的一种运输方式。

由于海洋运输具有运量大、通行能力强、运费低廉等特点,所以许多国家特别是沿海国家和地区都乐于采用海洋运输。海洋运输已成为目前国际贸易中最重要的运输方式。

一、海洋运输的经营方式

国际海洋货物运输按照船舶营运方式的不同,可分为班轮运输和租船运输两种。

(一)班轮运输(liner transportation)

班轮运输,又称定期船运输,是指船舶按照预定的船期表(sailing schedule),在特定的航线上和固定的港口之间往返运载货物的一种运输方式。该方式比较适合于承运批量小、批次多的件杂货物。其服务对象是非特定的、分散的众多货主,所以班轮公司具有公共承运人的性质。中远运输集团(China ocean shipping company,COSCO)

就是我国主要的公共承运人。

1. 班轮运输的特点

目前班轮航线已遍及世界各海域和主要港口,班轮运输已成为海洋运输中不可缺少的主要运输方式,有力地促进了国际贸易的发展。该运输方式具有如下特点:

(1) "四固定"即固定航线、固定港口、固定船期和相对固定的运费率,是班轮运输最基本的特征;

(2) 班轮运价中已包括装卸费用,即承运人负责货物的配载装卸,并支付装卸费用;

(3) 承运人对货物负责的期间是从货物装上船起,到货物卸下船止;

(4) 承托双方的责任和权利以班轮公司签发的班轮提单为依据。

2. 班轮运输中承运人与托运人的责任划分

班轮承运人是指班轮运输合同中承担提供船舶并负责运输的当事人。托运人是指在班轮合同中委托承运人运输货物的当事人。

承运人同托运人的责任和费用的划分界限一般在吊钩底下。也就是说,托运人只要将货物送达吊钩底下,就算完成交货义务,然后承运人负责装船。风险的划分一般以船舷为界,即货物在装运港越过船舷之前所发生的风险由托运人承担,越过船舷后的风险由承运人承担。

(二) 租船运输 (charter transport)

又称不定期船运输,是指租船人向船东租赁船舶用以运输货物的一种运输方式。租船有租赁整船和租赁部分舱位两种方式。实际业务中以租赁整船为多。在租船运输中,船东出租的是船舶的使用权,故租船业务是一种无形贸易。

当前在国际租船业务中,广泛使用的租船方式主要有两种,即定程租船和定期租船,还有一种光船租船,应用较少。

1. 定程租船 (voyage or trip charter) 简称程租,又称航次租船,是指以航次为基础的租船方式。这是租船的基本形式,被广泛采用。在该方式下,船方必须按时把船舶驶到装货港装货,再驶到卸货港卸货,以完成合同规定的运输任务。租船人按约定支付运费。运费一般按装运货物的吨数。定程租船又可分为单航次租船、来回程租船、连续航次租船等。

2. 定期租船 (time charter) 简称期租,是指按一定期限租赁船舶的方式。租赁期限可长可短,短则几个月,长则几年、十几年,甚至到船舶报废为止。在租赁期内,由租船人负责船舶的调度和营运工作,并按约定向船东支付租金。期租租金一般以船舶的每载重吨每月若干金额计算,通常都是预付的。

二、海洋货物运输费用

海上货物运输费用，根据船舶的不同营运方式，可分为班轮运费和租船费用两种，其中租船费用又可分为程租船运费和期租船租金。

班轮运费

班轮运费是班轮公司承运货物而向货主收取的运输费用。它包括货物从装运港船舷或吊钩下至目的港船舷或吊钩下所发生的全部运输费用（包括装卸费用）。习惯上称之为"船舷至船舷"或"钩至钩"费用。

1. 班轮运价表

班轮运费是按照班轮运价表（liner's freight tariff）的规定计收的。各班轮公司或班轮公会都有自己的运价表。我国目前广泛使用的外运3号本、中远1号本就属等级费率运价表。在该表中，商品分20个等级。1级费率最低，20级费率最高。

2. 班轮运费的构成

班轮运费有基本运费和附加费用两部分构成。

基本运费是班轮运费的主体，根据基本费率算出；附加费用是班轮公司在基本运费之外加收的费用，班轮附加费用名目繁多，主要有燃油附加费、港口附加费等。

3. 班轮运费的计算标准

基本运费的计算标准主要有以下几种。

（1）按货物的毛重计收。如以公吨为计算单位，以"W"表示。

（2）按货物的体积计收。如以1立方米为计算单位，以"M"表示，以上两种计费方法统称尺码吨。

（3）按货物的毛重或体积，选择其中较高者计收，运价表中以"W/M"表示。

（4）按货物的FOB总值的一定百分比计，称从价运费。以"A. V."或"Ad. Val."表示。

（5）按货物的重量、体积或总价值三者中最高的一种计，以"W/M or Ad. Val."表示等。

4. 班轮运费的计算方法

班轮运费除由双方临时议定之外，其具体的计算方法是：

（1）根据货物名称从货物分级表中查出货物等级和计算标准。

（2）从航线费率表中查出相应的基本费率。

（3）再查出附加费的计算方法及费率。

（4）算出货物的单位运价再乘以总运费吨数便得到该批货物的运费总额。

若是从价运费，则直接以规定的百分比乘以FOB总值即可。

举例：某企业出口一批蛋制品，毛重10公吨，体积为11立方米，从上海港装运，直航至英国普利茅斯港。求全部运费。

解：a. 查货物分级表知蛋制品为 12 级，W/M。

b. 查航线费率表知基本费率为 116 元/公吨。

c. 查附加费率表知直航附加费为 18 元/F. T.；燃油附加费 35%。

基本费率：116 元

直航附加费：18 元

燃油附加费：$116 \times 35\% = 40.6$ 元

运价：174.6 元

运费吨：因 10 < 11，故取 M

总运费：$11 \times 174.6 = 1\,920.60$ 元

第二节　集装箱运输

集装箱运输（container transport）是指以集装箱为整体运输单位，利用海陆空等运输方式将货物运到目的地的一种比较现代化的运输方式。

目前在国际联系上运用最广的是 IA 型 8'×8'×40'IAA 型，8'×8.6'×40'IC 型，8'×8'×20' 称之为 20 尺和 40 尺集装箱。为了统计计算，国际上都以 20 英尺集装箱作为计算标准单位。以 TEU（Twenty Equivalent Unit）表示。

1. 集装箱货物交接方式

实务中集装箱货物交接方式主要有以下四种。

（1）整箱交，整箱接（CY—CY），即发货人以整箱交货，收货人以整箱接货。

（2）整箱交，拆箱接（CY—CFS），即交货人以整箱交货，各收货人凭单拆箱接货。

（3）拼箱交，拆箱接（CFS—CFS），即发货人拼箱交货，各收货人凭单拆箱接货。

（4）拼箱交，整箱接（CFS—CY），即发货人拼箱交货，收货人整箱接货。

2. 集装箱运输费用

（1）FAK 包箱费率（freight for all kinds）：即不细分箱内货物类别，不计货量，只按箱型规定统一的费率。

（2）FCS 包箱费率（freight for class）：即按不同货物种类和等级制定的包箱费率。

（3）FCB 包箱费率（freight for class and basis）：即按不同货物的类别、等级及计算标准制定的包箱费率。

第三节 其他运输方式

在进出口贸易实践中,货物的运输除海洋运输方式外,多种运输方式得到了发展,主要有:

一、铁路运输

铁路运输(railway transportation)是我国对外贸易运输中的重要运输方式之一,其具有运量大、风险小、速度快及连续性强等优点,特别是内陆国家间的贸易,铁路运输的作用尤为显著,在进出口的贸易运输中占重要地位。

进出贸易中利用铁路运输有两种方式。

1. 国际铁路货物联运

国际铁路货物联运是指两个或两个以上国家,按照协定利用各自的铁路,联运起来完成一个货物的合理运输的方式。它使用一份统一的国际联运票据,由一国铁路向另一国铁路移交货物时,无须发、收货人参加,铁路方面为全程运输负责,"国际货约""国际货协"是国际铁路联运的两个国际条约。在我国国内凡可办理铁路货运的车站均可接受国际铁路货物联运。

2. 国内运输

国内运输是指进出口货物在全国范围内的铁路运输。出口货物铁路运输到装运港或进口货物卸船后由铁路运至目的地,称为国内铁路运输。我国大陆往中国香港、中国澳门的铁路货物运输也称国内运输。

中国香港发货由中国的外运公司各地方分支机构及香港中国旅行社联合组织进行,由深圳分公司接货,由其负责向海关申报,报关放行过关后,由香港中国旅行社负责办理。

澳门货物经中国澳门铁路运输,货物自发货地运往广州站,广东省外运公司接货,由其办理水路中转将货物运往澳门,货到澳门由南立集团运输部负责接货并交付收货人。

二、航空运输

航空运输(air transport)作为一种现代的运输方式,具有速度快、方向准确、节省费用、不受地面限制等优点,发展比较速度快。对于一些体积小、贵重、量大而异常的商品如电脑、电子商品和药品等,特别是易腐、鲜活和季节性等的商品适宜于航空运输。

航空货物运输的主要方式有：

1. 班机运输（airliner transport 或 scheduled airline）；
2. 包机运输（charter carrier transport）；
3. 集中托运（consolidation transport）；
4. 航空快运方式（air express）；
5. 陆空陆联运（TAT combined transport）等。

三、公路、内河、邮政和管道运输

1. 公路运输

公路运输也是陆上运输的一种基本方式，它运输机动灵活、方便，是港口、车站、机场集散进出口货物的重要手段，尤其在我国站点辽阔，在陆地上与许多国家相邻的情况下，它在邻国的进出口贸易交换中发挥着重要作用。

2. 内河运输

内河运输属于一种水上运输方式，具有成本低、运量大等优点，是连接内陆腹地与海边地区的纽带，在现代的运输中起着重要的辅助作用，如长江运输。

3. 邮政运输

邮政运输是通过邮局来运送货物的一种方式，进出口贸易利用该运输用于小件货物。

4. 管道运输

管道运输比较特殊，它主要用于运送液体和气体货物。

四、国际多式联运和大陆桥运输

1. 国际多式联运（international multi—modal transport）

国际多式联运是在集装箱基础上发展起来的一种高效、现代化的联合运输方式。通常以集装箱为媒介，把各种单一的运输方式有机结合起来，构成一种国际性的连贯运输。国际多式联运只需通过一次托运、一次计费、一张单证、一次保险就可完成货物的全程运输，也就是说，它把全程运输作为一个单一运输过程来安排。它表现出手续简单、货运速度快、结算方便等优越性，同时还能提高货运质量，有效实现门到门的运输，因而在国际上被越来越广泛地采用，有良好的发展前途。

2. 大陆桥运输（land bridge transport）

大陆桥运输是指以集装箱为媒介，以大陆上的铁路或公路运输系统为中间桥梁，把大陆两端的海洋运输连接起来的一种海—陆—海连贯运输方式，它属于一种国际多式联运。目前世界上主要的大陆桥运输线有横贯北美大陆的"美国大陆桥"、连接太平洋和大西洋两岸的"加拿大大陆桥"、横贯苏联、中东、欧洲的"西伯利亚大陆桥"（又称第一条欧亚大陆桥）、横贯中国大陆、欧洲的第二条欧亚大陆桥等。其中第二条欧亚大陆桥1992年正式开通，它东起我国的连云港市，西至荷兰的鹿特丹，全长10 800公里，主要途径我国中西部地区，很好地促进了沿途省份的经济发展。

第四节 海 运 提 单

伴随着国际货物运输，产生了种类繁多的运输单据，如海运提单、航空运单、铁路运单等。这些单据在进出口业务中发挥着重要作用，不可缺少。本节将重点介绍最重要的一种单据——海运提单。

一、海运提单的定义及作用

海运提单（ocean bill of lading）简称提单（bill of lading，B/L），是指用以证明海上货物运输合同和货物已经由承运人接收或装船，以及承运人保证凭以交付货物的单据。它是由承运人签发的具有法律效力的单据。

海运提单具有如下三方面的性质和作用。

（1）它是承运人签发的货物收据（receipt for the goods），证明承运人已按提单所列内容收到货物。

（2）它是代表货物所有权的凭证（document of title）。提单作为物权凭证，其持有者可凭以向承运人提货，亦可通过背书将其转让，以实现货物所有权的转让，或凭以向银行办理抵押贷款或叙做押汇。

（3）它是运输合同的证明（evidence of the contract of carriage），是承运人和托运人处理双方在运输中的权利和义务问题的主要法律依据。

二、海运提单的内容

目前各航运公司所制定的提单，格式上虽不完全相同，但其内容大同小异，主要包括正面内容和背面条款两部分。

1. 提单的正面内容

提单的正面内容具体包括以下各项：承运人名称及主营业所、托运人名称、收货人名称、被通知人名称、船名、航次及船舶国籍、装运港、目的港、货物的品名、唛头、件数、重量或体积、运费及其他费用、提单号码、份数和签发日期和地点、承运人或船长、或其代理人签字等。正面内容主要由承运人和托运人填写。

2. 提单背面条款

提单背面条款是处理承运人和托运人（或收货人、持单人）之间所发生争议的依据。目前大多数提单的背面条款是基于《统一提单的若干法律规定的国际公约》，简称《海牙规则》制定的。一般来说，主要包括：定义条款、首要条款、承运人的责任和豁免、运费条款、转运条款、包装与唛头条款、赔偿条款、留置权条款、特殊货物条款等内容。

三、海运提单的种类

海运提单可以从不同的角度进行分类。

（一）按货物是否已装船划分

1. 已装船提单（on board or shipped B/L）

已装船提单是在货物装上船后，由承运人签发的提单。这种提单必须注明船名、装船日期，并由船长或其代理人签字。另外也须有"货已装船"（on board）字样。实务中，买方一般要求卖方提供已装船提单。

2. 备运提单（received for shipment B/L）

备运提单是指承运人在收到托运货物等待装运时所签发的提单。在货物装船后，托运人可凭之向船公司换取已装船提单；也可经承运人在其上批注已装船字样，并注明船名、装船日期及签字后，变成已装船提单。

（二）按提单收货人的抬头方式划分

1. 记名提单（straight B/L）

记名提单又称"收货人抬头提单"，是指在提单收货人一栏内填写指定收货人名称的提单。这种提单只能由提单上指定的收货人提货，不可转让。一般只有在运输贵重物品或展览品是才使用该提单。

2. 不记名提单（Beare B/L）

不记名提单又称来人抬头提单，是指提单收货人栏内不填写具体收货人名称的提单，该栏或留空白，或填写"to bearer"。这种提单任何人持有皆可提货，而且仅凭交付即可转让，因而风险较大，实务中很少使用。

3. 指示提单（order B/L）

提示提单是指提单收货人一栏内只填写"凭指示"（to order）或"凭某某人指示"（to the order of ×××）字样的提单。这种提单经背书后可转让。在进出口业务中使用最广。背书的方法有两种，空白背书和记名背书。前者是仅有背书人（提单转让人）在提单背面签字盖章，而不注明被背书人的名称；后者是除背书人签章外，还须列明被背书人名称。当前实务中使用最广的是"凭指示"并经空白背书的提单，即"空白抬头、空白背书"的提单。

（三）按提单对货物外表状况有无不良批注划分

1. 清洁提单（clean B/L）

清洁提单是指货物在装船时外表状况良好，承运人未加注任何有关货物残损、包装不良或其他有碍结汇批注的提单。

2. 不清洁提单（unclean B/L）

不清洁提单是指承运人在提单上加注有货物表面状况不良或存在缺陷等批注的提单。

国际贸易中，卖方有义务提交清洁提单，也只有清洁提单才可以转让。

（四）根据运输方式的不同划分

1. 直达提单（direct B/L）

直达提单是指货物运输途中不转船，而是直接从装运港运至目的港的提单。

2. 转船提单（tranship B/L）

转船提单是指货物需中途转船才能到达目的港的情况下，承运人所签发的提单。提单上注有"转运"或"在某港转运"字样。

3. 联运提单（through B/L）

联运提单是指货物通过海陆、海空或海海的联合运输时，由第一承运人签发的、包括全程的、在目的地可以凭以提货的提单。各承运人只对自己运程内的货物运输负责。

（五）根据船舶营运方式不同划分

1. 班轮提单（liner B/L）

班轮提单是指货物由班轮公司承运时所签发的提单。

2. 租船提单（charter B/L）

租船提单是指承运人根据租船合同签发的提单。这种提单受租船合同条款的约束。

（六）按提单格式划分

1. 全式提单（long form B/L）

全式提单是指不但有完整的正面内容，而且有详细的背面条款的提单。国际贸易中使用的大多为全式提单。

2. 略式提单（short form B/L）

略式提单是指仅有正面内容而无背面条款的提单。

（七）按提单使用效力划分

1. 正本提单（original B/L）

正本提单是指提单上有承运人正式签字盖章并注明签发日期的提单。这种提单是具有法律效力的单据，上面须标明"正本"字样。一般签发一式两份或多份，凭其中任一份可提货。

2. 副本提单（copy B/L）

副本提单是指无承运人签字盖章，仅供参考之用的提单。提单上一般标明"副本"字样。

（八）其他提单

1. 过期提单（stale B/L）

过期提单是指超过规定交单日期或者晚于货物到达目的港的提单。通常情况下，迟于单据签发日期21天才提交的提单也算过期提单。银行一般不接受过期提单。在近洋国家间的贸易合同中，一般订有"过期提单可以接受"条款。

2. 倒签提单（anti-dated B/L）

倒签提单是指承运人应托运人要求，使提单签发日期早于实际装船日期的提单。这主要是为了使提单符合信用证对装运日期的规定，以顺利结汇。这属于伪造单据行为，违约又违法。

3. 舱面提单（on deck B/L）

舱面提单又称甲板提单，是指货物装在船舶甲板上时所签发的提单。由于货物在甲板上风险较大，所以买方和银行一般不接受甲板提单。

4. 预借提单（advanced B/L）

预借提单是指在信用证规定的装运日期和议付日期已到，而货物却未及时装船的情况下，托运人出具保函，让承运人签发已装船提单。这就属于预借提单，是违法的。

四、提单的国际公约

为了统一提单背面条款关于托运人和承运人之间的权利义务的规定，国际上先后签署了三个国际公约。

（1）1924年8月25日在布鲁塞尔签订了《统一提单的若干法律规则的国际公约》，简称《海牙规则》（Hague Rules）。

（2）1968年2月23日在布鲁塞尔签订的《修改统一提单的若干法律规则的国际

公约的议定书》，简称《维斯比规则》（Visby Rules）。

（3）1978年3月在汉堡通过的《联合国海上货物运输公约》，简称《汉堡规则》（Hamburg Rules）。

第五节　买卖合同中的运输条款

一、运输条款

在国际货物买卖中，双方必须在合同中就货物运输的相关问题做出明确、合理的规定和安排，这就构成了买卖合同中的运输条款。一般来说，买卖合同中的运输条款主要涉及如下内容：

1. 装运时间

规定有如下几种方法：

（1）规定在某月或某日装运；

（2）规定在某月月底或某日前装运；

（3）规定在收到信用证后一定期限内装运；

（4）近期装运术语，如"立即装运"（immediate shipment）等，应尽量避免使用。

2. 装运港（地）和目的港（地）

（1）装运港（地）实际业务中，应考虑多方面因素，根据合同使用的贸易术语和运输方式合理选择装运港（地）。

通常只规定一个装运港（地），如"装运港：青岛"（port of shipment：Qingdao）。有时因实际业务需要，也可规定多个装运港（地）。如"装运港：青岛和大连"（port of shipment：Qingdao and Dalian）

（2）目的港（地）在进出口业务中，目的港（地）一般由买方提出，经卖方同意后确定。

合同中一般只规定一个目的港，必要时也可规定两个或两个以上或作笼统规定，由买方在装运前通知卖方。

3. 分批装运和转运

根据国际商会第600号出版物《跟单信用证统一惯例》的有关规定：

（1）如信用证中没有规定禁止分批装运和转运，可视为允许分批装运和转运；

（2）对于同一船只、同一航次及同一目的港的多次装运，即使运输单据表面上注明不同的装运日期或不同的装运港口，也不应视为分批装运；

（3）对于分批装运的货物，如其中任何一批未按规定装运，则该批及以后各批均告失效。

4. 装运通知

以 FOB 条件成交的合同一般规定，买方应按约定的时间将装货船只的船名、船舶到港、受载日期等通知卖方，以便卖方及时安排货物出运和准备装船。

以上是进出口合同中有关货物运输的一些主要条款，应当很好地了解和掌握。

二、滞期/速遣条款

国际货物运输中，大宗货物一般采用程租船方式运输，而滞期/速遣条款是程租合同中（采用 FIO 条件时）必不可少的一项奖罚条款。在签订贸易合同时，应注意合同中的滞期/速遣条款必须与租船合同中的滞期/速遣条款相一致。此外，还应注意以下事项。

1. 装卸时间

即合同中规定的完成货物装卸所用的时间。

关于装卸时间的规定方法有很多，当前国际上较为普遍采用的方法是：按"连续 24 小时好天气工作日"计算，即在好天气情况下，连续作业 24 小时为一个工作日，不分昼夜。对于中间因坏天气而无法作业的时间予以扣除。这种规定比较合理，双方都愿接受，在我国也较多采用。

关于装卸时间的起算和止算。较为普遍的规定是：如船长递交"装/卸准备就绪通知书"（notice of readiness—NOR）在上午 8~12 点送达，则从下午 2 点起算；如在下午 2~6 点送达，则从次日上午 8 点起算。终止时间则以最后一件货物装上船或卸下船为准。

2. 装卸率

即每日装卸货物的数量。可用来表示装卸时间。合同中规定的装卸率一般应按照港口习惯的正常装卸速度来订明。

3. 滞期/速遣费

若租船人超出或提前于规定的装卸时间完成装卸作业，则应缴纳或获取相应的罚款或奖金，即滞期/速遣费。具体数额由双方商定，一般速遣费为滞期费的一半，不到一天，按比例计。

对于滞期时间，按航运界惯例，遵循："一旦滞期，始终滞期。"（once on demurrage, always on demurrage）的原则。对于速遣时间有两种计算方法：一是按节约的全部时间计算；二是按节约的工作时间计算。

以上是进出口合同中有关货物运输的一些主要条款，应当很好地了解和掌握。

英文参考教程
Delivery of Goods

Delivery of the goods refers to the act of the seller transferring the title of the goods to the buyer in accordance with the stipulations in the contract. It is realized through delivery of the goods by the seller and payment by the buyer. The procedure of delivery of the goods is quite complicated, as it involves the methods of the delivery and conditions of the delivery, etc.

A. Methods of the Delivery

Export goods have to be moved from the place of dispatch to the place of destination. This transportation has an international character. Goods may be moved by sea, land or air or by a combination of these modes of transportation.

In international trade practice, it is very important for the exporter to choose a correct method of delivery, because this concerns the safety of the goods, freight, time of arrival, sales of the goods and development of the business.

1. Ocean Transport

So far as foreign trade is concerned, goods transport is mostly done by ocean vessel——tramp or liner.

1) A tramp is a freight-carrying vessel which has no regular route or schedule of sailings. It is first in one trade and then in another, always seeking those ports where there is a demand at the moment for shipping space.

The shipper charters the ship from the shipowner and uses it to carry the goods. It falls into 3 kinds:

a) Voyage charter: It includes single voyage charter, return voyage charter and successive voyage charter.

According to the route stipulated in the charter party, the shipowner is responsible for delivering the goods to the port of destination and for managing the ship as well as bearing all expenses.

b) Time charter: The charterer charters the ship for a period of time during which the ship is deployed and managed by the charterer.

During the period of chartering, the ship is managed, deployed and used by the charterer. A series of work, such as loading, unloading, stowing and trimming and the so-caused fuel expenses, port expenses, loading and unloading expenses, etc., should be borne by the charterer. The shipowner should bear the wages and board expenses of the crew, and be responsible for seaworthiness during the period of chartering and the so-caused expenses and the vessel insurance premium.

c) Demise charter: Demise charter is also called bareboat charter, which belongs to time charter, but there are some differences; as to time charter, during the period of chartering, the shipowner provides the charterer with a crew, while as to bareboat charter, the shipowner only provides the charterer with a bareboat, the charterer shall employ the crew by himself.

The freight is usually stipulated according to the tonnage of the ship and the freight rate on the current chartering market.

There are 3 methods of stipulating the freight:

- Tonnage of the goods loaded;
- Tonnage of the goods unloaded;
- On all-round contract basis.

The charter party is a contract concluded between the shipowner and the charterer when the latter charters the ship or booking shipping space from the former. It stipulates the rights and obligations of the two parties.

The main terms in the charter party include the interested parties, name and flag of the ship, description and quantity of the shipments, time of chartering, freight, loading and unloading expenses, time limit of loading and unloading, de-murrage and dispatch money.

The freight may be stipulated in the charter party as follows:

- Freight can be paid in advance;
- Freight can be paid after the goods have arrived at the port of destination;
- Part of freight is paid in advance, the rest of which is paid after the goods have arrived at the port of destination.

Before the charterer pays off freight and other charges, the shipowner is entitled to refuse to deliver the goods, this kind of right is called lien.

There are 4 methods to be used to stipulate the expenses of loading and unloading:

- The shipowner bears gross terms;
- The shipowner is free in (F. I.);
- The shipowner is free out (F. O.);
- The shipowner is free in and out (F. I. O.). When adopting this method, the interested parties shall indicate who will bear the expenses of stowing and trimming. If they agree that the charterer shall be responsible for them, then the interested parties shall stipulate "shipowner is free in and out, stowed, trimmed (F. I. O. S. T)".

The time of loading and unloading will effect the turn-over rate of the ship, and thus, will effect the interest of the shipowner. Therefore it is the main clause specified in the charter party. The time limit of loading and unloading may be indicated by:
- Fixed days;
- Efficiency of loading and unloading;
- Customary quick dispatch.

During the time limit of loading and unloading, in case the chatterer does not finish the work of loading and unloading, in order to compensate the shipowner for his losses, the charterer should pay certain amount of fine to the exceeding time, this is the so-called demurrage.

During the time limit of loading and unloading, in case the charterer finishes the work of loading and unloading ahead of schedule, then the shipowner shall pay certain amount of bonus to the charterer, this is the so-called dispatch money.

2) Liner: A liner is a vessel with regular sailings and arrivals on a stated schedule between specific ports.

The main features of liners usually include:

a) The liner has a regular line, port, timetable and comparatively fixed freight.

b) The shipowner usually leases part of shipping space instead of the whole ship.

c) The carrier is responsible for loading and unloading operations, i.e. Gross Terms.

3) The B/L drawn by the shipping company is the shipping contract between the carrier and the consignor. The rights and obligations of the carrier and the consignor are based on the B/L drawn by the shipping company.

The basic standards for calculating freight are stipulated as follows:

a) According to gross weight, i.e., weight ton, which is indicated by "W" in the tariff.

b) According to volume, i.e., measurement ton, which is indicated by "M" in the tariff.

c) According to value of the cargo, i.e., a certain percentage of F.O.B price which is indicated by "A.V." (Ad Valorem) in the liner freight tariff.

d) According to gross weight or volume, i.e., choosing the higher rate between the two, which is indicated by "W/M" in the tariff.

e) According to gross weight or volume or A.V., i.e., choosing the highest rate of the three, which is indicated by "W/M or A.V.".

f) According to gross weight or volume, and then plus a certain percentage of A.V., which is indicated by "W/M plus A.V.".

g) According to the number of the cargo.

h) According to the temporary agreement entered into between the shipowner and the consignor.

Based on different draftsmen. Liner Freight Tariffs can be divided into 4 kinds:

a) Shipping Conference Freight Tariff;

b) Liner's Company Freight Tariff;

c) Cargo Owner's Freight Tariff;

d) Freight Tariff of Both Parties.

The method used for calculating liner freight is quite complicated. First, according to the English name of the goods, we must consult the Scale of Commodity Classifications so as to find out the grade and the calculating standard to which the cargo belongs. Then, according to the grade and the calculating standard, we should find out the basic rate in the scale of rates for the specific line service. Thirdly, we have to find out the additional or surcharge rate. On the basis of the basic rate and the additional rate, we can get the unit freight. Finally by using the weight or measurement of the goods times the unit freight, we can get the total amount of freight.

The main surcharges are shown as follows:

a) Heavy lift additional;

b) Long length surcharge;

c) Direct additional;

d) Transshipment surcharge;

e) Port congestion surcharge;

f) Port surcharge;

g) Bunker surcharge or bunker adjustment factor (BAF);

h) Optional fees;

i) Alternation of destination surcharge;

j) Deviation surcharge.

In addition to the above-mentioned surcharges, ice surcharge, cleaning tank surcharge, currency adjustment factor, fumigation surcharge etc. are sometimes included.

2. Railway Transport

Railway transport does not tend to be effected by weather conditions, so it is available for transportation for almost the whole year. Railway transport is fast, delivery quantity is large. It can guarantee the successive transport of the goods. Risks of damage to the goods are comparatively small.

Railway transport falls into 4 kinds:

1) Railway transport at home;

2) Railway transport to H. K. (China) and Macao (China);

3) International railway transport between two countries;

4) International railway through transport.

According to the stipulations of the International Union of Railways, the International Railway Cargo Through Transport Agreement and the International Convention Concerning the Carriage of Goods by Rail, the goods belong to the export country may be transported directly to the place of destination as long as the carrier issues a railway bill of lading at the place of dispatch.

The main transport documents are the railway bill and its duplicate. The railway bill is the transportation contract and binding upon the consignee, the consignor and the railway department. The railway bill together with the goods is transported from the place of dispatch to the place of destination and then is delivered to the consignee after he has paid off the freight and other charges. The consignor may make exchange settlement with the bank against the duplicate of railway bill.

3. Air Transport

Air transport is fast and safe, the risk of or damage to the goods is reduced to the lowest degree. It is not restricted by ground conditions. It is especially suitable for transporting fresh, live, perishable, and seasonable goods.

The airway bill is a document supplied by the carrier to the consignor. It is a transport contract signed between the consignor and the carrier. After the goods have arrived at the place of destination, the consignee may take delivery of the goods against the advice of arrival given by the carrier. The consignor fills in this document in triplicate, and one of these copies shall be sent with the goods.

1) "For the carrier": This is signed by the consignor. It is kept by the carrier for customs purposes.

2) "For the consignee": This is signed by the carrier, as well as the consignor, and is sent with the goods to the consignee.

3) "For the consignor": This is signed by the carrier and sent back to the consignor.

Contents of the airway bill mainly include:

1) The name and address of the consignor;

2) The name and address of the consignee;

3) The place of departure, the issuing carrier's name and address, and the destination;

4) The number of packages, their marks and numbers, packing nature and quantity (including dimensions or volume);

5) The value for customs purposes and for carriage;

6) The value declared by the consignor for insurance purposes;

7) Handling information;

8) The requested route and the agreed stopping places;

9) The signature of the shipper or his agent and the execution date.

4. Postal Transport

According to international trade practice, the seller fulfils the duty of delivery only if he delivers the parcel to the post office, pays off the postage, and gets the receipt.

Postal transport falls into 2 kinds:

1) Regular mail;

2) Air mail.

5. Highway or Inland River Transport

To some countries, it is particularly important. And in many cases, it is a complementary but necessary mode of transport to ocean, air and railway transport.

6. Combined Transport

Combined transport means the conveyance of cargo includes at least two modes of transport by which the goods are carried from the place of dispatch to that of destination on the basis of combined transport or a multimodal transport contract.

It usually includes:

1) Train – Air (or Truck – Air, or Ship – Air): The export goods are carried to Hongkong (China) by train or truck or ship and then loaded into airplanes at Hongkong. (China)

2) Train – Ship: The export goods from Chinese interior provinces may also be transported to Hongkong (China) by railway for transshipment to foreign ports by vessels.

3) Container Transport: With the expansion of international trade, the container service has become more and more popular. The use of container provides a highly efficient form for transport by road, by rail and by air, though its fullest benefits are felt in shipping, where costs may be reduced by as much as one half. Containers are constructed of metal and of standard lengths, mostly ranging from ten to forty feet. This service has the following advantages:

1) Containers can be loaded and locked at factory premises or at nearby container freight stations, making pilferage impossible.

2) There is no risk of goods lost or mislaid in transit.

3) Manpower in handling is greatly reduced, with lower costs and smaller risk of damage to the goods.

4) Mechanical handling enables cargoes to be loaded in a matter of hours rather than days, thus reducing the time ships spend in port and greatly increasing the number of sail-

ings.

Container transport falls into two kinds:

1) full container load (FCL);

2) less than container load (LCL).

7. Land Bridge Transport

Land bridge transport is a mode of transport that connects the ocean transport on the two sides of the land by the railway which runs across the continent, i. e., ship-train-ship.

Land bridge transport uses the container as a medium, so it has all advantages of container transport.

There are two main land bridges in the world:

1) American land bridge;

2) Siberian land bridge.

The delivery conditions for land bridge transport mainly include:

1) loaded in the container and free on railway wagon at the station;

2) loaded in the container at CY or CFS near the station;

3) loaded in the container and free on board the vessel at the port.

The advantages of land bridge transport are obvious:

1) Make exchange settlement earlier. As soon as the container is delivered, the seller may make exchange settlement against combined transport documents;

2) Save expenses;

3) The transport is speedy and safe;

4) The formality is simple. All that the consignor should do is to apply for consignment, and the general carrier will be responsible for arranging and transporting the goods from the place of delivery to the place of destination.

8. International Multimodal Transport

International multimodal transport means the conveyance of cargo between two countries by at least two modes of transport from the place of dispatch to that of destination on the basis of multimodal transport contract.

The basic conditions of international multimodal transport are:

1) Transport documents, i. e., combined transport documents shall cover the whole journey;

2) It includes two or more different modes of successive transportation;

3) It shall be international transportation;

4) The multimodal transport operator (MTO) shall be responsible for the whole journey;

5) The whole journey shall use a single factor rate.

B. Delivery Conditions

Delivery conditions refer to delivery clauses in the international sales contract.

Delivery conditions include the time of delivery, and in some cases including the time of loading and unloading, and the charges resulting from loading and unloading operations, the port of shipment, the port of destination, partial shipments and transshipment, shipping documents, etc.

1. Time of Delivery

The time of delivery refers to the time limit during which the seller shall deliver the goods to the buyer at the agreed place by the agreed methods.

1) Ways of delivery

a) Pysical delivery or actual delivery: The seller delivers the goods into the actual possession of the buyer, for example, delivery of the goods under EXW and DES trade terms.

b) Constructive delivery or symbolic delivery: After the seller loads the goods on board the vessel and presents the whole qualified documents which include certificates of title to the goods, the seller is said to have finished delivery of the goods. It is unnecessary for the seller to guarantee the goods to be received by the buyer actually. In the symbolic delivery contract, there are two different time limits, one is the time of shipment, the other is the time of delivery. In the contracts under F and C group trade terms, the time of shipment and the time of delivery belong to the same concept while in the contracts under D terms, they are different.

2) Ways of stipulating the time of delivery

a) Stipulate the definite time of delivery;

- Stipulate a fixed time, for example:

Shipment at or before the end of June;

Shipment on or before Sept. 15th;

Shipment not later than July 31st. the goods shall be shipped within a fixed.

- Stipulate a fixed period of time, for example:

Delivery or shipment during May 1995;

Shipment during May/June 1995;

Shipment during second half of April and first half of May.

b) Stipulate the goods shall be shipped without a fixed time, for example:

Shipment within 15 days after receipt of remittance;

Shipment by first available vessel;

Shipment within 30 days after receipt of L/C.

In order to prevent the buyer from opening L/C late, we should stipulate at the same time "the relevant L/C must reach the seller not later than …".

c) Stipulate the goods shall be shipped in the near future, for example:

Immediate shipment;

Shipment as soon as possible;

Prompt shipment.

But there are not unanimous explanations about these terms in the international trade, and thus, it is quite easy to result in disputes, so we should try to avoid using them.

2. Port of Shipment and Port of Destination

As the place of delivery concerns handling of formalities, payment of charges and transfer of risks, it is very important to stipulate it clearly in the contract.

The place of delivery is closely related to the trade terms.

1) In the case of the import and export business under EXW, DES trade terms, since the business directly involves delivery, the duties of the two parties are closely linked with the place of delivery.

2) In the case of the business under CFR, CIF, CPT, CIP, etc. trade terms, the business concerns the transportation of the goods, the two parties shall stipulate the place of shipment as well as the place of destination in the contract.

The port of shipment or the place of departure is usually chosen and determined by the seller, of course, it shall be agreed by the buyer.

The points that we should pay attention to when stipulating the port of shipment in an export contract:

1) The port of shipment shall be close to the origin of the goods.

2) We should take into consideration the loading and unloading, and specific transportation conditions and the standards of freight and various charges at home and abroad.

3) Under the FOB terms, the buyer is responsible for chartering a ship. However, when we stipulate the port of shipment, the depth of it shall be suitable to the ship chartered by the buyer.

The port of destination is usually proposed and determined by the buyer, which shall be convenient for reselling the goods and shall be the one at which the vessel may safely arrive and be always afloat.

When we determine the port of destination, we must pay attention to the following points:

1) We should not accept the port in the country with which our government does not permit to do business.

2) The stipulation on the port of destination shall be definite and specific. We should not use those ambiguous terms, such as "main ports in Europe" or "main ports in Africa".

3) If we have to choose a port which has no direct liner to stop by or the trips are few, we should stipulate "transshipment to be permitted" in the contract.

4) The port of destination shall be the one at which the vessel may safely arrive and be always afloat.

5) As to the business with an inland country, we usually choose a port which is nearest to the country. We usually do not accept an inland city as the place of destination unless through combined transportation for which the combined transport operator will be responsible.

6) In case the middleman abroad has not found a proper buyer when the contract is concluded, in order to make it convenient for him to sell the cargo afloat, the "optional port" may be accepted upon request of the foreign party, the buyer is allowed to choose one from the several ports of destination provided. In case the "optional port" is adopted, we must pay attention to the following points:

1) The port provided shall be in the same line and shall be the one that may be reached by ordinary liners, i.e., the port of call.

2) The number of optional ports prescribed shall not exceed 3.

3) When calculating the freight and surcharges, the highest rates for them shall be charged due to the option.

4) The consignee shall inform the liner company or its agent at the final port of destination before the liner has arrived at the first port provided, otherwise the shipowner has the right to discharge the goods at any port provided.

3. Shipping Documents

Shipping documents indicate that the goods have been loaded on board the vessel or have been delivered into the custody of the carrier. In the constructive delivery, shipping documents are the main foundation for the seller to prove that he has fulfilled the duty of delivery, as well as for the buyer to pay the purchase price.

According to different modes of transportation, shipping documents mainly refer to bills of lading, railway bills, airway bills, multimodal transport documents, etc.

1) Bill of lading

The document for sea transport is called B/L which is a receipt from the shipping company, giving details of a particular shipment.

a) Roles of B/L

- B/L is a receipt for the goods issued by the shipowner or his agent evidencing the receipt of the goods mentioned in the B/L.

- B/L is a document of title to the goods. Any lawful holder of the B/L may take delivery of the goods from the shipping company against the B/L, or transfer the title to the goods by transferring the B/L or secure loans against the B/L from the bank before the arrival of the shipment.

- B/L is evidence of the contract of carriage between the consignor and the shipping company. The rights and obligations of two parties are listed on the B/L.

b) Kinds of B/L

- According to whether the goods have been loaded on board the vessel, the B/L is divided into shipped on board B/L and received for shipment B/L.

A shipped on board B/L is evidence that the goods have been loaded on board a certain steamer. According to general foreign trade practices, only the shipped on board bill of lading is accepted by banks for payment under a letter of credit.

A received for shipment B/L is evidence given by the shipowner that the goods have been received for shipment but have not yet been actually loaded on a particular ship. It is therefore uncertain whether the goods would be shipped or loaded on board a ship within a short period of time.

- According to whether there are notes on the bill of lading, it falls into two kinds: clean B/L and unclean B/L.

* A clean B/L shows that the goods have been shipped on board a vessel in apparent good order and condition. A clean B/L is issued to the shipper when the goods do not have any exterior defects at the port of shipment. Actually on every B/L there are the words "shipped in apparent good order and condition". The carrier will not modify this statement if the goods are in good order, therefore making the bill clean. The carrier undertakes full liability for the goods and will carry and deliver them in the same good order as he received them. The carrier will be liable if the goods are found damaged.

* Unclean bills of lading are generally marked "insufficiently packed", "carton old and stained" "… packed in damaged condition" etc. But not all bills of lading which are noted are unclean bills of lading. The following 3 kinds of noted bills of lading are not regarded as unclean bills of lading.

* The notes do not indicate clearly that the goods or packing are unsatisfactory, e.g., "old packing" or "old carton", etc.

* The purpose of the note is to emphasize that the carrier shall not be responsible for the risks resulting from the quality of the goods or packing.

* The purpose of the note is only to deny that the carrier has any knowledge of the content, quantity volume, quality or technical specifications of the goods.

- According to whether the B/L is transferable, it is divided into 3 kinds: straight B/L, order B/L and blank B/L.

* A straight bill of lading is made out so that only the named consignee at the destination is entitled to take delivery of the goods under the bill. The consignee is designated by the shipper. The carrier has to hand over the cargo to the named consignee, not to any third party in possession of the bill. This kind of bill of lading is not transferable. The shipper cannot pass the bill to a third party by endorsement. So the bill is of very restricted application. When the goods are shipped on a non-commercial basis, such as samples or exhibits, or when the goods are extremely valuable, a straight bill of lading is generally issued.

* An order B/L indicates that the bill is made out to the order of any person named in such a bill. This kind of bill may be transferred after endorsement. When the bill is made out "to order of shipper" it is necessary for the shipper to endorse the bill either in blank or in full, to the consignee to whom he wishes the delivery of the goods is to be made. If the shipper does not endorse such a bill he reserves the right to dispose of the goods to himself.

* A blank bill of lading is also called open B/L or bearer B/L. It refers to the bill in which the name of a definite consignee is not mentioned. This kind of B/L can be transferred without endorsement. There usually appear in the box of consignee words like "to bearer" and the holder of the B/L can take delivery of the goods against the surrender of B/L.

- According to the modes of transport, it can be divided into 3 kinds.

* A direct B/L is evidence that the goods are shipped and carried by the steamer and transported from the port of loading direct to the port of destination without transshipment during the voyage. The buyer usually prefers such a B/L, because the possible cargo damage or losses is usually caused by transshipment.

* A transshipment B/L is a document showing that when there is no direct service between two ports, the goods are transited by another steamer during the voyage, generally at the port of transshipment mentioned in the B/L, to the port of destination where a ocean-going liner does not call during its voyage.

* A through bill of lading is issued when the entire voyage involves more than one carrier. The first carrier issues the bill and collects the freight for the entire voyage and arranges transshipment and forwarding of the goods at the intermediate port. The shipper prefers this kind of B/L because of the trouble having been saved to deal with other carriers by himself.

- According to the contents of the B/L, it can be divided in to 2 forms.

* A Long Form B/L refers to the bill of lading on the back of which all the detailed terms and conditions about the rights and obligations of the carrier and the consignor are listed as an integral part of the bill.

* A short form B/L is a document which omits the terms and conditions on the back of the B/L.

- According to the time for payment of freight, it can be divided into 2 types.

* A freight prepaid B/L means that all the freight is paid by the consignor when the B/L is issued by the carrier.

* A freight to be collected B/L refers to the B/L on which "freight payable at destination" is indicated.

- According to the types of the carrying vessels, it can be classified into a liner B/L and a charter party B/L.

- Other types of B/L

* A Groupage B/L and house B/L: The forwarding agent usually groups together particular compatible goods of consignees situated usually in the same area, and dispatches them as one consignment. After taking over the consignment, the shipowner will issue a groupage B/L to the forwarding agent. And then several house Bs/L are issued by the forwarding agent to the individual consignors. At the destination, the forwarding agent's representative or another agent will break bulk the consignment and distribute the goods, to their respective consignees on their production of the house Bs/L.

* A Ante-dated B/L: In order to avoid non-acceptance for negotiation of the B/L by the bank, when the actual loading date is slightly later than the date of shipment stipulated in the L/C, the carrier sometimes, at the request of the shipper, will issue to the shipper an ante-dated B/L so as to meet the requirement of the L/C. In this case, the carrier is liable for all risks arising from the issuance of such a B/L. Therefore, the carrier usually avoids this practice.

* A On Deck B/L: An on deck bill is issued when the goods are stowed on deck. The risks of the deck goods are great, the carrier shall not be responsible for the damage to and losses of the deck goods. So the buyer and the bank are usually unwilling to accept such a B/L. But some cargoes, such as inflammable goods, explosive goods and poisonous goods, cargoes in large volumes or of awkward sizes, live cattle, plants, etc., must be loaded on deck. In these cases, "loading on deck to be allowed" is usually stipulated in the contract and the relative L/C, and specific insurance should be taken out by the shipper.

* A Stale B/L: A stale bill of lading is a bill when it is presented to the consignee or bank later than a specified time after issuance. In order to safeguard the interest of its principal, the bank usually refuses to accept a stale B/L, because the delay in the presentation of the B/L might lead to additional costs, such as warehousing expenses etc. According to relevant stipulations of the Uniform Customs and Practice for Documentary Credits, the B/L shall be presented within a specified time after issuance. If no time limitation is specified, the bank may refuse the bill of lading presented to it later than 21 days after issuance of the B/L or other transport Documents.

c) Contents of B/L: Every liner company in the world has its own B/L form and clauses, but the basic contents are stipulated according to the International Convention for the Unifition of Certain Rules of Law Relating to Bill of Lading (Hague Rules).

- On the face of the B/L, the following particulars are to be noted:
* Consignor;
* Consignee;
* Party to be notified;
* Name of the vessel;
* Ship's nationality;
* Voyage;
* Port of shipment and port of destination;
* Freight;
* Number of the copies of the B/L, date, signature of the shipowner or his agent or captain of the steamer.
* main particulars regarding the goods loaded on the steamer: description, marks, number of package, weight or measurement.
* Declaration shall be made that the goods have been loaded on board in apparent good order and should be discharged at the port of destination or at the port as near as the vessel may safely get and be always afloat.
* After one of the original B/L has accomplished the formality of taking delivery, the others stand null and void.
* The consignor, consignee and bearer declare that they accept and agree the B/L and its stipulations and exclusion clauses printed, written or typed on the back of the B/L.

- Clauses on the back of the B/L;
* Obligation and responsibility of the carrier;
* Exceptions;
* Claim and action clauses;
* Duty and obligation of the consignor;
* Transportation clauses for special goods;
* Other clauses.

2) Multimodal Transport Document (M. T. D.)

The multimodal transport document is a document which evidences the combined transport contract and indicates that the multimodal transport operator shall take over the goods and shall be responsible for delivering the document according to the clauses in the contract. It appears to meet the requirements of container transport.

The differences between an M. T. D. and a through B/L are:

a) A through B/L is restricted to the combination of ocean transport with other modes of transportation; while an M. T. D. can be used either in combined transport of ocean and other modes or in the combination of modes of transport excluding ocean transport, but it shall include two or more different modes of transportation.

b) A through B/L is issued by the carrier, captain or agent of the carrier, while an M. T. D. is issued by the multimodal transport operator or his authorized person.

c) The issuer of a through B/L is only responsible for the first journey, while the issuer of an M. T. D. should be responsible for the whole journey. A through B/L is a whole journey B/L issued by the first carrier after the goods have been loaded on board the vessel, it is a shipped, on board B/L, while an M. T. D. may be a shipped on board B/L, but in most cases it is a received for shipment document.

（资料来源：丁溪，唐赛. 国际贸易理论与实务［M］. 中国商务出版社，2013.）

➢ 本章小结

国际货物运输是国际贸易不可缺少的重要环节。海洋运输是运用最广泛的一种运输方式，其经营方式有班轮运输和租船运输两种。除海运外，国际贸易中常用的运输方式还包括铁路运输、航空货物运输、集装箱运输、国际多式联运、邮包运输以及公路、内河、邮政和管道运输等。

在国际货物买卖合同中，买卖双方必须就交货时间、装运地和目的地、能否分批装运和转运等问题在合同中作出明确规定。明确、合理地规定装运条款，是保证进出口合同顺利履行的重要条件。

运输单据是承运人收到承运货物签发给出口商的证明文件，它是交接货物、处理索赔与理赔以及向银行结算货款或进行议付的重要单据。运输单据主要有海运提单、海运单、铁路运单、航空运单和多式联运单据等。

➢ 本章名词

班轮运输　租船运输　班轮运费　国际铁路货物联运　国际多式联运　装运期　装卸港　分批装运与转运　滞期费　速遣费　海运提单　多式联运单据

▶ 理论思考

1. 班轮运输中，承托双方的责任、费用和风险是如何划分的？
2. 租船合同中为什么订有"滞期/速遣"条款？
3. 进出口业务中，在出口业务中，使用选择港条款应注意哪些问题？
4. 集装箱运输具有哪些特点？

▶ 实训习题

一、判断题

1. W/M or A.V. 指按重量和体积中较高的一个收取运费后再加上一定百分比的从价费。（　）
2. 班轮运输较适合大宗货物的运输。（　）
3. 程租船和期租船的不同之处在于租船的期限不同。（　）
4. 规定具体、明确的日期是国际贸易中最广泛使用的规定装运期的方法。（　）
5. 凡装在同一航次、同一条船上的货物，即使装运时间和装运地点不同，也不作分批装运。（　）
6. CIF 伦敦/利物浦/安特卫普是指货物分别在三个港口卸货。（　）
7. 承运人在 B/L 上加注"货物用旧麻袋包装"是不清洁提单。（　）
8. 记名提单和指示提单同样可以背书转让。（　）
9. 航空运单不能作为货物所有权凭证进行转让和抵押。（　）
10. 海运提单的签发日是指货物开始装船日。（　）
11. 海运提单是托运人与承运人订立的运输契约，双方责任以提单背面条款为准。（　）
12. 我方出口某大宗商品，如 CIF 班轮条件成交时，则我方必须用班轮装运货物。（　）

二、案例分析题

1. 我国对新加坡按 CFR 合同出口一批化肥，合同规定 1~3 月装运，国外来证也如此，无它字样。但我方在租船订舱时发生困难，因出口量大一时租不到足够的舱位，需分三次装运。问在这种情况下，是否需要国外修改信用证的装运条款？

2. 我国向俄罗斯出口茶叶 9 000 箱，合同和信用证均规定"从 7 月开始，连续每月 3 000 箱"，问：我方于 7 月装 3 000 箱，8 月没装，9 月装 3 000 箱，10 月装 3 000 箱，可否？

三、填空题

1. 将货物从出口地运到进出口地的运输方式有_____运输、_____运输、

_____运输等。其中使用最多的是_____运输。

2. 海洋运输中的商船按其经营方式不同分为_____和_____两种。_____运输适合于少量货物的运输。

3. W/M or A.V. 表示_____收取运费。

4. 班轮运费包括_____费和_____两部分，其中附加费主要包括：_____附加费、_____附加费、_____附加费、_____附加费等。

5. 采用班轮运输货物，其运费应包括_____。

6. 在定期租船的租赁期间，船方负担_____等费用及_____费用，租船人负担船舶运营中的_____费、_____费、_____费等。

7. 国际上对分批装运的解释是_____的。《跟单信用证统一惯例》规定，除非信用证另有规定，否则视为_____分批装运。

8. 装运单据主要包括_____、_____、_____、_____和_____单据等。

9. 海运提单的性质和作用为提单是货物的_____；是货物所有权的_____和运输协议的_____。

10. 提单按收货人的抬头可分为_____提单、_____提单和_____提单等。

四、单选题

1. 下列"装船提单"日期正确的是（   ）。
   A. 货于5月24日送交船公司　　　B. 货于6月4日开始装船
   C. 货于6月5日全部装完　　　　D. 货于6月8日抵达日本

2. 海运提单和航空运单（   ）。
   A. 均为物权凭证
   B. 均为"可转让"物权凭证
   C. 前者作物权凭证，后者不可转让、不作物权凭证
   D. 前者不作物权凭证，后者作物权凭证

3. 按FOB术语签订的合同，采用程租船运输的大宗货物，应在合同中具体规定（   ）。
   A. 装船费由谁负担　　　　　　B. 卸货费由谁负担
   C. 运费由谁负担　　　　　　　D. 保险费由谁负担

4. 班轮条件是指货物装卸费由（   ）。
   A. 买方负担　　　　　　　　　B. 卖方负担
   C. 承运人负担　　　　　　　　D. 买卖双方各付一半

5. 我国出口到蒙古国的杂货运输应选择（   ）。
   A. 海洋运输　　　　　　　　　B. 铁路运输
   C. 航空运输　　　　　　　　　D. 管道运输

6. 航空运输的费用收取标准为（　　）。

A. 按 M 收取　　　　　　　　　　　B. 按 W 收取

C. 按 W/M 收取　　　　　　　　　　D. 按 W/M or A.V. 收取

五、计算题

某公司出口到澳大利亚悉尼港某商品 100 箱，每箱毛重 30 公斤，体积为 0.035 立方米，运费计算标准为 W/M 10 级。查 10 级货直运悉尼港基本运费为 200 美元，加货币附加费 35.8%，再加燃油附加费 28%，港口拥挤费 25%，求总运费。

六、阅读提高（阅读案例，提高分析、解决问题能力）

1. 某对外贸易中心集团诉××发展股份有限公司未尽义务案

2017 年 11 月，原告中国某对外贸易中心集团下属的 A 公司与新加坡 B 公司签订了 4 份进口合同，进口一批氨纶丝，由被告××发展股份有限公司承运。2017 年 12 月，该批货由××发展股份有限公司承运抵达目的港厦门。提单上记载的运输方式为 CFS/CY（即：由装运港的集装箱货运站运至目的港的集装箱堆场）。货物名称为 A 级氨纶丝。货物装在 20 英尺集装箱内。提单上作了"由托运人装箱和点数"以及"据说装有……"的批注。本案原告持正本提单向承运人要求提货，但海关查验货物时发现集装箱内装载的货物不是氨纶丝，而是涤纶丝。又经查，承运人交付的集装箱箱体完好无损，铅封完整，集装箱内的货物由纸箱包装，纸箱正面标有涤纶丝字样。原告因所载货物与提单不符，拒绝接货，并向法院起诉。

受理此案的厦门海事法院认为：提单上注明"CFS/CY"字样，表明所承运的货物为"站到场"交接方式。根据国际集装箱惯例和我国《海上国际集装箱运输管理规定实施细则》，在 CFS/CY 交接方式下，承运人有义务在装运港集装箱货运站接货并监督装箱。被告在提单上注明由托运人装箱"并点数""据说装有……货物"的批注，表明被告未尽到义务。最后判被告败诉。被告不服，向福建省高级人民法院提出上诉，省高院经二审后，决定驳回上诉，维持原判。

评析提示

本案的承运人忽略了一个要害问题：即国际惯例和我国相关法规均规定：当采用集装箱运输时，承运人必须亲自清点货物并负责装箱。

2. A 服装服饰有限公司诉××货运公司无单放货案

原告 A 服装服饰有限公司（简称 A）与美国一家贸易公司签订了货物买卖合同，价格条件为 FOB 上海。根据合同，A 将货物交给××货运公司上海办事处，委托其运至美国旧金山。××货运公司签发了以 A 为托运人的提单，并交给 A，同时××货运公司又将货物交给××总统轮船公司上海分公司实际承运，并取得了××总统轮船公司签发的以××货运公司为托运人的提单。货物由××总统轮船公司运抵目的港旧金山后，××总统轮船公司向××货运公司收回正本提单后向其交货。但××货运公司未收回其自己签发的提单就将货物交给美国的收货人，即无单放货，导致原告 A

未收回货款而提出诉讼。

请就此说明责任方并阐述理由。

评析提示：××货运公司以他自己的名义收取了运费，并签发了提单，当然应对无单放货造成的损失负全部责任。从另一角度讲，如果认定××货运公司是货运代理人身份，可能结果会更糟，因为货运代理人更不能享受实际承运人的免责和赔偿责任限额等保护，在对托运入进行赔偿时必须完全负责。

3. 倒签提单，客户拒绝收货案

我某公司向德国出口某冷冻商品1 500箱，合同规定1~5月按同等量装运，每月300箱，凭不可撤销即期信用证付款，客户按时开来信用证，我方1~3月交货正常，顺利结汇，但在4月时，由于船期延误，推迟到5月6日才装运出口，而海运提单则倒签为4月30日，并送银行议付，议付行也未发现问题。后在5月10日，我公司又同船装运300箱运往目的地，开具的提单为5月10日。进口商取单时发现问题，拒绝收货。问：我方的失误在哪里？进口商为何拒收货物并拒付？

评析提示

我方失误：

1. 拖延交货期；

2. 将5月6日装运出口的货物装船日期倒签为4月30日，这是违法行为；

3. 最严重的错误是5月10日以将信用证中规定分月等量装运的货物装在5月6日装的同一只船上，这个错误无疑告诉对方4月30日的提单是倒签的；

4. 将分批装运的货物装在同一只船上，从根本上违背了信用证关于分批装运的规定。

进口商拒收货物的理由：

1. 卖方倒签提单的行为成立，这是一种侵权行为；

2. 对5月10日装运的货物，虽然5月装运是按信用证规定的数量装运，但进口商以前批（4月）应装的货物未按时装运为由可判决5月10日所装的货物无效。因为《跟单信用证统一惯例》（UCP600）第41条规定：在规定分批装运条款时，具体订明每批装运的时间和数量，只要其中一期未按时、按量装运，则本期及以后各期均告失效，除非信用证另有规定；每批构成一份单独合同，否则，都可作为违约论。因此，买方有权拒收货物。

CHAPTER 6

第六章 国际货物运输保险

> **本章指导**
>
> 通过对本章的学习,要求能够了解国际货物运输中,所面临的各种风险以及由此可能产生的各种损失和费用;掌握保险公司所保障的各种险别和条款及具体内容;特别是共同海损构成的条件,CIC 条款中海运货物保险的基本险别及保险起讫条款;学会:
>
> 1. 正确订立合同中的保险条款;
> 2. 保险金额的确定、保险费的计算及保险索赔。

国际贸易中的货物在整个运输过程中,有的需要经过多次的装卸、存储、搬运,可能遇到各种自然灾害或意外事故,从而使货物遭受损失。为了保障货物在遭受损失后能得到经济上的补偿,通常由买方或卖方在货物装运前向保险公司投保货物运输险。因此,我们有必要对海上货物运输承保范围、我国海洋货物运输保险的险别、其他运输方式下的保险条款,以及我国进出口货物保险的具体做法有所了解。

第一节 海洋货物运输保险的风险、损失与费用

进出口货物在海运中常常会遇到各种风险而导致损失或丢失,但保险公司并非对任何保险都予以承保,对任何损失都予以赔偿。因此,熟悉海上运输货物保险的风险与损失,对于深入了解和掌握海运保险知识是十分必要的(见表 6-1)。

一、风险

海上运输货物保险的风险有两大类,即海上风险和外来风险。

表 6-1　　　　　　　　　　　　海上运输风险构成情况

海上风险	自然灾害（自然力量引起）	恶劣气候（heavy weather） 雷电（lightning） 海啸（tsunami） 地震或火山爆发（earth quake or volcanic eruption） 洪水（flood）		
	意外事故（偶然非意料中原因）	搁浅（grounding）规律性潮汛可继续航行除外 触礁（stranding）包括和残骸相触 沉没（sunk）如有航行能力除外 碰撞（collision）和海水或停靠时与其他船互相挤撞不算 失踪（missing）4~6个月 失火（fire）自然因素，货物特性或人为因素 爆炸（explosion）		
海上损失及费用	海上损失	全部损失 total loss	实际全损 actual total loss	①保险标的完全灭失 ②标的物损失无法挽回 ③失去商业价值或原有用途 ④船舶失踪达一定时期
			推定全损 constructive total loss	①修理费＞修复后价值 ②整理并运抵目的地费用＞到达目的地价值 ③实际全损无法避免或施救费用＞获救标的价值 ④失去所有权且收回所有权的费用＞价值
		部分损失	共同海损 单独海损	
	海上费用	施救费用 sue & labor expenses	有契约关系人	
		救助费用 salvage charge	无契约关系的第三方支付的报酬	
外来风险	一般外来风险	偷窃（theft & pilferage） 玷污（contamination） 渗漏（leakage） 破碎（breakage） 受潮受热（sweat & heating） 串味（taint of odor） 生锈（rusting） 钩损（hook damage） 淡水雨淋（fresh water & rain damage） 短少和损提货不着（short-delivery & non-delivery） 短量（shortage in weight） 碰损（clashing）		
	特殊外来风险	战争（war） 罢工（strike） 拒收和进口（rejection & import duty） 黄曲霉素（aflatoxin）		

(一) 海上风险

海上风险 (peril of the sea),又称海难,一般是指船舶或货物在海上航行中发生的风险,包括自然灾害和意外事故。

1. 自然灾害

自然灾害 (natural calamity),是指不以人的意志为转移的自然界力量所造成的灾害,在海运保险业务中,仅指恶劣气候、雷电、海啸、地震、洪水、火山爆发等人力不可抗拒的自然力量造成的灾害。

2. 意外事故

意外事故 (fortuitous accidents),一般是指装载有货物的船舶在海上航行中,由于偶然的、难以预料的原因造成的事故。如运输工具遭受搁浅、触礁、沉没、船舶与流冰或其他物体碰撞,以及失踪、失火、爆炸等原因造成的事故。

(二) 外来风险

外来风险 (extraneous risk) 是指海上风险以外的其他原因所造成的风险,外来风险包括以下两种类型:

(1) 一般外来风险。一般外来原因所造成的风险为一般外来风险。主要包括:偷窃、渗漏、短量、碰撞、破碎、钩损、生锈、玷污、串味、雨淋、受热受潮、发霉等。

(2) 特殊外来风险。特殊外来风险是指由于军事、政治、国家法令及行政措施等特殊外来原因造成的风险。如战争、罢工、拒收以及交货不到等。

二、损失与费用

(一) 海上损失与费用

海上损失又称海损,是指被保险人因被保险货物在运输途中遭遇海上风险而造成损坏或灭失而引起的费用。按各国保险业的习惯,海上损失也包括与海运相连的陆上或内河运输中所发生的损失和灭失。运输途中被保险货物本身遭到损坏或灭失的损失,按其损失程度可分为全部损失和部分损失。

1. 全部损失 (total loss)

全部损失简称全损,是指整批或不可分割的一批被保险货物在运输中全部遭受损失。全部损失又分为实际损失和推定损失。

(1) 实际全损 (actual total loss),是指该批被保险货物在运输途中完全灭失,或者受到严重损坏完全失去原有的形状、效用,或者不能再回归被保险人所拥有。被保险货物在遭受实际全损时，被保险人可按其投保金额获得保险公司全部损失的赔偿。

（2）推定全损（constructive total loss），是指被保险货物在运输途中受损后，实际全损已不可避免，或者为避免发生实际全损所需支付的费用与继续将货物运抵目的地的费用之和超过保险价值。

被保险货物发生推定全损时，被保险人可以要求保险人发出委付通知（notice of abandonment）。所谓委付，就是被保险人表示愿意将保险标的的一切权利和义务转移给保险人，并要求保险人按全部损失赔偿的一种行为。委付必须经保险人同意后方能生效，但是保险人应当在合理的时间内将接受委付或不接受委付的决定通知被保险人。委付一经保险人接受，不得撤回。

2. 部分损失（partial loss）

部分损失是指不属于实际全损和推定全损的损失，即没有达到全部损失程度的损失。在保险业务中，按照造成损失的原因不同，部分损失又分为共同海损与单独海损两种。

（1）共同海损（general average，GA），是指在同一海上航程中，船舶、货物和其他财产遭遇共同危险，为解除危险，有意识地合理地采取措施所直接造成的特殊牺牲和支付的特殊费用。

（2）单独海损（particular average，PA），是由承保风险直接导致的船或货的部分损失。该损失应由受损方单独负担。可以看出，单独海损在造成海损的原因及损失承担责任方面都与共同海损不同。

第二节　我国海洋运输保险条款与险别

一、我国海洋运输保险条款

我国现行的货物运输保险条款是中国人民保险公司1981年1月1日修订的《中国人民保险公司海洋运输货物保险条款》，简称"中国保险条款"（China Insurance Clause，CIC），该保险是参照国际保险市场习惯做法，并结合中国保险工作的实际而制定的。中国保险条款的主要内容包括保险公司承保责任范围、除外责任、责任起讫、被保险人的义务及索赔期限等。

保险险别是保险人对风险和损失的承保责任范围，它是被保险人与保险人履行权利和义务的基础，也是保险人承保责任大小和被保险人缴付保险的依据。我国的货物运输保险险别分为基本险和附加险两种。

二、我国海洋运输货物保险的基本险别

根据我国现行的《海洋货物运输保险条款》的规定，我国海洋运输货物保险的基本险别有平安险、水渍险和一切险三种（见表6-2）。

表6-2　　　　　　　　　　　我国海洋货物运输的保险险别

	险别	承保范围
基本险	平安险	①自然灾害、意外事故造成的全损 ②意外事故造成的全部和部分损失 ③只要发生意外事故，此前或此后自然灾害造成的部分损失 ④装卸转船过程中一件或数件落海造成的全部或部分损失 ⑤施救费用，以不超过保险金额为限 ⑥意外事故造成中途停靠引起的卸、装货、存仓、运送的特殊费用 ⑦共同海损引起的牺牲分摊费和救助费 ⑧运输契约订有船舶互撞条款据此应由货方偿还船方的损失
	水渍险	平安险责任+自然灾害造成的部分损失
	一切险	平安险水渍险责任+一般外来风险所致的全部、部分损失
一般附加险	偷窃和提货不着险	货物被偷窃及货运抵目的地后全部或整件未交
	淡水雨淋险	淡水、雨水和冰雪溶化，包括船上淡水舱、水管漏水、舱汗
	短量险	数量或重量短少，散装货要减除运输中的正常损耗
	混杂、沾污险	混进杂质
	渗漏险	流质、并流质、油类渗漏及湿肠衣因流体渗漏腐烂变质
	碰损破碎险	前者指金属、木质，后者指易碎物质
	串味险	同舱装载的货物受到一起堆放的商品的异味的影响如茶叶、香料、药材受到樟脑、毛皮的异味影响
	受热受潮险	气温变化或水蒸气的影响
	钩损险	装卸过程中使用手段或吊钩等工具造成的损失
	包装破裂险	包装破裂造成的短少沾污及候补包装、调换包装的费用。有免赔率
	锈损险	生锈但必须是在保险期发生的
特别附加险	战争险	战争或类似战争行为，和敌对行为武装冲突海盗行为及由此引起的捕获、拘留、扣押、禁制造成的损失或由于常规武器造成的损失，共同海损的牺牲，分摊和救助费用，核武器除外
	罢工险	因罢工者被迫停工，工人参加工潮暴动和民众战争人为采取行动造成的损失，包括恶意行为造成的损失
	交货不到险	投保该险别不论任何原因，以货物上船始6个月不能运到原定目的地交货，保险公司即赔偿，一切损失并取得代位权，但承保时要提供一切进口所需证件，否则无效

续表

	险别		承保范围
特别附加险	进口关税险		有的国家规定进口货物无论完好与否（短小、残损、变质）均须按完好，即价值纳税，如投保该险，保险公司则对此损失赔偿，但须另行规定一投保额和基本险数保额相互区别并以此为限
	舱面险		一般只在平安险的基础上加保，而不在水渍险或一切险的基础上加保。除上述险别的承保范围外，还包括被抛弃和被风浪冲击落水的损失
	拒收险		货物在进口时由于各种原因，被拒绝进口或没收所造成的损失，投保时，应持有进口所需的一切证件
	黄曲霉素险		药品中黄曲霉素超量会被拒绝进口，没收或强制改变用途
	出口货物到港九或澳门存仓火险扩展条款		出口至港澳货物运至保单载明之过户银行仓库时，存仓期间火险责任延长30天不另收保费，30天后如需延长存仓时间，每天按0.05%计收，不是一月按一天算
独立险别	卖方利益险		在采用托收方式时货物在运输过程中受损即买方不赎单时，保险公司负责赔偿损失并有向买方、第三者索偿的权利，这不是重复保险或双重保险
专门险别	冷藏货物险		承担冷藏货物因冷藏机器停止工作连续24小时以上造成的被保险货物的腐败和损失以及水渍险下的责任造成的损失赔偿，货物到达目的地卸离海轮后保险公司继续负责10天包括存入岸上冷藏库
	散装桐油险		对散装桐油不论何种原因造成的短少、渗漏（超过规定的免赔率）、玷污和变质负责，到运抵目的港岸上油库责任即行终止，如未卸载自海轮抵港15日止
	集装箱保险	全损险	全损险只对自然灾害、意外事故造成集装箱的全部损失负赔偿责任
		综合险	综合险对集装箱遭受灾害、事故造成的全部损失或部分损失均予赔偿并负责赔偿由于下列原因造成集装箱的机器部分的损失：①运输船舶的沉没、触礁、搁浅、碰撞引起的（包括同冰碰撞）②陆上或空中运输工具的碰撞、倾覆及其他意外事故引起的损失③外来的火灾、爆炸引起的损失
			集装箱保险的除外责任：①由于集装箱不符合国际标准或由于其内在缺陷和特性②或工人罢工或迟延所引起的损失和费用③正常磨损及其修理费用④集装箱战争险、条款规定的承保责任和除外责任⑤与投保集装箱经营有关的或由其引起的第三者责任和费用

（一）平安险（free from particular average，FPA）

保险公司对平安险的承保责任范围是：

（1）被保险货物在运输途中由于恶劣气候、雷电、海啸、地震、洪水等自认灾害造成整批货物全部损失或推定全损。被保险货物用驳船运往或远离海轮时，每一驳船所装的货物可视作一整批。

（2）由于运输工具遭受搁浅、触礁、沉没、互撞、与流冰或其他物体碰撞以及失火、爆炸等意外事故所造成的货物的全部或部分损失。

（3）由于运输工具发生搁浅、触礁、沉没、焚毁等意外事故，货物在此前后又在海上遭受恶劣气候、雷电、海啸等自然灾害所造成的部分损失。

（4）在装卸或转运时由于一件或数件甚至整件货物落海造成的全部或部分损失。

（5）被保险人对遭受承保责任内危险货物采取抢救、防止或减少货物损失的措施而支付的合理费用，但以不超过该批被救货物的保险金额为限。

（6）运输工具遭遇海难后，在避难港由于卸货所引起的损失，以及在中途港、避难港由于卸货、存仓以及运送货物所产生的特别费用。

（7）共同海损的牺牲、分摊和救助费用。

（8）运输契约订有"船舶互撞责任"条款，根据该条款规定应由货方偿还船方的损失。

（二）水渍险（with average or with particular average，W. A or W. P. A）

保险公司对水渍险的承保范围，除包括上述平安险的各项责任外，还负责被保险货物由于恶劣气候、雷电、海啸、地震、洪水等自然灾害所造成的部分损失。

（三）一切险（all risks）

一切险的责任范围是，除包括上述平安险和水渍险的各项责任外，还负责被保险货物在运输途中由于一般外来原因所造成的全部或部分损失。

从上述三种基本险别的责任范围看，平安险的责任范围最小，水渍险的责任范围比平安险的责任范围大，一切险的责任范围是三种基本险别中最大的一种。投保人可根据货物的特点、运输路线等情况选择投保平安险、水渍险和一切险中的任何一种。

对海洋运输货物保险的三种基本险别，保险公司均规定有除外责任（Exclusions）。所谓除外责任，是指保险公司规定不予承保的损失或费用。除外责任主要包括以下几种情况：①被保险人的故意行为或过失所造成的损失；②属于发货人责任所引起的损失；③在保险责任开始前，被保险货物已存在的品质不良或数量短差所造成的损失；④被保险货物的自然损耗、本质缺陷、特性以及市价跌落、运输延迟所引起的损失或费用；⑤属于海洋运输货物战争险条款和货物运输罢工险条款规定的责任范围和除外责任。

同国际保险市场的习惯做法一样，中国人民保险公司的海洋运输货物保险条款规定的保险责任起讫期限也是采用"仓至仓"条款（Warehouse to Warehouse Clause，W/W Clause），即保险公司的保险责任自被保险货物运离保险单所载明的起运地仓库或储存处所开始运输时生效，包括正常运输过程中的海上、陆上、内河和驳船运输在内，直至该项货物到达保险单所载明目的地收货人的最后仓库或储存处所或被保险人用作分配、分派或非正常运输的其他储存处所为止。如未抵达上述仓库或储存处所，则以被保险货物在最后卸载港全部卸离海轮后满60天为止。如在上述60天内被保险货物需转运至非保险单所载明的目的地，则该项货物的保险期限从开始运转时终止。

以上三种基本险别的索赔时效,自被保险货物在最后卸载港全部卸离海轮后算起,最多不超过两年。

三、附加险

附加险是对基本险的补充和扩展。投保人只能在投保一种基本险的基础上才可加保一种或数种附加险。目前,《中国保险条款》中的附加险有一般附加险和特殊附加险两种。

(一) 一般附加险 (general additional risks)

一般附加险承保一般外来风险所造成的全部或部分损失,其险别共有下列 11 种:

(1) 偷窃、提货不着险 (theft, pilferage and non-delivery, TPND)。指被保险货物在保险有效期内,被偷走或窃走,以致在目的地货物的全部或整件提货不着的损失,保险公司负赔偿责任。

(2) 淡水雨淋险 (fresh water and/or rain damage)。对被保险货物因直接遭受淡水或雨淋,以及由于冰雪融化所造成的损失负责赔偿。

(3) 渗漏险 (leakage)。承保被保险货物在运输过程中因容器损坏而引起的渗漏损失,或对用液体储藏的货物因液体的渗漏而引起的货物腐败等损失负责赔偿。

(4) 短量险 (shortage risk)。被保险货物在运输途中因外包装破裂或散装货物发生数量散失和实际重量短缺的损失保险公司负责赔偿,但不包括正常运输途中的自然消耗。

(5) 混杂、玷污险 (intermixture and contamination)。保险公司对被保险货物在运输途中因混进杂质或被玷污所造成的损失负责赔偿。

(6) 碰损、破碎险 (clash and breakage)。对被保险货物在运输过程中因震动、碰撞、受压所造成的破碎和碰撞损失,由保险人赔偿。

(7) 钩损险 (hook damage)。对被保险货物在装卸过程中因被钩损而引起的损失,以及对包装进行修补或调换所支付的费用负责赔偿。

(8) 锈损险 (rust)。对被保险的金属或金属制品一类货物在运输过程中发生的锈损负责赔偿。

(9) 串味险 (taint of odor)。对被保险的食品物品、中药材、化妆品原料等货物在运输过程中因受其他物品的影响而引起的串味损失负责赔偿。

(10) 包装破裂险 (breakage of packing)。对被保险货物在运输途中因装运或装卸不慎,致使包装破裂所造成的损失,以及在运输过程中,为保证运输安全需要修补包装或调换包装所支付的费用,均由保险公司负责赔偿。

(11) 受潮受热险 (sweat and heating)。对被保险货物在运输过程中因气温突变或由于船上通风设备失灵致使船舱内水汽凝结、发潮或发热所造成的损失负责赔偿。

当投保险别为平安险或水渍险时,可加保上述 11 种一般附加险中的一种或数种险别。但如已投保了一切险,就不需要再加保一般附加险,因为保险公司对于承保一般附加险的责任已包含在一切险的责任范围内。

(二) 特殊附加险 (special additional risk)

特殊附加险承保由于特殊外来风险所造成的全部或部分损失。中国人民保险公司承保的特殊附加险有下列 8 种:

(1) 战争险 (war risk)。根据中国人民保险公司《海洋运输货物战争险条款》,海运战争险承保直接由于战争、类似战争行为和敌对行为、武装冲突或海盗行为所致的损失,以及由此而引起的捕获、拘留、扣留、禁止、扣押所造成的损失。还负责各种常规武器(包括水雷、鱼雷、炸弹)所致的损失以及由于上述责任范围而引起的共同海损的牺牲、分摊和救助费用。但对使用原子弹或氢弹核武器所造成的损失和费用不负责赔偿责任。战争险的保险责任起讫以水上危险(waterborne)为限,直到目的港卸离海轮或驳船时为止。如不卸离海轮或驳船,则从海轮到达目的港的当日午夜起算满 15 天,保险责任自行终止;如在中途港转船,不论货物是否在当地卸货,保险责任以海轮到达该港或卸货地点的当日午夜起算满 15 天为止。

(2) 罢工险 (strike risks)。对被保险货物由于罢工、工人被迫停工或参加工潮、暴动等造成的直接损失,或任何人的恶意行为所造成的损失,保险公司予以赔偿。但对在罢工期间由于劳动力短缺或不能使用劳动力所造成的被保险货物的损失,包括因罢工而引起的动力或燃料缺乏而使冷藏机停止工作致使冷藏货物的损失,以及无劳动力搬运货物,使货物堆积在码头淋湿受损,不负赔偿责任。罢工险对保险责任起讫的规定与其他海运货物保险险别一样,采取"仓至仓"条款。按国际保险业惯例,已投保战争险后另加保罢工险,不另增收保险费。

(3) 黄曲霉毒素险 (aflatoxin)。指保险人对被保险货物因其所含有黄曲霉素超过进口限制标准,被限制进口、没收或强制改变用途而遭受损失所负的赔偿责任。

(4) 舱面险 (on deck)。是保险人对存放在舱面上的被保险货物,除应对保险单上所载明的条款负责外,还要对货物被风浪冲击落水造成的损失赔偿。

(5) 交货不到险 (failure to deliver)。指按照"仓至仓"条款,不论任何原因,保险人应对在保险期内不能交出货物负赔偿责任。

(6) 进口关税险 (import duty)。指在被保险货物遭受保险责任范围内的损失,而被保险人仍必须按完好货物价值完税时,保险公司对被保险人因部分货物损失而多缴的进口关税负责赔偿。

(7) 拒收险 (rejection)。指保险人对保险货物在进口港被进口国政府或有关当局拒绝进口或没收的情况下,应按货物的保险价值负责赔偿。

(8) 货物出口到中国香港（包括九龙）或中国澳门存仓火险责任扩展条款（fire risk extension clause，FREC-for Storage of Cargo at Destination Hong Kong (China)，including Kowloon or Macao (China)）。

第三节 我国陆、空、邮货物运输保险

在国际贸易中，不仅海洋运输的货物需要办理保险，陆上运输、航空运输、邮包运输的货物也都需要办理保险。我国陆、空、邮运输保险是在海上货物保险的基础上发展起来的。中国人民保险公司对不同方式的运输货物都规定相应的专门条款。

一、陆上货物运输保险条款与险别

中国人民保险公司1981年1月1日修订的《陆上货物运输保险条款》规定：陆上运输险分为陆运险和陆运一切险基本险别。

（一）陆运险与陆运一切险

陆运险（overland transportation risks）的责任范围是保险公司承保被保险货物在运输途中遭受暴风、雷电、洪水、地震等自然灾害或由于运输工具遭受碰撞、倾覆、出轨或在驳运过程中因驳运工具遭受搁浅、触礁、沉没、碰撞，或由于遭受隧道坍塌、崩溃或失火、爆炸等意外事故所造成的全部或部分损失。陆运险的承保责任范围与海洋运输货物保险条款中的"水渍险"相似。

陆运一切险（overland transportation all risks）承保的责任范围除上述陆运险的责任外，还包运输途中，由于外来原因造成的短少、短量、偷窃、遗漏、碰损、破碎、钩损、雨淋、生锈、受潮、受热等全部或部分损失，这与海洋运输货物保险条款中的"一切险"相似。

（二）陆上货物运输保险的除外责任

陆上货物运输保险中含有除外责任条款，主要包括下列三种情况：
（1）被保险人的故意行为或过失所造成的损失；
（2）属发货人责任范围的，或被保险的自然消耗所引起的损失；
（3）由于战争、罢工或运输延迟所造成的损失。

（三）陆上货物保险责任的起讫期限

陆上货物保险也采用"仓至仓"原则，即保险责任从被保险货物运离保险单所载

明的起运地发货人的仓库或储存处所开始运输时生效，包括正常陆运和有关水上驳运在内，直到该货物送交保险单所载明的目的地收货人仓库或储存处所，或者被保险人用作分配、分派或非正常运输的其他储存处所为止。如果没有运抵保险单所载明的收货人的仓库或储存处所，则以到达最后卸载车站之后60天为限。

在投保陆上货运保险时，还可加保一种或若干种附加险，如陆运战争险。陆运战争险是指承保直接由于战争、类似战争行为以及武装冲突所造成的损失，保险人的责任起讫期限为自货物装上火车时开始，到达目的地卸离火车为止。如果被保险货物不卸离火车，则以火车到达目的地的当日午夜起算，满48小时为止。

二、航空货物运输保险

中国人民保险公司1981年1月1日修订的《陆上货物运输保险条款》规定：航空运输货物保险分为航空运输险和航空运输一切险两种基本险别。

（一）航空运输险

航空运输险（air transportation risks）的责任范围与海洋货物运输保险条款中的"水渍险"相似，包括被保险货物在运输途中遭受雷电、火灾、爆炸或由于飞机遭受恶劣气候或其他危难事故而被抛弃，或由于飞机遭受碰撞、倾覆、坠落或失踪等自然灾害和意外事故所造成的全部或部分损失。

航空运输一切险（air transportation all risks）的承保责任范围与海洋货物运输保险条款中的"一切险"相似，除包括航空运输险的各项责任外，还包括被保险货物由于一般外来原因所造成的全部或部分损失，由保险公司负责赔偿。

（二）航空货物运输保险责任的起讫期限

航空货物运输保险责任起讫期限也采用"仓至仓条款"。不同的是，如果货物运达保险单所载明的目的地而未抵报保险单所载明的收货人仓库或储存处所，其保险责任则以被保险货物在最后卸离地卸离飞机后满30天为止。如在上述30天内被保险货物必须转运到非保险单所载明的目的地，则其保险责任从该项货物开始运转时终止。

在投保航空运输险时，还可加保战争险等附加险别。如果被保险货物不卸离飞机，战争险的责任起讫期限则以载货飞机到达目的地的当日午夜起算，满15天为止。

三、邮包运输保险

根据中国人民保险公司1981年1月1日修订的《邮包保险条款》规定，邮包保险基本险别分为邮包险和邮包一切险两种。

（一）邮包险与邮包一切险

保险公司对有保险的承保责任范围是负责赔偿被保险邮包在运输途中由于恶劣气候、雷电、海啸、地震、洪水等自然灾害，或由于运输工具搁浅、触礁、沉没、碰撞、出轨、倾覆、坠落、失踪，或由于失火、爆炸意外事故所造成的全部或部分损失。

（二）邮包险与邮包一切险的责任起讫

邮包险和邮包一切险的保险责任是自被保险邮包离开保险单所载起运地点寄件人的处所运往邮局时开始生效，直至被保险邮包运达保险单所载明的目的地邮局，自邮局签发到货通知书当日午夜算起，满15天终止，但在此期限内，邮包一经递交至收件人的处所，保险责任即行终止。

第四节　伦敦保险协会的海运货物保险条款

英国在国际保险业务中具有悠久的历史。英国伦敦保险业务所制定的《协会货物条款》（Insurance Cargo Clause，ICC），已被大多数国家所采用，有的国家在制定本国保险条款时经常会参考上述条款。《协会货物条款》最早制定于1912年，后来经过多次修订，最近一次的修订是在1982年1月1日完成的。新的海运货物保险条款与旧的条款相比，在名称与条款结构上都有很大变化。新修订的《协会货物条款》不再使用旧条款规定的平安险、水渍险和一切险三种险别，而是规定了六种险别，以英文字母A、B、C命名，这样可以有效避免因不确定的险别名称而引起的对条款内容的误解。在我国进出口业务中，特别是以CIF或CIP条件出口时，有的国外商人要求我出口公司按伦敦保险协会条款投保，我国出口企业一般可以接受。

一、伦敦保险协会修订的海运货物保险条款的种类

伦敦保险协会的海运货物保险条款主要有六项：
（1）协会货物条款（A）：Insurance Cargo Clauses（A），ICC（A）
（2）协会货物条款（B）：Insurance Cargo Clauses（B），ICC（B）
（3）协会货物条款（C）：Insurance Cargo Clauses（C），ICC（C）
（4）协会战争条款（货物）：Institute War Cargo Clauses
（5）协会罢工险条款（货物）：Institute Strikes Cargo Clauses
（6）恶意损害险条款：Malicious Damage Clauses

以上六种险别，除恶意损害险以外，其他五种险别在条款的结构和内容上都相似，基本包括下列八项内容：承包范围（risks covered）；除外责任（exclusion）；保险期限（duration）；索赔（claims）；保险利益（benefit of insurance）；减少损失（minimizing losses）；防止延迟（avoidance of delay）；法律与惯例（law and practice）。

根据现行的协会货物保险条款，在 ICC（A）、ICC（B）、ICC（C）条款和 ICC 战争险、罢工险条款中，以上八项内容中，除承保范围、除外责任和保险期限三项内容的规定有所不同外，其他各项内容完全相同。

二、协会货物保险的主要险别

（一）ICC（A）的承保风险与除外责任

1. ICC（A）的承保风险

根据伦敦保险协会对新条款的规定方法，对 ICC（A）是采用"一切风险减除外责任"的方法，即除了"除外责任"风险保险人不予负责外，其他风险均予负责。

2. ICC（A）的除外责任

（1）一般除外责任。ICC（A）的除外资责任主要包括以下几个方面：被保险人故意的不法行为造成的损失或费用；自然渗漏、自然损耗、包装不足或不当所造成的损失或费用；保险标的内在缺陷或特性所造成的损失或费用；直接由于延迟所引起的损失或费用；由于船舶所有人、经理人、租船人经营破产或不履行债务所造成的损失或费用；由于使用任何原子或核武器所成的损失或费用。

（2）不适航、不适货除外险责任。这里是指保险标的在装船时，如被保险人或其受雇人已经知道船舶不适航，以及船舶、装运工具、集装箱等不适货，保险人不负赔偿责任。

（3）战争除外责任。如由于战争、内战、敌对行为等所造成的损失或费用；由于捕获、拘留、扣留等（海盗除外）所造成的损失或费用；由于漂流水雷、鱼雷等所造成的损失或费用。

（4）罢工除外责任。由于罢工、被迫停工等所造成的损失或费用；由于罢工者、被迫停工工人等所造成的损失或费用；以及任何恐怖主义者或出于政治动机而行动的人所造成的损失或费用。

（二）ICC（B）的承保风险与除外责任

1. ICC（B）的承保风险

根据伦敦保险协会对 ICC（B）和 ICC（C）的规定，其承保风险的做法是采用"列明风险"的方法，即在条款的首部开宗明义地把保险人所承保的风险一一列出。

因此 ICC（B）的承保风险是灭失或损失合理，归因是属于下列之一者，保险人方予以赔偿：

（1）火灾、爆炸。

（2）船舶或驳船触礁、搁浅、沉没或出轨。

（3）陆上运输工具倾覆或出轨。

（4）船舶、驳船或运输工具同除去水以外的外界物体相碰撞。

（5）在避难港卸货。

（6）地震、火山爆发、雷电。

（7）共同海损的牺牲。

（8）抛货。

（9）浪击落海。

（10）海水、湖水或河水进入船舶、驳船、运输工具、集装箱、大型海运箱或储存处所。

（11）货物在装卸时落海或摔落造成整件的全损。

2. ICC（B）的除外责任

ICC（B）的除外责任与 ICC（A）的除外责任基本相同，只有下列两点区别：

（1）ICC（A）除对被保险人的故意不法行为所造成的损失、费用不负赔偿责任，对于被保险人之外的任何个人故意损害和破坏标的物或其他任何部分的损害要负赔偿责任。但在 ICC（B）下，保险人对此不负赔偿责任。

（2）ICC（A）对海盗行为列入保险范围，而 ICC（B）对海盗行为不负保险责任。

（三）ICC（C）的承保风险

ICC（C）的承保风险比 ICC（A）、ICC（B）要小得多。它只承保"重大意外事故"；而不承保"自然灾害及非重大意外事故"的风险。其具体的承保风险是：火灾、爆炸；船舶或驳船触礁、搁浅、沉没或倾覆；陆上运输工具倾覆或出轨；在避难港卸货；共同海损牺牲；抛货。ICC（C）险的除外责任与 ICC（B）完全相同。

综上所述，ICC（A）的承保风险，类似我国的"一切险"；ICC（B）类似"水渍险"；ICC（C）类似"平安险"，但比"平安险"的责任范围小。六种险别中，只有恶意损害险属于附加险别，不能单独投保，其他五种险别的结构相同，体系完整。因此，除 ICC（A）、ICC（B）、ICC（C）三种险别可以单独投保外，必要时，战争险和罢工险在征得保险公司同意后，也可作为独立的险别进行投保。

三、协会货物保险主要险别的保险期限

保险期限（period of insurance）也称保险有效期，是指保险人承担保险责任的起

止期限。英国伦敦保险协会海运货物条款（A）、（B）、（C）与我国海运货物保险期限的规定大体相同，也是"仓至仓"，但是我国条款的规定更为详细。

第五节 保险实务与合同中的保险条款

在进出口货物运输中，被保险人需要选择投保险别、确定保险金额、办理投保手续并交付保险费、领取保险单证以及在货损时办理保险索赔等。保险条款是进出口合同的重要组成部分之一，必须规定得正确合理。

一、保险实务

在国际货物买卖过程中，应根据买卖双方商定的价格条件来确定由买方还是卖方负责投保。在 FOB、FCA、CFR、CPT、EXW 或 FAS 条件下，由买方办理保险；若以 CIF 或 CIP 条件成交，应由卖方办理保险手续。办理货运保险的一般程序分为三步。

（一）确定保险险别及保险金额

1. 保险险别的选择

保险险别是保险人对风险的承保责任范围，保险公司承担保险责任是以投保人的险别为依据的。险别不同，保险承担的责任范围不同，收取的保险费与不同被保险人在保险货物受到损失时可能得到的补偿也不同。因此，如何适当地选择险别是一个十分重要的问题，基本原则是既要保证货物获得充分的安全保证，又要节省保险费用开支。在确定保险险别时应考虑以下几个要素：

（1）货物本身的性质和特点；
（2）货物的包装；
（3）运输工具所经过的路线；
（4）季节、气候等自然条件。

2. 保险金额的确定与保险费用的计算

（1）保险金额是被保险人对货物的实际投保金额，是被保险货物发生保险范围内的损失时，保险公司赔偿的最高限额，也是保险公司计算保险费的基础。保险费是保险公司依据不同的保险率向被保险人收取的费用，不同的商品，不同的地区，保险费率是有差别的。

《UCP 600》规定：如果信用证对投保金额未作规定，投保金额须至少为货物的 CIF 或 CIP 价格的 110%。如果从单据中不能确定 CIF 或者 CIP 价格，投保金额必须基于要求承付或议付的金额，或者基于发票上显示的货物总值计算，两者之中取金额

较高者。因此,保险金额的计算公式为:

$$\text{保险金额} = \text{CIF（或 CIP）价} \times (1 + \text{投保加成率})$$

对 CFR 或 CPT 价合同下的货物进行投保,需先把 CFR 或 CPT 转化成 CIF 或 CIP 价,再加成计算保险金额,可按下列公式计算:

$$\text{CIF（或 CIP）价} = \frac{\text{CIF（或 CIP）价}}{1 - [\text{保险费率} \times (1 + \text{投保加成率})]}$$

（2）保险费的计算。保险费是保险公司经营业务的基本收入,也是被保险人获得损失赔偿权的对价。投保人交付保险费,是保险合同生效的前提条件。在被保险人交付保险费之前,保险人可以拒绝签发保险单据。保险费的计算公式为:

$$\text{保险费} = \text{保险金额} \times \text{保险费率}$$

进口货物保险率有"进口货物保险率"和"特约费率"两种。进口保险费率分"一般货物费率"和"指明货物加费费率"两项。一般货物费率按不同运输方式,分险别和地区制定,但不分商品,除"指明货物加费费率"中列出的商品以外,还适合用于其他一切货物。至于"指明货物加费费率",是对一些指定的商品投保一切险时采用的。"特约费率"是各保险公司在进出口货物保险费率,主要适用于预约保险合同项下的进出口货物。

（二）办理保险和交付保险费

1. 保险的基本原则

保险的基本原则是保险人与被保险人在订立保险合同时必须共同遵守的一些原则。主要包括:

（1）保险利益原则。保险标的（subject matter insured）是保险所要保障的对象（保险利益原则）保险标的是保险所要保障的对象,它可以是任何财产及其有关利益或者人的寿命和身体。保险利益（insurable interest）,又称可保权益,是指投保人对保险标的具有法律上承认的利益。投保人对保险利益应当具有保险利益。如果保险人对保险标的不具有保险利益,则保险合同无效,这就是保险利益原则。就货物运输保险而言,反映在货物运输上的利益,主要是货物本身的价值,但也包括与此相关联的费用,如运费、保险费、关税和预期利润等。当保险标的安全到达时,被保险人就受益;当保险标的遭到损毁或灭失时,被保险人就受到损害。

（2）最大诚信原则。最大诚信（utmost good gaith）原则是指投保人和保险人在签订保险合同以及在合同有效期内,必须保持最大限度的诚意,双方都应恪守信用,互不欺骗隐瞒,保险人应当向投保人说明保险合同的条款内容,并可以就保险标的或者被保险人的有关情况提出询问,投保人应当如实告知。最大诚信原则主要有两方面的要求:一是重要事实的申报;二是保证。

（3）补偿原则。各种保险合同（人身保险合同除外）都是补偿性合同,所有补偿性合同都是建立在补偿基础之上的。当保险标的遭受保险责任范围内的损失时保险人应当依照保险合同的约定履行补偿义务。但保险人的补偿金额不得超过保险单上的保险金额或被保险人遭受的实际损失。保险人的补偿不应使被保险人因保险补偿而获得额外利益。

（4）近因原则。近因（proximate cause）原则是保险理赔工作中必须遵循的一项基本原则，也是在保险标的发生损失时，用来确定保险标的所受损失是否能获得保险赔偿的一项重要依据。这一原则是指保险人只对承保风险与保险标的的损失之间有直接因果关系的损失负赔偿责任，而对于保险责任外的风险造成的保险标的的损失不承担赔偿责任。

2. 投保手续

（1）进口货物的投保手续。进口货物一般按 FOB 或 CFR 条件成交，由买家办理保险。为了简化投保手续和防止出现漏保或来不及办理投保等情况，我国进口货物一般采取预约的做法，各进出口公司和中国人民保险公司都签订有预约保险合同。

按照海运进口货物预约保险合同的规定，投保人在获悉每批货物的起运消息后，只要准确将船名、开航日期、航线、货物品名及数量、保险金额等内容，以书面形式通知保险公司，就算向保险公司办理了投保手续，而无需填写投保单。如果被保险人未按预定保险合同的规定办理投保手续，则保险公司不负赔偿责任。

按空、邮运进口货物预约保险合同的规定，凡在预约保险合同范围内承保的货物，投保人必须逐笔向保险公司填送起运通知书，作为保险公司投保的手续和凭证。起运通知书的内容包括：运输方式、飞机运单号、开航日期或邮包收据日期、起运地及目的地、货物名称、贸易术语、价格等项目。保险公司获得起运通知书后，自动承担承保范围内货物损失的保险。

（2）出口货物的投保手续。出口货物如果按 FOB 或 CFR 条件成交，保险是买方的责任，则只能自己承担。因此，如欲确定此期间货运安全，就必须办理短途运输险。

如果按 CIF 条件成交，由我方办理保险，只要在装船前办理保险手续，就不违反贸易合同。然而 CIF 合同下的货运险是真正的"仓至仓责任"，因此，应该在货物运离仓库前办理投保手续，以便一旦在从仓库至码头的短途运输中发生货损，能够得到赔偿。

投保人向保险公司办理投保，须逐笔提出书面申请，填写投保单，写明投保人姓名、货物名称、包装、数量、标志、保险金额、船名、开船日期、航程、投保险别、赔款地点等。但在实际业务中，我国各外贸公司可以不必填写这些内容，只需填写装运出口的单据副本并加注保险金额和保险险别即可。如需填写投保单，则必须真实，并严格按照合同与信用证的规定办理。

(三) 取得保险单据

保险合同的形式一般以保险单据表示。保险单据是保险人和被保险人之间订立保险合同的证明文件，它反映了保险人和被保险人之间的权利与义务关系，也是保险人的承保证明。当发生保险责任范围内的损失时，它又是保险索赔和理赔的主要依据。

1. 保险单（insurance policy）

保险单俗称大保单，是使用最广的一种保险单据，用于承保一个指定的航程内某一批货物发生的损失，具有法律效力，对双方当事人具有约束力。其内容一般包括：(1) 当事人（投保人名称、地址）；(2) 保险标的（品名、数量、包装、标记）；(3) 船名或运输工具名称；(4) 保障的风险和事故种类；(5) 保险金额、保险费率、保险费；(6) 保险责任起止日期、期限；(7) 出单日期；(8) 保险公司签章；(9) 索赔所需提供的证据及规定，并应立即通知保险人查勘。保险单背面载有保险人和被保险人之间权利和义务方面的保险条款，如保险责任范围、除外责任、责任期限、损失处理、索赔理赔、争议处理等。

2. 保险凭证（insurance certificate）

保险凭证俗称小保单，是一种简化的保险单据。这种凭证除书面没有列明详细保险条款外，其余内容均与保险单相同。保险凭证具有与上述保险单据同等的法律效力。

3. 联合凭证（combined certificate）

联合凭证是一种将发票和保险单相结合，但比保险凭证更为简化的保险单据。保险公司将承保的险别、保险金额以及保险编号加注在投保人的发票上，并加盖印戳，其他项目均以发票上列明的为准。这种凭证只是在我国某些特定地区的出口业务中曾有使用，现已很少使用。

4. 预约保单（open policy）

预约保单，又称预约保险合同，是指被保险人（一般为进口人）与保险人之间订立的合同，凡属合同承保范围的货物，一经装运，在合同的有限期内自动承保。在实际业务中，预约保单适用于我国自国外进口的货物。凡属预约保单规定范围内的进口货物，一经起运，我国保险公司即自动按预约保单所订立的条件承保。

5. 批单（endorsement）

批单是指投保人在接受保险单后，如需要补充或变更其内容时，可根据保险公司的规定，向保险公司提出申请，经同意后即重新开出的一种内容经更改或补充的凭证。保险单经过修改后，保险公司即按此内容承担保险。

(四) 保险索赔

保险索赔（claim）是指被保险货物如在保险责任有效期内发生属于责任范围内

的损失，被保险人向保险公司提出索赔要求的行为。

保险索赔是一项重要而细致的工作，一定要实事求是，认真负责，确保双方的权利和义务的实现。在索赔工作中，被保险人应做好下列工作。

1. 损失通知和残损检查

当被保人获悉或发现被保险货物已遭损失，应立即通知保险公司或保险单上所载明的保险公司在当地的检验理赔代理人申请检验。保险公司或指定的理赔代理人在接到损失通知后应立即采取相应的措施，如检验损失。提出施救意见、核实损失原因、确定保险责任和签发检验报告等。

2. 承运人等有关方面提出索赔

被保险人或其他代理人在提货时发现被保险货物整件短少或有明显的残损痕迹，除向保险公司报损外还应立即向承运人或有关当局，如海关、港务局等，索取货损货差证明。如货损货差涉及承运人、码头、装卸公司等方面的责任，还应及时以书面形式向有关责任方提出索赔，并保留追偿权利。有时还要申请延长索赔时效。

3. 采取合理的施救、整理措施

被保险货物受损后，被保险人应迅速对受损货物采取必要合理的施救、整理措施，防止损失的扩大。被保险人收到的保险公司发出的有关采取防止或减少损失的合理措施的特别通知后，应当按照保险公司的要求处理。因抢救、阻止或减少货损的措施而支付的合理费用，可由保险公司负责，但以不超过该批被抢救货物的保险金额为限。

4. 索赔单证

被保险货物的损失经过检验，并办妥向承运人等第三者责任方的追偿手续后，应立即向保险公司或其代理人提出赔偿要求。提出索赔时，除应提供检验报告外，通常还必须提供其他单证，包括：保险单或保险凭证正本；运输单据，包括海运提单、铁路或公路运单、航空运单、邮包收据；发票；装箱单或重量单；向承运人第三者责任方请求赔偿的函电或其他必要的单证或文件；货损、货差证明；海事报告（sea protest）摘录；列明索赔金额及计算依据以及有关费用的项目和用途的索赔清单。

5. 应了解索赔免赔的一些规定。当货物发生全损时，应赔偿全部保险金额，如果部分损失，则应合理确定索赔比例。对易碎和易短量货物的索赔，应了解是否有免赔的规定；保险业有两种规定方法：一种是不论损失程度均予以赔偿；另一种是规定免赔率。免赔率是指保险人对于保险货物在运输途中发生的货损货差，在一定比率内不负赔偿责任。这是因为有些货物由于商品本身的特点或在转运作业过程中，必然会发生损失，这是正常现象，而非偶然事故，保险公司不予赔偿。

二、买卖合同的保险条款

保险条款是国际货物买卖合同中的重要组成部分之一，保险条款的内容应明确由谁办理保险，保险险别、保险金额、按什么保险条款保险等。除此之外，还应明确投保加成率，如超过10%，由此而产生的超额保险费应由买方负担。

保险条款的内容依据不同的贸易术语而有所区别，以 FOB、CFR 或 FCA、CPT 条件成交的合同，保险条款订为："保险由买方负责"（insurance to be covered by the buyer）。

如买方对货物或保险不熟悉，买方委托卖方代为办理保险，则应明确规定保险金额、投保险别、按什么保险条款以及保险费由买方支付。

以 CIF 和 CIP 条件成交的合同，在保险条款中必须规定由谁负责投保、投保险别、保险金额、按什么保险条款保险，并注明该条款的生效日期。保险条款订立的具体方法举例如下：

例1："保险由卖方按发票金额××%××险（险别），以中国人民保险公司×年×月×日的有关海洋运输货物保险条款为准。"

(Insurance：To be covered by the seller for ×% of total invoice value against × as per and subject to the relevant ocean marine cargo clauses of the people's insurance company of china, dated ….)

例2："保险由卖方按发票金额的××%投保陆运（火车，汽车）一切险和海洋运输货物一切险，按中国人民保险公司×年×月×日陆上运输货物保险条款和海洋运输货物保险条款负责，包括战争险，按×年×月×日陆上运输货物战争险（火车）条款和×年×月×日海洋运输货物战争险条款负责。

(Insurance：To be covered by Seller for ×% of total invoice value against Overland Transportation All Risks and All Risks as per Overland Transportation Cargo Insurance Clauses "Trains, Truck" and Ocean Marine Cargo Clauses of the people's Insurance Company of China date …, including War Risks as per Overland Transportation Cargo War Risks Causes (by train) date …, and Ocean Marine Cargo Clauses dated …)

例3："保险由卖方按发票金额的××%投保××险（险别）按伦敦保险协会×年×月×日货物××险条款负责。"

(Insurance：To be covered by the seller for ×% of total invoice value against …, … as per Institute Cargo Clauses … dated …)

Cargo Transportation Insurance

In international trade, the transportation of goods from the seller to the buyer by air, by land, or by sea is generally over a long distance and has to go through the procedures of loading, unloading, handling, and storing. During this process, it is quite possible that the goods will encounter various kinds perils or risks and sometimes suffer losses. In order to protect the goods against possible losses in case of such perils, the buyer or seller before the transportation of the goods must usually take out insurance with an insurance company on the goods.

International cargo transportation insurance refers to the fact that the insured covers insurance for the shipment with the insurer, i. e. , the insurance company before shipment. The insured pays insurance premium to the insurance company on the basis of insurance amount, insurance cover as well as insurance premium rate, and obtains the insurance policy. The insurer shall compensate the insured for the losses of, and damage to the goods, if any, during the transportation within the scope of insurance cover.

A. Perils and Losses

1. Perils

Perils refer to risks which occur at sea, or at the place where the ocean and land, or the ocean and the inland river, or the ocean and the lighter are connected.

Perils are mainly divided into two kinds, i, e. , general perils of the sea and extraneous risks.

1) General perils of the sea include natural calamities and fortuitous accidents. Natural calamities are caused by the forces resulting from the changes of nature, e. g. , vile weather, thunder, lightning, tsunami, earthquake, flood, etc. Fortuitous accidents include accidents resulting from unexpected causes, the carrying conveyance being grounded, stranded, or in collision with floating ice or other objects, as well as fire or explosion.

2) Extraneous risks include theft, fresh or rain water damage, shortage, leakage, breakage, sweating and heating, intermixture and contamination, odour, hook damage, breakage of packing, rusting, etc.

2. Ocean losses and expenses sustained

Ocean losses refer to the direct or indirect losses of the insured subject matter during the voyage owing to the perils of the sea.

1) **Total loss**

Total loss is usually classified into 2 kinds:

a) Actual Total loss: The insured subject matter is totally and irretrievably lost.

b) Constructive Total loss: It is estimated that the actual total loss of cargo is inevitable or the cost of salvage or recovery could have exceeded the value of the cargo.

In case of a constructive total loss, the insured may apply to the insurer for compensation according to partial loss or constrctive total loss. In case of the latter, the insured shall submit to the insurance company the notice of abandonment. In this way, the insured passes all the title to the subject matter to the insurer willingly, and applies to the insurer for compensation according to the total loss.

2) Partial loss

Partial loss includes general average and particular average.

a) General Average: When the word "average" is used in insurance, it means "loss or damage" at sea.

General average refers to a certain special sacrifice and extra expense intentionally incurred for the general interests of the shipowner, the insurer, and the owners of the various cargoes aboard the ship.

For example, a ship may have run aground and all efforts to refloat it have failed. In order to save the ship from breaking up, the master may decide to jettison part of the cargoes to lighten the ship. This loss is borne by all the parties concerned mentioned above in proportion. The same applies to additional expenses incurred for the common interests, for example, the cost of using a tug to tow the damaged vessel into a port; all the parties have to contribute in proportion to their interests.

The following conditions of general average must be provided with:

The carrying vessel must really run up against the risk that threatens the safety of the ship and the cargoes.

The sacrifice of general average must be a willing and intentional action.

The sacrifice of general average and the expenses outlaid must be reasonable.

The purpose of the sacrifice and expenses incurred is only restricted to the general safety of the vessel and cargoes.

Losses shall be the direct result of the general average.

The purpose of the sacrifice and expenses is to save the ship, cargoes and freight, so G. A. contribution shall be made by the three parties in proportion to the final value saved.

b) Particular average: Particular average means that a particular cargo is damaged by any cause and the degree of damage does not reach a total loss, i. e., only a partial loss, which shall be borne by the owner of this individual consignment.

3) Maritime charges

Maritime charges are usually incurred in saving the insured cargoes.

a) Sue and labour charges: When the insured cargo suffers natural calamities or fortuitous accidents within the scope of insurance cover the insured or his agent or any employees pays the expenses caused in saving the insured cargo in order to prevent the losses from further expanding. These charges shall be covered by the insurer.

b) Salvage charges: When the insured cargo suffers a natural calamity or a fortuitous accident within the scope of insurance cover, the third party who has no contracted relations with the insured and the insurer salvages the cargo successfully. According to the relative laws, existing in the world, the insurer shall pay to the salvor. But there is a principle, i. e., "no cure-no pay".

B. Marine Insurance Clauses

The contents, of our marine insurance clauses include the scope of cover, exclusions, commencement and termination of cover, duty of the insured, time of validity of a claim, etc.

1. The Insurance Coverage Includes Basic Insurance and Additional Insurance

1) Basic risks

Basic insurance is also called main insurance which may be underwritten independently. It is classified into three conditions, i. e., Free From Particular Average, with Particular Average and All Risks. Where the goods insured hereunder sustain loss or damage, the People's Insurance Company shall undertake to indemnify there-for according to the Insured Condition specified in the Policy and the Provisions of the clauses.

a) Free from particular average (F. P. A.)

The scope of F. P. A. includes:

- Total loss or constructive total loss of the whole consignment hereby insured caused in the course of transit by natural calamities, such as vile weather, thunder and lightening, tsunami, earthquake and flood.

- Total or partial loss caused by accidents, ——the carrying vessel being grounded, stranded, sunk, or in collision with floating ice or other objects, as well as fire or explosion.

- Partial loss caused by vile weather, lightning and/or tsunami, etc. where the conveyance has been grounded, stranded, sunk or burnt, irrespective of whether the event or events to take place before or after such accidents.

- Total or partial loss consequent on falling of entire package or packages into sea during the process of loading, unloading or transshipment.

- Sacrifice in and contribution to general average, and salvage charges resulting from the above mentioned accidents as well as other reasonable expenses in salvaging the cargoes from perils.

- Such proportion of losses sustained by the shipowners as is to be reimbursed by the cargo owner under the contract of Affreightment "Both to blame collision" clause.

b) With particular average (W. P. A. or W. A.¹): It covers partial loss due to vile weather, lightning, tsunami, earthquake and/or flood as well as the risks covered under F. P. A. condition as mentioned above.

c) All risks: Aside from the risks covered under the F. P. A. and W. A. conditions as above, this insurance also covers all risks of losses or damage to the insured goods whether partial or total, arising from external causes in the course of transit.

In practice, while taking out insurance for a specific shipment, we must differentiate one coverage from another, especially must be clear as to the differences between the clauses of F. P. A. and those of W. P. A.

Policies embodying clauses of the former type can be obtained at a lower rate of premium than those embodying W. A. clauses, but do not provide such comprehensive insurance cover as the latter. The exporter has to decide in each particular case whether F. F. A. terms are sufficient or a W. A. insurance is required; when fragile or more delicate goods are shipped, e. g., glassware, plywood etc,, a W. A. policy is generally apposite, even if the goods are expertly packed. When rough cargoes are shipped, e. g., sheet iron, coal, etc., an F. P. A. policy is usually sufficient.

2) Additional risks

Additional risks can not be, covered independently, they shall be underwritten depending on one kind of the basic risks.

a) General additional risks:

- Theft, pilferage and non-delivery;
- Fresh water and rain damage;
- Shortage;
- Intermixture and contamination;
- Leakage;
- Clash and breakage;
- Odour;
- Sweating and heating;
- Hook damage;
- Loss or damage caused by breakage of packing;
- Rust.

b) Special additional risks.

- Failure to delivery;
- Import duty risk;
- On deck risk;

- Rejection risk;
- Aflatoxin risk;
- Survey in customs risk;
- Survey at jetty risk;
- Strike, riot and civil commotion (SRCC);
- War risk;
- "Contingency insurance" cover seller's interest only.

2. Exclusions

Exclusions refer to losses and expenses for which the insurance company declares clearly not to be responsible.

Exclusions usually include:

1) Loss or damage caused by intentional act or fault of the insured;

2) Loss or damage due to the responsibility of the consignor;

3) Inferior quality or shortage in quantity before the commencement of the insurance duty;

4) Natural loss, inherent vice or nature of the insured goods;

5) Loss of the market price of the insured goods;

6) Loss due to delay in transportation and any expenses arising therefrom.

3. Commencement and Termination of Insurance Duty

1) Commencement and Termination of Basic Insurance

The commencement and termination of basic insurance are usually stipulated by adopting the customary "W/W" clause. By the clause warehouse to warehouse, the liability of the insurer is extended to cover pre-shipment and post-shipment risks. The insured goods are covered from the time when they leave the warehouse at the place named in the policy for the commencement of the transit and continue to be covered until they are delivered to the final warehouse at the destination named in the policy, but the policy provides an overriding time limit of sixty days after the completion of discharge of the insured goods from the seagoing vessel at the final port of discharge. On the expiration of that time limit of 60 days the cover ceases to protect the goods even though they have not reached the final warehouse.

2) Commencement and termination of marine war insurance

The insured goods are covered from the time when they are loaded on board the ship or lighter at the port of shipment named in the policy and continue to be covered until they are discharged at the port of destination named in the policy. If the cargoes are not discharged from the ship or lighter, then the time of insurance duty shall be limited to 15 days counting from the midnight of the day when the vessel arrives at the port of destination.

C. London Insurance Institute Cargo Clauses

The newly revised London Insurance Institute Cargo Clauses include 6 kinds:

- Institute Cargo Clause A;
- Institute Cargo Clause B;
- Institute Cargo Clause C;
- Institute War Clause – Cargo;
- Institute Strikes Clause – Cargo;
- Malicious Damage Clause.

1. Institute Cargo Clause A

The scope of clause A is comprehensive, so the method of "all risks except exclusions" is adopted.

1) Risks covered

a) All risks except exclusions;

b) General average and salvage expenses;

c) Proportion of losses under the contract of affreightment "Both to Blame Collision" Clause.

2) Exclusions

a) General exclusions

- Loss or damage due to wilful misconduct of the insured;
- Natural leakage of the subject matter, natural wear and tear, or wastage of the subject matter;
- Insufficient or improper packing;
- Delay;
- Inherent vice of the subject matter;
- Insolvency of the owner of the ship, the carrier or the charterer;
- Nuclear or atomic weapons.

b) Unseaworthiness and unfitness of the carrying vessel or lighter, including the containers;

c) War, capture, hostile behavior, distraint and conventional weapons;

d) Strike, terrorists.

2. Institute Cargo Clause B

Clause B lists all risks covered so that the insured may choose the proper insurance cover.

1) Fire, explosion;

2) Ship or lighter colliding with rocks, running aground, sunk or capsized;

3) Conveyance overturned or derailed;

4) Ship, lighter or other conveyance colliding with any external object excluding water;

5) Loss or damage due to unloading at the port of refuge;

6) Loss of damage due to earthquake, eruption of volcano, lightning or thunder;

7) Sacrifice in general average;

8) Loss of the subject matter due to jettison and washing overboard;

9) Loss of the subject matter due to being plunged into water by waves;

10) Loss of the subject matter insured due to water entering the ship, lighter, conveyance, container or storage place;

11) Total loss caused by falling of the entire package or packages into sea during the processes of loading and unloading.

Exclusions of clause B are those mentioned in clause A, but the following two are not included:

1) Piracy;

2) Malicious damage.

3. Institute Cargo Clause C

Institute Cargo Clause C only covers major casualties. Comparing with clause B, it excludes the following risks:

1) Loss or damage due to earthquake, eruption of volcano, lightning or thunder;

2) Falling of the goods into sea during the processes of loading and unloading, water entering the ship, lighter, conveyance, container, storage plane, etc.

Exclusions of clause C are the same as those in clause B.

D. Marine Insurance Business In China and Insurance Clauses in the Contract

1. Marine Insurance Business

1) Choosing Insurance Coverage

The liability undertaken by the insurance company is on the basis of insurance coverage.

We should take into consideration the following conditions when choosing insurance coverage:

a) Quality and characteristic of the goods: The coverage usually varies according to the type of goods and the circumstances; delicate goods, such as breakable crockery, cotton piecegoods or perishable foodstuffs, obviously have to be covered against more risks than sturdy articles like steel girders, tin ingots etc.

b) Conveyance and line: On the goods carried by different kinds of conveyance we should take out different insurance coverages. Different lines influence the goods as well, e. g. , the goods tend to be heated in equatorial areas.

c) Changes of international political and economic situations: Sometimes, international political and economic situations will menace the safety of the goods directly. For example, in case of war, we shall cover insurance on the goods against war risks.

d) Regularity of damage: We can obtain the regularity on the basis of investigation and research on the previous cases of damage.

e) Package conditions of the cargo: The packing of the goods must be sufficient for enduring a long distance transportation.

2) Determining insurance amount and calculating insurance premium:

The insurance amount is the highest compensation amount undertaken by the insurer, and it is also the foundation for calculating the insurance premium. The insured may usually determine the insurance amount by himself.

In principle, the insurance amount should be the actual value of the insured goods. However, in international trade practices, it is rather difficult to accurately calculate the actual value of the goods. Therefore, the insurance amount is usually determined on the basis of the CIF invoice value. But if we only take the CIF value as the insurance amount, the operating expenses and profit in expectancy by the insured cannot be compensated by the insurance company in case of loss or damage. So both the insurance clauses adopted in different countries and the international trade practices stipulate that the insurance amount may be marked up by a certain percentage on the basis of the CIF value. Then the insurance amount under CIF trade term includes:

a) Invoice value which is made up of 3 parts, i. e. , cost of the goods, amount of freight, insurance premium.

b) Markup percentage which is usually 10 percent of the CIF value.

The formula used to calculate the insurance amount under CIF trade terms is shown as follows:

$$\text{Insurance amount} = \text{CIF price} \times (1 + \text{markup percentage})$$

But at present, most of our import contracts are concluded under FOB or CFR terms. In order to simplify procedures and make calculations convenient, foreign trade enterprises usually sign open cover policies with the insurance company in which an average freight rate and an average insurance premium rate are stipulated, and the insurance amounts will not be marked up any more.

If under FOB trade terms:

$$\text{Insurance amount} = \text{FOB price} \times (1 + \text{average freight rate} + \text{average premium rate})$$

If under CFR trade terms:

$$\text{Insurance amount} = \text{CFR} \times (1 + \text{average premium rate})$$

The insurance premium being the name given to the sum of money paid by the insured, is the basic proceeds earned by the insurer.

Premium is usually calculated according to two kinds of rates, i. e., the general premium rate and the named cargo premium rate.

Under CIF terms, the formula for calculating the premium will be:

$$\text{Premium} = \text{CIF price} \times (1 + \text{markup percentage}) \times \text{premium rate}.$$

As mentioned above, the premiums of the imports in China are usually calculated in a simplified way.

If under FOB terms, the formula will be:

$$\text{Premium} = \text{FOB price} \times (1 + \text{average premium rate} + \text{average freight rate}) \times \text{average premium rate}.$$

If under CFR terms, the formula will be:

$$\text{Premium} = \text{CFR price} \times (1 + \text{average premium rate}) \times \text{average premium rate}.$$

3) Taking out insurance

Cargo transport insurance is usually taken out on "warehouse to warehouse" basis, so the goods under CIF terms shall be covered before being loaded on board the vessel. The insurance on export goods under CFR and FOB terms shall be taken out by the buyer, therefore the shipping advices shall be sent to the buyer by the seller before or when the goods are loaded on board the vessel.

Taking out insurance with the insurer is a contracted legal action of the insured, who usually applies for insurance in a written form. This kind of written form is called Application for Marine Insurance.

When the insured fills in the application, he should pay attention to the following points:

a) Details of the insured goods shall be provided on the principle of utmost good faith.

b) Contents shall be in conformity with the stipulations in the contract and L/C.

c) The insurer holds no liability for any wilful fault or negligence of the insured.

d) The venture must be legal.

e) The insurance amount, insurance coverage, the name, quantity, packing of the insured goods, the name of the vessel, sailing date, etc, must be filled in correctly.

4) Insurance clauses

Under FOB, CFR or CIF trade terms, the contract insurance clauses may be stipulated as follows:

a) Insurance to be effected by the buyer;

b) Insurance to be effected by the seller on behalf of the buyer for 110% of the invoice value against FPA (WFA, or All risks);

Premium to be for the buyers account.

c) Insurance to be effected by the seller for 110% of the invoice value against FPA (WPA or Alt risks) and war risk as per Ocean Marine Cargo Clauses of The People's Insurance Company of China.

E. Forms of Marine Insurance Contract

There are 5 kinds of Forms of Marine Insurance Documents.

1. Insurance Policy

The insurance policy is the most widely used insurance document. It legally binds upon both parties.

Contents of the insurance policy usually include:

1) Names and addresses of the insured and the insurer;
2) Subject matter insured;
3) Kinds of risks and accidents covered;
4) Commencement date of insurance as well as time limit;
5) Insurance amount;
6) Insurance premium;
7) Date and place of taking out the policy;
8) Signature of the insurer;
9) Words evidencing the establishment of the insurance relationship between the insured and insurer;
10) Particulars of the insured goods: the name, description, mark, quantity, packing, name of ship, port of shipment, port of destination, date of shipment, etc. ;
11) Coverage, place of claim satisfaction place and declaration of the insurer that the insured goods will be compensated in case of any loss or damage due to any risk within the scope of insurance cover.

There are rights and obligations of the two parties on the back of the insurance policy. It mainly includes the scope of insurance, the exclusion, the commencement and termination of the duty, the obligations of the insured and the time limit for claim.

2. Insurance Certificate

It is a kind of simplified insurance policy. The insurance certificate only indicates the name of the insured, name of the insured cargo, quantity, mark, conveyance, place of shipment, place of destination, insurance cover, and insurance amount. But the rights and obligations of the two parties are omitted. The insurance certificate has the same legal validity as the insurance policy.

3. Open Policy

This type of policy is of great importance for export business, it is a convenient method for insuring the goods where a number of consignments of similar export goods are intended to be covered. An open policy covers these shipments, as soon as they are made, under the previous arrangement between the insured and the insurance company. The particulars of these shipments should be supplied to the insurance company later on in the form of shipment advices which include the names of cargoes, quantities, insurance amounts, kinds of conveyance, ports of shipment, destinations, dates of shipment, etc. An open policy only indicates the scope of insurance coverage, insurance pemium rate and highest insurance amount of each lot, calculating method of the insurance premium, etc.

4. Combined Certificate

When the goods are exported to Hong Kong (China), and some countries in Southeast Asia, the insurance company sometimes adds the coverage, insurance amount and serial number of insurance on the commercial invoice which is made out by a foreign trade company. This is a certificate which combines the invoice with the insurance policy. It is the simplest insurance certificate in use.

5. Endorsement

After insurance has been taken out, if the insured wants to replenish or change the contents of the policy, he may apply to the company for the same. After agreement by the company, another certificate which indicates the relative amendment will be issued. This certificate is called endorsement.

F. Insurance Claim

Lodging or filing a claim means that in case the insured goods suffered losses within the scope of insurance cover, the insured can claim for indemnity from the insurer on the strength of the insurance contract.

1. Formalites for Claim

In case of loss or damage, the consignee shall determine who will be responsible for the same and thus determine the object whom he should raise a claim against.

The object may be the seller or consignor in case loss or damage is due to inferior quality, insufficient packing or shortage as well as inherent vice; or may be the carrier if loss or damage is due to improper transportation; or may be the insurer if loss or damage is due to natural calamities or fortuitous accidents within the scope of insurance.

1) Advice and inspection of goods damaged

After the insured goods have arrived at the port of destination, the insured or his agent should inspect the goods in time. If he finds any loss or damage within the scope of insurance, he should inform the inspector or the satisfaction agent of the insurer of the same at the port of destination. That the insured advises the insurer of the loss or damage is a necessary procedure of application for indemnity.

The following parties should be responsible for inspection:

a) The carrier or tally department;

b) The insurer and other relevant parties;

c) The authentic surveyor.

2) Evidence of lodging a claim

When the insured lodges a claim against the insurer, besides the written application for claim and detailed list of claim, he should also provide the following documents to indicate and evidence the degree of loss or damage, and the compensation duty of the insurer:

a) The inspection declaration of loss or damage;

b) The insurance policy or insurance certificate;

c) The invoice, B/L, packing list or weight memo;

d) The sea protest;

The sea protest is the true record of vile weather, fortuitous accidents or other perils during the voyage, the purpose of it is to indicate that the ship or cargoes may suffer losses due to the perils, and declare that the captain and the crew have already taken all necessary and reasonable measures. If the losses are due to force majeure events, the shipowner should be exempted from any obligations.

e) The detailed list of expenses;

f) The relevant documents and circular letters to the carrier and other third party to lodge a claim.

3) Protecting the interests of the insurer

a) Any person who files a claim should have the insurance interest.

b) Loss of or damage to the subject matter shall be the direct result of the perils within the scope of the insurance cover.

2. Points Should Be Paid Attention to When Filing Claims

1) As to fragile goods, there are two ways to stipulate the method for compensation. One is franchise, i.e., in case of breakage, the insurer is free from a certain percentage of compensation. The franchise includes relative franchise and deductible franchise. Both are free from compensation if the amount of loss does not exceed the franchise. But they have one im-

portant difference. In case the amount of loss exceeds the franchise under the relative franchise the insurer will not deduct the franchise and compensate the total loss, while under the deductible franchise the insurer will deduct the franchise and only compensate the exceeding part. Another stipulation is irrespective of percentage (I. O. P.) i. e., the insurance company will compensate in case of breakage irrespective of percentage but the insurance premium will be higher.

2) When the loss or damage suffered by the subject matter insured comes up to the constructive total loss, the insured may submit to the insurer the notice of abandonment, and pass all the rights and interests of the damaged goods to the insurer and ask him to compensate on the basis of the constructive total loss.

（资料来源：丁溪，唐赛. 国际贸易理论与实务 [M]. 中国商务出版社，2013.）

▶本章小结

保险的基本原则主要有可保利益原则、最大诚信原则、补偿原则等。国际贸易货物在海上运输过程中，可能会遭受各种不同风险，而海上货物运输保险人主要承保海上风险和外来风险所造成的损失与费用。海上损失按损失程度的不同，可分为全部损失和部分损失；按性质可分为共同海损和单独海损。海上货物保险保障的费用包括施救费用和救助费用。

在我国，进出口货物运输最常用的保险条款是中国保险条款。该条款按运输方式，可分为海洋、陆上、航空和邮包运输保险条款四大类。我国海洋货物运输保险条款包括三种基本险别，即平安险、水渍险和一切险。附加险别包括一般附加险、特殊附加险和特别附加险。

▶本章名词

可保利益原则　最大诚信原则　补偿原则　海上风险　外来风险　实际全损　推定全损　共同海损　单独海损　施救费用　救助费用　仓至仓条款

▶理论思考

1. 保险的基本原则是什么？
2. 简述风险的种类和内容。
3. 我国海上货物运输保险的险别有哪几种？各自的责任范围有何区别？
4. 什么是"仓至仓"条款？
5. 在什么情况下才能构成共同海损？共同海损与单独海损的区别是什么？

实训习题

1. 请翻译下列合同中的保险条款

Insurance: To be covered by the sellers for 110% of the total invoice value against as per Ocean Marine Cargo Clause of the People's Insurance Company of China.

2. 请阅读以下案例

案例1：

2017年，我国WK外贸公司向中国香港出口罐头一批共500箱，按照CIF HONGKONG向保险公司投保一切险。但是因为海运提单上只写明进口商的名称，没有详细注明其地址，货物抵达香港后，船公司无法通知进口商来货场提货，又未与WK公司的货运代理联系，自行决定将该批货物运回起运港天津新港。在运回途中因为轮船渗水，有229箱罐头受到海水浸泡。货物运回新港后，WHHK公司没有将货物卸下，只是在海运提单上补写进口商详细地址后，又运回香港。进口商提货后发现罐头已经生锈，所以只提取了未生锈的271箱罐头，其余的罐头又运回新港。WK外贸公司发现货物有锈蚀后，凭保险单向保险公司提起索赔，要求赔偿229箱货物的锈损。保险公司经过调查发现，生锈发生在第二航次，而不是第一航次。投保人未对第二航次投保，不属于承保范围，于是保险公司拒绝赔偿。保险公司的做法是否合理？公司应吸取什么教训？

案例2：

某外贸公司按CIF术语出口一批货物，装运前已让保险公司按发票总值110%投保平安险，6月初货物装妥顺利启航。载货船舶于6月13日在海上遇到暴风雨，致使一部分货物受到水渍，损失价值为2 100美元，数日后，该轮又突然触礁，致使该批货物又遭到部分损失，价值为8 000美元。试问：保险公司对该批货物的损失是否赔偿？为什么？

案例3：

我某外贸公司与荷兰进口商签订一份皮手套合同，价格条件为CIF鹿特丹，向中国人民保险公司投保一切险。生产厂家在生产的最后一道工序将手套的湿度降低到了最低程度，然后用牛皮纸包好装入双层瓦楞纸箱，再装入20英尺集装箱，货物到达鹿特丹后，检验结果表明，全部货物湿、霉、沾污、变色，损失价值达8万美元。据分析，该批货物的出口地不异常热，进口地鹿特丹不异常冷，运输途中无异常，运输完全属于正常运输。试问：(1) 保险公司对该批货损是否负责赔偿？为什么？(2) 进口商对受损货物是否支付货款？为什么？(3) 你认为出口商应如何处理此事？

案例4：

我国A公司与某国B公司于2015年10月20日签订购买52 500吨化肥的CFR合同。A公司开出信用证规定，装船期限为2016年1月1日至1月10日，由于B公司租来运货的"雄狮号"在开往某外国港口途中遇到飓风，结果装货至 2016 年 1 月 20 日才完成。承运人在取得 B 公司出具保函的情况下签发了与信用证条款一致的提单。"雄狮号"于 1 月 21 日驶离装运港。A 公司为这批货物投保了水渍险。2016 年 1 月 30 日"雄狮号"途经达尼尔海峡时起火，造成部分化肥烧毁。船长在命令救火过程中又造成部分化肥湿毁。由于船在装货港口的延迟，使该船到达目的地时赶上了化肥价格下跌，A 公司在出售余下的化肥时价格不得不大幅下降，给 A 公司造成了很大的损失。试分析：（1）保险公司对于货物的损失是否赔偿？为什么？（2）货物的损失中哪部分属于单独海损，为什么？（3）哪部分属于共同海损，为什么？

3. 保险查询

（1）登陆中国人民保险公司、平安保险公司网站，浏览网站内容。回答：（1）三个网站主页地址是什么？（2）这些公司网上投保手续（流程）是什么？（3）哪家保险公司有英文保险（险别）条款？

（2）请查询出口货物保险费率表查询下列出口商品的保险费率。

①出口韩国的一批纯棉布匹（海运、陆运、空运、邮包）。

②出口马来西亚的一批成衣（海运、陆运、空运、邮包）。

③出口澳大利亚的一批玩具（海运、陆运、空运、邮包）。

④出口到巴基斯坦的一批生丝。

⑤出口到新西兰的一批计算机。

⑥出口到意大利的一批白金钻戒。

⑦出口到芬兰的一批景泰蓝。

⑧出口到俄罗斯的一批挂毯。

⑨出口到墨西哥的一批装框装饰画。

⑩出口到日本的一批桶装原油。

（3）经研究，公司决定将出口美国货物交平安保险公司承保；将出口毛里塔尼亚货物交太平洋保险公司承保。阅读两家公司网上投保流程说明，（模拟）完成两笔货物出口投保手续。（切勿真的提交/发送！）

4. 计算题

（1）我某出口合同，报价 CIF Losangles，要求投保一切险和战争险，如出口发票金额为 15 000 美元，一切险保险费率为 0.6%，战争险费率为 0.03%。问：①投保金额是多少？②应付保险费多少？

（2）一批出口货物 CFR 价为 250 000 美元，现客户要求改 CIF 价加二成投保海运一切险，我保险公司均同意办理，如保险费率为 0.6% 时，问题：①我应报 CIF 价多少？（保证外汇净收入不变）②我方应向客户收多少保险费？

CHAPTER 7

第七章　国际货款的结算

> **本章指导**
>
> 通过对本章的学习，要求能够了解有关货款支付方面的国际贸易惯例，各种支付方式的原理、利弊区别，特别注意对信用证的收付程序、种类及跟单信用证统一惯例的有关规定的了解，掌握并能够在国际结算业务中运用：
>
> 1. 汇票
> 2. 托收
> 3. 信用证

第一节　货款结算的支付工具

不同的货款结算方式均依赖于一定的支付工具。国际贸易中使用的支付工具包括货币和票据，目前基本上都采用非现金结算，即以票据作为结算工具。票据可分为汇票、本票和支票三种，在国际货款结算中，以使用汇票为主。

一、汇票

（一）汇票的定义

汇票（Bill of Exchange，简称 Draft 或 Bill）是由一人签发给另一人的无条件书面命令，要求受票人在见票时或于未来某一规定的或可以确定的时间，向某人或其指定的人或持票人支付一定的金额。

（二）汇票必须具备以下内容

（1）票据主文中列有"汇票"一词；（2）无条件支付一定金额的命令；（3）受

票人的姓名；（4）付款日期；（5）付款地点；（6）受款人或其指定人的姓名；（7）出票日期和地点；（8）出票人的签名。

（三）汇票的当事人

汇票有三个基本当事人：

1. 出票人（drawer）

签发汇票的人，一般是出口商。在汇票承兑前出票人是主债务人，如果汇票遭到拒付，他将保证偿付票款给持票人或被迫付款的任何背书人。

2. 受票人（drawee）

接受支付命令的人，又称付款人，一般是进口商或其指定的银行。受票人在汇票上未签名之前，不是汇票的债务人，有拒绝承担付款责任的权利。

3. 受款人（payee）

收取汇票金额的人，即汇票的收款人，一般是出口商或其指定的银行。收款人作为汇票的第一持票人，因持有汇票而拥有所有的票据权利，即请求付款权、追索权和票据转让权。

除了上述基本当事人之外，随着汇票的流通转让，又出现了背书人、被背书人、承兑人、保证人和持票人等其他当事人。

（四）汇票的使用

汇票的使用包括出票、提示、承兑、付款等票据行为，如需转让，一般通过背书行为转让，遭到拒付时，还要涉及发出退票通知、制作拒绝证书和行使追索权等票据行为。

1. 出票（issue）

指出票人签发票据并将其交付给收款人的票据行为。出票时必须逐一写明汇票的各项必备内容，对于收款人有以下三种写法。

（1）限制性抬头。这种抬头的汇票不能流通转让，只能由抬头人收取票款，有如下形式：ⅰ．"Pay C Co. only"（仅付 C 公司）。ⅱ．"Pay C Co. not transferable/negotiable"（付给 C 公司，不可转让）。ⅲ．"Pay C Co."（付给 C 公司）并在汇票正面注明"not transferable/negotiable"（不可转让）字样。

（2）指示性抬头。

这种抬头的汇票可以经过持票人背书后转让给第三者，有如下形式。

ⅰ．"Pay C Co. or order"（付给 C 公司或其指定人）。

ⅱ．"Pay to the order of C Co."（付给 C 公司的指定人）。

ⅲ．"Pay to C Co."（付给 C 公司）。

（3）持票人或来人抬头。

这种汇票无须持票人背书，仅凭交付既可转让，有如下形式：

ⅰ．"Pay to bearer"（付给持票来人）。

ⅱ．"Pay to C Co. or bearer"（付给 C 公司或持票来人）。

2. 提示（presentation）

持票人向付款人或其他人出示汇票要求承兑或付款的行为。付款人看到汇票即为见票（Sight）。提示可分为承兑提示和付款提示两种。

3. 承兑（acceptance）

远期汇票的付款人承诺在汇票到期日支付汇票金额的行为。承兑的手续由付款人在汇票正面写上"承兑"字样，注明承兑日期，并签名或盖章，交还持票人。

汇票承兑后承兑人是主债务人，出票人则为从债务人。承兑人承诺了票据的有效性，对票据的文义负责，不得以出票的签字是伪造的、背书人无行为能力等理由来否认汇票的效力，到期足额付款。

汇票的承兑可以是普通承兑或一般承兑，也可以是限制性承兑或保留性承兑。承兑人对于出票人的命令不加限制的同意确认即为普通承兑，限制性承兑是指附加有修改汇票文义的保留性付款记载的承兑。常见的限制承兑有有条件承兑、部分承兑、限定付款地点承兑和修改付款时间承兑四种。

4. 付款（payment）

持票人在到期日或规定的期限内提示汇票，经付款人或承兑人付款后，汇票上的一切债权债务即告结束。持票人获得票款时，应当在汇票上签收，并将汇票交给付款人。

5. 背书（endorsement）

背书是持票人在汇票的背面签上自己的名字，或再加上被背书人的名字，并把汇票交给被背书人或受让人的票据转让行为。经背书转让后，受让人享有汇票的收款权力，还可通过再次背书继续转让汇票。对于受让人来说，所有在他以前的背书人和出票人都是他的"前手"，对于出让人来说，所有在他以后的受让人都是他的"后手"。任一背书人都是汇票的债务人之一，"前手"对"后手"负有担保汇票必然会被承兑或付款的责任。

背书的方式有以下三种：

（1）限制性背书，有以下几种写法：

ⅰ．"Pay to C Co. only"（仅付 C 公司）。

ⅱ．"Pay to C Co. not transferable/negotiable"（付给 C 公司，不可转让）。

ⅲ．"Pay to C Co. not to order"（付给 C 公司，不得付给其指定人）制作成限制性背书的汇票，被背书人不得将汇票再行流通转让，而只能凭票取款。

（2）特别背书，又称记名背书，有以下几种写法：

ⅰ．"Pay to the order of C Co."（付给 C 公司的指定人）。

ⅱ."Pay to C Co. or order"（付给 C 公司或其指定人）。

ⅲ."Pay to C Co."（付给 C 公司）。

汇票经特别背书后，即可交付转让给被背书人，被背书人可继续将汇票背书转让给他人。

（3）空白背书，又称不记名背书。背书人只在汇票背面签名而不记载受让人名称，制作成空白背书的汇票仅凭交付即可转让。

远期汇票承兑后尚未到期时，持票人如想提前取得票款，可以通过背书将汇票转让给银行或贴现公司，并从票面金额中扣减按照一定贴现率计算的贴现息后获取部分余款。这种票据转让行为被称为贴现，贴现银行待贴现汇票到期时，再行提示给承兑人要求全额付款。

6. 拒付（dishonour）与追索（recourse）

无论持票人提示汇票要求承兑时遭到拒绝承兑，还是持票人提示汇票要求付款时遭到拒绝付款，均称为拒付，也称退票。除了明确表示拒付外，付款人逃避不见、死亡或宣告破产，一直到付款事实上已不可能执行时，也可视为拒付。

持票人是汇票的唯一债权人，如在合理的时间内提示承兑，或在到期日提示付款，遭到拒付，可向其任一前手背书人、出票人和承兑人行使追索权，要求偿还汇票金额及费用。持票人行使追索权之前，必须及时发出退票通知，将拒付事实书面通知其前手，需要时还须及时制作拒绝证书。拒绝证书是由汇票拒付地点的法定公证人或其他有权作出证书的机构作出的证明拒付事实的文件，它是持票人凭以向其前手进行追索的法律依据。

（五）汇票的种类

可以根据汇票的不同特征，从不同的角度来对汇票做分类。

1. 按照汇票出票人和付款人的不同，汇票可分为银行汇票和商业汇票。

银行汇票（Banker's Bill）的出票人和付款人都是银行，商业汇票（Commercial Bill）又称商号汇票（Trader's Bill），其出票人是工商企业或个人，付款人可以是工商企业或个人，也可以是银行。

2. 按照汇票是否附有商业单据，汇票可分为光票和跟单汇票。

光票（Clean Bill or Draft）是不附带商业单据的汇票，附有商业单据的汇票称为跟单汇票（Documentary Bill or Draft）。光票的流通完全依靠当事人的信用，银行汇票多是光票。跟单汇票的付款以提交货运单据为条件，商业汇票一般为跟单汇票。

3. 按照付款时间的不同，汇票可分为即期汇票和远期汇票。

即期汇票（Sight Bill or Demand Draft）是指在见票时即持票人提示汇票的当天立即付款的汇票，即期汇票无须承兑。

远期汇票（Time Bill or Usance Bill）是指在一定的期限或特定日期付款的汇票，

分为以下几种情况：（1）见票后若干月/天付款（At ×× Days/Months after Sight）；（2）出票后若干天/月付款（At ×× Days/Months after Date）；（3）汇票注明日期后若干天（At ×× Days/Months after Date）或提单签发日后若干天付款（At ×× Days after Date of Bill of Lading）；（4）指定日期付款（Fixed Date）。

远期汇票须由持票人向付款人提示要求承兑，以明确承兑人的付款责任。见票后若干天/月付款的远期汇票，要从承兑日起算，确定付款到期日。

4. 按照汇票承兑人的不同，可分为商业承兑汇票和银行承兑汇票。

商业承兑汇票（Trader's Acceptance Bill）是由企业或个人承兑的远期汇票，它建立在商业信用的基础之上。银行承兑汇票（Banker's Acceptance Bill）是由银行承兑的远期汇票，它建立在银行信用的基础之上。

二、本票

（一）本票的定义

《英国票据法》关于本票的定义是：本票是一人向另一人签发的，保证于见票时或定期或在可以确定的将来的时间，对某人或其指定人或持票人支付一定金额的无条件的书面承诺。

（二）本票的内容

根据《日内瓦统一法》，本票必须具备以下内容：

1. 票据主文中列有"本票"一词；
2. 无条件支付一定金额的承诺；
3. 付款日期；
4. 付款地点；
5. 受款人或其指定人的姓名；
6. 签发本票的日期和地点；
7. 制票人的签名。

（三）本票的种类

本票按出票人的不同分为商业本票和银行本票两种。商业本票的出票人是企业或个人，银行本票的出票人是银行。银行本票如果开成不记载收款人名称或来人抬头本票，即可代替现金流通。为了限制银行本票的签发，有的国家对本票的发行规定最低限额，只允许开出一定金额以上的大额本票，或禁止发行来人抬头的银行本票，以免当作纸币在市场上流通。

我国《票据法》只允许使用银行本票，不承认银行以外的工商企业、组织机构或个人签发的本票。

（四）本票与汇票的比较

本票与汇票在基本内容上有许多相同之处，《票据法》关于汇票的背书、到期日、付款、追索等票据行为的规定同样适用于本票。尽管如此，本票和汇票仍是两种不同性质的票据，有以下不同。

1. 本票是出票人的无条件支付承诺，是承诺式票据；汇票是出票人要求受票人无条件付款的支付命令，是命令式或委托式票据。

2. 本票有两个基本当事人，即出票人和受款人；汇票的基本当事人有三个，即出票人、受票人和受款人。

3. 本票的出票人既是付款人，远期本票不需要承兑；远期汇票必须承兑。

4. 本票的出票人是主债务人；汇票在承兑前，出票人是主债务人，承兑后，承兑人是主债务人。

三、支票

（一）支票的定义

《英国票据法》关于支票的定义是：支票是以银行为付款人的即期汇票。即存款人对其开户行签发的，授权该银行对某人或其指定人或持票人即期支付一定金额的无条件书面支付命令。

（二）支票的内容

根据《日内瓦统一法》，支票必须具备以下内容：

1. 票据主文中列有"支票"一词；
2. 无条件支付一定金额的命令；
3. 受票人的姓名；
4. 付款地点；
5. 出票日期和地点；
6. 出票人的签名。

如果支票的出票人所签发的支票金额超过付款时其在银行处实有的存款金额，称为空头支票。签发空头支票是被各国法律所禁止的。

(三) 支票的种类

支票按抬头的不同性质，可分为记名支票、不记名支票；按支票签发人的不同，可分为银行支票、商业支票；按支票本身的基本特征，可分为划线支票、保付支票等。具体如下：

1. 记名支票

记名支票在其收款人一栏写明具体收款人姓名，如 Pay A Co. or order（付 A 公司或其指定人），取款时须由收款人签章。

2. 不记名支票

不记名支票又称空白支票，收款人一栏只写明 Pay bearer（付来人）。持票人无需在支票背后签章即可支取票款，此种支票可以仅凭交付而转让。

3. 划线支票

正面划有两道平行线的支票称为划线支票。一般支票可以委托银行收款入账，也可由持票人自行提取现款，支票不带划线者，称为现金支票。划线支票只能委托银行代收票款入账，在支票遗失或被人冒领时，使用划线支票可以通过银行代收的线索追回票款，从而保障了持票人和出票人的资金安全。

4. 保付支票

保付支票是由付款银行在支票上加盖"保付"戳记，保证在支票提示时付款。支票一经保付保付银行就承担付款责任，出票人、背书人都可免于追索。付款银行对支票保付后，既将票款从出票人账户中提出，转入专户存储，以备付款。

5. 银行支票

银行支票是由银行签发，并由银行付款的支票。银行代理客户办理票汇时，可开立银行支票。

(四) 支票和汇票的区别

1. 付款人的身份不同。

支票的付款人只能是银行，汇票的付款人可以是工商企业或个人，也可以是银行。

2. 付款期限不同。

支票只能是即期付款，一经提示，除正当理由可以拒付外，通常是见票即付，汇票既有即期付款也有远期付款，远期汇票必须提示承兑。

另外，支票可以划线、支付，汇票在法律上无划线和支付的规定。

第二节 支付方式

货款的支付方式根据资金的流向与支付工具的传递方向是否相同，可以分为顺汇和逆汇两种方法。顺汇是由债务人或付款人主动通过银行将款项支付给债权人或收款人的结算方式，其资金的流动方向与结算工具的传递方向相同。逆汇是由债权人以出具票据的方式，委托银行向债务人收取款项的结算方式，其资金的流动方向与结算工具的传递方向相反。

国际货款的结算方式有汇付、托收和信用证三种，其中汇付属顺汇法，托收与信用证属逆汇法。这三种方式虽然都是通过银行办理，但银行的作用并不相同。在汇付和托收方式下，银行只是提供服务，并未承担任何第一性的付款责任，买卖双方是在根据贸易合同相互提供信用的前提下，各自履行进口商付款和出口商提供货运单据的责任，所以汇付和托收以商业信用为基础。而信用证以银行信用为基础，因为在信用证方式下，开证行在一定的条件下承担第一性的付款责任。

一、汇付

汇付（remittance）又称汇款，是指债务人或付款人通过银行将款项汇交债权人或收款人的结算方式。采用汇付方式结算货款时，进口商通过银行汇款给出口商，出口商直接将货物交付给进口商，货运单据也由出口商自行寄送进口商，银行并不传递和处理与货物有关的单据。

（一）汇付方式的当事人

汇款人（remitter）：汇出款项的人。在进出口贸易中，通常是进口商。

收款人（payee or beneficiary）：接受汇款的人。在进出口贸易中，通常是出口商。

汇出行（remitting bank）：接受汇款人的委托，汇出款项的银行。在进出口贸易中，通常是进口地的银行。

汇入行（paying bank）：又称解付行，即接受汇出行的委托解付汇款的银行。在进出口贸易中，通常是出口地银行。

在上述当事人中，汇款人和收款人可以是同一人，即汇款人将款项汇出后，可以自己到异地取款。

汇款人在委托汇出行办理汇款时，要出具汇款申请书。汇款申请书是汇款人与汇出行之间的一种契约，汇出行一经接受申请就有义务按照汇款申请书的指示通知汇入行。汇出行与汇入行事先订有代理合同，在合同规定范围内，汇入行对汇出行承担解付汇款的义务。

（二）汇付方式的种类及业务程序

汇付方式按照汇出方式的不同分为信汇、电汇和票汇三种。

1. 电汇

电汇（telegraphic transfer，T/T）是指汇出行应汇款人的申请，用加押电报或电传的形式指示汇入行付款给收款人的一种汇款方式。

电汇具有交款迅速、安全可靠的优点，但汇款人要承担较高的电汇费用。电汇方式资金的在途时间极短，有利于资金的充分利用，适用于金额大、需求急的汇款。

2. 信汇

信汇（mail transfer，M/T）：是指汇出行应汇款人的申请，用邮寄信汇委托书或支付委托书的方式指示汇入行付款给收款人的一种汇款方式。

在处理程序上，信汇与电汇基本相同，所不同的是汇出行不是用电报而是以航邮方式将信汇委托书或支付委托书寄给汇入行。委托书上不必加密押，而是加具有权签字人的签字或印鉴，汇入行经核对证实无误后，解付汇款。

电汇和信汇的业务程序如图7-1所示：

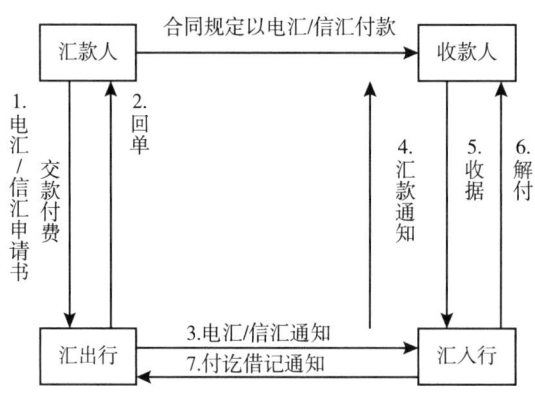

图7-1 电汇/信汇业务程序

信汇具有费用较电汇低廉，但汇款在途时间长、收款人收款较迟等特点。由于电讯的发展，大多数发达国家目前已不再使用和接受信汇，我国除对个别国家或除非有特殊要求外，对外也已基本不使用信汇方式进行结算。

3. 票汇

票汇（remittance by banker's demand draft，D/D）：是指汇出行应汇款人的申请，开立以汇出行的海外分行或代理行为付款人的银行即期汇票，交由汇款人自行寄交给收款人，凭票向付款行取款的一种汇付方式。

票汇结算方式有很大的灵活性，只要抬头允许，汇款人可以将汇票带到国外亲自取款，也可由汇款人将汇票寄给国外收款人取款。票汇的收款人还可以到任何一家能核对汇票的真实性、愿意买入该汇票的国外银行取款，而不必像信汇、电汇那样，只能到汇入行取款。

票汇与电汇、信汇的不同在于：第一，汇票的传递不通过银行，汇入行无需通知收款人前来取款，由收款人自行持票上门取款，而电汇、信汇的汇入行在收到汇出行的委托或支付通知后，必须通知收款人取款；第二，票汇的收款人可以通过背书的方式转让汇票，而信汇委托书则不能流通转让。

由于票汇方式使用的汇票是可在市场上流通转让的银行汇票，如果汇票在到达解付行手中之前，已经过多次转让，那么银行利用汇款资金的时间也较长，因此，票汇为银行提供了更多的利润。

(三) 汇付方式在国际贸易中的运用

在国际贸易结算中，无论是电汇、信汇还是票汇，银行都不经手货运单据，而由出口商自行寄交进口商，这种支付方式被称为单纯支付。由于银行只提供服务而不提供信用，使用汇付方式完全取决于买卖双方中的一方对另一方的信任，并在此基础上进行交易和支付，因此汇付方式建立在商业信用基础之上，风险较大。

在国际贸易中以汇付方式结算买卖双方债权债务时，根据货款的交付和货物运送时间的关系可分为预付货款和货到付款两种。

1. 预付货款和随订单付款

预付货款（payment in advance）：是指进口商将货款的一部分或全部汇付给进口商，进口商收到货款后再发货的支付方式。预付货款是对进口商而言，从出口商来说，就是预收货款，即出口商先收款、后发货的支付方式。

通常有两种情况使用：一是进出口双方关系十分密切，双方互相信赖；二是双方交易的是紧俏商品，在货源有限时，进口商为了保证购到货物，占领市场，不得不答应出口商提出的预付货款条件。在这种情况下，进口商为降低风险会采取一定的措施，如要求出口商提供银行保函或书面保证，按规定交货及交单等。

随订单付款（cash with order）是指进口商把现金或银行汇票随订单一起寄给出口商。随订单付款多用于客户提出特殊加工要求的商品或小额贸易，如工艺品等。进口商对于那些市场畅销而又稀缺的商品，也乐意采用这种方法以优先取得供应。

2. 货到付款（或：凭单付款）

货到付款（payment after arrival of the goods）是指出口商先发货，进口商收到货物后，立即或在一定的时间内将货款汇付给出口商的一种结算方式。

货到付款对进口商极为有利，进口商不用承担资金风险，在整个交易中处于主动地位，如迟付货款，还可占用对方资金。而对出口商来说，不仅要占压资金，还要承担货物已发出而货款不能或不能按时收回的风险，所面临风险较大。

货到付款常用于售定、寄售和赊购等贸易方式下。

此外，在预付货款的交易中，进口人为了减少预付风险，还可使用凭单付汇的做法。凭单付汇（remittance against document）是指进口商通过当地的汇出行将货款汇给出口地的汇入行,指示汇入行凭出口商提供的符合指定要求的商业单据和装运凭证付款给出口商。汇入行根据汇出行的指示向出口商发出汇款通知书,并以此为依据,有条件的向出口商付汇。

由于汇款在尚未被收款人支取前是可以被撤销的,按一般的银行惯例,汇款人有权在收款人取款前随时通知银行将汇款退回,所以,出口商在受到汇入行的汇款通知后,应尽快发运货物,并从速向汇入行交单取款,以防汇款被撤销,而招致风险和损失。有鉴于此,凭单付汇通常只适用于现货交易。

二、托收

托收(collection)是指债权人(一般为出口商)开具汇票或者连同货运单据,委托当地银行通过它在进口地的分行或代理行向债务人(一般为进口商)收取票款的一种支付方式。

由于在托收业务中,汇票是从出口地开向进口地的,而资金要从进口地流向出口地,结算工具汇票与资金流向相反,所以,托收属逆汇方式。

(一)托收方式的当事人

委托人(principal),委托银行办理托收的一方,通常是开立汇票委托银行向国外进口商收取货款的出口商。

托收行(remitting bank),接受委托人的委托办理托收业务的人,通常是出口地银行。

代收行(collecting bank),接受托收行的委托向付款人收取票款的银行,通常是进口地银行,并且多数是托收行在进口地的分行或代理行。

付款人(drawee),根据托收指示被提示单据并被要求付款或承兑汇票的人,即汇票的受票人,通常是进口商。

委托人与托收行的关系、托收行与代收行的关系都是委托代理关系。

委托人与托收行的委托代理关系以委托人提交的托收申请书确定,托收行与代收行之间通常签订代理合同并按托收委托书确定双方的委托代理关系。

付款人和代收行之间不存在任何契约关系,付款人也不受代收行的任何约束。如果付款人拒付,代收行除将拒付情况通知托收行并由托收行通知委托人外,并不承担付款责任。

(二)托收的种类及其流转程序

在托收业务中,银行处理的单据有两类:一类是资金单据,包括汇票、本票、支票、付款收据或其他类似用于取得付款的凭证;另一类是商业单据,包括发票、运输单据、所有权凭证或其他类似如"非金融"方面的单据,保险单据等。

托收方式按其是否带有商业单据可分为光票托收和跟单托收两种。

光票托收(clean collection)是指不附带商业单据的资金单据的托收。光票托收主要用于货款尾数、小额货款、贸易从属费用和索赔款的收取。

跟单托收(documentary collection)是指附有包括货运单据在内的商业单据的托收。跟单托收可以是带有资金单据(汇票)的跟单托收,也可以是不带有资金单据的跟单托收,即以发票代替汇票连同有关的货运单据交银行托收。

跟单托收的汇票,可以是即期汇票,也可以是远期汇票。

如果是即期汇票,代收行应于收到汇票后立即向受票人提示,要求付款。受票人如无正当拒付理由,应立即付款赎单。

如果是远期汇票,代收行应在收到汇票后立即向受票人提示,要求承兑,以确定到期付款责任。承兑后代收行收回汇票,到期日再作付款提示,承兑人应即付款。

在国际贸易支付中采用的托收方式通常都是跟单托收,其中的货运单据代表了货物的所有权,交单即等于交货,因此,对于交单的规定非常重要。

根据代收行向进口商交付货运单据的条件不同,跟单托收的交单方式可分为付款交单和承兑交单两种。

1. **付款交单**(documents against payment,D/P)

指在代收行提示跟单汇票后,只有在进口商付清货款时,才能将货运单据交给进口商的一种交单方式。

按付款时间的不同,付款交单又可分为即期付款交单和远期付款交单两种。

(1) 即期付款交单(D/P at sight),是指出口商发货后开具即期汇票,连同货运单据通过银行向进口商提示,进口商见票即付,在付清货款后领取货运单据。其业务程序如图 7-2 所示:

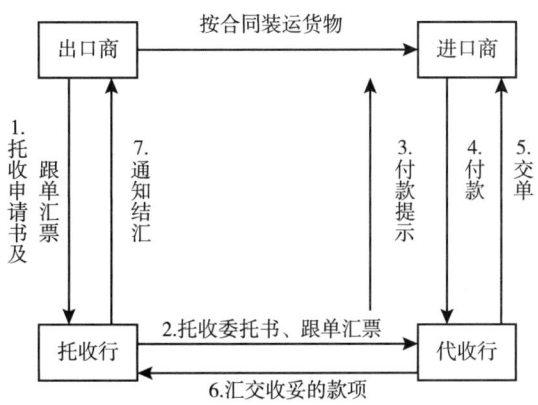

图 7-2 即期付款交单业务程序

(2) 远期付款交单（D/P after sight），指出口商发货后开具远期汇票，连同货运单据通过银行向进口商提示，进口商先在汇票上承兑，然后于汇票到期日付清货款后再领取货运单据。远期付款交单的业务程序如图7-3所示：

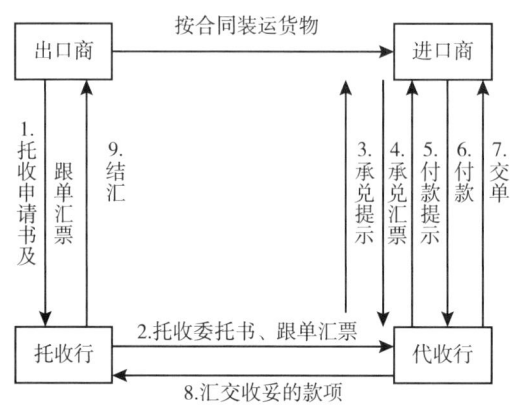

图7-3　远期付款交单业务程序

在远期付款交单的情况下，当到货日期早于付款日期时，如要提前取得货运单据以便及时转售或使用，进口商可采取以下作法：一是在付款到期日之前付款赎单；二是进口商开立信托收据交给代收银行，凭以借出货运单据先行提货。所谓信托收据（trust receipt，T/R），就是进口商借单时提供的一种书面信用担保文件，用来表示愿意以代收行的受托人的身份代为提货、报关、存仓和销售，并承认货物的所有权仍属银行，保证取得的货款应于汇票到期日交付代收行。

远期付款交单方式下的凭信托收据借单提货实质上是委托人或代收行对进口商提供的一种资金融通方式，这种方式只有在出口商对进口商的资信、偿款能力等十分了解并确信能如期收回款项时才能使用。

如果是出口商提出或同意可以凭信托收据借单提货，并在托收委托书上写明"付款交单，凭信托收据借单提货"（D/P，T/R）字样，代收行以此指示办理托收业务而产生的风险应由出口商承担。

如果出口商和托收行未曾在托收委托书上允许这一融资条件，而是代收行想为其本国进口商提供融资，同意进口商凭信托收据借单提货的话，则一切后果应由代收行自行负责。

2. 承兑交单（documents against acceptance，D/A）

指进口商在远期汇票上承兑后，即可向银行领取货运单据，然后于汇票到期日再行付款。

承兑交单的业务程序如图7-4所示：

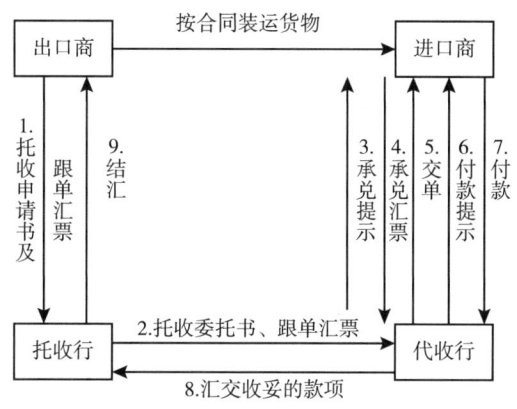

图7-4 承兑交单业务程序

(三) 托收的风险及其防范

在跟单托收方式下,出口商先行发货,然后委托银行收取货款。而银行只负责提示单据,代收货款,对能否收回款项并无责任,出口商能否安全及时地收回货款,完全取决于进口商的信用。

根据国际惯例,银行只需核实所收到的单据在表面上与托收委托书所列内容一致,对出口商所叫单据的真伪及是否发运伪劣货物概不负责,进口商能否安全取得合格的货物,完全依赖于出口商的信用。因此,跟单托收建立在商业信用基础之上,交易双方均存在相应的风险。

托收方式对出口商风险较大:因为出口商在发运货物后,在一定程度上失去了货物和资金两方面的主动权,如进口商倒闭或无力付款,或有意拒不付款赎单,出口商就有可能收不回或晚收到货款。在货物抵达目的地时还会产生存仓、转售或不得已运回出口地的费用和损失。在承兑交单或远期付款凭信托收据借单提货方式下,出口商的风险更大,因为进口商只要办理了承兑或提交了信托收据,即可取得单据并提取货物,一旦到期不付款,出口商就会钱货两空。

托收方式对进口商比较有利:由于托收方式费用低廉,进口商可免去开立信用证的手续,不必付银行押金,减少了资金支出。如果采用远期托收,还可以不必占用自有资金,有利于资金周转。实际出口业务中采用托收,是出口商对进口商提供融资,以此作为竞争的一种手段,有利于调动进口商采购货物的积极性,促进成交和扩大出口。

为了防范风险,确保安全收汇,应采取以下措施:

1. 做好售前调查工作。

出口商必须详细调查进口商的资信情况、进口国的贸易和外汇管制法令、海关规定,以及进口商是否能领到所购货物的进口许可证,或是否能申请到足额的外汇等,并注意避免市场风险。

2. 正确确定交单方式和价格条件。

出口商如确定采用托收方式，应尽量争取采用即期付款交单（D/P at sight）方式，而避免使用承兑交单（D/A）方式，以确保进口商付款赎单。

世界上有些地区，如拉美地区，习惯上将 D/P 远期按 D/A 方式处理，使原来的只有进口商付款后才交单的付款交单方式，实际上变成了只凭承兑就交出货运单据的方式，使出口商面临着货、款两空的风险。如不得已采用了 D/P 远期，应采取措施避免出现上述问题，如在 D/P 远期中不使用远期汇票，或在托收指示中要求进口商在付款前提供"付款保函"后取单等。

在使用 D/P 远期方式时，争取以 CIF 价格条件成交，由出口方办理保险，如货物出现风险，还可向保险公司索赔。如以 FOB 或 CFR 价格条件成交，应加保卖方利益险，以求当货物在运输途中受损而买方又不支付货款时，由保险公司承担赔偿责任。

3. 把托收方式与银行保函、信用证等方式结合起来，以降低风险。

为了使收取货款有保障，可以要求进口商申请开立出口商认可的银行保函，一旦进口商在规定的时间内拒绝赎单或承兑取单提货后拒不付款，出口商有权向开立保函的银行索赔。

（四） 托收的国际惯例

在国际贸易中，银行与委托人之间，托收行与代收行之间，往往由于各方对权利、义务和责任的解释有分歧，加上不同银行的具体做法也有差异，从而容易导致误会、纠纷和争议。国际商会为调和各有关当时人之间的矛盾，以利于商业和金融活动的开展，曾于 1958 年草拟并于 1967 年公布了《商业单据托收统一规则》，从而在银行托收业务中取得了统一的术语、定义、原则和程序，并建议各国银行采用。国际商会于 1978 年对该规则作了修订，改名为《托收统一规则》。目前使用的《托收统一规则》（Uniform Rules for Collection）以国际商会第 522 号出版物的形式颁发，于 1996 年 1 月 1 日起实施。

《托收统一规则》分"总则及定义""托收的方式及结构""提示方式""义务与责任""付款""利息""手续费及费用""其他规定"七大部分，共计 26 条。

《托收统一规则》（URC522）自公布实施以来，被各国银行广泛采纳和使用。但应当指出的是，作为国际惯例，《托收统一规则》并不是国际上公认的法律，只有在当事人事先约定的条件下，才受该惯例的约束。我国银行在进出口业务中使用托收方式时，也参照这个规则的解释办理。

三、信用证

随着经济的增长和国际贸易的发展，银行参与国际贸易结算时，从仅提供服务演变到既提供服务、又提供信用和资金融通，在这一过程之中，逐步形成了信用证支付方式。

（一）信用证的含义

信用证（Letter of Credit，L/C）是进口方银行（开证行）根据进口商（开证申请人）的申请和要求，向出口商（受益人）开立的，凭规定的单据，在一定期限内，支付一定金额的书面保证文件。简言之，信用证是一种银行开立的有条件的书面付款承诺。具体的条件体现在受益人必须提交符合信用证规定的各种单据。

（二）信用证的当事人

每一张信用证至少涉及三个基本当事人：申请开证人、开证行和受益人，在使用过程中，又产生了通知行、议付行、付款行和保兑行等其他当事人。

1. 开证申请人（applicant）

又称开证人（opener），是向银行申请开立信用证的人，通常是进口商，即贸易合同的买方。

2. 开证行（opening bank，issuing bank）

是应开证申请人的要求，开立信用证并承担付款责任的银行，通常是进口地银行。开证行是各当事人的"中心"人物，开证人与开证行的委托代理关系通过开证申请书确定，开证行与受益人的权利和义务由信用证确定。开证人通过开证申请书委托开证行向受益人提供信用，开证行同时代开证人行使请求受益人交付单据的权利。

3. 受益人（beneficiary）

接受信用证并享有信用证下合法权利的人，通常是出口商或实际供货人，即交易合同的卖方。受益人有按信用证规定签发汇票向所指定的付款银行索取价款的权利。

4. 通知行（advising bank，notyifying bank）

是受开证行的委托将信用证转交或通知出口商的银行，通常是出口地的银行。通知行只负有合理审慎地鉴别信用证表面真实性的责任，并不承担其他义务。

5. 议付行（negotiating bank）

是指自己垫付资金买入或贴现受益人开立和提交的符合信用证规定的跟单汇票的银行。议付行可以是信用证上指定的银行，也可以是非指定的银行。议付行有权向开证行或付款行索偿，若遭拒付，可向受益人追索。

6. 付款行（paying bank，drawee bank）

是开证行授权进行信用证项下付款或承兑并支付受益人出具的汇票的银行。付款行可以是开证行自己，也可以是接受开证行委托的另一家银行。付款行的验单付款是终局性的，即使对受益人误付了与信用证的要求不符的单据，也无权向受益人追索。

7. 保兑行（confirming bank）

是应开证行的请求在信用证上加具保兑的银行，它具有与开证行相同的责任和地位。保兑行对信用证独立负责，在付款后，不论开证行倒闭或无理拒付，都不能向受益人追索。在实际业务中，通知行往往兼任保兑行的职责。

（三）信用证支付方式的业务程序

一笔信用证业务从发生到终结大体上要经过以下基本环节：

1. 进口商申请开证（application for credit）

进口商在与出口商签订贸易合同后，应根据合同条款向银行申请开立信用证。申请开证时，进口商应填写开证申请书，内容包括两部分：第一部分是要求开立信用证的基本内容，是开证行开证的主要依据。第二部分是开证人对开证行的声明或保证，以明确自己应承担的责任，其基本内容是承认在其付清货款前，开证行对单据及其所代表的货物拥有所有权，若到期不付款，开证行有权没收一切抵押物，作应付款项的一部分。

开证申请人申请开证时，开证行可根据开证人的资信状况，要求提供一定的担保品或一定比例的押金，并收取手续费。

2. 进口方银行开立信用证（issuance of credit）

开证行开立信用证时，必须严格按照开证申请书的要求开立，否则，开证行的权益不能得到可靠保障。

开立信用证的方法有信开、全电开两种。信开是指开证行将信函形式的信用证通过航邮寄送给出口商或通知行。全电开是指开证行通过 SWIFT 系统（环球银行金融电讯协会）或电报电传等电讯方式将信用证内容传至通知行。

3. 出口方银行通知信用证（advice of credit）

出口方银行收到开证行开来信用证时，经核对密押和印鉴相符，确认其表面真实性后，应及时将信用证通知受益人。开证行在开立信用证时可以指定另一家银行加具保兑，此时，保兑行通常由通知行兼任。

受益人收到信用证后，应仔细审核信用证。如发现其内容有与合同条款不符或不能接受之处，应及时要求开证人通过开证行对信用证进行修改或拒绝接受信用证。如接受信用证，应立即备货，并在信用证规定的装运期限内，按照信用证规定的条件装运发货。然后，缮制并取得信用证所规定的全部单据，开立汇票，连同信用证正本和修改通知书，在规定的期限内送交：信用证规定的议付行或付款行、或保兑信用证的保兑行、或任何愿意议付该信用证下单据的银行。

4. 出口方银行议付信用证（negotiation of credit）

议付行对出口商提交的单据进行仔细的审核后，确认单证相符、单单相符后，即可进行议付。

议付是指议付行以自有资金按照汇票金额扣除各项费用和利息后,垫付款项给受益人,并获得受益人提交的汇票及单据的所有权的行为。议付表面上是银行的购票行为,实际上是银行为受益人融通资金的一种方式。银行议付单据后,有权向开证行或其指定的付款行索偿,如遭拒付,可向受益人追索议付款项。

5. 进口方银行接受单据(documents taken up by issing bank)

开证行(或其指定的付款行)收到议付行寄来的汇票和单据后,如审单后发现单证或单单不符,有权拒付,但必须及时将拒付事实通知议付行。

如未发现单据中的不符点,应无条件付款给议付行后,取得汇票和单据的所有权。

6. 进口商赎单提货(take delivery of goods against documents retired)

开证行接受单据后,应立即通知进口商备款赎单。进口商核验单据无误后,将全部票款及有关费用付给开证行,即可取得所有单据并提货。此时,开证行和进口商之间由于开立信用证而形成的契约关系就此终止。

如果进口接受单据但无力赎单,一般可要求开证行凭其出立的信托收据先取得单据提货。如开证行在付款后进口商发现单证不符,亦可拒绝赎单,这时开证行就有可能遭受资金损失。因为开证行的审单付款是终局性的,如事后发现有不符,亦无权向议付行追索。

进口商付款赎单后,如发现任何有关货物的问题,不能向银行提出赔偿要求,应分具体情况向出口商、保险公司或运输部门索赔。跟单信用证的业务程序如图7-5所示。

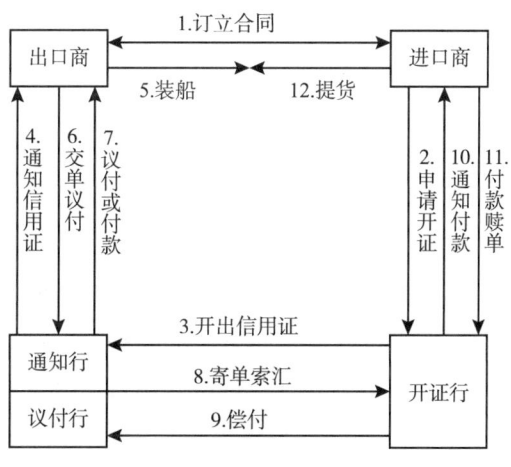

图7-5 跟单信用证业务程序

(四)信用证的内容

根据不同交易的需要,各银行习惯使用的信用证格式各不相同。国际商会曾先后设计并介绍过四种信用证标准格式,其中包括:即期付款信用证、承兑信用证、延期付款信用证和议付信用证。但是,现在各国银行基本上还是按照其过去的习惯开立信用证,同时参照国际商会推荐的标准格式略加修改。

虽然目前信用证尚无统一格式,但其基本内容大致相同,主要包括以下几个方面:

1. 对信用证本身的说明

如信用证的编号、种类、金额、开证日期、到期日和交单地点等。

2. 信用证的当事人

如开证申请人、受益人和开证行,以及开证行指定的通知行、议付行、付款行、偿付行和保兑行等。

3. 货物条款

如货物的名称、规格、数量、包装、价格等。

4. 装运与保险条款

如运输方式、起运地、目的地、装运日期、可否分批装运、可否转运等。以 CIF 或 CIP 贸易术语达成的交易项下的保险要求,及投保的金额和险别等。

5. 单据条款

包括:对汇票的要求,如使用汇票,应列明汇票的必要项目;对货运单据的要求,包括商业发票、海关发票、提单或运输单据、保险单证等;此外,还有包装单据、产地证、检验证书等。

6. 特别条款

主要是根据进口国政治经济贸易状况的变化或不同业务需要规定的一些条款。

7. 开征银行的责任条款以及适用的国际惯例

目前,银行开出的信用证都注有"该证受国际商会第 600 号出版物《跟单信用证统一惯例》的约束"字样。

(五) 信用证的特点

信用证支付方式具有以下三个特点:

1. 信用证是一种银行信用,开证行承担第一性付款责任。

在信用证支付方式下,则由开证行代进口商承担第一性的付款责任。出口商仅凭信用证及合格单据即可直接向开证行要求付款,而无须先向进口商进行付款提示。开证行的第一性付款责任是有条件的,这个条件就是出口商提交的单据与信用证的要求必须完全相符。

2. 信用证是一项独立自足的文件,它不依附于贸易合同而存在。

信用证通常都是以交易合同为基础开立的,但信用证一经开出,就成为独立于买卖合同之外的另一种契约。信用证的各当事人的权利和责任完全以信用证所列条款为准,不受买卖合同的约束。

3. 信用证是一种单据业务，它处理的对象是单据。

根据《UCP600》第 5 条规定："银行仅处理单据，而不是与单据有关的货物、服务或其他行为"。因此，信用证是一种纯粹的单据业务，银行只对信用证承担付款责任，凭表面上完全符合信用证条款规定的单据付款。至于单据的真伪、法律效力以及单据所代表的货物状况等，银行概不负责。

（六）信用证的性质及作用

采用信用证支付方式，只要出口商按信用证的要求提交单据，银行即保证付款。所以，信用证建立在银行信用之上，由开证银行代进口商承担第一性的付款责任。这种银行信用并以自有资金直接参与到支付过程中的支付方式，一定程度上解决了交易双方权利和义务不对等的问题，并为买卖双方融通资金提供了多种途径和便利。信用证支付方式较易被进出口双方所接受和采用，有利于双方贸易活动的顺利进行，进而促进了国际贸易的发展。

信用证在国际贸易结算中可以起到以下两个主要作用：一是保证作用；二是资金融通作用，具体体现如下：

对出口商来说，只要按信用证规定发运货物，向指定银行提交单据，收取货款就有了保障。发货后将汇票和单据交议付行议付，通过押汇可及时收回货款，有利于加速资金周转。在货物装运前，还可以凭信用证向银行申请打包放款（packing credit），这是对出口商业务开展极为有利的一种融资方式。

对进口商来说，申请开证时只需交纳少量押金或免交押金，大部分或全部货款在单据到达后支付，减少了资金占用。如为远期信用证，还可凭信托收据向开证行借单提货出售或使用，到期后再向开证行付款。可以通过信用证条款控制出口商的交货时间、交货方式以及所交货物的质量和数量。可以保证进口商付款后即获得代表货物的单据。

对银行来说，开证行贷出的是信用，不必占用资金，即可取得开证手续费的收入，还可将收取的开证押金加以利用；虽然面临一定的垫款风险，但开证时已收取一定的押金，付款后即获得出口商提交单据所代表货物的所有权，因而，风险已经得到有效的控制。至于出口地的议付行，议付出口商提交的单据后，可向开证行索偿，只要出口商交来的单据符合信用证规定，就可以对出口商进行垫款、叙做出口押汇，还可以从中获得利息和手续费等收入。

（七）信用证的种类

在国际贸易买卖中所使用的信用证种类很多，从不同的角度来看，分类如下：

1. 跟单信用证和光票信用证

根据付款凭证的不同，信用证可分为跟单信用证和光票信用证两种。

跟单信用证（Documentary L/C）是指银行凭跟单汇票或仅凭单据付款、承兑或议付的信用证。这里的单据包括：代表货物所有权的单据，如海运提单；或证明货物已发运的单据，如铁路运单、航空运单等；以及商业发票、保险单据、产地证书等。在国际贸易结算中，大都使用跟单信用证。

光票信用证（Clean L/C）是指开证行仅凭受益人开具的汇票而无须附带货运单据就付款的信用证，主要用于贸易总公司与各地分公司间的货款清偿和贸易从属费用的结算。

2. 可撤销信用证和不可撤销信用证

按开证行对受益人保证的性质不同，信用证可分为可撤销信用证和不可撤销信用证。

可撤销信用证（Revocable L/C）。是指开证行在付款、承兑或被议付以前，可以不经受益人同意也不必事先通知受益人而随时修改或撤销的信用证。由于可撤销信用证的开证行可以随时取消或修改，对受益人缺乏足够的保障，因而在国际贸易中极少采用。

不可撤销信用证（Irrevocable L/C）。是指信用证一经通知受益人，在有效期内未经受益人及有关当事人的同意，对信用证内容不得随意修改或撤销的信用证。只要受益人提交的单据符合信用证规定，开证行或其指定银行必须履行付款责任。使用这种信用证，受益人的权益有可靠的保障，因而在国际贸易中不可撤销信用证得到广泛的使用。

每份信用证在开立时应清楚地表明是可撤销的还是不可撤销的，若信用证上对此未写明，按《UCP600》的最新规定，该信用证将被视作是不可撤销的。

3. 保兑信用证和不保兑信用证

按是否有另一家银行对信用证加具保兑，信用证可分为保兑信用证和不保兑信用证。

保兑信用证（Confirmed L/C）是指一家银行开出的信用证，由另一家银行保证对符合信用证规定的单据承担付款责任。只有不可撤销信用证才可加具保兑。信用证一经保兑，保兑行与开证行一样都承担第一性的付款责任。对受益人来说，同时取得了两家银行的付款保证，安全收汇更有保障。保兑行通常是通知行，有时也可以是出口地的其他银行或第三国银行。

不保兑信用证（Unconfirmed L/C）是指未经除开证行以外的其他银行保兑的信用证，即一般的不可撤销信用证。

4. 即期付款信用证、延期付款信用证、承兑信用证和议付信用证

按兑付方式的不同，信用证又可分为即期付款信用证、延期付款信用证、承兑信用证和议付信用证四种。

（1）即期付款信用证（Sight Payment L/C）是指开证行或付款行在收到符合信用

证规定的跟单汇票或单据时，立即履行付款义务的信用证。这种信用证的特点是出口商收汇迅速安全，有利于资金周转。即期付款信用证可以是开证行自己付款，也可由其他银行付款，还可以视付款行所在地和到期地点的不同，由开证行指定、或不指定或不需要由另一家银行议付。

（2）延期付款信用证（Deferred Payment L/C）又称迟期付款信用证，是指开证行保证在受益人交单一定时期后付款的信用证。日期的确定有从运输单据出单日期起算和从单据到达开证行的日期起算两种方法。这种信用证不要求受益人开立远期汇票，无开证行承兑汇票的票据行为，故又称无承兑远期信用证。

使用延期付款信用证，受益人不能获得票据贴现的便利，此外，受益人一般要求由另一家银行对延期付款信用证加具保兑。在实践中，延期付款信用证大多用于金额较大而且付款期限较长（往往长达一年或数年）的资本货物交易，常与政府出口信贷相结合。

（3）承兑信用证（Acceptance L/C）是指付款行在收到符合信用证规定的远期汇票和单据时，先在汇票上履行承兑手续，待汇票到期日再行付款的信用证。这种信用证规定以银行为汇票上的付款人，又称为银行承兑信用证。

银行承兑信用证项下，出口商可以等承兑汇票到期后再收回资金，也可以将承兑汇票在市场上贴现以融通资金。有时进口商为了融资方便，或利用银行承兑汇票以取得比银行放款利率更为优惠的贴现率，往往要求开立银行承兑信用证，证中规定"远期汇票可即期付款，所有贴现和承兑费用由买方负担"，实际上是进口商将承兑后的远期汇票贴现后，向出口商即期付款。这种特殊的银行承兑信用证被称为"买方远期信用证"，又被称为"假远期信用证"。

（4）议付信用证（Negotiation L/C）是指开证行在开立信用证时指定该信用证可由另一家银行或由出口地任何银行议付的信用证。按是否限定议付银行，又可分为公开议付信用证和限制议付信用证两种。前者是指任何银行均可办理议付，后者是指仅由被指定的银行办理议付。

5. 可转让信用证和不可转让信用证

可转让信用证（Transferable L/C）是指开证行在信用证上明确注明"可转让"字样，授权通知行在受益人（第一受益人）的要求下，可将信用证的全部或部分转让给第三者（第二受益人）的信用证。

可转让信用证只能转让一次，如信用证不禁止分批装运，在累计不超过信用证金额的前提下，可以分成几个部分分别转让给一个以上的第二受益人。可转让信用证的受益人，往往是中间商，要求国外进口商开立可转让信用证，以转让给实际供货人（第二受益人），由实际供货人直接装运。

不可转让信用证（Non-transferable L/C）是指受益人不能将信用证的权利转让给他人的信用证。凡未在信用证上注明"可转让"字样者，将被视为不可转让信用证。

6. 循环信用证

循环信用证（Revolving L/C）是指在被全部或部分使用后，其金额又恢复到原金额并再次使用，直至达到规定的次数或规定的总金额为止的信用证，通常在定期均衡供货、分批结汇的长期合同下采用。使用这种信用证，进口商可节省开证手续和费用，减少押金，一次开证，长期反复使用，有利于买卖双方交易的进行。

循环信用证有按时间循环和按金额循环两种。

按时间循环的信用证规定受益人在规定的期限内每隔一定的时间可使用一次信用证上规定的金额。

按金额循环的信用证是指受益人在规定的总额内使用完信用证规定的金额后，可以恢复到原金额再继续使用的信用证。

7. 对背信用证

对背信用证（Back to Back L/C）是指中间商收到进口商开来的信用证后，要求该证的通知行或其往来银行，以原证为根据，另行开立的以实际供货人为受益人的新信用证。往往是在中间商收到进口商开来不可转让信用证的情况下，不得不向实际供货人开立对背信用证。

8. 对开信用证

一国商人向另一国商人出口商品的同时，又向对方购进另一批货物，这样双方可以互以对方为受益人分别开立两张信用证，即称为对开信用证（Reciprocal L/C）。其特点是：第一张信用证的受益人和开证申请人就是第二张回头证的开证申请人和受益人，第一张信用证的开证行和通知行一般也是回头证的通知行和开证行。两证金额可以相等，也可以不等，两证可以同时生效也可以先后生效。对开信用证一般用于易货贸易、来料加工和补偿贸易等。

9. 预支信用证

预支信用证（Anticipatory L/C）是允许出口商在装货交单前可以支取全部或部分货款的信用证。一般情况下，预支信用证的开证行授权出口地的通知行或保兑行在交单以前，向出口商预先垫付全部或部分金额的款项。出口商交单议付时，出口地银行在从议付金额中扣除预先垫付款的本息，再将余额付给出口商。倘若出口商届时不能装货、交单议付，垫款银行可向开证行追索，开证行保证偿还出口地银行的垫款本息，然后向开证人索要此款。为引人注目，预支信用证的上述条款通常都是用红字打成的，故又称为"红条款信用证"。

（八）国际商会《跟单信用证统一惯例》

在信用证的初始阶段，由于没有一个共同遵守的统一准则，各国银行往往根据各自的习惯和利益按自行规定办事，信用证各有关当事人之间的纠纷和争议经常发生。为此，国际商会在1930年拟订了《商业跟单信用证统一惯例》，对跟单信用证有关当事人的权利、责任以及有关条款和术语进行了统一解释，并于1933年以第82号出版物公布，建议各国（地区）银行采用。在随后的几十年间多次进行修订，1983年此惯例被重新命名为《跟单信用证统一惯例》，以《国际商会400号出版物》的形式公布实施。

近年来，随着国际上运输工具和运输方式的发展变化，通信工具的电子化、网络化和电子计算机的广泛使用，国际贸易、运输、保险、单据处理和结算工作也发生了巨大的变化。国际商会于1993年又对《跟单信用证统一惯例》进行了第五次修订，出版了国际商会第500号出版物，于1994年1月1日开始实施。2007年国际商会对《跟单信用证统一惯例》进行了第六次修改，出版了国际商会第600号出版物（UCP600）。

《跟单信用证统一惯例（UCP600）》经过多次修订，日趋完善，目前被世界上大多数国家和地区所采用。

四、银行保函

在国际贸易中，当一方担心对方不履行合同义务，需要银行出具保证文件而又不宜使用信用证方式时，往往要求对方通过银行开具银行保函或备用信用证。银行保函和备用信用证都是建立在银行信用之上，通常使用于期限较长、金额较大、交易条件比较复杂的项目，而且不仅适用于货物买卖，也使用于承包工程项目、融资等一切有关国际经济交往的业务中。

（一）银行保函的含义

银行保函（Banker's Letter of Guarantee，L/G）又称银行保证书，是银行根据申请人的请求，向受益人开立的担保申请人正常履行合同义务的书面保证文件。如申请人未向受益人履行某项义务时，由担保银行承担保证书中所规定的付款责任。

（二）银行保函的当事人

银行保函有三个基本当事人：申请人、担保行和受益人。

（1）申请人（applicant），又称委托人（principal）、被保证人，是要求银行开立保函的一方。

（2）担保行（guarantor bank），是根据申请人的请求，开立保函的银行。

（3）受益人（beneficiary），是接受保函，并且当申请人未履行合同义务时有权向担保行提出索赔的一方。

除了以上三个基本当事人之外，银行保函还有可能涉及转递行、保兑行和转开行等其他当事人。

(三) 银行保函的种类

银行保函根据不同用途，概括起来，主要有投标保函和履约保函两种。

1. 投标保函（Tender L/G）

是在工程项目进行招标时担保银行应投标人（申请人）的请求，向招标人（受益人）出具的保函，保证投标人在开标前不中途撤销投标或片面修改投标条件，中标后按时与招标人签订合同并提交履约保函或交付履约保证金。否则，担保银行负责赔偿招标人一定金额的损失。投标保函的金额一般为投标报价的1%~5%。

2. 履约保函（Performance L/G）

是银行应申请人的请求，向受益人开立的保证申请人履行某项合同项下义务的书面保证文件。在保函有效期内如发生申请人违反合同的情况，银行将根据受益人的要求向受益人赔偿保函规定的金额。履约保函的适用范围很广泛，不仅用于一般的进出口贸易，而且还用于工程项目建设、国际租赁、技术贸易、对外加工贸易和补偿贸易等。履约保函的担保金额一般为合同金额的5%~10%。

在进出口贸易中，履约保函又分为进口保函和出口保函两种。

（1）进口保函（Import L/C）是银行应进口商的申请，开给出口商的信用文件，保证出口商按交易合同交货后进口商一定如期付款，否则由担保行负责偿付一定金额的款项。

（2）出口保函（Export L/G）是银行应出口商的申请开给进口商的保证文件，保证出口商按约履行交货义务，如出口商未能交货，担保行负责赔偿进口商一定金额。这种银行保函又可称作还款保函。

（四）银行保函与跟单信用证的区别

（1）跟单信用证主要用于贸易货款的结算；银行保函既可用作货款结算工具，又可用于其他各种信用担保。

（2）跟单信用证的支付在正常情况下是必然发生的；银行保函的支付具有必然性。

（3）跟单信用证一概独立于贸易合同；银行保函却未必独立于基础合约。

（4）跟单信用证的开证行负有第一性的付款责任；银行保函的担保行未必负有第一性的付款责任。

（5）跟单信用证的交单地点可以是议付行、代付行或保兑行所在地，有多种款项的支付方式，并可作为融资工具使用；银行保函只能向担保行索偿或索赔，其到期地点只能是担保行所在地。

五、备用信用证

备用信用证（Standby L/C）起源于美国，因为美国法律只允许"担保公司

(bonding company)"开立信用证而禁止银行开立信用证,银行为争取这方面的业务,就采取变通的办法创立了具有保函性质的备用信用证。

(一)备用信用证的含义

备用信用证是开证行对受益人承担某项责任的凭证。在此凭证中,开证行承诺偿还开证申请人的借款、预收款或其他负债,或在开证申请人未履约时向受益人支付一定金额的款项。

自1983年起,备用信用证的使用一直遵循《跟单信用证统一惯例》。国际商会于1998年4月又颁布了《国际备用信用证惯例(ISP98)》,并于1999年1月生效,为备用信用证的使用提供了单独的规则。

(二)备用信用证与银行保函的区别

1. 银行保函可以有从属性保函;备用信用证是独立于交易合同的自足性契约。
2. 银行保函的担保行,可能承担第一性付款责任,也可能承担第二性付款责任;备用信用证的开证行负有第一性的付款责任。
3. 银行保函通常不要求受益人在索偿或索赔时出具汇票;备用信用证常常要求受益人在索偿或索赔时出具即期汇票。

六、国际保理

随着国际贸易买方市场的普遍形成,贸易竞争已发展到了付款条件方面,越来越多的进口商拒绝使用信用证方式,使出口商不得不更多地依赖于托收和赊销方式结算货款,从而增加了出口商的商业风险和资金负担。为了帮助出口商减少风险和获得资金融通的方便,一种新的支付方式——国际保理业务应运而生。

国际保理(international factoring)又叫国际付款保理、保付代收或承购应收账款业务等。是指在以赊销为支付方式的贸易中,由保理商向出口商提供的一种集融资、结算、财务管理和信用担保为一体的综合性贸易支付方式。

国际保理业务主要包括以下几方面的内容:

(1)对进口商进行资信调查及评估,并对其确定一个合理的信用额度;

(2)代收账款并负责账务管理,保理商买断出口商的票据,所有应收账款的催收和账务管理的责任由保理商承担;

(3)风险担保,又称坏账担保,即在进口商信用额度内所有风险均由保理商承担,如进口商在付款到期日拒付或无力付款,由进口保理商在一定期限内无条件地支付不超过其核定信用额度的货款;

(4)提供出口商所需的资金融通,收到出口商提交的票据后,保理商可提供不超过货款 80% 的无追索权的预付融资款，余款在进口商付清全部货款后支付。

在国际货款结算中采用保理方式，有助于进口商掌握客户资信，增加交易机会，解除了托收方式下具有收款风险的后顾之忧，还有利于加速资金周转，因而，逐渐在国际货款结算中得到广泛的使用。

第三节 支付方式的选用及贸易合同中的支付条款

在对外贸易实际业务中，根据不同国家和地区、不同客户、不同交易的实际情况，正确和灵活地选用货款结算的支付方式是一个关系到交易成败的重要问题。

一、选择支付方式时的考虑因素

各种不同的支付方式，在不同的情况下，对进出口商双方各有利弊。各当事人在选择和使用某种支付方式时需要考虑多种不同的因素，首先，安全是第一重要问题，其次，是占用资金时间的长短及能否获得融资便利，最后，办理手续的繁简，银行费用的多少也是必须考虑的因素之一。具体地说，在选择支付方式时需要考虑以下问题：

（一）客户信用

要在出口业务中做到安全收汇，在进口业务中做到安全用汇，安全收到符合合同的货物，就必须事先做好对国外客户即交易对手的信用调查，以便根据客户的具体情况，选用适当的结算方式。对于信用不是很好或者尚未对他有充分了解的客户，就应选择风险小的方式与其进行交易，如在出口业务中，一般可采用跟单信用证方式，必要时也可争取以预付货款方式支付。若与信用很好的客户交易时，由于风险较小，就可选择手续比较简单、费用较少的方式；又如在出口业务中可以采用付款交单（D/P）的托收方式等。至于承兑交单（D/A）的托收方式或赊账交易，应尽限于本企业的联号或分支机构，或者确有把握的个别对象，一般客户原则上不能采用。

（二）经营意图

选用支付方式，应结合企业的经营意图。出口商在货物畅销时，不仅可以提高售价，而且卖方还可选择对己最有利的结算方式，包括在资金占用方面最有利的方式；而在货物滞销时或竞争激烈的商品，不仅售价可能要降低，而且在结算方式上也需作必要让步，否则就可能难以达成交易。

(三) 贸易术语

买卖合同中采用不同的贸易术语,所表明的交货方式和适用的运输方式是多种多样的,但并不是每一种交货方式和运输方式都能适用于任何一种结算方式。仍以出口业务为例,在使用 CIF、CFR 等属于象征性交货或称推定交货术语的交易,出口商交货与进口商收货不在同时发生,转移货物所有权是以单据为媒介,就可选择跟单信用证方式,在进口商信用较好时,也可采用跟单托收,如付款交单(D/P)方式收取货款。

但在 EXW 这种属于实际交货方式术语的交易中,由于是出口商直接向出口商交货,无法通过单据控制物权,因此一般不能使用托收。如果通过银行向进口商收款,实质上是一笔货到付款,出口商承担的风险极大。在以 FOB、FCA 条件达成的买卖合同中,虽然在实际业务中也可凭运输单据付款交货,但这种合同的运输方式由进口商安排,当出口商将货物装上进口商指定的运输工具或交给进口商指定的承运人后,出口商或接受委托的银行实际上已经很难控制货物,在这种情况下,出口商也不宜采用托收方式。

(四) 货运单据

当货物通过海上运输或多式联合运输,所使用的海运提单或可转让的多式联运提单都是货物所有权凭证,在交付进口商之前,出口商可以控制货物,可适用于信用证和托收方式结算货款。当货物通过航空、铁路或邮政运输时,所使用的单据,包括海上运输所使用的不可转让的海运提单,都不是货物所有权凭证,收货人不需要这些单据也可以提取货物,在这些情况下,除非这些单据上的收货人是银行,否则都不适宜做托收。即使采用信用证,也必须以开证行作为运输单据的收货人,以便银行控制货物。

二、不同支付方式的结合使用

一般情况下,一笔交易只使用一种支付方式,但在特定的情况下,也可以在一笔交易中把两种甚至两种以上不同的支付方式结合起来使用。

(一) 信用证和汇付的结合使用

是指部分货款在货物装运后即采用信用证支付,另一部分货款在货物运抵目的地并经过商品检验确定其品质或数量后,余额采用汇付方式支付。

这种方式多用于交货数量不宜控制的初级产品贸易上。对于特定商品或特定交易需进口商预付定金的,也可将预付定金部分以汇付方式支付,其余货款用信用证结算。

(二) 信用证与托收的结合使用

是指一笔交易的部分货款以信用证支付，余额用托收结算。实际做法是，出口商签发两张汇票，凭光票支取信用证款项，凭跟单汇票采用 D/P 方式支取余款。即信用证采用光票信用证的方式，跟单托收必须是付款交单方式。

这种做法对进口商来说，可减少开证金额，少付押金，减轻了资金周转的压力；对出口商来说，有部分信用证付款的保证，且进口商必须付清全部货款后才能获得货运单据，因此，出口商安全收汇较有保障。

(三) 跟单托收与预付押金的结合使用

在进口商预付部分货款或一定比率的押金为保证的前提下，采用跟单托收的方式结算货款。出口商收到预付款或押金后发运货物，并从货款中扣除预付押金，其余金额通过银行托收。如托收金额被拒付，出口商可将货物运回，并以预收押金抵偿运费、利息及其他损失。

(四) 跟单托收与备用信用证或银行保函的结合使用

跟单托收与备用信用证或银行保函的结合使用，可以保证跟单托收项下的货款被拒付时，出口商可以利用备用信用证或银行保函的有关条款，签发进口商拒付的声明书并开立汇票要求银行付款。

使用这种方式时，备用信用证或银行保函的有效期必须晚于托收付款期限，以便被拒付后能有足够的时间办理追偿手续。

(五) 汇付与备用信用证或银行保函的结合使用

这种支付方式一般用在大型设备、成套设备以及飞机与轮船等大型运输工具的交易中。

由于这种交易具有货物金额大、制造生产周期长、检验手段复杂、交货条件严格，以及质量保证期限长等特点，往往采用两种甚至两种以上不同的结算方式，如汇付与备用信用证或银行保函的结合使用，再结合使用分期付款或延期付款的方法支付货款。

三、贸易合同中的支付条款

国际货物买卖合同中有关货款收付的规定通常以"支付条款"（terms of payment）的形式出现，支付条款是合同中的一项重要内容。本节就实际业务中常用的支付条款简单举例如下。

（一）汇付条款

例1：买方应不晚于××年×月×日将全部货款用电汇（信汇或票汇）方式预付给卖方。

The Buyers shall pay the total value to the Sellers in advance by T/T（M/T or D/D）not later than … .

例2：买方应不迟于10月15日将100%的货款由票汇预付至卖方。

The buyers shall pay 100% of the sales proceeds in advance by Demand Draft to reach the Sellers not later than Oct. 15.

例3：买方同意在本合同签字之日起，1个月内将本合同总金额××%的预付款，以电汇方式交卖方。

×% of the total contract value as advance payment shall be remitted by Buyer to the Seller through telegraphic transfer within one month after signing this contract.

（二）托收条款

跟单托收一般先列明由卖方负责在装运货物后，开立汇票连同货运单据办理托收。例如：

货物装运后，卖方应将以买方为付款人的汇票连同本合同的各种货运单据，通过卖方银行寄交买方银行转交买方，并托收货款。

After delivery, the Seller shall send through the Seller's bank a draft drawn on the Buyer together with the shipping documents to the Buyer through the Buyer's bank for collection.

之后，再按不同交单条件、付款期限，及买方的付款、承兑责任等作具体规定。

例1：即期付款交单

买方应凭卖方开具的即期跟单汇票于见票时立即付款，付款后交单。

Upon first presentation the buyers shall pay against documentary draft drawn by the Sellers at sight. The shipping documents are to be delivered against payment only.

例2：远期付款交单（见票后××天）

买方对卖方开具的见票后××天付款的跟单汇票，于提示时应即予承兑，并于汇票到期日即予付款，付款后交单。

The Buyers shall duly accept the documentary draft drawn by the Sellers at × days sight upon first presentation and make payment on its maturity. The shipping documents are to be delivered against payment only.

(三) 信用证支付条款

例1：即期信用证支付条款

买方应通过为卖方所接受的银行于装运月份前××天开立并送达卖方不可撤销即期信用证，有效至装运月份后第15天在中国议付。

The Buyers shall open through a bank acceptable to the Sellers an Irrevocable Sight Letter of Credit to reach the Sellers × days before the month of shipment, valid for negotiation in China until the 15th day after the month of shipment.

例2：远期信用证支付条款

买方应通过为卖方所接受的银行于装运月份前××天开立并送达卖方不可撤销见票后30天付款的信用证，有效至装运月份后第15天在上海议付。

The Buyers shall open through a bank acceptable to the Sellers an Irrevocable Letter of Credit at 30days sight to reach the Sellers × days before the month of shipment, valid for negotiation in Shanghai until the 15th day after the month of shipment.

例3：循环信用证支付条款

买方应通过为卖方可接受的银行于第一批装运月份前××天开立并送达卖方不可撤销的即期循环信用证，该证在20××年期间，每月自动可供××（金额），并保持有效至20××年1月15日在北京议付。

The Buyers shall open through a bank acceptable to the Sellers an Irrevocable Revolving Letter of Credit at sight to reach the Sellers × days before the month of first shipment. The Credit shall be automatically available during the period of 20× for … (value) per month, and remain validity for negotiation in Beijing until Jan, 15, 20×.

英文参考教程

Payment of Purchase of Price

Settlement of the purchase price in foreign trade is realize by collection and payment of foreign exchange. In every contract for the sales of goods abroad, the clause dealing with payment of the purchase price embodies four elements: time, mode, place and currency of payment.

A. Instrument of Payment

In international trade, the main instrument of payment in settlement of the purchase price is the currency and bill.

1. **Currency**

There are three different cases in using currency: adopting the currency of the seller's country, or that of the buyer's country, or even that of a third country.

When we decide which currency should be used, we should take the following two points into consideration: one is the convertibility and stability of the currency; the other is the tendency of fluctuation of the currency adopted.

2. **Bill**

1) **Bill of Exchange.** The bill of exchange (draft) has played a vital part in the world's commercial and financial life for some centuries.

A bill of exchange is an unconditional order in writing, addressed by one person to another, signed by the person giving it, requiring the person to whom it is addressed to pay on demand, or at a fixed or determinable further time, a sum certain in money to, or to the order of, a specified person, or to any bearer.

In conjunction with the definition, the specimen may be dissected as follows:

- An unconditional order in writing;
- Addressed by one person/party (the drawer)

Thomas Jones;

- To another (the drawee) James Arthur, Manchester;

Specimen Bill of Exchange

No. 9, 340

£ . Stg. 100　　　　　　　　London, 15th July, 1995

On demand pay to John Wood or bearer the sum of One

Hundred Pound

(English Currency) only.

　　　　　　　　(Signed) Thomas Jones

To: Mr James Arthur

Manchester

- Signed by the person (the drawer) giving it;
- Requiring the person to whom it is addressed (the drawee, or the payer) to pay;
- On demand, or at a fixed or determinable future time;
- A sum certain in money, £ . Stg. 100;
- TO, or to the order of, a specified person, or to bearer (the payee), John Wood.

a) Parties to a bill of exchange.

It will be seen that there are three parties to a bill of exchange:

- The drawer, i. e., the person who draws the bill and he is usually the exporter or his banker in import and export trade.

- The drawee (payer), i.e., the person who is to pay the money and he is usually the importer or the appointed banker under a letter of credit in import and export trade.
- The payee, i.e., the person who is to receive the money, he may be, and often is, the same person as the drawer and he is usually the exporter himself or his appointed banker in import and export trade or he may be the bearer of the bill.

b) Classification of bills of exchange.

- Clean bill and documentary bill: A bill of exchange is called a clean bill, when no shipping documents are accompanied with it.

A documentary bill is the bill which is accompanied with shipping documents (chiefly the bill of lading, commercial invoice, insurance policy, etc.).

- Sight (demand) bill and time (usance) bill: According to the time of payment, a bill of exchange may be either a sight bill or a time bill. If the draft is payable at sight on presentation, it is a sight bill. If the drawee is required to pay the bill at a later date, the bill is called a time or usance bill. It requires acceptance before payment. The time is generally fixed as follows:

  * The drawee is required to pay the bill a certain number of days after sight, such as 30 days, 60 days, 90 days, 120 days, etc.;

  * Payable certain days after the date of draft;

  * Payable certain days after the date of bill of lading;

  * Payable certain days after the date of arrival of goods;

  * Payable certain days after the fixed date.

- Commercial bill and banker's bill: If the drawer is a commercial firm, the bill is called a commercial bill.

When the drawer is a bank, the bill is called a banker's bill.

- Commercial acceptance bill and banker's acceptance bill: In time commercial bills, when the drawer is a commercial firm and the drawee is another commercial firm, the bill after acceptance by the drawee is called a commercial acceptance bill.

When the drawer is a commercial firm or a bank and the drawee is a bank, the bill after acceptance by the bank is called a banker's acceptance bill.

c) General procedures in handling a bill of exchange.

- **Drawing**: Drawing means the act of the drawer in filling up the bill of exchange with particulars as to the name of the drawee, the amount payable, the date of payment and the name of the payee, and after signature, the drawer may present the bill to the drawee through the medium of the payee or a banker.

With regard to the payee, the drawer may use one of the following methods:

* Restrictive payee, such as (pay ABC Co. Ltd. only) or (pay ABC Co. Ltd., not negotiable). Such a bill of exchange can not be negotiated or transferred to another party by endorsement and only the payee named can collect the amount.

* To order, such as (pay ABC Co. Ltd. or Order) or (pay to the order of ABC Co. Ltd.). Such a bill of exchange can be negotiated or transferred to another party after endorsement by the payee or the amount may be collected by the payee himself.

* To bearer, such as (pay to bearer) or (pay to ABC Co. Ltd. or bearer). Such a bill of exchange does not need the endorsement by another party and can be negotiated or transferred merely by delivery.

- **Presentation**: Presentation refers to the act of the holder of the bill of exchange presenting the bill to the drawee, asking the latter either to pay or to accept the bill. The drawee's receiving or seeing the bill is called "sight". If the bill is a sight or demand bill, the drawee has to pay the amount at once; if it is a usance or time bill, the drawee has to make his acceptance and pay the amount on the date due.

- **Acceptance**: Acceptance means the act of the drawee to show his responsibility by accepting the usance bill for payment at a fixed future date by writing the word "accepted", marking the date of acceptance and signing on the face of the bill. The drawee after making the acceptance is called the acceptor and is responsible for paying the amount on the due date of the usance bill.

- **Endorsement**: A bill of exchange may be a negotiable instrument, and may be transferable in the international money market. In the case of a "to order" bill of exchange, endorsement is needed in the procedure of negotiation or transfer by the payee by signing his name on the back of the bill, either blank endorsement which makes the bill payable to the bearer or holder, or full endorsement with the name of the transferee and his order, who is called the endorsee. The right of receiving the amount is transferred to the endorsee or the holder in due course.

The holder of a bill of exchange has several choices open to him. He can keep the bill until it is due for payment and then present it to the acceptor. He can transfer the bill to another person, i.e., he can "negotiate" the bill, the other person becomes a holder in due course. A special form of negotiation exists where the holder passes the bill to a bank or discount company, and this is the third choice. The bank or discount company concerned may be prepared to "discount" the bill by paying immediate cash for the bill at a little less than its face amount, i.e., after deducting charges and interest based on the current rate of discount, and then, will in the due date of the bill collect the full amount from the acceptor. The holder may be satisfied to receive a slightly smaller amount as he can get the money before the bill falls due. The new "holder in due course" may hold the bill until it matures or may rediscount the bill in turn.

- **Protesting**: When a bill has been duly presented for acceptance or payment and the acceptance or payment has been refused, the bill is said to be dishonoured. Upon dishonour the holder has an immediate right to take action against all parties to the bill. The holder must normally give a formal notice of dishonour to all the parties he wishes to make liable. In order to exercise the right of recourse, the holder should apply for a letter of protest from the notary public on the strength of which he may recover the purchase price.

2) **Promissory Note.** A promissory note is an unconditional promise in writing made by one person to another signed by the maker, engaging to pay, on demand or at a fixed or determinable future time, a sum certain in money to, or to a order of, a specified person or to a bearer.

A promissory note is the promise, but a bill of exchange is an order of the one who issues it. A promissory note has no drawee, hence there is no "acceptance" involved.

3) **Cheque.** A cheque is an unconditional order in writing drawn on a banker signed by the drawer, requiring the banker to pay on demand a sum certain in money to or to the order of specified person or to a bearer.

A cheque is also defined as "a bill of exchange drawn on a bank payable on demand".

A cheque is crossed when two parallel lines are drawn across it. When this is done, payment of the cheque will not be made in cash over a bank-counter, but will be made only through somebody's account.

B. Modes of payment

In international trade, the main methods of payment are remittance, collection and letter of credit.

1. Remittance

Remittance means that the buyer remits money to the seller through a bank on his own initiative.

According to the terms and time stipulated in the contract, remittance is classified into three kinds:

1) Mail transfer (M/T): The buyer gives money to a local bank which sends a trust deed for payment to its correspondent bank at the seller's end by mail and entrusts it with the task to pay money to the seller.

2) Telegraphic transfer (T/T): At the request of the buyer, a local bank sends a trust

deed for payment by cable directly to its correspondent bank at the seller's end and entrusts the work to it to pay money to the seller.

3) Demand draft (D/D): The buyer buys a draft from a local bank and sends it by mail to the seller, the seller or his appointed person can collect money from the relative bank at his end against the draft sent by the buyer.

In international trade remittance is usually used in Payment in Advance, Cash with Order (C. W. O.), Cash on Delivery (C. O. D.) and Open Account Trade. Under Payment in Advance and C. W. O., the importer gives credit to the exporter; while, under C. O. D. and Open Account Trade, the exporter gives credit to the importer.

2. Collection

Normally, the buyer does not remit the purchase price, but allows the exporter to draw a bill of exchange, with or without documents attached on him. In such a case, the exporter asks his bank to arrange for the acceptance or payment of the bill overseas, and the bank will carry his task through its own branch office abroad or a correspondent bank. This procedure is termed as collection of proceeds of sales.

1) Parties involved in collection

a) The principal or exporter;

b) The remitting bank or the bank appointed by the exporter to collect the proceeds of sales;

c) The collecting bank or the bank appointed by the remitting bank to collect the proceeds from the importer, usually a branch office abroad or a correspondent bank of the remitting bank;

d) The payer or importer.

2) Kinds of collection

a) Collection on clean bill: It means that the exporter collects the purchase price against the draft only, without any shipping documents attached thereto.

This method is usually used in collecting balance under L/C, advance, commission and costs of samples.

b) Collection on documentary bill: It means that the exporter collects the purchase price against the documentary bill.

It can be subdivided into two kinds:

• Documents against payment (D/P): D/P calls for actual payment against the transfer of shipping documents.

There is D/P at sight, and D/P after sight.

∗ D/P at sight: After shipment of the goods, the exporter shall draw a sight bill of exchange, and send it as well as shipping documents to a local bank, through which and whose correspondent bank the documentary draft is presented to the importer. The importer shall pay against the documentary draft drawn by the seller at sight.

D/P at sight requires immediate payment by the importer to get hold of the documents.

* D/P after sight: After shipment of the goods, the exporter shall draw a usance bill of exchange and send it as well as shipping documents to a local bank, through which and whose correspondent bank the documentary draft is presented to the importer. The importer shall accept the usance draft, and make payment on the due date of the usance bill.

Under D/P after sight, the importer is given a certain period to make payment, such as 30, 45, 60 or 90 days after the first presentation of the documents, but he is not allowed to get hold of the documents until he pays.

In this case, in order to push sales of the goods in time, the importer may consult with the collecting bank to borrow the bills of lading before the maturity of the drafts against the trust receipts (T/R), and make payment on the due dates of drafts. This method is called accommodation.

The so-called "Trust Receipt" is a written guaranty provided by the importer to the collecting bank for the purpose of borrowing B/L from the latter, in which the importer declares that he will take delivery of the goods, declare to the customs, store the goods, take out insurance on and push sales of the goods as the consignee of the collecting bank, and acknowledge the title to the goods and proceeds of the sale belonging to the collecting bank and will guarantee to make payment on the date due.

• Documents against acceptance (D/A): D/A calls for delivery of documents against acceptance of the draft drawn by the exporter. D/A is always after sight.

D/A makes the importer get hold of shipping documents and take delivery of the goods before payment. So the exporter would have to take great risks.

As far as the sellers benefit is concerned, D/P at sight is better than D/P after sight, whereas D/P is far better than D/A. In international trade, payment through collection is accepted only when the financial standing of the importer is sound or where a previous course of business has inspired the exporter with confidence that the importer will be good for payment.

The processes of different modes of collection may be simply explained through the following diagrams:

D/P at sight

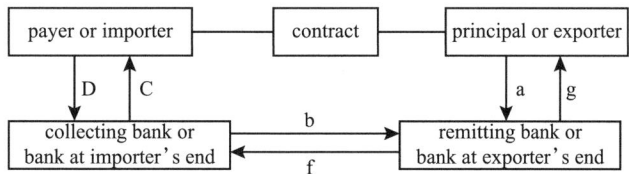

Explanations:

a. After shipment, the exporter applies to the remitting bank for collecting the invoice value by sending an application, a sight bill and shipping documents to the remitting bank.

b. The remitting bank draws up a collection order and transfers it as well as the sight bill and shipping documents to the collecting bank.

c. The collecting bank presents the draft and shipping documents to the importer according to the instructions in the collection order.

d. The importer pays the purchase price at sight to the collecting bank.

e. The collecting bank delivers the documents to the importer.

f. The collecting bank transfers accounts to the remitting bank.

g. The remitting bank transfers the accounts to the principal.

D/P after sight

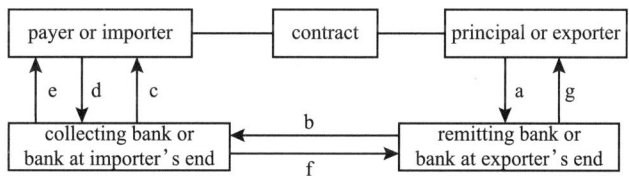

Explanations:

a. After shipment, the exporter applies to the remitting bank for collecting the invoice value by sending an application, a time draft and shipping documents to the remitting bank.

b. The remitting bank draws up a collection order and transfers it as well as the time draft and shipping documents to the collecting bank.

c. The collecting bank presents the drafts and shipping documents to the importer and the importer accepts the draft.

d. The importer pays in due course to the collecting bank.

e. The collecting bank delivers the documents to the importer.

f. The collecting bank transfers accounts to the remitting bank.

g. The remitting bank transfers accounts to the principal.

D/A

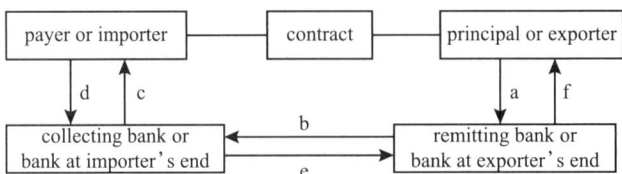

Explanations:

a. After shipment the exporter applies to the remitting bank for collecting the invoice value by sending an application, a time draft and shipping documents to the remitting bank.

b. The remitting bank draws up a collection order and transfers it as well as the time draft and shipping documents to the collecting bank.

c. The collecting bank presents the draft and documents to the importer. After the importer accepts the draft the bank will deliver the shipping documents to the importer, while taking back the draft.

d. The importer pays the purchase price in due course.

e. The collecting bank transfers accounts to the remitting bank.

f. The remitting bank transfers accounts to the principal.

3. Letter of Credit (L/C)

The most commonly used method of payment in the financial business of international trade is the letter of credit which is a reliable and safe method of payment, facilitating trade between unknown parties and giving protection to both the seller and the buyer.

1) The feature common to all kinds of L/C

The feature common to all kinds of L/C is that the buyer arranges with a bank to provide finance for the exporter in the country of the latter on delivery of the shipping documents. On presentation of the shipping documents, the banker will pay the purchase price, normally by paying a sight bill on presentation or by accepting a time bill drawn on the buyer.

2) The parties relating to a letter of credit are named as follows:

a) The applicant, generally the buyer or importer, who applies to the bank for issuance of a letter of credit.

b) The originating bank or opening bank or issuing bank, which is the bank receiving the application from the applicant to issue the L/C and will be responsible for payment. It is usually a bank at the place where the importer's premises are located.

c) The advising bank or correspondent bank, which is a bank at the place where the exporter resides and may usually be a branch of the issuing bank or its correspondent. The advising bank hands the letter of credit to the exporter under the instructions from the issuing bank. It only proves the authenticity of the L/C and is not responsible for anything else.

d) The beneficiary, who is empowered to use the L/C and is usually the exporter.

e) The negotiating bank which is a bank ready to accept or discount the documentary bill drawn by the beneficiary under the L/C. The negotiating bank may be the advising bank or another bank appointed to negotiate under the L/C. If there is no specific stipulation in the L/C, the exporter may present the documentary bill to any bank which is ready to put through the transaction.

f) The paying bank, which is a bank responsible for the payment specified in the L/C. It is usually the issuing bank or it may be another bank appointed by the issuing bank according to the stipulation in the L/C.

3) Where payment under a banker's commercial credit is arranged, four stages can normally be distinguished:

a) The exporter and the overseas buyer agree in the contract of sales that payment shall be made under a commercial credit.

b) The overseas buyer instructs a bank at his place of residence (the originating bank) to make available a commercial credit for another country's exporter on the terms agreed upon in the contract of sales.

c) The originating bank arranges with a bank at the residence of the exporter (known as the advising bank) to negotiate, accept or pay the exporter's draft upon delivery of the shipping documents by the seller.

d) The advising bank advises the exporter that it will negotiate, accept or pay his draft upon delivery of the shipping documents.

Procedure of L/C

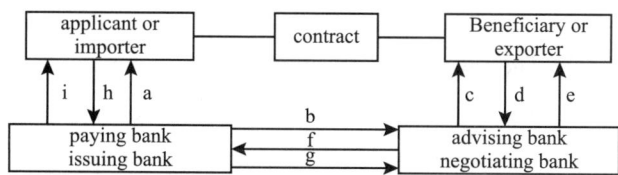

Explanations:

a. The importer applies to a local bank for opening an L/C in favour of the exporter and provides a certain amount of deposit and formality fees.

b. The opening bank sends the L/C opened to the advising bank.

c. The advising bank transfers the L/C to the exporter.

d. After examining the L/C, the exporter delivers the goods according to the stipulations of L/C. After shipment, the exporter makes out a draft and draws up the documents in accordance with the L/C, and delivers them to the negotiating bank within its validity.

e. If the documents are in conformity with the L/C, the negotiating bank will advance the purchase price to the exporter.

f. The negotiating bank transfers the draft and documents to the opening bank or the bank appointed by the opening bank applying for payment.

g. The opening bank will pay to the negotiating bank after examining the documents.

h. The opening bank informs the applicant of the same and asks him to make payment so as to get hold of the shipping documents.

i. The applicant makes payment to get hold of shipping documents, and takes delivery of the goods against the documents.

4) In the letter of credit, the following points are generally stipulated expressly:

a) The definition of the L/C, its kind, validity, expiry date and place of negotiation;

b) Descriptions of the goods to be shipped: name, specification, quality, quantity, packing, price, etc. of the goods;

c) The latest shipment date, the port of loading and port of destination, types of transportation, partial shipments or transshipment to be or not to be allowed;

d) Evidence and documents for payment; bill of exchange, commercial invoice, packing list (weight memo), certificate of origin, inspection certificate, customs invoice, consular invoice, B/L, insurance policy or certificate, or other documents such as a copy of telegram to the the dispatch of goods, if required;

e) Any special requirements;

f) Clauses covering the responsibility of payment by the issuing bank in favour of the beneficiary or holder of the bill of exchange.

5) Kinds of L/C

a) Revocable L/C: The revocable L/C means that the opening bank may amend or revoke the credit before negotiation, acceptance or payment without agreement of the beneficiary.

b) Irrevocable L/C: The irrevocable L/C means that once the L/C is opened, without agreement of the beneficiary, the opening bank cannot amend or revoke the L/C within its-validity. As long as the beneficiary provides the documents in accordance with the stipulations in the L/C, the opening bank shall perform its duty of payment.

c) Documentary L/C: The documentary L/C stipulates that the bill of exchange drawn by the seller should be accompanied with shipping documents. This kind of L/C is most widely used in international trade.

d) Clean L/C: If the bill of exchange is a clean bill, the L/C is called a clean L/C.

e) Confirmed L/C: The confirmed L/C should be an irrevocable L/C confirmed by another bank named by the opening bank.

The bank authorized or requested by the opening bank to confirm the L/C is called the confirming bank. Once an L/C is confirmed, there are two banks to be responsible for payment of the purchase price, i. e. , the opening bank and the confirming bank. The confirmation constitutes a definite undertaking of the confirming bank, in addition to that of opening bank, that as long as the documents presented by the seller are in accordance with the stipulations of the L/C, the confirming bank shall be responsible for negotiation, acceptance or payment. This is the type of commercial credit most favourable to the exporter, because the bank guarantees that it will honour the exporter's drafts provided that they are drawn and presented in conformity with the terms of the letter of credit.

The nature of the credit being irrevocable and confirmed is reflected in the fact that the credit cannot be revoked within its term of validity without the consent of the beneficiary and that the advising or correspondent bank undertakes to honour the drafts of the exporter.

The confirmed L/C is popular in modern export trade because it reduces the credit risk borne by the exporter, it serves in many trades as the normal terms of settlement. The banks have made an invaluable contribution to the smooth discharge of export transactions by perfecting this type of commercial credit.

f) Sight L/C: This kind of L/C stipulates that the beneficiary may collect the purchase price from the bank against a sight draft.

g) Usance L/C: This kind of L/C stipulates that the beneficiary may collect the purchase price from the bank against a usance draft.

There is a special usance L/C under which the beneficiary opens a time draft, the paying bank abroad should be responsible for discount while the discount charges and interest owing to deferred payment should be undertaken by the opening bank or its applicant. As to the beneficiary, this type of L/C still belongs to payment at sight, while for the applicant belongs to payment after sight. So it is also called a buyer's usance L/C.

The clause under this type of L/C is usually stipulated as "Drawee banker discount charges and acceptance commission are for the account of the applicant and therefore the beneficiary is to receive the value for the usance draft as if drawn at sight".

h) Transferable L/C: This type of letter of credit allows the beneficiary to transfer the amount partly or wholly of the letter of credit to one or more than one parties, i. e. , the second beneficiary. This is because the original beneficiary is only a middleman or broker and has to transfer the L/C to the; actual suppliers of the goods, who will attend to the shipping procedures while the first beneficiary will obtain a commission or a difference between the amount payable to him under the letter of credit and the actual amount payable to the second beneficiary.

i) Revolving L/C: Where the export sale is not an isolated transaction but the overseas buyer is a regular customer of the exporter, the buyer will arrange a revolving credit in favour of the seller. The buyer gives the bank standing instructions to arrange for a credit in favour of the exporter, which at no time shall exceed a fixed maximum. The advantage of this arrangement is that no renewal is required and much clerical labour is saved.

j) Reciprocal L/C: When the two parties conclude a transaction in which they act as importers and exporters mutually and the trades are related and equal or almost equal. The two parties open Ls/C in favour of each other. So the two Ls/C are conditioned on each other.

Features of reciprocal L/C:

- The two Ls/C must be valid simultaneously.
- The drawer and beneficiary of one L/C is usually the drawee and payer of another L/C.
- The opening bank of one L/C is usually the advising bank of another.

This type of L/C is often used in barter trade, compensation trade, processing trade, etc.

k) Back to back L/C: The exporter sends the L/C established by the importer in his favour to a bank as sole security, requiring the local bank to reopen an L/C in favour of the actual exporter. The L/C opened by the importer is called the original L/C, while the second L/C issued in favour of the actual exporter at the request of the exporter is called the subsidiary L/C.

This type of L/C is suitable for business through a middleman, i.e., a broker or commission man.

l) Anticipatory credit: It is also called the packing credit. The opening bank allows the beneficiary to collect the purchase price against the draft or other evidence, but he must give a receipt and an undertaking to present the required shipping documents within the validity of the credit.

This kind of L/C is mainly used in the following cases:

When supply cannot meet demand the importer usually makes payment in advancein order that he may get hold of the goods in urgent need earlier; or, the makes payment in advance in order that the seller may buy the materials for manufacture of large machines, vessels or aircraft ordered or, he does in order to transfer foreign exchange through the bank.

It can be subdivided into two kinds:

• clean payment credit: It means that the importer pays in advance the whole amount under the L/C against a clean bill.

• partial payment credit: It includes the red clause credit and the green clause credit.

Under the red clause credit, the opening bank allows the beneficiary to collect the partial purchase price against a declaration of shipping documents to be sent afterwards and a sight draft and the bank will pay off the balance against shipping documents after shipment.

The green clause credit is almost the same as the red clause credit except that in the case of the green clause credit, the opening bank requires the beneficiary to store the goods in the customs warehouse in the place of export. Then the beneficiary can require the bank to advance the partial purchase price against a godown warrant or warehouse receipt.

m) Stand by L/C: It is also called the commercial paper L/C, which is a guaranty issued by the opening bank on behalf of the applicant declaring that the bank will undertake certain obligations. It is a special L/C which Northern American countries usually use instead of a letter of guarantee. The roles assumed by the standby L/C not only include making payment, but also include guaranteeing to perform a contract making repayment for loan, and fulfilling other agreed obligations.

6) Letter of guarantee (L/G)

The letter of guarantee is a written document issued by the bank on behalf of the importer or exporter in favour of the latter or the former guaranteeing to undertake payment, conlusion or performance of a contract, etc.

It includes two types:

(1) L/G for performance of import and export contract:

• L/G for performance of import contract: It is a guaranty issued by the bank (guarantor) on behalf of the importer to the beneficiary, which stipulates that if the importer fails to pay duly after delivery of the goods by the exporter, the bank shall be responsible for the payment.

It can be subdivided into the following kinds:

* L/G opened for import of equipment;
* L/G opened for compensation trade;
* L/G opened for assembly and processing trade;
* L/G opened for credit purchasing.

• L/G for performance of export contract:

It is a kind of guaranty issued by the bank on behalf of the exporter to the importer which stipulates that if the exporter fails to deliver the goods in time, the bank should be responsible for making compensation for the losses incurred by the importer.

It includes performance guarantee for important export business, plant export guarantee, repayment guarantee etc.

(2) L/G for bid and loan: It is a kind of guaranty issued by the bank to the invitor for tender on behalf of the bidder which guarantees that the bidder will not withdraw the bid halfway or amend the bidding conditions unilaterally and will not refuse to sign a contract and pay performance bond after winning the bid, otherwise the bank shall be responsible for making compensation for losses sustained by the inviter for tender.

Besides the above mentioned guarantee for bid, the bank L/G is also used in loan business. But some countries forbid the use of bank L/G, for example, the U.S. and Japan, instead, they adopt the stand-by L/C.

Differences between the bank L/G and the L/C:

- Under the L/C, the bank shall undertake the duty of payment; while under the letter of guarantee, the bank shall be responsible for payment only in the case of non-performance of the contract by the applicant. So the issuing bank of the L/C is responsible for payment as the first payer, while the opening bank of the L/G is usually responsible as the second payer.

- Under the L/C, the issuing bank handles business according to the stipulations of the L/C only and has nothing to do with the contract, while the opening bank of the L/G will handle business according to the contract. If the two parties to the contract cannot agree with each other upon some matters, or one party breaches the contract or fails to perform his obligations stipulated in the contract, the opening bank of the L/G will be likely to be involved in the disputes of the contract.

- Under the L/C, the beneficiary can often get accommodation through negotiation, while under the L/G, the beneficially can not do through negotiation.

Differences between the stand-by L/C and the common L/C:

In 1977 the International Chamber of Commerce recognized that the stand-by L/C is regarded as being belonging to the scope of the documentary L/C. The stipulations in "The Uniform Customs and Practice for Documentary Credits" are suitable for the stand-by L/C as well. Therefore, the standby L/C, like other forms of L/C, should be governed by its provisions. At the same time, it should also clearly stipulate whether it is irrevocable or not, what the highest amount is and when it reaches its maturity.

But there are some differences:

The L/C is usually used in specific trade, while the stand-by L/C is used only in the case of non-performance of duty by the applicant, such as non-delivery, non-payment, non-repayment for loan or refusing to sign the-contract after winning the tender or refusing to pay the performance bond, etc.

Differences between the stand-by L/C and the letter of guarantee:

They both belong to bank credit in which the bank guarantees that the applicant performs the contract or repays for debt.

But they are different in qualities.

- The opening bank of the L/G usually acts as the subsidiary payer. It undertakes the duty of payment only in the case of non-performance by the principal while the stand-by L/C is opened by the opening bank in favour of the beneficiary. As long as the beneficiary's written statements or evidence are in conformity with the stipulations in the stand-by L/C he can get the agreed amount or loan from the bank when the applicant fails to fulfil his duty.

- The opening bank of the L/G would have to pay in the case of non-performance of the relevant contract or a certain promise by the applicant, so the opening bank is likely to be involved in the contract disputes or even a legal action.

The opening bank of the stand-by L/C would have to pay as long as the beneficiary presents a statement or evidence of breach by the applicant stipulated in the L/C within the validity, so the bank has nothing to do with the contract.

C. Combination of Different Modes of Payment

In import and export business, it is very important for us to choose different modes of payment.

In order to get in foreign exchange safely, make payment properly, fasten capital turnover and expand business, we should choose proper modes of payment based on our foreign trade policy.

In export business, we usually adopt the sight L/C, because it can guarantee to get in foreign exchange safely and rapidly. If we have to adopt the usance L/C, we should take interest into consideration. In order to promote foreign trade and expand sales, sometimes we may adopt D/P, if the buyers are in sound credit standing. In order to push sales of inventory, sometimes we may accept D/A as well. In the case of consignment, if necessary, we should require the consignee or agent to issue an L/G, then we may entrust him with the consignment business against the L/G opened. In import business, we may adopt L/C, collection, remittance or L/G to meet different cases.

The combination of various modes of payment:

1. Combination of Remittance and L/C

In this case, the partial amount is paid by L/C, the balance is settled by remittance. For example as to the business of ore, the two parties may agree that the buyer will pay the partial amount by L/C against shipping documents. The balance will be settled after the goods arrive at the port of destination or after the goods are reinspected.

2. Combination of L/C and Collection

In this case, the partial amount is paid by L/C the balance is settled by collection. The exporter will draw two drafts, the amount under the L/C will be paid against a clean draft, while the full set of shipping documents will be attached to the sight draft or time draft under collection. In most cases, the major part of the value of goods will be payable by irrevocable L/C and the remaining amount will be settled on collection basis, D/P at sight, the full set of shipping documents are to accompany the collection item. All the documents are not to be delivered to the buyer until the full payment of the invoice value. In case of nonpayment of balance for the collection item, the documents shall be held by the issuing bank at the entire disposal of the seller.

3. Combination of Remittance and L/G

As to full sets of equipment big machinery, vessels, airplanes etc., owing to the large amount and a long production period, the buyer, according to the procedures of production and delivery, usually adopts the combined modes of remittance and L/G to pay periodically. In our import business, a foreign exporter often requires us to pay 5% ~ 10% of the value of the goods by remittance, the remaining amount is to be settled through progressive payment or deferred payment against the L/G issued by our bank.

The so-called progressive payment or payment by installments means that the importer pays the purchase price periodically according to the processes of production and delivery. In the case of progressive payment, the last part of amount should be paid off after the exporter fulfils its duty completely.

The so-called deferred payment means that the importer should pay a deposit first, then according to the processes of production and delivery, pay a certain amount of the purchase price periodically. But most of the purchase price is paid off a certain number of days, months, or even years after the delivery of the goods.

Differences between progressive payment and deferred payment are:

1) In the case of progressive payment, the importer pays the purchase price in an agreed mode periodically. When the exporter fulfils the duty of delivery, the importer has already or nearly paid off the price value, so it is also called cash on spot delivery. In the case of deferred payment, most of the purchase price is amortized in a long period after the delivery of the goods, so it is a credit given to the importer by the exporter, but the importer shall undertake the interest resulting from the deferred payment.

2) In the case of progressive payment, the importer will not obtain the whole title to the goods until he pays off the last part of the purchase price. In the case of deferred payment, the

goods will be transferred to the importer automatically as soon as the exporter performs the delivery of the goods.

D. Terms of Payment in the Contract

1. Stipulation of Remittance

Under remittance, we should stipulate clearly the method, time and amount in the contract. For example, "The consignment agent shall remit 50% the sales proceeds by M/T to reach the consignor not later than 15th, Feb. 2002".

2. Stipulation of Collection

All documents sent for collection must be accompanied by a collection order giving complete and precise instructions. Banks are only permitted to act upon these instructions, therefore, the clauses as to collection must be stipulated clearly.

1) Stipulation of D/P at sight: "Upon first presentation, the buyer shall pay against the documentary draft drawn by the seller at sight. The shipping documents are to be delivered against payment only."

2) Stipulation of D/P after sight: "The buyer shall duly accept the documentary draft drawn by the seller at … days sight upon first presentation and make payment on its maturity. The shipping documents are to be delivered against payment only."

"The buyer shall pay against the documentary draft drawn by the seller at ×× days after the date of B/L. The shipping documents are to be delivered against payment only."

"The buyer shall pay against the documentary draft drawn by the seller at ×× days after the date of draft. The shipping documents are to be delivered against payment only."

3) Stipulation of D/A:

"The buyer shall duly accept the documentary draft drawn by the seller at ×× days sight upon first presentation and make payment on its maturity. The shipping documents are to be delivered against acceptance only".

3. Stipulation of L/C

When the L/C is adopted, we should indicate the type, opening date, validity of the L/C as well as the place of negotiation.

1) Stipulation of sight L/C: "The buyer shall open with a bank acceptable to the seller an irrevocable sight L/C to reach the seller … days before the month of shipment, valid for negotiation in China until the 15th day after shipment."

2) Stipulation of usance L/C: The buyer shall open with a bank acceptable to the seller an irrevocable L/C available by draft 30 days after sight, to reach the seller … days before the month of shipment, to be valid for negotiation in China until the 15th day after shipment.

4. Combination of L/C and Collection

In the case of payment by the combination of L/C and collection, the bank will not deliver the documents until the whole purchase price is paid off. For example, "The buyer shall open with a bank acceptable to the seller an irrevocable L/C to reach the seller … days before the month of shipment, 80% of the invoice value available by clean draft at sight while the remaining 20% on D/P at sight basis. The full set of the shipping documents of 100% invoice value shall accompany the collection item and shall only be released until payment of the full amount of invoice value. If the buyer fails to pay the full amount of invoice value, the shipping documents shall be held by the issuing bank at the seller disposal."

5. Combination of L/C and Remittance

In international trade, this kind of combination of payment mode is sometimes adopted to meet the requirements, of a particular trade: "80% of invoice value by irrevocable L/C, available by sight draft against surrender of full set of shipping documents to the negotiating bank at port of shipment, the remaining 20% by remittance after arrival of cargo and reinspection of cargo up to the stipulated standard."

6. Combination of Remittance and L/G

Under these terms and conditions the contents of the payment terms are usually expressed as follows: "10% of price value by payment in advance through Mail Transfer (M/T), 90% of amount shall be paid within 18 months in installments after shipment."

(资料来源：宋秀峰. 国际贸易（双语版）[M]. 中国发展出版社，2010.)

➤ 本章小结

国际贸易结算中使用的票据包括汇票、本票和支票，以汇票为主。汇票是一种要式票据，所以必须要式齐全，其基本原理和法律规则同样适用于本票和支票。

汇付属于商业信用，由于使用的结算工具不同，汇付通常可以分为电汇、信汇和票汇三种。托收在国际贸易中只是有条件地使用；在实际业务中，托收能调动进口商采购的积极性，有利于提高出口商的竞争力。信用证的特点表现为独立性、单据买卖和银行信用。信用证结算方式的主要当事人有四个，即开证申请人、开证行、通知行、受益人。

银行保函是银行作为担保人向受益人开立的，保证被保证人向受益人尽到某项义务，否则将有担保人负责支付受益人损失的保证文件。国际保理业务是集合会计结算、财务管理、信用担保和贸易融资为一体的综合性售后服务。

在国际贸易业务中，一笔交易的货款结算可以只使用一种结算方式，也可以根据需要，将两种以上的结算方式结合使用，从而有利于促成交易和及时收汇等。

▶本章名词

汇票　本票　支票　信汇　电汇　票汇　付款交单　承兑交单　信用证　UCP600　不可撤销信用证　议付信用证　可转让信用证　银行保函　备用信用证　国际保理

▶理论思考

1. 什么是汇票？汇票的内容有哪些？
2. 汇票的抬头有几种写法？各起什么样的作用？
3. 什么是背书？背书的种类有哪些？
4. 为什么说汇付和托收分属顺汇和逆汇，但又都属商业信用性质？
5. 什么是信用证？简述信用证方式的基本业务程序。
6. 信用证方式具有哪些特点？

▶实训习题

一、训练材料

以下材料分别是关于合同和信用证的主要内容，试根据合同的主要内容修改信用证。

下面是××号合同的主要内容：

卖方：山东艺术品进出口公司

买方：CED International Limited, Hongkong

品名：Art. No. 99-104XZ

数量：3 500 件

单价：每件 6.75 美元成本加运费加保险到鹿特丹，含佣金 3%

总金额：23 625 美元

交货期：不迟于 2017 年 6 月 10 日由青岛装运，可分批，可转运

支付条款：以不可撤销的，即期信用证付款，于 2017 年 6 月 25 日前在中国议付有效

IRREVOCABLE DOCUMENTARY CREDIT

To: Shandong Artware Import and Export Corporation

Advising Bank: Hongkong and Shanghai Banking Corp. Ltd., Qingdao Branch Dear Sirs,

We hereby open our Irrevocable Letter of Credit No. HKH344802EB in favour of Shandong Artware Import and Export Corporation for account of CED International Limited, Hongkong, up to an aggregate amount of US $21,625 (Say US Dollars Twenty-One Thousand Six Hundred Twenty Five Only) for 110% of the invoice value relative to the shipment of

3,500 pcs of Art. No. 92102XZ at US $6.75 PER PIECE CIFC5% Rotterdam as per Contract No. 1 – UP.

Drafts to be drawn at sight on our bank and accompanied by the following documents:

1) Signed commercial invoice in triplicate showing a deduction of 5 percent commission on CIF value.

2) Full set original clean on board ocean Bills of Lading made out to shipper's order, endorsed in blank, marked freight prepaid.

3) Marine Insurance Certificate in triplicate for full CIF value plus 10 percent covering All Risks and War Risks Shipment form Rotterdam to Qing dao.

Partial Shipments: allowed

Transhipment: allowed

Shipment must be effected not later than 10 May.

This L/C is valid until 20 June, 2000 in China.

二、翻译合同条款

1. D/P at sight

Upon first presentation the Buyer shall pay against documentary draft drawn by the Seller at sight. The shipping documents are to be delivered against payment only.

2. D/P after sight

The Buyer shall duly accept the documentary draft drawn by the Seller at ×× days upon first presentation and make payment on its maturity. The shipping documents are to be delivered against payment only.

3. D/A

The Buyer shall duly accept the documentary draft drawn by the Seller at ×× days upon first presentation and make payment on its maturity. The shipping documents are to be delivered against acceptance.

4. 即期付款的信用证

The Buyer shall open through a bank acceptable to the seller an Irrevocable Sight Letter of Credit to the Seller 30 days before the month of shipment. Valid for negotiation in China until the 15th day after the month of shipment.

5. 远期付款的信用证

The Buyer shall open through a bank acceptable to the seller an Irrevocable Sight Letter of Credit at 45 day's sight to reach the Seller ×× days before the month of shipment. Valid for negotiation in Shanghai until the 15th day after the month of shipment.

6. 托收与信用证结合

The Buyer shall open through a bank acceptable to the Seller an Irrevocable Sight Letter of Credit to reach the Seller 30 days before the month of shipment, stating that 50% of the invoice value available against clean draft at sight while the remaining 50% on D/P at sight. The full set of the shipping documents of 100% of invoice value shall accompany by the collection item and shall only be released after full payment of the invoice value, If the Buyer fail to pay full invoice value, the shipping documents shall be held by the issuing bank at the Sellers disposal.

三、案例分析

1. 我某公司与外商签订某商品出口合同，合同规定装运期为10月，即期信用证付款，但未规定具体开证日期。A商拖延开证，我方见装运期快到，从9月底开始，连续多次催外商开证。10月15日，收到信用证的简电通知，我方因怕耽误装运期，即按简电将货物装运出口。10月28日，我方才收到信用证证实本，该证实本对有关单据作了与合同不符的规定。经办人员审证时未予注意，交银行议付时才被银行发现。由于该证有效期已到，只得凭担保请银行办理议付手续。最终被开证行以单证不符为由拒绝付款，遭受损失。你认为，我方应从此事件中吸取哪些教训？

2. 某公司向外国某商行进口一批货物。合同规定，货物分两批装运，支付方式为不可撤销即期议付信用证。我方按时开出了有关的信用证，证中规定货物分两批装运，受益人分两次支款。第一批货物装运后，卖方在有效期限内向银行交单议付，议付行审核单据后，即向该商议付货款，随后中国银行对议付行作了偿付。我方在收到第一批货物后，发现货物品质不符合同，因此要求开证行对第二批货物的单据拒绝付款，但遭到开证行拒绝。你认为开证行这样做是否合理？

3. 我某公司出口按CIF条件，凭不可撤销议付信用证支付方式向某外商出口货物一批。该商按合同规定开来的信用证经我方审核无误。我出口公司在信用证规定的装运期限内将货物在装运港装上开往目的港的海轮，并在装运前向保险公司办理了货物运输保险。但装船完毕后不久，海轮起火爆炸沉没，该批货物全部灭失。外商闻讯后来电表示拒绝付款。你认为，我出口公司应如何处理？并根据《INCOTERMS2010》和《UCP600》说明理由。

4. 中国某公司采用CIF价出口价值25 000美元货物去新加坡，2017年10月31日，美国花旗银行新加坡分行开来L/C，12月初，中方从有关方获悉，开证申请人倒闭。此时，货物已在装运港，中方果断决定装船。12月8日，取得海运B/L。12月10日，接到开证行撤销L/C的通知，中方复电货物已经发运，不可撤销。接着业务员认真制单，经银行仔细审单，最终顺利收汇。

5. 中国某公司出口啤酒一批，采用L/C方式付款，卖方发运货物后备齐单据准备议付，买方认为啤酒这种货物的运输存储要求很高，必须做到检验之后，才能付款。卖方认为根据信用证的规定，只需所交单据符合信用证要求就可议付到货款。最后买方同意付款，再处理争议。

四、打开中国银行网查出国际结算进口业务收费标准

五、打开中国银行网查出对背信用证与可转让信用证的区别

CHAPTER 8

第八章 争议的预防和处理

> **本章指导**
>
> 通过本章的学习,要求能够了解商品检验检疫、索赔、不可抗力、仲裁的基础知识,运用所了解的上述知识在合同中签订好相关条款,还要重点掌握:
> 1. 出入境检验检疫程序及检验时间和地点规定;
> 2. 不可抗力时间的认可、不可抗力的法律后果;
> 3. 仲裁协议的作用和仲裁裁决的效力。

第一节 商品检验

商品检验(commodity inspection)是指在国际贸易买卖中由商检机构或国家商检部门对卖方交付给买方货物的品质、数量和包装进行检验,以确保合同的标的物符合买卖合同规定;有的还对装运技术条件或货物在装卸运输过程中发生的残损、短缺进行检验或鉴定,以明确事故的范围和责任的归属;商品检验还包括依据一国法律或行政法规对某些进出口货物实施的强制检验或食品、动植物及其相关产品的检疫,是买卖合同中必须订明的一项内容。以下主要介绍买方的检验权、检验时间及地点、商检机构、商检证书及商检条款等内容。

一、买方的检验权

按照各国有关法律的规定,国际贸易中的买方都有权对卖方所交货物在合理时间内进行检验,除非双方在买卖合同中对此另有约定。《联合国国际贸易销售合同公约》第36、第37条对卖方交货的品质担保义务范围及责任期间及保证合同约定数量交货作出了明确规定:卖方所交货物必须符合合同规定,在此也指出法律关于买方对货物的检验权的规定并非强制性的,不是买方接受货物的前提条件。若买方没有利用合理机会检验货物，就表明他放弃了检验权，也就丧失了拒收货物的权利。

二、检验的时间和地点

如前所述，国际上一般都承认买方在接受货物之前，有权对货物进行检验，但是对买方应在何时、何地检验货物，各国法律并无统一规定。结合以上有关制约检验时间、地点的各因素分析和当前国际上的习惯做法，关于合同中货物检验的时间和地点的规定，基本做法有以下几种：

（1）在出口国检验，又可分为在产地检验和装运前或装运时在装运港（地）检验；
（2）在进口国检验，分为在目的港检验和在买方营业地或最终用户所在地检验；
（3）在出口国检验，在进口国复验。
（4）在装运港检验重量，目的港检验品质。

三、检验机构

1. 国外检验机构

美国食品药物管理局（Food and Drug Administration，FDA）；法国国家实验室检测中心；日本通商产业检查所等官方机构，以及当今世界最大的检验鉴定公司，瑞士日内瓦通用鉴定公司（Secrete General De Surveillance，SGS）；美国保险人实验室（Underwriters Laboratory，UL）；英国劳氏船级社（Lloyd's Register of Shipping）；日本海事鉴定协会（Nippon Kanji Kentei Kyokai，NKKK）；英之杰检验集团（Inch cape Inspection and Testing Service，IITS）等民间检验机构。

2. 我国的检验检疫机构及其基本任务

2001年4月10日，国务院又将原国家质量技术监督局和原国家出入境检验检疫局合并为中华人民共和国质量监督检验检疫总局。自2018年4月20日起，出入境检验检疫系统统一以海关名义对外开展工作，完成旅检监管、通关作业申报查验放行"三个一"、运输工具登临检查、辐射探测、邮件监管、快件监管、报关报检企业资质注册以及对外"一个窗口"办理7个业务领域完成优化整合，实现"一口对外、一次办理"，并完成业务单证及印章的统一替换。

根据《中华人民共和国进出口商品检验法》的规定，地方检验检疫机构在进出口商品检验方面的基本任务有三项：

（1）实施法定检验，其范围包括：①列入《商检机构实施检验的进出口商品种类表》（简称《种类表》）规定的商品；②出口食品卫生的检验；③出口危险品的包装容器的性能鉴定和使用鉴定；④对装运出口易腐烂变质食品，冷冻品的船舱和集装箱等运载工具的适载检验；⑤有关国际条约或协议规定须经商检机构检验的进出口商品的检验。

（2）实施监督管理，其内容包括：①对法定检验以外的进出口商品进行抽查检验并实施监督管理；②开展进出口商品的质量认证工作，颁发认证证书，准许使用进出口商品质量认证标志等。

（3）办理鉴定业务，鉴定业务是指检验检疫机构凭对外贸易关系人（如出口生产企业、供货部门、进出口商品的收货、用货部门、运输、保险契约的有关各方）的申请或国外检验机构的委托，办理进出口商品鉴定业务，并签发各种鉴定证书，作为对外贸易关系人办理进出口商品交接、结算、计费、理算、报关、纳税、索赔、仲裁的有效凭证，还有签发产地证明（普惠制原产地证、一般原产地证及配额原产地证等）、价值证明、签封样品等。鉴定业务不是强制性的，故不同于法定检验。对外贸易关系人委托商检机构办理鉴定业务，应当提供合同、信用证以及有关单证。

四、检验证书

进出口商品经出入境检验检疫机构检验，鉴定后出具的证明文件，称为检验证书（inspection certificate）。常见的检验证书主要有：

（1）品质检验证书；
（2）重量或数量检验证书；
（3）包装检验证书；
（4）兽医检验证书；
（5）卫生检验证书；
（6）消毒检验证书；
（7）熏证书；
（8）价值证明书等。

五、检验依据和检验方法

1. 检验依据

对进出口商品进行检验并出证，必须先确定检验的依据。在国际贸易中：

（1）凡我国法律或行政法规所规定的强制性检验标准或其他必须执行的检验标准或对外贸易合同中所约定的检验标准；

（2）成交样品、合同、信用证、卖方提供的品质证明书、使用说明书、图纸等技术资料；

（3）海运提单、运单、卖方的发票、装货清单、重量明细单（磅码单）是对商品数量、重量检验的依据,均构成进出口商品检验的主要依据。

2. 检验方法

鉴于对同一项目、同一检验可能有多种方法可供选用,而所得结果却不尽相同,所以最好在合同中订明相应的检验方法。

六、买卖合同中的检验条款

国际货物买卖合同中的检验条款繁简不一,但主要内容包括:有关买方复检权的规定;检验或复验的地点;检验项目、检验依据和检验证书等,在此一例出口合同中的检验条款以供参考。

双方同意以装运港中国出入境检验检疫局签发的品质和数量(重量)检验证书作为信用证项下议付单据的一部分。买方有权对货物的品质、数量进行复验。复验费用由买方负担。如发现品质和/或数(重)量与合同不符,买方有权向卖方索赔,索赔期限为货到目的港××天内。

It is mutually agreed that the Inspection Certificate of quality and quantity (weight) issued by the China Exit and Entry Inspection and Quarantine Bureau at the port of shipment shall be part of the documents to be presented for negotiation under the relevant L/C. The buyers shall have the right to reinspect the quality and/or quantity (weight) be found not in conformity with that of the contract, the buyers are entitled to lodge with the Sellers a claim which should be supported by the sellers. The claim, if any, shall be lodged within ×× days after arrival of the cargo at the port of destination.

第二节 索 赔

国际货物买卖程序烦琐,履约时间长,外界环境变化较快,所以难免在履约过程中会碰到各种问题。当一方履约被对方认为与合同不符时,就可能发生争议(disputes)。而一方不履约或履约不符(即违约)(breach of contract)给对方造成损害时,对方就可能也可以依据相关法律对此损失提出索赔(claim),与此对应,对方受理此项索赔即为理赔。

一、有关违约的法律规定

违约(breach of contract)就是指合同双方当事人中任何一方不履行或不按合同约定履行合同义务。各国法律均认为依法有效成立的合同对当事人均具有法律约束力。

（1）英国法：将合同条款依其重要性分为条件（condition）和担保（warranty），违反合同的主要的、重要的条款及其义务视为违反条件（breach of condition），对方当时人有权解除合同并请求损害赔偿（赔偿损失）；如违反次要条款，则认为违反担保（breach of warranty）。对方在此种情况下，只能要求损害赔偿，不得解除合同。

（2）美国法：对违约的区分是从违约后果的严重程度，将违约分为重大违约（material breach）和轻微违约（minor breach），若属前者，对方当事人可解除合同并要求损害赔偿。否则，只能要求损害赔偿。

（3）《联合国国际货物销售合同公约》：第25条将违约分为根本性违约和非根本性违约。对于根本性违约，对方当事人可以解除合同并要求损失赔偿，若只构成非根本性违约，则只能请求损害赔偿。

（4）我国《合同法》第94条第2、第3款规定："当事人一方迟延履行主要债务，经催告在合理期限内仍未履行；当事人一方迟延履行债务或者有其他违约行为使合同不能实现目的。"对方可以解除合同，按照我国合同法，解除合同可以同损害赔偿并用。

二、合同中的索赔条款

在合同中订好索赔条款，对日后发生的索赔或理赔处理起来是十分有利的。

进出口合同中的索赔条款一般有两种规定方式：一种是异议和索赔条款（discrepancy and claim clause）；另一种是罚金条款（penalty clause）。大多数合同中只签订有异议和索赔条款，只有在买卖大宗商品和机械设备等商品时，合同中才会同时订立上述两种条款。

前者是针对卖方交货质量、数量或包装与合同规定不符而订立的。其内容包括：一方违约，对方有权索赔、索赔依据、索赔限期、赔偿办法及赔偿金额等；后者是国际货物买卖合同的罚金条款订立，一般是针对卖方延期交货或买方迟延付款或迟延接货等情况。在出现上述约定情形时，违约方（迟延履行合同义务一方）应支付给对方约定的金额，并且，同时免除卖方实际交货或买方付款或接货的义务。

一般情况下，我国的进出口合同只订立"异议与索赔条款"或"检验与索赔条款"，而对于连续分批交货的大宗货物买卖合同和机械设备一类商品的合同，才同时订立"罚金条款"。

第三节 不可抗力

国际货物买卖合同从签订到双方履约通常有一定的时间间隔，如自然灾害及突发战争等直接影响到当事人履行合同，甚至使其不能履行合同，这就要考虑是否予以免责或在何种情况下予以免责。在实践中，为了防止这类事件引发不必要的纠纷，双方当事人有必要在合同中订立不可抗力免责条款。

一、不可抗力的意义及认定

不可抗力（force majeure）又称人力不可抗拒。它是指在合同签订后，不是由于订约者任何一方的过失或疏忽，而是由于发生了当事人既不能预见和预防，又无法避免和克服的意外事故，以致不能履行或不能如期履行合同，遭受意外事故的一方，可以免除履行合同的责任或延期履行合同。

不可抗力通常分为两类：一类是由于自然力量引起的，如水灾、火灾、暴风雨、大雪、地震、泥石流等；另一类是由于社会力量引起的，如战争、罢工、政府禁令等。对于社会原因引发的意外事故，则解释上存在较大分歧。由于不可抗力条款是免责条款，又是法律的一项原则，所以，双方当事人尤其是卖方常常在援引不可抗力条款时有意扩大其范围，以减少自己的责任。因此，在合同中订入不可抗力条款就显得十分重要。但总体来说，对于不可抗力事件的认定原则基本相同，那就是：①意外事故必须是合同签订之后发生的；②不是由于合同双方当事人自身的过失或疏忽所致；③事件的发生及造成的后果是当事人无法预料、不能控制、无法避免和无法克服的。

二、不可抗力的处理

按照英、美、法合同落空原则，大陆法情事变更原则及其他各国法律的相关规定，当发生不可抗力致使合同一方当事人不能履行或不能按约定履行合同义务时，遭受不可抗力的一方当事人得予解除合同或变更合同履行条件，并免除其损害赔偿责任。

但究竟是解除合同还是变更合同履行条件，需视事故的原因、性质、规模及对履行合同所产生的影响程度而定，并明确规定在合同中。

三、合同中的不可抗力条款

国际货物买卖合同中的不可抗力条款主要规定以下内容：不可抗力事件的范围，不可抗力事件的处理原则和方法，不可抗力事件发生后通知对方的期限和方式，及出具相应证明文件的机构等。

我国进出口合同中的不可抗力条款，基本上有以下三种规定方法：

（1）概括式规定："由于不可抗力的原因，致使卖方不能全部或部分装运或延迟装运合同的货物，卖方对于这种不能装运或延迟装运合同货物不负责任。但卖方须用电报或电传通知买方并须在××天内以航空挂号信件向买方提交由中国国际贸易促进委员会出具证明此类事故的证明书。

（2）列举式规定："由于战争、地震、水灾、火灾、暴风雨、雪灾的原因，致使卖方不能全部或部分装运或延迟装运合同货物，卖方对这种不能装运或迟缓装运本合同货物不承担责任。但卖方须用电报或电传通知买方，并须在15天内以航空挂号信件向买方提交由中国国际贸易促进委员会出具证明此类事故的证明书"。

（3）综合式规定："如因战争、地震、水灾、火灾、暴风雨、雪灾或其他不可抗力的原因致使卖方不能全部或部分装运或延迟装运合同货物，卖方对这种不能装运或迟缓装运本合同货物不承担责任。但卖方须用电报或电传通知买方，并须在15天内以航空挂号信件向买方提交由中国国际贸易促进委员会出具证明此类事故的证明书"。

第四节 仲 裁

在国际贸易中，买卖双方因履行合同义务或对合同规定，发生争议是难免的事，如何正确处理这些争议，事关买卖双方和各自国家（地区），利益和声誉。国际贸易中争议的处理通常有：当事人进行协商解决、由第三人从中调解、提交仲裁和提起诉讼，尽管和解与调解省事省力，但有时却未必有用。所以，通常提交仲裁解决争议是国际货物买卖中争议处理的常用方法。

一、仲裁的含义及特点

仲裁（arbitration）又称公断，是指买卖双方在争议发生之前或之后，签订书面协议，自愿将争议提交双方同意的仲裁机构予以裁决，以解决争议的一种方式。这种裁决是终局性的，对双方当事人均有约束力，当事人双方必须遵照执行。

在国际货物买卖的争议和纠纷处理上。仲裁与诉讼相比，具有以下特点：仲裁以争议双方自愿为原则；提交仲裁和受理事件以仲裁协议为依据；仲裁机构和仲裁员由双方协议选定和仲裁具有终局效力。

二、仲裁形式与机构

目前，国际贸易仲裁绝大多数都通过常设的仲裁机构进行的，我国的涉外经贸仲裁机构是中国国际经济贸易仲裁委员会（China International Economical and Trade Arbitration Commission，CIETAC），委员会设在北京。世界上许多国家地区和一些国际组织都设有专门的常设仲裁机构，如英国伦敦仲裁院，瑞典斯德哥尔摩商会仲裁院等。这些机构一般都是民间社会性组织，其中许多仲裁机构与我国仲裁机构已有业务上的联系，在仲裁业务中有过合作。

三、仲裁程序

仲裁程序（arbitration procedure）是指进行仲裁的程序和做法。主要包括仲裁申请，组织仲裁庭，仲裁审理及仲裁裁决。对于一些争议金额较小，案情简单的案件，可以简化仲裁程序，以尽快结案。

四、国际货物买卖合同中的仲裁条款

我国在订立国际货物买卖合同时常用的仲裁条款有下列三种规定方法：

（1）在我国仲裁的条款，凡因本合同引起的或与本合同有关的任何争议，均应提交中国国际经济贸易仲裁委员会或其分会进行仲裁。仲裁裁决是终局的，对双方均有约束力。

（2）在被申请一方所在国仲裁的条款，凡因执行本合同所发生的或与本合同有关的一切争议，双方应通过友好协商解决；如果协商不能解决，应提交仲裁。仲裁在被申请一方所在国进行。如在中国，则由中国国际经济贸易仲裁委员会根据其仲裁规则进行仲裁。根据该仲裁机构规则进行仲裁。仲裁裁决是终局的，对双方均有约束力。

（3）在第三国仲裁的条款，凡因执行本合同所发生的或与本合同有关的一切争议，双方应通过友好协商解决；如果协商不能解决，应提交××××××（某第三国某地某仲裁机构）。根据该仲裁机构的仲裁规则进行仲裁/仲裁裁决是终局的，对双方都有约束力。

英文参考教程

Disputes, Claims, Arbitration and Force Majeure

A. Disputes and Claim

1. Disputes

In international trade, disputes often arise between the two parties when one party thinks that the other fails to carry out the duties stipulated in the contract wholly or partially, which very likely leads to claim, arbitration and legal action.

As to the main reasons which lead to disputes; the laws of different countries and international practices have different explanations. They can be generalized as follows:

1) Whether the contract is tenable.

2) Stipulations of the contract are unclear such as "prompt shipment", "quantity about 10,000 M/T", "destination European main ports" etc. which may bring about different interpretations.

3) During the performance of the contract, force majeure events arise which result in non-performance and delay performance of the contract, while as to the legal consequence of force majeure, the two parties may have different explanations.

4) Non-performance or incomplete performance of the contract is touched off by the seller, in such cases as inferior quality or discrepancy in quality, deficient or poor packing, insufficient quantity and delayed delivery, etc.

5) Non-performance or incomplete performance of the contract is caused by the buyer, for instance, the buyer does not dispatch a vessel to carry the goods or does not name the carrier in time, or does not open an L/C in time or rejects the goods unreasonably.

6) The carrier is liable for damage to or shortage in weight of the goods.

7) The insurer is liable for loss of, or damage to the goods.

The main contents of the disputes include breach of contract, facts concerning breach of contract, liabilities and legal consequences resulting from breach of contract.

The settlement of disputes should be made in a restrained and tactful way so that future relationships are not prejudiced. The two parties should negotiate amicably on the basis of equality and mutual benefit, or make conciliation through a third party; in case no settlement can be made through negotiation, the case shall be submitted to arbitration.

2. Claim and Satisfaction

Claim means that in international trade, one party breaks the contract and causes losses to the other party directly or indirectly, the party suffering the losses may ask for compensation for the losses.

Satisfaction means that the party breaking the contract declares that he will accept and handle the claim.

Generally speaking, in international trade, if any party does not fulfil the contract or cannot wholly fulfil the contract, his act amounts to breach of the contract.

There are two ways to determine the nature of breach. One way is based on the trade terms of the contract; the other is based on to the consequence of breach.

1) Based on trade terms: There are two kinds of undertakings entered into in every con-

tract. The more important of the two is called a condition.

A condition is a clause to which the parties, when making the contract, attribute such importance that it can truly be described as being of the essence of the contract. It goes to the root of the contract. To break a condition is to break the foundation of the contract and leads to an action for fundamental breach of contract.

The less important type of undertaking is called a warranty. A warranty does not go to the root of the contract, so the injured party cannot cancel the contract, but it does entitle him to compensation for breach of warranty.

Some countries, e. g., the United Kingdom, adopts this method. But British law does not stipulate clearly which belongs to "condition", which belongs to "warranty", so this method is quite flexible and at will.

2) Based on consequences of breach of contract: If one party breaks the contract and makes the other party unable to obtain the main profit, then this is called "material breach". In this case, the injured is entitled to cancel the contract and asks for compensation for losses.

If one party breaks the contract, but the case is not so serious and the other party will not lose any main profit, this is called "minor breach". In this case, the party suffering the losses is not entitled to cancel the contract, but he may ask for compensation for losses.

In "United Nations Convention on Contracts for the International Sale of Goods", these two undertakings are termed fundamental breach and non-fundamental breach.

3. The Points that We Should Pay Attention to in Handling Claim and Satisfaction

If we wish to lodge a claim, and the basis of our claim is that the goods or services have not delivered or offered in accordance with the contract in some vital way, which amounts to a breach of condition, or a breach of warranty, then we should prove it by a detailed presentation of the facts. This will leave the supplier very little alternative for compensation, if he wishes to avoid arbitration or action.

It is rather a complicated issue to handle claims of compensation in trade. A buyer, for instance, may make claims from different motives and under different circumstances. The buyer is justified to make claims of compensation if the seller is held responsible for inflicting losses on him. But there are cases in which the buyer intentionally finds fault with the seller due to the decline of the market price and other unfavorable factors. Such claims are commonly known as market claims. The seller, on the other hand, may also try to find fault with the buyer and make market claims. Thus the claims department or agent should be careful in handling such cases with special attention to the following points:

1) The contract and its clauses should be carefully studied, because a trade contract

signed by the seller and the buyer provides evidence of both parties' obligations. When one party makes claims against the other party, it is important to consult the contract to see whether such claims are justified.

2) A careful study should be made on the compensation claims including facts and reasons and documents that support them. The accuracy of the facts and circumstances should be scrutinized.

3) If the claims against an act in breach of the contract are justified, a further study should be made on its legal consequence that the side making the breach has to face. For instance, according to the standpoint of British law only a breach of condition can lead to the revocation of a contract and compensation for claims, while a breach of warranty, that is, a violation of the secondary terms of the contract, can only lead to compensation for claims and not the revocation of the contract. Therefore, it is very important to study the nature of a breach in handling cases of compensation for claims.

4) Once the nature of breach and responsibility for losses are determined, a further study should be made on the correct standards and methods to calculate the losses. It goes without saying that justified compensation should be made and the amount of compensation should be reasonable, and this involves whether the calculation standards and methods are correct or not.

4. Claim Clauses in the Contract

The most commonly used claim clauses are the discrepancy &, claim clause and the penalty clause.

1) The discrepancy & claim clause is stipulated in case the quality, quantity or packing of the goods delivered by the seller is not in conformity with the contract. The discrepancy & claim clause mainly includes the claim foundation and time limitation. For example, "Any claim by the buyers on the goods shipped shall be filed within 30 days after the arrival of the goods at the port of destination and supported by a survey report issued by a survey or approved by the sellers. Claims in respect of matters within responsibility of the insurance company and/or shipping company will not be considered or entertained by the sellers."

2) Penalty clause: The penalty clause is stipulated in case of delayed delivery by the sellers or delayed taking over the goods by the buyers. Its feature is that the two parties shall stipulate a certain percentage of penalty in advance in the contract. For example.

"In case of delayed delivery, the sellers shall pay to the buyers for every week of delay a penalty that amounts to 0.5% of the total value of the goods whose delivery has been delayed. Any fractional part of a week is to be considered a full week. The total amount of penalty shall not, however, exceed 5% of the total value of the goods involved in late delivery and be to be deducted from the price amount by the paying bank at the time of negotiation, or by the buyers directly at the time of payment. In case the period of delay exceeds 10 weeks after the stipulated delivery date, the buyers have the right to terminate this contract. But the sellers shall not thereby be exempted from the payment of penalty. "

5. Settlement of Claim

In some contracts, the two parties often stipulate clauses on settlement of claim as well as inspection & claim clauses.

In case the sellers are liable for the nonconformity of the goods with the contract and a claim is made by the buyers within the period of claim or the period of quality guarantee stipulated in the contract, the sellers may settle the claim upon the agreement of the buyers in the following ways:

1) Agree to the rejection of the goods and refund to the buyers the value of the rejected goods in the same currency as contracted herein, and bear all direct losses and expenses incurred from the rejection, including interest, banking charges, freight, insurance premium, inspection charges, storage charges and all other necessary expenses required for the custody and protection of the rejected goods.

2) Devaluate the goods according to the degree of inferiority, extent of damage and amount of losses suffered by the buyers.

3) Replace the defective goods with new ones which conform to the specification, quality and performance as stipulated in the contract, and bear all expenses incurred and direct losses sustained by the buyers. The sellers shall, at the same time, guarantee the quality of the replaced goods for a further agreed period.

B. Force Majeure Clause

Both parties to a legal contract have the obligations to fulfil the contract. Whichever party that fails to perform the prescribed obligations and acts in violation of the contract will hold legal liabilities. However in international trade practices, rules have formulated to deal legally with total or partial frustration of a contract resulting from no fault of any parties but from supervening forces. They are allowed to relieve liabilities of the nonperformance in certain circumstances. In the U.S., the American Uniform Commercial Code admits the excuse of "commercial impracticability"; in France, it is termed "force majeure"; and the German law uses the notion of collapse of the basis of transaction. These rules, when applied to trade, usually mean forces unforeseeable and unavoidable, termed "force majeure". It means that the frustration of the contract by the party in question results from natural or social forces including flood, earthquake, typhoon, fire, war and government decrees of prohibition beyond the control of man. This party shall be free from liability for performance, or be given an option of prolonging the performance of the contract owing to the above-mentioned event or series of events. In clause 1, article 79 of "the United Nations Conventions on Contracts for the International Sale of Goods", for example, it is stipulated:

"A party is not liable for a failure to perform any of his obligations if he proves that the failure was due to an impediment beyond his control and that he could not reasonably be expected to have taken the impediment into account at the time of the conclusion of the contract or to have avoided or overcome it or its consequences".

The party that is free from the liability according to the force majeure clause should satisfy the following two requirements. In the first place, the party should timely inform the other party right after the accident so that the latter is able to take necessary remedial measures. Otherwise, the former will still be held responsible for tqe loss or extended loss thus caused. Secondly, the party that failed to perform the contract should provide effective documentation describing the frustrating events and their consequences. If he fails to do this, or if the facts identified are not in conformity with his descriptions, the liability of his failure to perform the contract will not be exempted or exempted totally.

In case of force majeure events which only hinder the performance of the contract temporarily, "Warsaw – Oxford Rules 1932" stipulates:

"In the event of any of the said causes, accidents or hindrances preventing, hindering or impeding the production, the manufacture, the delivery to the seller, or the shipment of the goods contracted to be sold or any part thereof, or the chartering of any vessel or part of vessel, notice thereof shall be given to the buyer by the seller and on such notice being given the time for shipment or delivery into the custody of the carrier, as the case may be, shall be extended until the operation of the cause, accident or hindrance preventing, hindering or impeding the production, the manufacture, the delivery to the seller or the chartering of any vessel or part of vessel has ceased."

However, if any of the accidents continues for more than fourteen days from the time or from the expiration of the period Specified or reasonable for the shipment of the goods or their delivery into the custody of the carrier, the whole contract or such part thereof as shall remain to be fulfilled by the seller may, at the option of either party, be determined, such option shall be exercised and notice to that effect shall be given by either party to the other party at any time during the seven days next succeeding the period of fourteen days herein before mentioned but thereafter.

There are 3 ways to stipulate force majeure clauses: in a general way, in a way to list the contents or in a comprehensive way.

1) Stipulate the force majeure clause in a general way. For example, "If the shipment of the contract goods is prevented or delayed in whole or in part due to force majeure, the seller shall not be liable for non-shipment or late shipment of the goods of this contract. However, the seller shall notify the buyer by cable or telex and furnish the latter within 15 days by registered airmail with a certificate issued by the China Council for the Promotion of International Trade attesting such event or events."

2) Stipulate the force majeure clause in a to list the contents way. For example, "If the shipment of the contracted goods is prevented or delayed in whole or in part by reason of war earthquake, flood, fire, storm, heavy snow, the seller shall not be liable for non-shipment of the goods of this contract. However, the seller shall notify the-buyer by cable or telex and furnish the latter within 15 days by registered airmail with a certificate issued by the China Council for the Promotion of International Trade attesting such event or events."

3) Stipulate the force majeure clause in a comprehensive way, for example, "If the shipment of the contract goods is prevented or delayed in whole or in part by reason of war, earthquake, flood, fire, storm, or other causes of force majeure, the seller shall not be liable for non-shipment or late shipment of the goods of this contract. However, the seller shall notify the buyer by cable or telex and furnish the latter within 15 days by registered airmail with a certificate issued by the China Council for the Promotion of International Trade attesting such event or events."

C. Arbitration

In international trade practice, in case of disputes, the two parties should try to settle the disputes through amicable negotiations. In case no settlement can be reached through negotiation, the case shall then be settled through conciliation, arbitration or even litigation.

Arbitration means that the two parties, before or after the disputes arise, reach a written agreement that they will submit the disputes which cannot be settled through amicable negotiations to the third party for arbitration.

Arbitration has two characteristics. First, an agreement must be reached between the two parties on solving the disputes through arbitration. The agreement may be reached before or after the occurrence of the disputes, that is by signing a written arbitration agreement between the interested parties. When applying for arbitration, the party concerned must submit the contract which includes a clause for arbitration or a temporary agreement on arbitration i. e., submission, otherwise the application will be rejected. Secondly, the ruling of arbitration is in general final. That is, the arbitrators to whom the two parties have agreed to resort shall make the final award. The interested parties cannot refuse the ruling or appeal to the court unless they can prove with facts that the arbitration is against the law or the arbitrators have acted unfairly.

In comparison with negotiations, arbitration is more likely to settle the disputes and the binding force is much stronger; in comparison with legal actions, arbitration is more flexible, quicker and cheaper. Arbitration is of the will of the two parties themselves, so the future business relationships are not jeopardized.

The differences between arbitration and legal actions can be generalized as follows: the legal action has jurisdiction, while arbitration has not; arbitration is of the two parties'own will; in case no agreement can be reached, any party cannot force the other party to submit to arbitration while resorting to judicial proceedings the plaintiff may take a unilateral action against the defendant without agreement between the two parties inadvance, arbitrators are appointed by the two parties, while judges are appointed by the government arbitration can be handled according to commercial practices so arbitration is more flexible and permissive; thus, in international trade, in case no settlement can be reached through amicable negotiations, the two parties would like to submit to arbitration, while a case is tried in accordance with the law if it is brought to a court. According to international commercial practices an arbitration agreement is a prior arrangement and a precondition.

The arbitration agreement is a written agreement in which the two parties declare that they are willing to submit to arbitration. It is used as evidence for cognizance of the disputes.

There are two types of arbitration agreement, one is called arbitration clause which is concluded before the disputes arise, in which the two parties declare that in case of disputes, they are willing to submit to arbitration. This type of agreement is generally included in the contract. The other type is called submission which is concluded after the disputes arise, in which the two parties declare that they are willing to submit to arbitration. This type of arbitration agreement is independent of the contract.

The China Foreign Trade Arbitration Commission stipulates in its "Provisional Rules of Arbitration Proceedings" that the effect of the arbitration clause in the contract and that of arbitration clauses concluded in other forms are completely the same.

The functions of arbitration agreement mainly show in the following aspects:

1) In case disputes arise, arbitration agreement is the basis for settlement of disputes, and is binding upon both parties.

2) It is the warranty for arbitration authorities and arbitrators to obtain the jurisdiction.

3) The arbitration agreement eliminates the jurisdiction of the court over the relative case. In case an arbitration agreement is reached, the interested parties cannot appeal to the court any more.

The above mentioned 3 functions are closely related, but the third is the most important one.

The arbitral proceedings usually include the plaintiff's application, the defendant's defence or countercharge, the formation of arbitral tribunal, the hearings and the award-making.

1) Application for arbitration and defense: The plaintiff or complainant shall submit an arbitration application to the arbitration authority which should include the names and addresses of plaintiff and defendant, the arbitration agreement supporting facts and evidence, requirements of the plaintiff.

After receiving the application, the arbitration authority should ask the defendant to defend himself by the statement of defense and the documentary evidence against the questions mentioned in the application. If the defendant wants to make a counter claim, he should lodge within 45 days after receiving the application and other documents sent by the arbitration authority.

2) Formation of arbitration tribunal and hearings: After disputes have been submitted to the arbitration authority, the interested parties shall appoint arbitrators to give hearings to the case for arbitration. According to international practices, the parties concerned shall determine the number of arbitrators and the way to appoint the arbitrators.

There are usually 3 arbitrators, of whom two are appointed by the interested parties, while the third one is appointed by the chairman of the arbitration authority or by the two appointed arbitrators. The third one is usually the chief arbitrator or umpire 53. In case of sole arbitrator, i.e., only one arbitrator hears the case and makes the award, the arbitrator can be appointed by the interested parties or the arbitration authority.

3) Award: The arbitrate tribunal shall give hearings to the case in accordance with the arbitration rules. The award is decided by majority votes and the minority opinion, if any, may be in writing and docketed into the arbitral file. The tribunal may render an interim or provisional award, part award and final award, as the case may be. The conclusion of the award shall be declared to the parties at the closing session of the hearings. The award shall be in writing and signed by the presiding arbitrator and the arbitrators or by the sole arbitrator. The award is usually final and has the force of law binding upon both parties. The award shall be executed by the parties within the time fixed in-the award. In case it is not executed by one party after the expiration of the fixed time limit, the other party may ask the relative court to enforce it in accordance with the law.

Arbitration clauses in the contract shall stipulate clearly the place of arbitration, arbitration authority, arbitration rules and the effectiveness of award.

The place of arbitration, in some degree, decides which rules and proceedings should be adopted in arbitration. In our export trade, we should try to make arbitration in our country. Of course, according to different cases, we can also agree to make arbitration in the country of the defendant or in a third country.

1) In Our Country

"All disputes arising out of the performance of, or relating to this contract, shall be settled amicably through negotiation. In case no settlement can be reached through negotiation, the case shall then be submitted to the China International Economic and Trade Arbitration Commission, Beijing, China, for arbitration in accordance with its Rules of Arbitration. The arbitral award is final and binding upon both parties."

2) In the Country of Defendant

"All disputes arising out of the performance of, or relating to this contract, shall be settled amicably through friendly negotiation. In case no settlement can be reached through negotiation, the case shall then be submitted for arbitration. The location of arbitration shall be in the country of the domicile of the defendant. If in China, the arbitration shall be conducted by the China International Economic and Trade Arbitration Commission, Beijing, China, in accordance with its rules of arbitration. If in … the arbitration shall be conducted by … in accordance with its arbitral rules of procedure. The arbitral award is final and binding upon both parties."

3) In the Third Country

"All disputes arising out of performance of, or relating to this contract shall be settled amicably through friendly negotiation. In case no settlement can be reached through negotiation, the case shall then be submitted to … for arbitration, in accordance with its arbitral rules of procedure. The arbitral award is final and binding upon both parties."

（资料来源：丁溪，唐赛. 国际贸易理论与实务 [M]. 中国商务出版社，2013.）

▶本章小结

在国际贸易中，引起争议的原因可归纳为卖方违约、买方违约、买卖双方均负有违约责任。索赔条款的规定一般有两种方法：异议和索赔条款、罚金条款。

不可抗力是一项免责条款。当发生不可抗力使合同无法履行或如期履行时，发生事故的一方可据此免除责任。不可抗力的发生可能是社会力量引起的，也可能是自然力量引起的。解决国际贸易争议的方式包括友好协商、调解、仲裁和司法诉讼四种。

➤ 本章名词

对外贸易争议　根本性违约　异议和索赔条款　违约金　定金　不可抗力　对外贸易仲裁　仲裁协议　仲裁程序

➤ 理论思考

1. 确定检验时间和地点的方法有哪些？
2. 商检证书的作用有哪些？
3. 我国实施法定检验的范围如何？
4. 索赔和理赔的含义是什么？
5. 买卖合同中不可抗力条款的内容有哪些？
6. 书面仲裁协议有哪几种形式？

➤ 实训习题

一、熟悉以下网站名称

1. 中华人民共和国海关总署　　　　　http：//www.customs.gov.cn
2. 中商外贸商机网　　　　　　　　　www.chinaccm.com
3. 中华涉外网　　　　　　　　　　　www.trade.9c9c.com.cn
4. 中国国际经济贸易仲裁委员会　　　www.cietac.org.cn
5. 中国国际经贸仲裁委员会深圳分会　www.cietac-sz.org.cn

二、利用网络内容办理、处理检验索赔的具体工作

贵单位有进出口货物各一批，报关前需商检，根据如下情况写明具体程序：

1. 出口货物：大米木桶装——输往美国、自理报检、冬季装运；
2. 进口货物：牛皮中底（做皮鞋用）货已到岸、因工作忙需代理报检、皮底属动物类产品；

（提示：报检地点、联系电话、出境货物出运期限、此类产品及包装进出口有特殊要求及规定、能否免检以及检验时应提供什么单据）

3. 当你单位一批价值23 000美元的货物出现索赔仲裁时，帮你单位寻一知名仲裁机构，名称_____仲裁机构处理仲裁案件收费是_____。

三、写出世界上知名检验机构的名称各二个

官方机构：

半官方机构：

非官方机构：

四、写出权威性标准组织各二个

国际标准：　　　　　　　区域标准：

行业标准： 国家标准：

五、翻译下列证书英文名称

1. 品质检验证书
2. 重量检验证书
3. 数量检验证书
4. 卫生检验证书
5. 原产地证明书
6. 普惠制产地证明书

CHAPTER 9

第九章 出口合同的履行

> **本章指导**
>
> 通过本章的学习,要求能够了解出口业务的基本运作程序,特别是从实际业务的角度了解每个环节的操作要点和注意事项,重点学会:
>
> 1. 如何备货,如何安排运输;
> 2. 怎样落实、审核信用证;
> 3. 对违约的处理办法。

在出口合同的履行过程中,涉及银行、海关、港务、船务公司等各个部门的配合与协助,才能做到科学管理、细致严谨,尽量避免工作脱节,以确保安全收汇等项任务的顺利实施,保证出口合同的有效履行。

在我国出口合同中大多数采用 CIF(CFR)或 CIP/(CPT) 贸易术语和 L/C 结算方式下,实施出口合同履行过程中,必须切实做好货(备货)、证(信用证的各项工作)、运(租船订舱、办理货运手续)、款(制单结汇)四个环节的工作。本章以上为参考,将出口合同履行所涉及的业务环节逐一阐述如下。

第一节 备 货

备货是出口合同履行的第一个主要的步骤,要求出口方根据合同和信用证的规定,按时、按质、按量地准备好应当交付的货物,主要包括:与生产加工及仓储部门联系,安排货物的生产、收购等事宜,向专门的机构办理有关单据的签证和认证等手续。

一、安排货物的生产与收购

正式合同签订之后,在进口方准备办理开信用证的同时,出口方即可以着手进行备货的各项安排，具体做法是：向生产加工及仓储部门下达联系单（有些公司称其为加工通知单）。如需要临时生产的，应通知厂方安排生产，并进行必要的整理、包装，落实交货期；如仓库有现货的，应通知仓库按合同的要求提取规定数量的商品，进行整理、加工和包装。在具体操作中要做到：

（一）准确理解合同有关交货品质的具体规定

在联系单中准确填写货物的品名、规格、花色等内容，定期对生产、加工等部门进行检查和督促，及时发现问题并加以解决，保证商品的品质符合合同规定的要求。

（二）确切把握合同中有关交货数量的具体规定

备货时应考虑有一定的备用量，以防装运时可能发生的调换和适应舱容之用。

（三）认真研究合同中有关货物的包装条款

在下达联系单时，详细列明对货物的唛头要求。如合同或信用证中对包装仅作笼统规定，应根据双方订立合同时所协商一致的意见办理，或按同类货物通用的方式包装。货物交付前，应仔细检查货物的包装是否牢固，如发现有破漏、松腰、开包、水渍等不良情况，应及时进行修整或换装。

仓库或工厂在备妥货物后，将整批货物的箱数、箱号、每箱数量、尺寸、色别搭配等内容填入尺码单后，再填制"货物出仓单"或"货物出运委托书"。这是商品出口在储存地点提货及内部销账、核算所留用的凭证。这种单据无统一格式，基本内容包括商品的名称、数量、件数、唛头、发货仓库等。一般根据进出口的工作程序一式数联不等，通常情况下有六联。

第一联在托运时交外运公司作工作单用，以便外运公司正确安排车运。第二联为出货报告单之主联，由出口公司的储运部门加盖提货印章后作提单用。外运公司根据船期及进栈在上面注明出货日期、船名、关单号，在出货前一天将此单送达进出口公司或其厂方、仓库，以备货待运。第三、第四、第五联，由出口公司的财会部计算成本、配制发票以及批销栈单，作记账凭证之用。第六联，由出口公司的业务部门作商品的细账记录及留底之用。

二、办理出口签证和认证

在出口合同的履行过程中，有时为了执行国家的有关规定或根据信用证的要求，必须向专门机构办理有关单据的签证和认证手续。

（一）办理许可证

对属于我国出口许可证管理目录中的商品，应办理出口许可证，它包括计划配额、一般许可证管理或主动配额出口许可证等。对输往国家、地区有配额限制的商品，应办理配额出口许可证。一般应事先向有关外贸主管部门申请办理相关手续。

（二）办理产地证

对享受普惠制待遇的商品应办理普惠制产地证，一般由中华人民共和国海关总署签发。对享受最惠国待遇或其他关税优惠待遇的商品应办理普通产地证，又称原产地证。它一般由中国国际贸易促进委员会（亦称中国国际商会）或海关总署签发即可。

（三）办理商检证书

对属于法定检验或合同中明确规定要求经过检验的商品，要在货物备妥后向中华人民共和国海关总署或其他商检机构申请报验。凡属法定检验的商品，应在指定的商检机构，按规定的日期、地点报验；属公证鉴定业务，则可根据买卖合同的规定确定申报机构。鉴定业务可选择上海英斯贝克商品检验有限公司、上海东方天祥检验服务有限公司等机构。申请检验的手续为：出口方先填写"出口报验申请单"，一般要求用中文和英文或另外一种外文填写，并附合同或信用证副本及有关单据，向检验机构申报。商检部门则在检验合格后，签发检验证书或在报关单上加盖印章，海关凭此放行。

三、备货过程中的注意事项

（1）商品的备货数量必须符合合同交货数量的规定，并且备妥货物的数量应按合同规定的交货数量稍许增加以留有适当的余地，以备装运过程中货物出现损坏或短少时，需要进行调换和增补之用。

（2）商品的包装既要符合合同的规定，又要适合运输的要求。如发现包装不良或损坏，应及时进行整修或换装。唛头等运输标志应严格按合同规定的式样印刷。

（3）货物备妥的时间必须严格按照出口合同和信用证规定的交货时间和期限，结合运输条件（如通过海运的货物应结合船期）进行安排。为防止意外，一般还应适当留有余地。

第二节　落实信用证

在采用以信用证方式收汇时，出口方于准备货物的同时，也要关注信用证的落实。进出口业务中有这样的说法："信用证不到不备货，信用证没有修改好不装船。"这是指如果进口方不按时开来信用证，货备好了也没法装运出去；信用证来迟了，会给安排装运方面的一系列工作造成忙乱与被动，甚至影响到整个交易的完成。所以，必须在备货的同时，兼顾信用证的落实情况，必要时向进口方进行催促。这就是通常所说的"催证"环节。对方开来信用证后，还应进行审核和修改，这是落实信用证中的"审证"和"改证"环节。

一、催证

催证就是以某种通信方式催促进口方办理开证的手续，以便出口方履行交货义务。按合同规定及时开证是进口方的重要义务，在正常情况下无须催证。但在实际业务中，由于合同规定的装运期限较长，进口方准备工作迟缓，进口商遇到本国市场发生变化或资金发生短缺等情况时，往往拖延开证。对此，出口方有必要在适当的时候，提醒和催促对方按合同规定开来信证。必要时还可在催证通知中提醒其不能按期开证所应承担的法律后果。大宗商品交易或按买方要求而特制的商品交易，更应结合备货情况及时进行催证。

开证时间一般应在出口方装运期前的一定时间（例如30天）。如果出口方根据备和承运船舶的情况，可以提前装运时，也可商请对方提前开证。

催证的方式，除直接向国外客户发函电通知之外，也可商请中国银行驻外分支机构或我国驻外商务机构等予以协助。

二、审证

在出口方通过通知行收到进口方开来的信用证之后，应当先对信用证的内容进行全面的审核，而不是急于去联系出运货物，这是由进出口贸易的复杂性决定的。因为买卖虽说有合同作为信用证条款的依据，但是进口方（开证申请人）、开证银行往往会有疏忽；某些国家、地区的贸易习惯、规定与出口方所在国会有所不同，以及对出口方所在国的有关政策、规定可能不了解；有时甚至是出于进口方有意识的欺骗行为，开来的信用证内容会有许多与合同内容不相一致的地方。所以出口方当事人必须对国外来证逐字、逐句、逐项进行仔细、认真的审核。

（一）审证的依据

信用证审核的依据是货物买卖合同及《跟单信用证统一惯例 UCP600》的规定。一张信用证能否接受，或是否需修改，主要取决于四个条件。

（1）证内有无政治上对我方歧视或我国不能接受的条款，开证行资信是否可靠。

(2) 对安全、迅速收汇是否有影响。

(3) 对同我国签订贸易、支付协定的国家的来证，其内容是否与协定的精神有矛盾。

(4) 证内所要求的各项条件和对单证的要求等，是否与销售合同一致，以及我们在实际执行中有无困难。

（二）银行的审证

在实际业务中，由有关银行和出口公司共同承担审证业务，其中通知银行着重审核开证行的政治背景、资信能力、付款责任和索汇路线等方面的内容。具体包括以下几个方面。

1. 来证是否符合我国的对外政策。

如果信用证来自与我国签有贸易协定国家的银行时，应该检查开证行是否属于协定中指定的银行，所使用的货币与记账方式是否符合协定的规定等。不符合规定的应拒绝接受。

2. 开证行的资信，包括资金储备情况，支付能力及商业信誉等。

如系支付能力差或商业信誉不好的开证行，建议受益人（即出口方）向进口方要求，信用证由资信情况好的银行进行保兑。

3. 信用证的真伪。

审核信用证的签字、印鉴是否真迹，电开证的密押是否符合，等等。

4. 索汇路线是否可靠。

审核开证银行与通知银行之间是否有代理或其他业务往来关系，信用证的付款责任是否明确，索汇路线是否完全可靠。

（三）出口企业的审证

如果银行审查没有发现问题，便可在信用证正本上加盖证实书戳印后交出口公司进行审核。出口公司着重审核信用证内容与买卖合同是否一致。具体包括：

1. 信用证的性质和种类是否与合同规定相符。

我国一般要进出口贸易中的信用证，必须具有不可撤销的性质。如果对方开来的是不可撤销的信用证，但证内有限制条款，如"接到我方通知后生效"或"领取进口许可证后生效"等，原则上不予以接受。

如果合同规定采用即期付款的办法，而来证却要求开远期汇票，则应判断是真远期还是假远期。凡在信用证条款中列明由开证行保证贴现，所有利息和贴现费由申请人负担，受益人可以即期收汇的，被认为是假远期信用证，一般对此出口方可以考虑接受。否则不可接受，应要求其改证。

对于对开信用证，应查明证的生效时间，以防止出口方履行了交货义务后，进口方却不再履行其义务。如果没有关于生效时间的限制性文句，则应要求对方加列。

对于循环信用证，应审核循环次数、金额、循环方式是否与合同相符，否则应要求对方改证。

2. 开证申请人和受益人名称、地址是否与合同相符。

开证申请人大都是买卖合同的对方当事人（买方），但也可能是对方的客户（实际买户或第二买主）；受益人通常是出口公司，是买卖合同中的卖方，但有时也可能有名称、地址上的更改，所以应当仔细核对，以防错发错运。

3. 信用证中的商品名称、规格、数量、包装是否与合同中的规定相一致。

如有差错，应要求对方修改，不能简单地按照办理。

4. 价格部分。

总金额、货币种类是否与合同规定的相符；总金额是否与单价、数量的乘相等；金额的大小写的值是否一致；有的没有考虑溢短装的情况；在货币的种类不一致时，是否规定有合理的折算的方法，我方能否接受等。

5. 信用证的装运期，有效期和到期地点。

注意有效期一般比装运期晚15天左右，但最迟不超过21天。以出口方能在装运货物后有足够的办理单证时间，又不至于耽误进口方及时提取货物。如来证的装运期太近，无法按时备货，应及时通过开证行要求进口方延展日期。信用证的到期地点应在我国境内，如规定在进口地或第三国到期，应考虑我方是否有能力接受。不然，可不予接受。

6. 信用证中的装船与分批条款，保险条款以及选港费，港口拥挤费等费用的支出，是否与合同规定的相一致。

如果不一致，我方能否接受。

7. 信用证所列的单据与出票条款。

来证中要求提供的单据种类、份数及填写方法，是否与合同规定的相一致，有无添加或更改。如果有，我方能否接受。例如，信用证如果要求整加合同中未列的产地证书，对于转口贸易的卖方则有可能办不到，导致发货后无法议付。对此，出口方应要求改证。

8. 信用证责任条款及其他特殊条款。

审证有开证行保证付款的声明。如出现指定船公司，指定船籍、船龄等。或不准在某个港口转船等，实施中不易办到的，一般不应轻易接受。不同的信用证，内容各不相同，出口方应对此作出认真地对待。

三、改证

信用证经审核后，如果发现有问题，应区别问题的性质，分别同银行、运输、保险、商检等有关部门研究，作出恰当妥善的处理。凡是属于不符合我国对外贸易方针政策，影响合同的履行和收汇安全的问题，必须要求国外修改信用证。

信用证条款涉及有关当事人的权利和义务，所以修改信用证必须符合一定的法律程序。《跟单信用证统一惯例》（以下简称《统一惯例》）第9条规定，未经开证行、保兑行（若已保兑）和受益人同意，不可撤销信用证既不能修改，也不能取消。这句话表明，虽然信用证可由受益人提出修改，也可由开证申请人主动要求改变内容，但这种修改内容的确定，必须要在有关当事人全部确认后方能实现。因此，改证的程序应当是：

（1）受益人向开证申请人提出或开证申请主动提出；

（2）经开证行传递到通知行，转告受益人；

（3）受益人认可修改意见。

凡受益人经审核确实需要修改的各项内容，如果不止一处，应做到一次性向开证人提出，尽量避免因考虑不周而提出多次修改要求，以便减少对方的手续办理时间和费用负担。

开证行同意开证申请人意见修改信用证后，即发出修改通知书，以信件、电报、或电传等方式通知通知行，再由通知行转告受益人。一般开证行不能直接接受通知受益人，开证申请人也不能将修改通知书直接寄送受益人。如受益人受到由开证申请人或开证行直接寄来的修改通知书，应提交原证给通知行核实。

根据《跟单信用证统一惯例 UCP600》规定："对同一修改通知书中的修改内容不允许部分接受。因此，部分接受修改内容当属无效。"为此，当受益人认为修改通知书中的内容部分符合要求，部分仍与自己提出的要求相违背时，除认为可全部接受对方要求之外，应及时向指定通知行作出全部不接受的表示，提醒对方推倒重来，而不能作出只接受其中一部分，拒绝其余部分的表态。

根据《跟单信用证统一惯例 UCP600》的新规定，受益人应对接受或拒绝修改做出表示。这种表示既可在收到修改书后立即做出，也可以延至交单时做出，在时间上并无具体限制，考虑到原信用证条款（或先前接受过修改的信用证），在受益人发出接受修改表示之前，仍对受益人有效，所以，受益人应在收到修改通知书并经审核认可后才可以发运货物，切忌仅凭对方"已经修改"的通知就装运发货，以免造成出口方工作上的分歧和经济上的损失。

第三节　安　排　运　输

出口公司在收妥信用证并备妥货物后，即可根据信用证的装运期安排运输事宜。这一阶段主要应办理货物运输手续，按国家的有关规定申报出口报关等事项，如由出口方负责投保，还应办理保险手续。

一、托运

在需要由出口方安排运输的出口合同履行中，出口方按合同规定负责租订运输工具，办理托运手续。在我国，有关外贸运输事宜一般都委托中国对外贸易运输公司，或其他经营外贸业务的企业代办。鉴于目前我国的出口合同一般仍以海运为主要运输方式，而在这类合同中除出口商品数量较大的合同需要租船装运外，一般均通过租定班轮舱位安排货物运输，故以下着重介绍订班轮舱位和托运的一般程序。

（1）查看船期表，填写"托运单"。班轮公司或外运机构一般每月都编制一份船期表，其中列有航线、船名及航次、船舶抵港及离港日期、截止收单期、沿途停靠港口等内容。出口公司在完成备货、收到信用证后，按信用证和合同的有关内容与条款，填写海运出口托运单，送交外运机构作为订舱依据。

（2）外运机构收到"托运单"后，会同中国外轮代理公司，根据配载原则、货物数量与品质特性、装运港与目的港情况，结合船期，具体安排船只和舱位。船方据此编制配载图。然后由外轮代理公司减法"装货单"（也称"下货纸"），作为船方收货装运的凭证。

（3）出口公司在申请货物出口报关并经海关签章放行后，即组织人力将货物运往指定的口岸码头，准备装船。如果此笔交易应由卖方投保，这时应联系办理保险手续。如由买方自办保险，则应向买方发出装船通知。

（4）在海关人员的现场监督下，出口货物开始装船。港区按配载图（又称货物积载图）所列舱位堆置货物，船方有专职理货员负责监督装船，具体核对所装货物的唛头、件数、包装方式、质量等。出口公司此时应派人员现场查看，一旦发现上船货物有问题，即作适当的补救处理。必要时亦可申请海关的检验部门在装船前验舱，防止船舱污秽、串味，影响出口商品品质。

（5）货物装船完毕，理货员在装船单上填入实际装船的时间、数量、舱位等，签名后转交船方。船长或大副据此签发"收货单"（也称"大副收据"）。托运人收取"收货单"后，凭此向外轮代理公司交付运费，换取正式提单。

（6）船舶办妥离境港手续后，出口方应向对方发出通知，以便进口方接货，办理进口报关手续等。

托运过程中委托方必须提供与出运货物有关的必要单据和资料，其中最主要的是具有委托书性质的托运单。按照不同的运输方式，托运单的形式及格式不尽相同。其中陆运无固定格式的托运单，空运使用空运托运单，海运使用海运托运单。后者一式共12联，第一联由外轮代理公司配船后留底，凭以编制装货清单和出口载货清单。第二、第三联是出运后的运费通知。外运公司审核无误后，将其中一联送出口公司收取运费，另一联由外运公司自己留底。第四、第五联为装货单与收货单。装货单由船代理配船后签章，即成为有效的装货凭证。两份单据都要在货物装上船时，注明装载船名、舱位、实收件数和理货员签字后，交大副签收。大副留下装货，并在收货单上签字后，交还外运公司，凭以换取提单。第六、第七联各为出口公司与外运公司代理订舱后的留底。第八、第九联在配船订舱完毕后，由船代理填入有关内容后，退还货主或外运公司。其中一联外运公司凭以缮制订舱记录卡（船卡），办理保险（由外运公司代理保险时），或寄发装船通知；另一联供出口公司凭以预制轮船公司格式的提单和填制报关单。第十联为缴纳出口货物港务费申请书，是货物进码头仓库而未装船前，存仓时的码头存仓记录；在货物装船后，凭以收取港务费用。最后两联是空白无格式的，其中一联在货物进仓后贴于桩脚上以备查用；另一联作码头仓库存查之用。

二、报关

货物装运出口前必须向海关申报，习称"通关"。按照我国海关法规定，一切进出口的货物都必须由设有海关的港口、车站、空港、国际邮件交换站或国界孔道进出，向海关办理申报手续，经海关查验后才可予以放行。

凡需要向海关办理报关手续的出口公司，都应事先填写《报关注册登记申请书》，随附国务院各省、自治区、直辖市有关主管部门批准的开业证件、工商行政管理部门核发的营业执照副本或影印件，向海关办理"报关注册登记证明书"后方可向所在地区各口岸海关办理报关手续。

海关对出口货物的监管，要经过申报、查验、放行等通关环节。

（一）出口公司申报

出口货物发货人一般应在装运的 24 小时前，向海关申报。集装箱通常要求在装运的 3 天前申报。出口报关企业应填写"出口货物报关单"一式两份，作为报关的基本依据，并交验下列单证。

（1）出口许可证和国家规定的其他批准文件；
（2）提单、装货单或运单；
（3）发票一份；
（4）装箱单一份，散装货物或单一品种且包装内容一致的件装货物可免交；
（5）减税、免税或免验的证明文件；
（6）对应施行商品检验、文物鉴定或受其他管制的进出口货物，应交验有关主管部门签发的证件（如商检证、卫生检验证、原产地证、品质证、配额证书等）。

海关在认为必要时，还可调阅买卖合同、产地证明和其他有关单证、账册等。在报关单证齐全有效、填报内容正确无误，并符合政策规定的情况下，海关才接受申报。

（二）海关查验货物

一切出口货物除经海关总署特准免检者外，必须接受海关查验，以确定实际货物是否与所申报的内容相一致，是否符合有关规定，能否满足审价、征税的需要等。查验货物一般应在受海关监管上进行。特殊情况下也可在海关同意的有关场所进行，但此时须向海关缴纳规费。

海关查验时，报关员应按照海关指定的时间，到现场协助海关查验，并按照海关的要求负责搬移货物、开拆或重封货物的包装等。

（三）海关放行

海关在审核单证、查验货物后，如没有发现不正常的情况即通知报关企业按章纳税。报关员在规定时间内办理缴纳关税、其他税费或海关罚款手续后，海关在"装货单"上盖章，签后即可放行。对已经海关放行的出口货物，因故未能装运出口，待运输工具装货完毕后，承运人或货方应立即向海关申报撤销该货的出口，作退关处理。

三、投保

在出口货物装船出运前，如果属出口方负责运输保险的，应按照合同规定的要求办理保险手续，填写保险单据，交由保险公司签发。当货物所有权转移时，出口企业应在保险单上背书，办理过户手续。

投保人在投保时，应将货物名称、保额、运输路线、运输工具、开航日期、投保险别等一一列明。我国业务量较大的出口公司，为简化手续、节省时间，可经与中国人民保险公司事先协商，改用有关出运货物的单据副本，如商业发票、出口货物明细单、报关单等，再加注保险金额、保险险别等内容，代替投保单。保险公司接受投保后，签发保险单据一式若干份，除一份留底，其余交投保人。

当货物抵达目的港（地）发现残损时，进口方作为保险单的合法受让人，应就地向保险公司或其代理人要求赔偿。中国各保险公司为便利我国出口货物运抵国外目的地及时检验损失，就地给予赔偿，已在100多个国家建立了检验或理赔代理机构。

第四节 制单结汇

在信用证、托收等支付方式下，出口方于货物装运之后，都应按照有关规定正确缮制各种单据，及时送交银行办理结算，从而完成一笔有效的出口贸易。它一般包括制单与结汇两个环节。

一、制单

制单是指出口方按信用证或/和合同的规定，制作凭以向银行议付货款或通过银行向进口方收款单据。

在采用象征性交货方式的条件下，凭单交货、凭单付款是这类交货方式的基本特征。银行在处理业务中，处理的主要是单据，特别是在信用证支付的条件下，银行只根据信用证条款办事，而不管合同的规定；只凭单据支付货款，而不问实际的货物。所以出口公司在制单过程中，一定要准备好所需的单证，做到单证一致、单单一致、单货一致。否则，则可能遭到银行拒付或进口方拒付。因此，在制单过程中，应做到正确、完整、及时、简明、整洁。这样不仅可以提高结汇速度，而且不易引起误解与争议。

出口单据种类繁多，一般主要有汇票、发票、海关发票、海运提单或其他运输单、保险单、产地证书、商品检验证书以及包装单、扣佣通知书等，其中有些单据只在特定的条件下使用。现介绍常见的出口单据如下。

（一）汇票

汇票（bill of exchange，draft）无论是在托收项下还是在信用证下，都由出口公司填写。一般汇票有两张正本，具有同等效力，银行在寄送单据时，分两次寄发汇票，以防丢失。付款人只据其中一张汇票付款，一份付讫后另一份自动失效。在信用证的支付方式下，汇票上可注明开证行的名称、信用证号码及开证日期。汇票的付款人为开证行，受款人应为出口公司。如属托收方式，汇票上应注明有关合同号码。

（二）发票

发票有多种，常用的有商业发票、海关发票、领事发票、厂商发票、形式发票等。

1. 商业发票（commercial invoice）

它是出口方向进口方签发的对所装运货物作全面细节说明的货款价目总清单。它可作为出口商发货的书面凭证；供进口方作为验收、核对货物数量、重量、规格等的依据；可作为双方收付款记账的凭证；供双方办理报关手续、缴纳出口税和清点的依据；在既期汇款又不需要出具汇票时，代替汇票办理付款的手续；亦可作为中心单据，成为其他单据缮制、核对的依据。

我国出口公司的商业发票没有统一格式，但主要项目基本相同，主要包括发票编号、开制日期、数量、包装、单价、总价和支付方式等内容。在制作发票时应注意：

（1）发票的抬头，如采用信用证付款方式，通常为开证人；如果是托收方式则为合同中的买方。

（2）对货物的描述。凡属信用证方式，必须与来证所列各项要求完全相符。以托收方式收款，则应与合同货物描述相一致。

（3）提交的发票份数应正确。

（4）由于各国法令或习惯不同，有的来证要求在发票上加注"证明所列内容真实无误"（或称"证实发票"，certified invoice），"货款已经收讫"（或称"收妥发票"receipt invoice），或有关出口人国籍、原产地等证明文句，应在不违背我国方针、政策和法令的情况下，酌情办理。出具"证实发票"时，应将发票下端通常印有的"有错当查"（E. &O、E）字样删去。

发票一般用英文制作，如来证中要求品名用法文、德文等，发票可以该外文照抄，有时加注英文名附于品名栏。

2. 海关发票（customs invoice）

它由出口方负责填制，是进口国家海关为掌握进口商品原价值、原产地情况而指定的一种特定格式的发票。海关发票供进口方向海关作进口报关、纳税之用。进口国海关可据此核定货物的产地，以采取不同的国别政策，根据所提供的货物成本价确定是否享受优惠税待遇，考核货物是否属于倾销。

3. 领事发票（consular invoice）

它是指由进口方在出口国家所设的领事馆所签发的发票。东南亚、拉丁美洲的国家规定，凡输往该国的货物，国外出口方必须向该国海关提供该国领事签证的发票，其中有的国家的发票设计有固定格式，有的则规定签证于出口商业发票之上。其作用与海关发票基本相同。

（三）运输单据

运输单据是指证明货物已经装船或发运或已由承运人接受监管的单据。根据运输方式的不同，其种类也有多种。其中用于海洋运输的海运提单（bill of lading）内容一般有正反两面，正面的内容主要包括船名、装运港、目的港、托运人、收货人以及货物的名称、数量、包装等；反面是具体运输条款，对有关承运人的责任、托运人的责任、索赔与诉讼等问题均有详细的规定。

海运提单的填写要注意抬头及背书的正确，装运货物与发票规定一致，不能显示"装运甲板"字样，不能有船方的不良批注。运费项目，若CIF或CFR条件，应注明"运费已付"（freight prepaid）；如成交价格为FOB时，则注明运费到付（freight collect）。

（四）保险单

保险单（insurance policy）。是保险人（即保险公司）与被保险人（即投保人，一般为进出口商）之间订立的保险合同的书面证明。当被保险货物遭受保险合同责任范围以内的损失时，保险单是被保险人向保险人提出索赔、保险人理赔的依据。在 CIF、CIP 合同中，出口商在向银行或进口商收款时，提交符合销售合同及/或信用证规定的保险单据是他的重要义务。

保险单的被保险人应是信用证上的受益人，并加空白背书，便于办理保险单转让。

保险险别和保险金额应与信用证规定一致。UCP600 规定，在单据的表面上 CIF 和 CIP 的金额能够被确定时，保险单必须表明投保最低金额，该项金额应为货物的 CIF 或 CIP 的金额加 10%。否则银行接受的最低投保金额，应为根据信用证要求而付款、承兑或议付金额的 110%，或发票金额的 110%，以两者之中较高者为准。保险单所表明的货币，应为信用证所规定的货币相符。

保险单的签发日期应当合理，在保险单上，除非表明保险责任单日期迟于货物装船或发运或接受监督之日起生效外，银行将拒收出单日期迟于装船或发运或接受监督日期的保险单。

（1）在信用证支付方式下，如来证无其他规定，保险单的被保险人应是信用证上的受益人，并加空白背书，便于保险单办理过户转让。

（2）保险险别和保险金额，要与合同和/或信用证的规定相符。保险单上的运输标志、包装及数量、船名、装运港（地）、目的港（地）等项内容，应与运输单据相一致。

（3）保险单的签发日期，应早于运输单据签发日。在信用证支付条件下，银行将拒收出单日期迟于装船或发运或货交承运人的保险单。

（五）产地证明书

这是证明货物原产地和制造地的文件，也是进口国海关采取不同的国别政策和关税待遇的依据。产地证一般分为普通产地证、普惠制产地证和欧洲纺织品产地证等多种，它们在使用范围和格式方面有所不同。

1. 普通产地证，又称原产地证（Certificate of Origin，C/O）。

通常不使用海关发票或领事发票的国家，要求提供产地证明可确定对货物的征税税率。有的国家为限制从某个国家或地区进口货物，要求以产地证来确定货物来源。

我国自 1996 年 7 月 1 日始，签证机构使用统一的带有长城标记的新版原产地证格式。其中共有 12 个栏目，右上角有年度流水号，不能跨年度使用。

2. 普惠制单据（Genernalized System of Preferences Documents C/O）。

普惠制简称 GSP。目前有许多发达国家给我国以普惠制待遇，对这些国家的出口货物，需提供普惠制单据。享有普惠关税的商品，其证书按照联合国贸发会议规定的格式和内容编制，由出口国家指定的机构签发。

在我国，一般商品的普惠制产地证书采用"格式 A"（Form A）形式，以英文或法文出具，背面允许使用中文印制。此证书除同其他单据一样要填写进出口双方的名称、地址全称、运输路线及货物的品名、数量、包装、唛头等内容之外，还要填写第八栏"原产地标准"。虽然此栏要求填写的字数不多，却是进口国家海关审查的核心项目。按照有关规定，如果商品完全由出口国自产，则在此栏中填上"P"代号；如果商品含有进口成分，但符合原产标准，则填"W"并加打四位数税目号。对新西兰、澳大利亚出口货物可以不填此栏。

我国出口商在填写第十二栏出口商声明时，生产国应填"China"，进口国必须填给惠国，均不能以地区或城市名称代替。

特殊商品的出口，若要享受普惠制待遇，需填写其他形式的证明书。如纺织品，一般产品必须填写"纺织品产地证"，手工制品则填写"手工制纺织品产地证"，这种证书在我国由中国进出口商品检验局出具。受配额限制的纺织品，应申请填写"纺织品出口许可证"，无配额控制的毛呢产品，则要求填写"纺织品装船证明"证书，这些证书由出口地外贸主管部门签发。

出口公司应对上诉各类规定有准确的了解，以便在填制此类单据中符合各个项目的要求。如一旦填错，就可能丧失享受普惠制待遇的机会。

（六）装箱单和重量单

这两种单据是用来补充商业发票内容不足的，便于进口方在货物到达目的港时，供海关检查和核对货物。装箱单又称花色码单，列明每批货物的逐件花色搭配，又称为内容明细表；重量单则列明每件货物的毛、净重。进口商核对货物，都要以装箱单为依据。如果整批货物的品种相同，只是重量不同，也可以用重量单代替。

装箱单可以单独制作，也可以合并在发票上，但货物的项目必须分别记载，以便于进口地的海关和收货人核对。

（七）检验证书

检验证书（inspection certificate）的提供，能起到分别证明商品的品质、数量、重量、卫生条件等作用。它一般由国家指定的商检机构出具，也可根据不同情况和不同要求，由出口公司或生产企业出具。证件名称视检验的内容而定，应注意证书名称及所列项目、检验结果与买卖合同、信用证规定的一致性。

上诉单据，并非每项都是信用证交易下的必备文件，究竟哪些是所需的，还应根据信用证中所开立的条件而定。

单证工作是出口工作中的最后一个环节，从交易磋商、签约到备货、国外开证、审证、装运货物，其中的任何一个环节发生问题，或未能及时发现并纠正，最后都会在单据中暴露出来，有的还可以采取必要的措施进行补救，所以单证工作在出口业务中实际上起到了把关的作用。

二、结汇

结汇是指出口企业制妥单据送交银行审单，银行在审核无误后，一方面向国外银行收款，另一方面按约定办法向出口公司付款的过程。按照《跟单信用证统一惯例（UCP600）》规定，信用证支付方式，开证行应在不超过从收到单据次日起算的 7 个银行工作日内，完成单据审核事宜。

（一）结汇方式

我国出口业务中，信用证项下的结汇方式，早期多采用定期结汇的做法。

具体做法：议付银行根据向不同国家（地区）索汇所需的往返天数、加上国内外银行的合理工作时间，预先确定一个固定的结汇日期。到期后无论是否收妥国外票款，都应主动将货款按当时外汇牌价折成人民币，交付出口方或收入出口方账户。

以后，我国又采用了"收妥结汇"的方法，也称"先收后结"。

具体做法：议付行经审查出口公司交来的单据，认定单、证一致后，将单据寄往国外付款行索汇，待接到国外关系银行通知已将票款收入议付行账户时，再按当日外汇牌价，把货款折成人民币交付出口公司。

《跟单信用证统一惯例（UCP600）》规定，信用证项下的汇款结算必须采用议付方式，"仅审核单据而未付出对价并不构成议付"（第10条第2款）。它指出议付在审单无误后，应按信用证条款买入出口公司的汇票和票据，按照票面扣除议付期和从议付日到估计收到货款日的利息，将净数按议付日外汇牌价折算成某种货币，交出口公司，然后再向国外开证行索取货款。这种做法被称为"买单结汇"或"出口押汇"。近年来，我国的银行业务中也逐渐采用这种方法，为出口企业垫款融资。

（二）单证不符的补救措施

在信用证付款方式下，由于主客观原因，致使发生单证不符是难以完全避免的。为此，可采用以下一些补救办法：

（1）在时间和其他条件许可的情况下，出口公司应立即更正或重新制单，力争在规定的有效期内重新交单结汇。

（2）如"不符合"性质一般受益人可在征得开证人同意的前提下，出具保证书请求议付行保通融议付，并承担日后遭开证行拒付的一切后果。

（3）如"不符点"的情况较为复杂，可请议付行先向国外开证行拍发电报或电传，列明单、证不符点，征得开证行的同意后，再将单据寄出。这种方法在我国银行业务中习称"电提"。如经电提开证行不同意付款，那么就只能改做跟单托收；或由出口方采取转售货物、原船运回等其他措施进行补救。

第五节　对违约的处理

出口交易在结汇之后大致完成整个业务处理过程，但有时也会出现一些意外的情况。例如，由于出口方没有完全尽到交货责任，以致出现事故，造成损失，导致进口方提出了索赔的要求；由于进口方在履约过程中出现问题，如不按时开立信用证、不按时付款赎单、无理拒收货物等，致使进口方遭受损失。对于这些违约行为，交易双方均有权向对方提出赔偿的要求，直至解除合同。

对于出口方而言，如因对方违约造成己方损失的，可根据不同对象、不同原因以及损失大小，实事求是地向进口方提出索赔。

进口方索赔中以出口方所交货物不符合合同规定者居多。在对方向己方索赔时，出口方理赔应注意以下问题。

（1）要认真研究分析对方所提索赔理由是否充足，情况十分属实，是否确因我方违约而使对方遭受损失，是否符合合同规定或法律规定。如属逾期才提出的索赔我方可以不予受理。

（2）仔细审核对方所提出的索赔证件和有关文件，如出证机构是否符合要求，检验标准和检验方法是否符合双方规定，单证是否齐全、清楚，有无夸大损失等。

（3）合理确定赔付方法。如确定属己方责任，应公平合理，实事求是地研究理赔方案，与对方协商确定。赔偿办法可采取赔付部分货物、退货、换货、修整，赔付一定金额，对索赔货物给予价格折扣或按残损货物百分比对全部货物降价等办法处理。

英文参考教程

Performance of Export Contract

The performance of export contract refers to the whole Process from the exporter's delivery of the goods to the collection of payment. A legal contract shall bind upon both parties, so the interested parties shall fulfil the agreed duties according to the contract. Any party cannot change or cancel the contract unilaterally without sound reason. In case one party does not perform the contract or the performance is not in conformity with the stipulations of the contract, his act amounts to breach of the contract. The party who breaks the contract shall undertake certain legal responsibilities according to different cases and consequences.

The performance of the export contract is the last step in export business. It involves several important stages and complicated formalities. Whether the performance of the export contract is good or not will influence the credit standing and interest of our country, therefore, we should pay close attention to the following points in the performance of the export contract.

1) We should honour the contract and keep our promises, and make performance strictly according to the stipulations of the contract.

2) We should strengthen the cooperation with relative parties, such as the customs authority, inspection institution, bank, insurance company, shipping company, etc.

3) We should prepare for the goods according to the L/C and the contract.

4) We should establish close relations with customers.

The main steps in the general process in performance of the export contract are (under CIF terms, payment by L/C) as follows:

At the request of the importer, the L/C is opened by the issuing bank and sent to the advising bank. After receiving the L/C the advising bank examines the L/C and transfers it to our import and export company.

If our company finds that the L/C is not in conformity with the contract it requires the foreign importer to amend the L/C.

1) Our company prepares for the goods and applies for inspection.

2) The commodity inspection bureau examines the goods and issues the inspection certificate.

3) Our import and export company fills in the consignment bill or cargo shipping application, and entrusts the Foreign Trade Shipping Company with the task of chartering a ship or booking shipping space. The China Ocean Shipping Agency issues the shipping order.

4) Our import and export company takes out insurance.

5) The insurance company issues the insurance policy.

6) Our import and export company fills in the customs declaration and renders the shipping order, inspection certificate, commercial invoice, packing list, export permit, copies of the contract and L/C to the customs authority for examination.

7) The customs authority examines the goods, L/C and documents and seals on the inspection certificate, release permit, customs declaration or shipping order.

8) According to the shipping order, the Foreign Trade Shipping Company loads the shipment on board the vessel.

9) After the goods have been Preloaded on board, the captain or mate issues the mate's receipt to our import and export company. The company exchanges it for the bill of lading from the Ocean Shipping Agency.

10) Our import and export company presents, the draft, bill of lading, invoice, customs invoice, certificate of origin, packing list together with the inspection certificate, insurance policy to the negotiating bank for negotiation.

11) The negotiating bank collects payment from the issuing bank and transfers accounts to our import and export company.

A. Preparation of the Goods

1) We must prepare for the goods according to the time limit stipulated in the contract.

2) The quality of the goods shall be in accordance with the stipulations of the contract we should examine the article number, specification and assortment of the goods carefully before packing.

3) The quantity of the goods shall be in conformity with the stipulation of the contract.

4) As to the packing of the goods, we should deal with it more carefully in export trade than in home trade.

B. Applying for Inspection

"The China Commodity Inspection Law" stipulates that all import and export products shall be inspected. The Contents of inspection of the goods include the quality, quantity, weight, packing, etc. of the goods.

If the contract stipulates clearly the inspection clause, the goods shall he inspected according to the contract. If the contract does not stipulate the inspection clause, the goods may be inspected according to the relative standards commonly accepted in international trade.

C. Implementing Payment Terms

The major steps include urging the customer into establishing an L/C, examining the L/C sometimes involving the amendment to the L/C, as the case may be.

When a contract is concluded, the buyer is usually under the obligation to establish an L/C with his bank within the time limit stipulated in the sales contract. However, since there are circumstances where the buyer fails to establish the L/C, or it does not reach the seller in time, we can usually urge him to expedite the establishment of the L/C or to ascertain its whereabouts by letter, telex or cable. For example:

S/CTE151 SHIRTS L/C UNRCVD PLS RUSH;

S/S1211 AIR CONDITIONERS 1,000 SETS GDSRDY PLS OPEN L/C;

S/C5014 ISSUANCE OVERDUE PLSOPEN L/C BYCBL AT ONCE;

S/C1099 YR ODR4UI: 3SHPMT [1S3DRAWING NEAR PLSRUSH L/C.

All letters of credit opened by foreign companies shall be examined by our banks and our import and export companies respectively.

Our bank mainly examines whether the opening bank has business relationship with us previously as well as its credit standing, political background, liabilities and responsibilities of payment, and also the genuineness of the signature in the L/C. If our bank finds no fault in the L/C, it will seal on the original L/C and transmits it to our import and export company.

Our import and export company should examine the L/C again according to the sales contract. The sales contract and the L/C are two different documents. The sales contract is the legal document which binds upon both the buyer and the seller, while the L/C is the document which binds upon the opening bank and the beneficiary.

The examination of the L/C includes the type, number, date of issuing, applicant, beneficiary, amount, expiration date, presentation period 11173, place of expiration, issuing bank, etc. in the L/Ct the number of the contract, the name, specification, unit price, packing, shipping mark, quantity of the cargo f the time of shipment, port of shipment, port of destination, partial shipments or transshipment to be allowed or not, etc.; the drawer, drawee, time of payment, etc.; the commercial invoice, bill of lading, insurance policy, inspection certificate, other documents, etc.; the undertaking of the issuing bank, instructions to the negotiating bank, etc.; and other stipulations, such as commission, discount, interest, etc. Our import and export company should examine the L/C completely and carefully.

When we find that there are some discrepancies or some unforeseen special clauses to which we do not agree in the L/C, we should send an advice to the buyer, asking him to make the necessary amendment. Sometimes unexpected situations with regard to the supply of goods, shipping space, transportation documents, expenses etc., may arise. In this case, an amendment to the original L/C will also be required.

For example:

L/C3524 PLS CBL AMENDMENT ALLOWING TRANSHPMT PARTSHPMTS;

PLSASK YRBK TOAMEND L/C41427 TOREAD QUOTE THROUGH B/L ACPTBL UNQUOTE; YRL/C44012 PLSDELETE QUOTE ALLBANK COMM AND CHARGES AREFOR BENEFICIARYS ACCT UNQUOTE STOP THESE SHLBEPAID BYBYRONLY.

In practice, the expiration date of the L/C and the time of shipment, owing to various causes, are often needed to make an extension by the opener. For example:

YR L/C15923 CVRG S OSS RCVD STOP SHPMTDATE ONORBFR 31ST MAY LEAVGONLY 15DYS FORARNGMT CANT COMPLYWITH STOP PLSEXTEND TO 15TH JUNE;

NO DRCTS/S1351 SAIL FOR YRPORT ZSMNTH PLSEXTEND L/C6295HZ VALIDITY TO 30TH JUNE.

D. Chartering a Ship and Booking Space

In case the quantity of the goods is large, especially when bulk cargoes are to be carried it may be of a great advantage to have a whole ship at our disposal, while as to the shipment whose quantity is not so large, we may entrust the Foreign Trade Shipping Company with the task of booking space.

The procedure for booking space is as follows:

1) The Foreign Trade Shipping Company publishes an export sailing schedule every month and hands out to import and export companies. On the sailing schedule, the route, name and nationality of the vessel, date of arrival, closing date of receiving, expected date of shipment, name of port of call, etc. for import and export companie's reference.

2) As soon as the goods are ready and the L/C has been received, the import and export company can entrust the Foreign Trade Shipping Company with the work of handling booking space formalities. According to the relative shipping clause in the L/C and the contract, the import and export company fills in the name, package number, gross weight, measurement of the goods, port of destination, time of shipment etc. on the consignment bill and sends it to the Foreign Trade Shipping Company before the closing date of receiving as a foundation for booking space.

3) The Foreign Trade Shipping Company, together with the China Ocean Shipping Agency arranges the shipping space for the goods on the basis of stowage principle 211, nature and quantity of the goods, port of shipment, port of destination in accordance with the sailing schedule.

4) The Foreign Trade Shipping Company delivers the goods to the dock warehouse on behalf of the import and export company.

5) After the scheduled ship arrives at the port, the Foreign Trade Shipping Company delivers the goods from the dock warehouse to the side of the vessel. After being checked out by the customs, the goods are loaded on board against the shipping order.

6) After shipment, the master or mate issues the mate's receipt which indicates that the shipment has been received in apparent good order and condition. This is a temporary receipt which must be exchanged for a regular bill of lading before the vessel sails.

E. Taking out Insurance

Under CIF trade terms, our import and export company shall cover insurance for the goods with the China Insurance Company. The insurance clauses, coverages, insurance amounts and mark-up percentage shall be handled according to the stipulation of the L/C.

F. Making Declaration to the Customs

Before shipment our import and export company shall fill in the customs declaration for export, and send it to the customs together with the shipping order, copy of the contract, copy of the L/C, commercial invoice, packing list, weight memo, inspection certificate, export licence, etc. After the goods have been inspected by the customs, if the goods are in conformity with the L/C and other legal documents, the customs shall sign and seal on the shipping order, and then the goods may be loaded on board the vessel.

G. Sending out the Shipping Advice

Immediately after shipment, our import and export company shall send out again the shipping advice to the buyer by cable according to the stipulation of the L/C. Sometimes the buyer may require our import and export company to send out again the shipping advice by letter so that he can get the details of the shipment. Especially under CFR trade terms, we must send out the shipping advice in time so that the buyer may take out insurance on the goods in time, otherwise if the goods suffer losses during the transport, we shall be responsible for them. The shipping advice usually includes the number of the L/C, number of the contract, name, quantity, measurement, gross or net weight, total value of the goods, name of the vessel, date and number of the bill of lading, etc.

H. Making out Documents for Settlement

After shipment, according to the stipulation of the L/C, our import and export company shall draw up all kinds of documents required and shall present them to the bank for negotiation and settlement.

The so-called negotiation means the bank at the exporter and purchases the bill of exchange and shipping documents drawn by the exporter.

The settlement means the exporter sells foreign exchange proceeds to the bank appointed by the country at the banker current buying rate.

At present, we have three means to make settlement:

1. Make settlement after the payment is made

After the bank at the exporter end checks out the shipping documents and finds no fault, the bank will airmails the documents to the opening bank or the appointed reimbursing bank to collect the purchase price. Then after the bank at the exporter's end receives the credit note from abroad, the bank changes the foreign exchange into RMB at the current buying rate and enters in the exporter's account.

2. Make time settlement

The bank at the exporter's end determines a fixed date for settlement in advance according to the mail distance the bank will go over for collecting the purchase value from the paying bank abroad. If the bank at the exporter's end finds no fault in the documents, it will usually change the purchase value into RMB and transfer it to the exporter account within 10 – 20 days after checking out the documents, no matter whether the bank has collected the purchase value.

3. Make settlement through negotiation

In case of no fault in shipping documents, the bank at the exporter's end buys the bill of exchange and shipping documents presented by the beneficiary under the L/C and changes the denomination of the bill of exchange into RMB at the current buying rate after deducting the interest incurred from the date of negotiation to the actual date of collection. According to international practices, the negotiating bank may take recourse to the beneficiary. The Bank of China also keeps the right to take recourse. In case the paying bank abroad finds any discrepancies and refuses to pay, the negotiating bank has to take recourse to the beneficiary for recovering the payment. So the beneficiary shall make out documents with more care to make sure that the documents are in conformity with each other with the L/C and with the goods consigned.

The points that we shall pay attention to when making out the main documents are introduced briefly as follows:

1. Draft or Bill of Exchange

1) The "drawn under" clause of the draft: It is the foundation for drawing a draft. The L/C usually stipulates that the draft drawn under the credit shall be marked "Drawn under … bank L/C No … dated …" The words "drawn under" are usually printed on the draft, then we may just type the contents of the draft according to the L/C. In case the L/C does not include the above mentioned stipulation, we shall still type the name and address of the opening bank, the number of the L/C as well as the date of issuing the L/C. Under collection, we shall type the words "for collection", serial number and D/P or D/A on the draft.

2) Drawer: The drawer, i.e., the beneficiary is to be indicated in the right lower corner on the draft.

3) Time limit of payment: It is usually indicated by "at sight", "at 30 days sight", "D/P at sight", "D/P at 45 days sight", etc.

4) Payer: Under the L/C, the payer shall be typed according to the stipulation of the

L/C. In case no payer is stipulated, we shall take the opening bank as the payer. Under collection, the payer of the draft is the importer, while under collection in connection with the L/C, the payer is the opener.

5) Draft amount: The sum of money written in words and in figures shall be in conformity with each other. The sum of money on the draft shall be written according to the stipulation of the L/C and in conformity with the invoice value. If an interest clause is included, payable with interest ... % per annum shall be indicated on the draft.

6) Payee: No matter whether under the L/C or under collection, the negotiating bank or remitting bank shall be typed on the draft, i. e., the Bank of China.

2. Commercial Invoice

In international trade correct invoicing is very important. The successful performance of the sales contract will often rely on it.

A commercial invoice is a detailed list made out by the exporter in the name of the importer which declares the details of the shipment so that the importer may examine whether the goods delivered by the exporter are in conformity with the contract.

A commercial invoice is a certificate of sale of the goods, it can also be used as the foundation for keeping accounts and making declaration to the customs. When payment under a letter of credit is agreed, it is normal that the commercial invoice is one of the documents which have to be rendered to the nominated bank.

The commercial invoice should always include the names and addresses of the seller and the buyer, drawing date and running number, reference number of the buyer's order, ports of shipment and destination, details of the goods exact marks and numbers on the packages, the invoice amount, and, if possible, the details of transportation, such as the name of the ship and the route.

The following is an example of the commercial invoice:

Invoice: 4 Containers of Office Machines by Great Tide Co. Ltd., Dalian to Messrs Mathews &. Wilson, Chicago, U. S. A. to be shipped per SS. Red Star from Dalian, Order Number 2HS/1246.

On the bottom of the commercial invoice, there are words "E. & O. E." In case the L/C requires the exporter to issue a certified invoice, the above mentioned words shall be deleted.

When drawing up a commercial invoice, the following points should be noticed:

1) Drawer: The drawer must be in conformity with the stipulation in the L/C.

2) Number and date: The number of the invoice is usually decided by the drawer. The date shall be earlier than that of the B/L or insurance policy, but not later than the expiration

date of the L/C.

3) Consignee or importer: The consignee or importer on a commercial invoice is usually the accountee or the applicant under the L/C.

There are several expressions which may be used to indicate the opener in the L/C, e. g. , issuer, applicant, accountee, for account of …, by order of …, etc. In case "For account of … and" By order of … "appear on the same L/C, the name after" For account of … shall be taken as the consignee of the invoice. If a bank opens an L/C on behalf of a certain importer, the consignee of the invoice shall be the importer instead of the bank. If there are two importers, i. e. , the middleman and the real buyer, unless otherwise stipulated in the L/C, we shall type the two buyers on the invoice.

4) Port of shipment and port of destination: The port of shipment and port of destination shall be in conformity with the stipulations in the L/C and the names given in the B/L.

5) Description of the goods: The description and specification of the goods shall be typed on the invoice according to the L/C strictly. Unless the L/C stipulates "other terms as per contract No …" the commercial invoice usually does not give the specific description of the goods which is not stipulated in the L/C. But in case the L/C only stipulates the general name of the goods, the commercial invoice may list the specific name, varieties, or article numbers of the goods.

In case the L/C requires the description of the goods be written in French, or Spanish, or other languages, we must comply with the requirement according to the stipulation.

6) Quantity of the goods: The quantity of the goods typed on the commercial invoice shall be in conformity with the L/C. In case the L/C permits the quantity latitude but does not permit the amount latitude, then the quantity of the goods in the commercial invoice usually can only be reduced by 5%.

7) Invoice value, and commission: Unless otherwise stipulated, the bank may reject the commercial invoice issued for the amount in excess of the amount permitted by the credit. The currency employed in the commercial invoice shall be in accordance with the stipulation of the L/C.

The invoice price has to be stated in line with the agreed terms of the contract as explained earlier it may be the F. O. B. price or C. I. F. price, etc. In case the trade terms stipulated in the L/C are not in conformity with those of the contract, for example, the trade terms in the L/C are "CIF C3% London" while the trade terms in the contract are "CIF London" we should ask the opener to make an amendment to the L/C.

There are various ways to indicate the commission in the commercial invoice. In case the commission has already been deducted form the amount in the L/C, the invoice value shall not include the commission either. In case the L/C does not deduct the commission nor does the invoice, the commission shall be paid after the seller has collected the purchase price. In case the commission and discount appear in the commercial invoice simultaneously, they shall be stated in the commercial invoice respectively. In case the L/C requires the credit note or credit memorandum be provided, the commission be not deducted from the invoice value, in this case the seller may agree to recover exchange on the basis of net value by deducting the commission from the draft amount, and make out the credit note and tender it together with the documents to the bank. In case the L/C stipulates that the commission shall be deducted by the bank, the invoice shall be made out in gross value, the seller may recover exchange on the basis of net value, i. e. after deducting the commission.

8) Shipping marks and packing of the goods: In case shipping marks are stipulated in the L/C, the invoice shall be made out in conformity with the L/C in case shipping marks are not stipulated in the L/C but agreed in the contract, the invoice shall be made out in conformity with the contract; in case shipping marks are not stipulated in the L/C or in the contract, they may be determined by the seller in conformity with the usage of a particular trade.

9) Signature and authentication: The invoice is usually signed; and sealed by the exporter. Sometimes the L/C only required the invoice be sealed by the China Council for the Promotion of International Trade. Sometimes it also requires the invoice be signed by the notary public. We must pay due attention to these clauses in the L/C. In case of "issued by", "signed by" or "drawn by", the invoice is all right when it is sealed by the appointed authority on the right of the invoice; In case of "certified by", "attested by" or "approved by", the invoice shall also be sealed on the left of it in order to certify it as correct and true. In case signature by hand is required, the invoice shall be signed by hand by the appointed signatory.

3. Customs Invoice

The customs invoice is one of the documents required by the customs in some import countries which has an unified form and shall be filled in according to the stipulations of the L/C.

The customs invoices include the formal customs invoice, combined certificate of value and origin certified invoice in accordance with customs regulations.

The customs invoice is mainly used as a foundation for customs statistics, customs valuation, taxation and certifying the origin of the goods, making sure whether there is dumping tendency. When we fill in the customs invoice, the following points shall be paid attention to:

1) Form of the customs invoice: Different countries and different regions adopt different forms. The specific form is usually stipulated in the L/C.

2) Contents of the customs invoice: The contents of the customs invoice shall be in conformity with those of the commercial invoice.

3) Formation of customs invoice price: The customs invoice usually requires that the detailed statement of the breakdown value be shown. In case under the CIF price, the freight, insurance premium and FOB price shall be listed respectively. In addition, the packing expenses, baling charges, handling expenses, if any, shall also be stated. The prevailing home market price shall be shown in domestic currency, while it shall be 5% – 10% lower than the FOB price, otherwise there is an risk of being considered pushing sales at an irregular low price.

4. Bill of Lading

The bill of lading is the most important shipping document. We should take care as to the following points when making out the bill of lading.

1) Kinds of the B/L: The L/C issued by the foreign bank usually requires that the full set of clean "on board" Bs/L be provided.

2) Consignor in the B/L: In case of no specific stipulation, the beneficiary of the L/C is the consignor.

3) Consignee in the B/L: According to different Ls/C, there are different ways to indicate the consignee.

a) In case of no clear stipulation in the L/C, the box of consignee may be completed by filling in "To order" and the B/L shall be endorsed by the import and export company.

b) In case the L/C stipulates "To order" or "To Order of Shipper" is typed in the box of consignee, the B/L shall still be endorsed by the import and export company.

c) In case the L/C stipulates the B/L shall be made out in the manner of "To order, deliver to the order of … bank", in the box of consignee "To order" shall be typed and "deliver to the order of … bank" shall be typed on the back of the B/L, and then the B/L shall be endorsed by the consignor.

d) In case the L/C stipulates the B/L shall be made out "To order of negotiating bank", in the box of consignee in the B/L "To order of Bank of China" may be typed and the B/L shall be endorsed by the bank.

e) In case the L/C stipulates the B/L shall be made out "Endorsed in blank" the box of consignee shall remain blank and the B/L shall be blank endorsed by the consignor. In case the L/C stipulates "Endorsed to", the consignor shall make endorsement in full.

f) In case the L/C stipulates that a set of original documents shall be sent to the buyer direct, the consignee shall be the opening bank.

4) Notify party: The notify party is usually the consignee or his agent at the port of des-

tination. The details of the name and address of the notify party shall be stated on the copy of the B/L. In case the L/C does not stipulate the notify party, the box on the original B/L may be blank, while on the copy of the B/L, the name, address, telephone number and telex number of the consignee or opening bank or middleman shall be clearly indicated so that the shipping company agency may send the advice of arrival to the notify party.

5) Description of the goods, mark, number and date of the B/L: The general description of the goods is usually required to be filled in the B/L.

The mark is usually filled in the B/L according to the stipulation of the L/C. As to the bulk cargo, "N/M (no mark)" and "Cargo in Bulk" shall be typed on the B/L.

In case a full set of Bs/L is required by the L/C, two originals shall be made out. In case of the ocean transport, the date of B/L shall be the date on which the goods are shipped on board.

6) Port of destination: Except under FOB trade terms, the port of destination in the B/L, for example, under CIF or CFR trade terms, shall be clear and definite.

There are several cases in filling in ports of destination.

a) If the L/C requires "free zone" be added after the port of destination, except Aden, Beirut, Colon, Aqaba, Port Said etc., the shipping company usually does not allow "Free Zone" to be listed in this column.

b) If the L/C requires "In transit … to" be added, it shall be typed on the free space, instead of after the port of destination, because the seller is responsible for shipping the goods to the port of destination only, while the responsibility and charges due to the transshipment shall be borne by the buyer.

c) Some American Ls/C require "OCP" be typed after the port of destination. OCP (Overland Common Point) refers to the inland area on the east of Rocky Mountains. All the goods transshipped from the west sea cost to the inland area will enjoy the preferential freight rate.

7) Freight: Under CIF or CFR trade terms, the freight shall borne by the consignor. "Freight prepaid" or "Freight paid" shall be filled in the B/L under FOB trade terms, the freight shall be borne by the consignee, so "Freight to collect" or "Freight payable at destination" shall be filled in the B/L.

5. Insurance Policy

1) Unless otherwise stipulated in the L/C or unless the insurance policy shows that the insurance will be effective no later than the date of shipping the goods on board or making delivery or delivering into the custody of the carrier, the bank will reject the insurance policy whose issuing date is later than the date of shipping the goods on board or making delivery or

delivering into the custody of the carrier stated in the shipping documents. So the date of insurance policy shall be earlier than the date of the B/L.

2) As to the goods which have franchise, the franchise shall be stated in the insurance policy, otherwise IOP (irrespective of percentage) shall be stipulated in the L/C.

3) In case of no clear stipulation in the L/C, the insured shall be the beneficiary of the L/C, who shall make blank endorsement so as to make it negotiable; in case the L/C requires it be made out "To order", the insurance policy shall be endorsed by the beneficiary.

The insurance coverage and amount shall be in conformity with the stipulation of the L/C. The mark, number of the packages, quantity, description of the goods, name of vessel, date of shipment, port of shipment and port of destination shall be in conformity with those in the B/L.

6. Packing List and Weight Memo

The packing list and weight memo are used for examining the goods when the goods arrive at the port of destination. In some degree, they make up the deficiency of the commercial invoice.

The packing list states the assortment of each individual lot; the weight memo states the gross weight and net weight of each piece.

7. Certificate of Origin

Generally speaking, there are two kinds of certificates of origin:

1) Certificate of origin: Those countries which do not use the customs invoice or consular invoice may determine the rate of duty according to the certificate of origin and make sure where the goods come from.

According to the requirements of the L/C or contract, there are two authorities concerned in our country issuing the certificate of origin; one is the Import and Export Commodity Inspection Bureau; the other is the China Council for the Promotion of International Trade.

2) Generalized system of preference certificate of origin form A: This kind of certificate must be filled in by our import and export company and be issued by the China Import and Export Commodity Inspection Bureau as a basis for reduducing or remitting the duty on import commodities. At present, there are 27 countries adopting this kind of certificate.

(资料来源：宋秀峰. 国际贸易（双语版）[M]. 中国发展出版社，2010.)

▶ 本章小结

出口合同的履行的一般程序主要包括备货、催证、审证、改证、租船订舱、报验、投保、装船和制单结汇等。其中货、证、船、款四个环节最为重要。

制单结汇时收取货款必不可少的一个环节。以信用证项下的交易为例，通常需要缮制的单据主要有：汇票、发票、装箱单、保险单等。缮制结汇单据时，要求做到正确、完整、即时、简明和整洁。

➢ 本章名词

出口合同履行　备货　报验　催证　审证　改证　报关　制单结汇　商业发票　普惠制单据　出口收汇核销　出口退税

➢ 理论思考

1. 出口业务中，备货的重要性何在？应注意哪些问题？
2. 审核信用证的依据是什么？通常应审核哪些内容？
3. 简述班轮运输下办理出口托运的程序？
4. 出口业务中的结汇单据主要有哪些？在制作这些单据时，应着重注意哪些问题？
5. 试述在出口贸易中，不能按合同规定按时、按质、按量交货的危害性。

➢ 实训习题

一、模拟业务背景

请使用"世格模拟操作软件"和网络来模拟练习进出口合同的全部履行过程。

1. 设定使用 CIF 信用证，出口一批松香到美国。要求查询如下内容：

A. 出口公司网上（中国商务部对外贸易司）办理出口许可：出口公司为（三强服装进出口公司）网上申请配额、许可证手续；

B. 出口公司发盘；

C. 进口公司的网上名址；

D. 合同的签订并 H.S 编码；

E. 出口商的制单与结汇手续；

F. 商检、海关、保险、外运公司、国税、外汇管理局等网上相关业务的手续。

二、模拟训练任务

根据所给资料及要求，以闽江纺织品进出口公司业务员身份，模拟完成出口合同履行。

1. 完成出口合同下的备货任务（包括收购货源、办理货物检验及产地证手续）；
2. 完成信用证的落实（包括审证、改证等必要工作）；
3. 完成货物装运出口任务（包括办理运输、保险、通关手续、发装运通知等）；
4. 整理、制作出口结汇单据，办理出口结汇手续。

三、模拟训练单据及资料

1. 货源收购资料

（1）合同供方——福州纺织十厂；

（2）签约时间地点——2010年4月29日；

（3）合同号码——100034；

（4）购销价格——每码7.65元；

（5）交货期——2010年7月底以前；

（6）其他——自拟。

2. 商检资料

（1）申请日期——2010年10月5日；

（2）联系人、电话——李萌，26745678；

（3）报验号——000349678；

（4）商品名称编码——1376.0001。

3. 产地证资料

（1）申请单位注册号——1003607637；

（2）证书号——12340071320；

（3）发票号——DK1073-476；

（4）发票日期——2010年11月6日；

（5）发票（FOB）总值——USD8914.00；

（6）拟出运日期——2010年11月17日；

（7）申请日期——2010年11月6日。

4. 模拟训练单据

购销合同

供方：　　　　　　　　　　　　　　　　　　合同编号：

需方：　　　　　　　　　　　　　　　　　　签订地点：

　　　　　　　　　　　　　　　　　　　　　签订时间：

年　月　日

产品名称	牌号商标	规格型号	生产厂家	单位	数量（码）	单价（元）	总金额（元）	交（提）货时间与数量	
								合计	

合计人民币金额（大写）

1. 产品名称、商标、型号、厂家、数量、金额、供货时间及数量；
2. 质量要求、技术标准、供方对质量负责的条件和期限；
3. 交（提）货地点、方式；
4. 运输方式及到达港站和运费负担；
5. 合理损耗及计算方法；
6. 包装标准、包装物的供应和回收；
7. 验收标准、方法及提出异议期限；
8. 随机备品、配件工具数量及供应办法；
9. 结算方式及期限；
10. 如需提供担保，另立合同担保书，作为本合同附件；
11. 违约责任；
12. 解决合同纠纷的方式；
13. 其他约定事项。

供方	需方	签（公）证意见：
单位名称（章）	单位名称（章）	
单位地址：	单位地址：	
法定代表人：	法定代表人：	经办人：
委托代理人：	委托代理人：	
电　　话：	电　　话：	
电报挂号：	电报挂号：	
开户银行：	开户银行：	
账　　号：	账　　号：	签（公）证机关（章）
邮政编码：	邮政编码：	年　月　日

CHAPTER 10
第十章　进口合同的履行

> **本章指导**
>
> 通过对本章的学习,要求能够了解进口业务的基本环节和运作程序,特别是从实际业务的角度了解每个环节的操作要求和注意事项,掌握开证、托运、投保、审单、付款、报关提货的程序,运用所学知识重点学会:
> 1. 如何解决单证不符;
> 2. 处理常见的信用证修改问题。

在进口业务中,作为进口商,同样要坚持"重合同、守信用"的原则,及时履行合同中进口商应该承担的义务;同时,还要随时注意卖方履行合同的情况,督促卖方按合同规定履行其应承担的义务。

在以 FOB 贸易术语和信用证支付方式成交的进口合同的履约过程中,主要有开立信用证、办理运输与保险、审单付款及接货、报关等工作程序。

第一节　开证、托运和投保

一、开证

进口合同签订后,按合同规定,买方作为开证申请人在向开证行开立信用证时,应填写开证申请书,按 UCP 600 规定,开证申请书的内容应与合同条款一致,例如:品质、规格、数量、价格、交货期、装运期、装运单据等,应以合同条款为依据,详细列明。开证申请书的内容必须完整,明确,为防止混淆和误解,开证申请书中不应罗列过多的细节。

信用证的开证时间,应按合同规定办理,如合同规定在卖方确定交货期后开证,买方应在接到卖方上述通知后开证,如合同规定在卖方领到许可证或支付履约担保金后开证,买方应在收到卖方已领到许可证的通知或银行通知保证金已照收后开证。

信用证开出以后,如发现内容与开证申请书不符,或因情况发生变化或其他原因,需对信用证进行修改,应立即向开证银行递交修改申请书,要求开证银行办理修改信用证的手续。如受益人收到信用证后,提出要求修改信用证中的某些条款,则应区别情况予以同意或不同意。如同意修改,应及时向开证银行办理改证手续,如不同意修改,也应及时通知受益人。信用证经修改后,开证行即不可撤销地受该修改条款的约束,买卖双方也应按修改后的信用证规定办理。

信用证最常见的修改内容举例如下:

1. 展延信用证的装运期和有效期。

例如:"信用证装运期和有效期分别延至"

(Shipment and expiring date extended to respectively)

2. 变更装、卸港口。

例如:"货物自××至××代替以前通知的内容。"

(Shinpment to be made from to instead of previously advised)

3. 对分批装运/转运的修改。

例如:"允许分批装运/转运"

(Partial shipment/transshipment are allowed)

4. 增加货物数量或金额。

例如:"增(或减)信用证金额(或数量)至"

[Increase (decrease) credit amount (the quantity) to]

5. 修改出口商名称、地址。

例如:"请将受益人名称和地址改为"

(Please amend the beneficiary's name and address to read)

在我国进口业务中,除使用信用证支付方式外,也有将汇付、托收或各种不同支付方式结合使用的。如使用汇付方式,买方应按合同规定,以信汇、电汇或票汇方式将货款汇付卖方;如采用托收支付方式,买方应根据合同规定,以付款交单或承兑交单方式及时付清货款,取得货运单据。

二、托运

在进口业务中,货物大多通过海洋运输方式,因此凡以 FOB 或 FCA 贸易术语成交的合同,应由买方负责租船或订舱工作。租船订舱工作可委托对外贸易运输公司办理,也可直接向远洋运输公司或其他运输机构办理。在办理租船订舱时,要填写《进口订舱通知单》,履行委托订舱手续。填写该项通知单时,要做到完整、准确,并与合同内容一致。

租船订舱工作应按合同规定及时办理,大宗货物一般应在交货期45天向运输机构提出;零星货物应在交货期前30天提出,以使运输机构有足够时间落实舱位工作。如有的合同规定,卖方在交货前一定时期内,应将预计装运日期通知我方。我方在接到上述通知后,应及时向运输机构办理租船订舱手续。在办妥租船订舱手续后,应按规定的期限将船名及船期及时通知对方,以便对方备货装船。同时,为了防止船货脱节和出现船等货的情况,还应随时了解和掌握卖方备货和装船的准备工作情况,注意催促对方按时装运。对数量大或重要物资的进口,如有必要,亦可请我驻外机构就地了解,或派员前往出口地点检验、监督装运,以督促对方根据合同规定按时、按质、按量履行交货义务。

国外装船后,卖方应及时向我方发出装船通知,以便我方及时办理保险和接货等项工作。

三、投保

FOB、FCA、CFR和CPT条件下的进口合同由进口企业负责向保险公司办理货物的运输保险。进口货物运输保险一般有以下两种形式。

(一) 预约保险

为了简化手续,防止进口货物在国外装运后因信息传递不及时而发生漏保或来不及办理保险等情况,我国外贸进出口公司与中国各保险公司签有海运、空运、陆运、邮运等不同运输方式的进口货物预约保险合同,简称"预保合同"(Open Policy),在预约保险合同中,各进出口公司对进口商品应投保的险别、保险费率、适用条款以及赔付的办法等,都作了具体规定。因此,对每批进口货物,当买方收到国外装船通知后,只要将船名、提单号、开船日期、商品名称、数量、装运港、目的港等项内容通知保险公司,即作为已办妥保险手续,保险公司则对该批货物负责保险。

(二) 逐笔投保

当进口数量不大时,进口单位可采用逐笔保险方式,外贸进口公司接到国外卖方发货通知后,应立即填写《进口货物国际运输预约保险起运通知书》,并送交保险公司。此项通知书经保险公司签章后,即完成投保手续。但是,如果买方未及时办理投保手续和支付保险费,则货物发生损失后保险公司不负赔偿责任。

进口货物的保险金额,原则上是按进口货物的CIF货值计算,但在实际业务中,我国进口合同大多采用FOB条件,为便于计算,在各进出口公司与保险公司签订的预约保险合同中,共同议定平均保险费率和平均运费率,也可按实际运费计算。保险金额的计算公式为:

保险金额 = FOB 价格 × (1 + 平均保险费率 + 平均运费率)

这里的保险金额仅指估算的 CIF 价，不另加减。如投保人要求在 CIF 价基础上加减投保，保险公司也可接受。

办理保险时，投保人应交付保险费，保险费是按保险公司规定的保险费率计算的。保险公司对不同商品、不同目的地、不同的运输工具和不同险别制定有不同的保险费率。进口货物保险费率有进口货物保险费率和特约费率两种。特约费率是各保险公司在进口货物保险费率的基础上，与各外贸进出口公司协商拟订的，是一种优惠的费率，主要适用于预约保险合同项下的进口货物。

第二节　审单和付款

国际贸易中进口出口业务绝大部分使用信用证方式结算货款，这就要求卖方提交的单据必须完全符合买方开立的信用证条款。为保证买方的权益，必须认真做好审单工作，而审单是银行与企业的共同责任，因此必须密切联系，加强配合。

在信用证付款方式下，国外卖方在货物装出后，将信用证规定的汇票及全套单据提交开证行。银行必须合理谨慎地审核信用证所规定的单据，以确定单据是否在表面上与信用证条款相符、单单相符，银行即对外付款。开证行经审单后付款是最终的付款，即无追索权。银行在对外付款的同时，通知外贸进出口公司向开证行付款赎单，进出口公司凭银行出具的"付款通知书"与订货部门进行结算。

银行在审单时如发现表面上与信用证规定不符，决定拒绝接受单据，按照《跟单信用证统一惯例（UCP600）》规定，开证行或其他指定的银行必须在收到单据次日起第七个银行工作日以内，以电信方式或其他快捷方式，通知寄单银行或受益人（如单据由受益人直接向银行提交），并说明其拒受单据的所有不符合点，还须说明单据是否保留，以待交单人处理，或退回交单人等。

在实际业务中，经审单如发现单证不符，根据具体情况，银行可与外贸公司密切配合，共同协商，作出适当的处理。处理的办法很多，例如：

（1）开证行可以与外贸企业（开证申请人）联系，为使交易能顺利进行，使开证申请人对不符点予以接受，指示开证行对外付款。

（2）开证行通过寄单行与卖方（受益人）联系，允许受益人在有效期内更改单据。

（3）凭国外议付行书面担保后付款，保留追索权即同意在议付行出具担保后先行付款，如收到货后发现与规定不符，可以把已付的货款追回。

（4）改为货到后经检验再付款。如果卖方提供货物的品质证明书与规定不符，可以向卖方提出，待货到后经检验符合规定后才支付货款。

（5）卖方同意降价后，接受单据（一般是修改后的单据）并支付货款。

应该指出，单证不符、单单不符，是拒付的唯一理由，而不应涉及货物。拒收单据和拒付货款，均须以开证行的名义办理，而不能以"开证申请人声称议付单据不符合信用证要求"为由拒付货款。

第三节 报关、提货

对进出境货物的监管是海关的重要任务之一，凡进出境的货物必须通过设有海关的地方（港口）进境或出境，接受海关的监管。因此，进口货物抵达后，通常由外贸公司或委托外运公司办理报关。货物经海关查验无误后，才予放行。凡属法定检验的进口货物，还需先行报检。

一、进口报关

所谓进口报关，是指进口货物的收货人或其代理人向海关交验有关单证，办理进口货物申报手续的法律行为。除另有规定外，进口报关必须由海关准于注册登记的报关企业或者有权经营进口业务的企业负责办理，报关单位指派的报关员应经海关培训并考核认可。未经海关准予注册登记的单位和未经海关考核认可的人员，不得直接向海关办理报关手续。

（一）申报手续

进口货物的收货人或其代理人待货物抵达卸货港后，应填具"进口报关货物报关单"向海关提供齐全、正确、有效的单据。法定申报时限为自运输工具申报进境之日起14天内，超过14天期限未向海关申报的，海关按日征收进口货物CIF（或CIP）价格的0.5‰的滞报金。超过3个月未向海关申报的，由海关提取变卖，所得价款在扣除运输、装卸、储存等费用和税款后，尚有余款的，自货物变卖之日起1年内，经收货人申请允予发还。

（二）报关单的填写

填写"进口货物报关单"是报关人向海关办理报关手续的一种法律行为。报关人员必须按海关规定和进口货物的实际情况，如实向海关申报。

填写《进口货物报关单》的一般要求。

（1）填报的项目要正确、齐全，字迹要清楚、整洁、端正。不可用铅笔或红墨水笔填写。已填报项目，凡有更改的，应在更必处加盖单位校对章。

（2）不同合同的货物，不能填报在同一份报关单上。同一批货物中如采用不同的贸易方式的，须填制不同的报关单。

（3）一份合同中如有多种不同商品，应分别填报。一张报关单上一般不超过五项海关统计商品编号的货物。

（4）要做到单证相符及单货相符。即报关单填报项目要与合同、批文、发票、装箱单相符；报关单中所报内容要与实际进口货物相符。

进口货物报关单的主要内容。

报关人员要正确填写"进口货物报关单"中的下列项目。

（1）进口口岸。填写货物入境的口岸名称。

（2）经营单位。填写经营进口货物业务的企业和单位的名称。经营单位是指对外签订和履行合同的企业和单位。

（3）收货单位。填写经营进口货物收货人的名称和所在地。

（4）贸易方式。按进口货物的实际贸易性质或方式填写，如一般贸易、寄售贸易、补偿贸易、来料加工等。

（5）贸易国别（地区）。一般是指直接购至国或地区。从 1994 年 1 月 1 日起这一栏变更为起运国别（地区）。起运国别（地区）是指把货物起始发出包括直接运往或运输路途经中转国但未发生任何商业性交易的情况下运往进口国的国家（地区）。

（6）原产国别。指进口货物的生产、开采或制造的国家。

（7）外汇来源。指进口货物实际使用的外汇来源。

（8）运输工具名称、提单或运单号。海运填写船名、航次、提单号；陆运填写车号、运单号；空运填航班号、货运单号。

（9）合同号、批准机关及文号。填写合同的详细年份、编号，批准进口的单位及批准文件的文号。

（10）商品名称、规格、数量、重量、包装及标记唛头。应将合同规定的商品名称和规格的主要项目、实际进口数量和数量单位、毛重和净重、包装种类、件数、标记唛头，一一填写清楚。

（11）交价格和到岸价格（指 CIF 价）。成交价格填写合同规定的成交单价并注明所使用的贸易术语及货币名称。到岸价格包括货价、运费、保险费。

（12）海关统计商品编号。按照国际贸易商品分类目录《商品名称及编码协调制度》填报。

（13）运杂费及保险费。按实际支付金额填写。以 CIF 条件进口的，此栏可不必填写。

（14）进口日期、申报单位、集装箱号等。

除填写"进口货物报关单"外，还应交验有关单证，如：提货单、装货单或运单；发票；装箱单；进口货物许可证；减、免税证明或免验货物的证明；海关认为有必要提供的进口合同、厂家发票、产地证明及其他文件等。

报关员在报关时须出示报关员证,并在报关单上加盖"HS"报关员专用名章,否则,海关将不接受报关。

(三) 查验

根据我国《海关法》规定,进口货物除非特殊原因经海关总署批准的以外,都应当接受海关的查验。海关查验货物主要是海关在接受申报后,以进口货物进行实际的核对查验,以确定货物的物理性能或化学成分以及货物的数量、规格等是否与报头单证所列相一致。

查验进口货物应在海关规定时间和场所进行,即在海关监管区域内的仓库、场地进行。验关时,进口货物的收货人或其代表应该到场并负责拆开包装。对散装货物、大宗货物或危险品等,可在船边等现场查验。在特殊情况下,由报关人申请,经海关同意,也可由海关派员工到收货人的仓库、场地查验。

(四) 结关

结关又称放行,是指进口货物办完向海关申报,接受查验,缴纳关税后,由海关在货运单据上签字或盖章放行,收货人或其代理人持海关签章放行的货运单据提取进口货物。海关在放行前,需再派专人将该票货物的全部单证及查验货物记录等进行全面的复核审查并签署认可,才在货运单上签章放行,交收货人或其代理人签收。放行意味着办完了海关手续,未经海关放行的进口货物,任何单位和个人不得提取或发运。

对违反国家法律、行政法规的进口货物,海关不予放行。对准许进口的货物,除另有规定者外,由海关根据我国《海关进出口税则》和《关税条例》规定的税率,征收进口税,进口货物应按规定纳税的,必须在缴清税款或提供担保后,海关方可签章放行。

二、验收货物

进口货物运达港口卸货时,港务局要进行卸货核对。如发现短缺,应及时填制"短卸报告"交由船方签认,并根据短缺情况向船方提出保留索赔权的书面声明。卸货时如发现残损,货物应存放于海关指定仓库,待保险公司同商检局进行检验,明确残损程度和原因,并由商检机构出证,以便向责任方索赔。

凡属于法定检验的进口货物,必须在合同规定的期限内由商检机构或指定的检验机构检验。未经检验的货物不准投产、不准销售和使用。法定检验的进口货物到货后,收货人必须向卸货口岸或到达站的商检机构办理登记。商检机构在报关单上加盖

"已接受登记"的印章,海关凭此验放。凡不属于法定检验的进口货物,买卖合同约定由商检机构检验的,依照法定检验商品办理报验、检验事项。如进口货物经商检局检验,发现有残损短缺,应凭商检局出具的证书对外索取赔。对于合同规定在卸货港检验的货物,如已发现残损短缺有异状的货物,或合同规定的索赔期即将期满的货物等,都需要在港口进行检验。

三、办理拨交手续

在办完上述手续后,如订货或用货单位在卸货港所在地,则就近转交货物;如订货或用货单位不在卸货地区,则委托货运代理将货物运内地并转交给订货或用货单位。关于进口关税和运往内地的费用,由货运代理向进出口公司结算后,进出口公司再向订货部门结算。

第四节 进口索赔

进口商品到货后,经检验,如品质、数量、包装等不符合合同规定的,需要向有关方面提出索赔。对外索赔,进口公司应加强与商检局的配合,商检局应认真检验,鉴定货损情况,出具商检证书,并根据有关事实,确定责任归属。

一、索赔对象

进口索赔应根据造成损失的原因,分别向有关责任方索赔。进口索赔的对象主要有以下三个方面。

1. 向卖方索赔

卖方不交货或不按期交货或交货的品质、数量、包装与合同规定不符等,均构成卖方违约,卖方应承担违约的法律责任。根据有关法律和国际公约的规定,买方可以根据卖方违约所造成的结果,区别情况,依法提出撤销合同或提出损害赔偿。

2. 向承运人索赔

承运人是指在运输合同中,通过铁路、公路、航空、内河运输或这些方式的联合运输,承担履行运输任务或办理运输队业务的任何人。进口的货物,如发生残损或到货数量少于提单所载数量,而运输单据是清洁的,则表明是承运人的过失所造成货物残损、缺少,买方即可根据不同运输方式的有关规定,及时向有关承运人提出索赔。

3. 向保险公司索赔

如由于自然灾害、意外事故或运输装卸过程中发生事故等致使货物受损,并属于承保范围以内的，应向保险公司索赔。凡属于承运人的过失造成的货物残损、遗失，而承运人不予赔偿或赔偿金额不足抵补损失的，只要属于保险公司承保范围内的，也应向保险公司提出索赔。

二、进口索赔应注意的问题

在进口索赔工作中，应注意下事项。

1. 索赔证据

对外提出索赔需要提供证件，首先，应制定备索赔清单，随附商检局签发的检验证书、发票、提单副本。其次，对不同的索赔对象，还要另附有关证件。向卖方索赔时，应在索赔证件中提出确切的根据和理由，如 FOB 或 CFR 合同，尚须随附保险单一份；向轮船公司索赔时，须另附由船长及港务局理货员签证的理货报告及船长签证的短卸或残损证明；向保险公司索赔，须另附保险公司与买方的联合检验报告等。

2. 索赔金额

按照国际惯例，买方向卖方索赔的金额，应与卖方违约所造成的实际损失相等。即应根据商品的价值和损失程度计算。所以，索赔金额除包括受损商品的价值外，还包括其他有关费用。例如商品检验费、装卸费、银行手续费、仓租、利息等，都包括在索赔金额内。至于具体应包括哪几项，应根据实际情况确定。

3. 索赔期限

对外索赔必须在合同规定的有效期限内提出，过期无效，责任方有权不予受理。如因商检工作有困难，可能需要更长的时间，可向对方要求延长索赔期限，或在合同规定索赔有效期内向对方提出保留索赔权。

按照《联合国国际货物销售合同公约》规定，如买卖合同中未规定索赔期限，买方行使索赔权的最长期限为自实际收到货物起不超过两年；向轮船公司的索赔期限为货物到达目的港交货后一年之内；向保险公司提出海运货损的索赔期限为被保险货物在卸载港全部离海轮后两年之内。

4. 索赔的责任方

进口货物发生了损失，除属于轮船公司及保险公司的赔偿责任外，如属卖方必须直接向卖方要求赔偿，防止卖方制造借口推卸理赔责任。

目前，我国的进口索赔工作，属于船方和保险公司责任的，一般由货运代理或运输公司代办；属于卖方责任的则由进出口公司直接办理。为了做好索赔工作，要求进出口公司、外贸运输公司、订货部门、商检局等各有关单位密切协作，做到检验结果正确，证据属实，理由充分，赔偿责任明确，并要及时向有关责任方提出，以挽回货物所受到的损失。

Performance of Import Contract

1. Application for Opening the L/C

At present, in our import transportation payment is made through collection, or partly by deposit and partly by the banker's L/G. But in most cases, payment is made through the L/C. After the conclusion of an import contract, our foreign trade enterprise shall apply to its bank to issue an L/C in favour of the exporter. The importer shall fill in an application for opening the L/C on the basis of the contract, which includes the type of the L/C, credit number, by full telex or airmail, date of application, applicant, beneficiary, advising bank, amount in figures and in words, date of expiry, place of expiry, draft, shipping documents, particulars evidencing shipment of the cargo, including the contract number, name of commodity, specification, quantity, packing, shipping marks, etc., terms of shipment, date of shipment, terms of price, special instructions, etc. In addition to the above-mentioned contents in the L/C, a statement of establishment of the L/C shall also be made by the applicant, in: which his promissory warranty is given.

The kind of L/C and the time of opening the L/C shall be handled according to the stipulation of the contract. In case the contract stipulates that the L/C shall be established after the seller gets the export licence or pays the performance bond, we shall open the L/C after we have received the advice of the seller's having got the export licence or the seller's performance guarantee money.

2. Conclusion of the Transport Contract

In case of ocean transport, most import transactions adopt FOB terms. In case of land transport or air transport, most transactions adopt FCA terms.

Under FOB or FCA terms, we shall be responsible for concluding the transport contract. The time of chartering a ship or booking space shall be in conformity with that stipulated in the contract. In case the contract stipulates that the seller shall advise us of the expected time of shipment, we shall charter a ship or book space with the Foreign Trade Shipping Company in time after receiving the above advice. After the work is done, we shall advise the seller of the name of the ship and the time of shipment, etc.

3. Insurance

Under FOB. FCA, CFR or CPT, we shall take out transport insurance. There are two ways to take out transport insurance for import goods.

1) Open policy The open policy specifically stipulates the proper coverage, premium rate, etc. of different kinds of import goods as well as ways of compensation for them.

The open policy covers the import goods in accordance with the previous arrangement between the insured and the China Insurance Company. On receiving the shipping advice from abroad, our import enterprise informs the insurance company of the name of vessel, sailing date, name of the commodity, quantity, port of shipment, port of destination, etc. as a formality for taking out the insurance.

2) Cover insurance for each individual lot: If without the open policy after receiving the sellers shipping advice our import enterprise shall cover insurance on the import goods with the insurance company.

3) Examination of documents and payment for the purchase price: After the delivery of the goods, the seller will present the draft and the full set of documents to the opening bank through his bank for recovery of the price value. After receiving the documents, the opening bank will examine the documents according to the stipulations of the L/C. In case the documents are in conformity with the L/C, the opening bank will pay the purchase price at sight or pay at a future date in case of the documents payable at a tenor other than at sight.

In case the documents are not in conformity with the L/C, the opening bank shall return the draft and the documents to the bank abroad and put the matter at its disposal.

4) Customs entry, taking delivery and allocation: After arrival of the goods, the foreign trade enterprise will fill in a declaration for importation and send it to the customs together with the commercial invoice, B/L, insurance policy, inspection certificate, etc. for examination.

While unloading, the port authority will check the goods discharged. In case of shortage, the port office will fill in a short-landed memo and then send it to the master for identification. In case of loss of or damage to the goods, the goods shall be stored in the warehouse named by the customs and the matter will be handled by the Insurance Company together with the Commodity Inspection Bureau.

If the consignee is at the port of destination, the foreign trade shipping company will allocate the goods to him and the foreign trade company will make settlements with the consignee. If the consignee is not at the port of destination, the foreign trade shipping company will carry the goods to the inland city and allocate the goods to the consignee, and at the import duties from the foreign trade company. Then the foreign trade company will make settlements with the consignee.

（资料来源：宋秀峰. 国际贸易（双语版）[M]. 中国发展出版社, 2010.）

▶ 本章小结

进口合同履行的主要环节包括开立信用证、租船订舱、通知船期和催船、装运、办理保险、审单付款、接货报关、检验、进口索赔等。

制单结汇是收取货款必不可少的一个环节。以信用证项下的交易为例,通常需要缮制的单据主要有:汇票、发票、装箱单、保险单等。缮制结汇单据时,要求做到正确、完整、及时、简明和整洁。

▶ 本章名词

进口合同履行　审单付款　进口付汇核销　进口索赔

▶ 理论思考

1. 在 FOB 条件下,采用即期信用证方式支付时,履行进口合同有哪些主要环节?
2. 进口公司在开立及修改信用证时,要办理哪些手续?
3. 审单时对"不符点"应如何处理?
4. 进口报关的一般程序包括哪些步骤?
5. 进口索赔的对象有哪些?在进口索赔中应注意哪些问题?
6. 我某进口公司以 CIF 鹿特丹进口食品 1 000 箱,即期信用证支付。国外卖方按时发货并向银行交单结算了货款。我方收到银行提示的单据(包括已装船清洁提单、保险单等),经审核无误后即履行了付款手续。货到目的港后,我方复验时发现下列情况:

(1) 该批货物共有 10 个批号,抽查 20 箱,发现其中有 2 个批号及 200 箱货物内含沙门氏细菌超过进口国标准。

(2) 收货人实收 998 箱,短少 2 箱。

(3) 15 箱货物外表状况良好,但箱内货物短少 60 千克。

根据上述情况,我方应分别向谁提出索赔?为什么?

▶ 实训习题

一、模拟业务背景

华兴进出口天津公司与韩国大宇公司于 2017 年 6 月达成进口 50 公吨白卡纸合同。请以华兴进出口天津公司业务员身份,模拟完成该合同下的各项履约任务。

二、模拟训练任务

1. 根据买卖合同要求,请中国银行向大宇公司开立信用证。
2. 根据客户"装出通知",向中国人民保险公司办理货物进口投保手续(有预约保险协议)。

3. 审核客户单据是否存在问题。

4. 向海关办理货物进口通关手续。

三、模拟训练单据与资料

（一）开立信用证

1. 开证资料——华兴进出口天津公司与大宇公司达成的白卡纸进口合同

CONTRACT

ORIGINAL   NO. N8TB336

Tianjin Date：JUNE 15, 2017

The buyers：HUAXING IMP. AND EXP. TIANJIN COMPANY

    107, XINGYAN ROAD, HEXI DISTRICT, TIANJIN, CHINA

Telex：2876TJPAC CN Fax：(86) - (022) - 3954

The seller：DAYUSN CORPORATION

    91TH FL, KWANGHWAN BLDG, 344 SELLER - RO

    CHONGRO - KU, SEOUL, KOREA

Telex：   Fax：

（1）COMMODITY：   DUPLEX BOARD WITH GREY BACK

（2）BRAND：   HANSOL HI - O

（3）SPECIFICATIONS： 250GSM, 31" *47" L. G

（4）QUANTITY：   100. OMTS

  （2% MORE OR LESS IN QUANTITY AND AMOUNT IS ALLOWED）

（5）PACKING：   STANDARD PACKING IN CONTAINER

（6）UNIT PRICE：   USD 415/MT CFR XINGANG, CHINA

（7）TOTAL VALUE：   USD 41, 500. 00

（8）TIME OF SHIPMENT： BEFORE THE END OF JULY

（9）PORT OF SHIPMENT： KOREA MAIN PORT

（10）PORT OF DESTIANTION：XINGANG, CHINA

（11）INSURANCE：   TO BE EFFECTED BY THE BUYER

（12）ENT：The buyers upon receipt from the sellers of the delivery advice, shall, in 15 - 20 days prior to the date of delivery, open an irrevocable Letter of Credit with the Bank of China, in favour of the Sellers, for an amount equivalent to the value of the shipment. The Credit shall be payable against the presentation of draft drawn on the opening bank and the shipping documents. The Letter of Credit shall be valid until the 15th day after the date of shipment is effected. By L/C at 90 DAYS AFTER DATE OF B/L.

REMARKS：

（1）PACKING：To be packed in strong wooden case (s) or in carton (s), suitable for long distance ocean marine transportation and to change of climate, well protected against moisture and shocks.

The Sellers shall be liable for any damage of the commodity and expenses incurred on account of improper packing or inadequate and improper protective measure taken by the Seller in regard to the packing.

(2) SHIPPING MARK: The Sellers shall mark on each package with fadeless paint the package number, gross weight, net weight, measurement and the wordings: "KEEP AWAY FROM MOISTEURE" "HANDLE EITH CARE" ect. and the shipping mark:

N8TB336
XINGANGCHINA

SELLERS	BUYERS
HANSOL CORPORATION	FUSHENG PAKING IMP. &EXP
	TIANJING COMPANY

2. 训练单据——信用证开证申请书

APPLICATION FOR ISSUING LETTER OF CREDIT

To: BANK OF CHINA

DATE:

Please issue on our behalf and for our account the following IRREVOCABLE LETTER OF CREDIT

by ( ) TELEX/( ) AIRMAIL: L/C NO.   (left for bank to fill)

Beneficiary: (full name & detailed address)	Advising bank: (left for bank to fill)
Applicant: (full name & detailed address)	Date of Expiry:
	Place of Expiry
Amount (both in figure and words)	

Dear Sirs,

We hereby issue our IRREVOBLE LETTER OF CREDIT in your favour for account of the above applicant available by your draft (s) drawn [ ] at sight/[ ] _____

On [ ] us/[ ] advising bank/[ ] applicant for _____% of invoice value marked as drawn under this L/C accompanied by following documents marked with X;

A1 [ ] Signed commercial invoice in _____ copies indicating Contract No. _____.

A2 [ ] Full set 3/3 clean on board Bills of Lading _____ [ ] made out to order and endorsed in blank/［ ］ notifying ［ ］ China National Foreign Trade Transportation Corp, at destination/［ ］ to collect/［ ］ prepaid ［ ］ indicating freight amount.

A3 ［ ］ Airway Bill _____ consigned to ［ ］ China National Foreign Trade Transportation Coro. At destination/［ ］ applicant/［ ］ us marked.

Air freight ［ ］ to collect/［ ］ prepaid ［ ］ indicating freight amount.

A4 ［ ］ Memorandum, issue by China Travel Service (H.K). Ltd., Hongkong _____ .

A5 ［ ］ Forwarding Agent's cargo receipt _____ .

A6 ［ ］ Insurance policy or certification in _____ copies endorsed in blank covering ［ ］ All Risks/( ) Air Transportation All Risks/［ ］ Overland Transportation All Risks, War Risks including _____ per _____ clause for _____ % of invoice value.

A7 ［ ］ Packing list/weight memo in _____ copies indicating quantity/gross and net weight of each package.

A8 ［ ］ Quality certificate in _____ copies issued by ［ ］ below mentioned manufacturer/［ ］ pubic recognized surveyor/［ ］ _____ .

A9 ［ ］ Copy of your telex advising applicant within _____ hours after Shipment indicating Contract No., L/C No., goods name, quantity invoice value, vessel's name/air flight No., package, loading port and shipping date.

AA ［ ］ Copy of applicant's/ZHONGZU's/or it's agent's shipping instruction indicating vessel name, Contract No., approximate shipment. stipulations/［ ］ _____ .

AC ［ ］ Other documents if any：

B. Evidencing shipment of：

Packing：   Price term：CIF/CFR/FOB _____

Manufacturer：   Shipping mark：

C. Special instructions：(if any marked with X)

C1 ［ ］ Your signed receipt instead of draft is acceptable.

C2 ［ ］ The remaining _____ % of invoice value _____ .

C3 ［ ］ Both quantity and amount _____ % more or less are allowed.

C4 ［ ］ All banking charges ［ ］ outside China/in. Hongkong are for beneficiaries' account

C5 ［ ］ Prepaid freight drawn in excess of L/C amount is acceptable against presentation of original charges voucher issued by shipping Co./Air Line/or it's agent.

D. Documents should be presented within _____ days from the date of shipment, but in any event the validity of this L/C..

E. Shipment from _____ to _____ not later than _____ transshipment is ［ ］

allowed/[ ] not allowed partial shipments are [ ] allowed/[ ] not allowed on deck shipment is [ ] allowed/[ ] not allowed; third party transport documents are [ ] allowed/[ ] not allowed.

* May leave in blank.

Sealed & Signed by: _____

Account No. _____ with _____

Telephone No.: (name of bank)

(二) 办理货物进口投保手续

1. 投保资料——客户装船通知

DATE: JUL. 24, 2017

HUAXING IMP. & EXP. TIANJIN COMPANY

DEAR SIRS,

WE ARE PLEASED TO ADIVISE YOU OF THE SHIPPING DETAILS AS FOLLOWS:

L/C NO.: N8TB336

INVOICE NO.: SKC990723/1

COMMODITY: 167 PLTS OF DUPLEX BOARD WITH GREY BACK

B/L NO.: SKLU805007

NAME OF VESSEL: GLORY STAR 841W

DATE: ON/ABOUT JUL. 24, 2017

FROM: BUSAN, KOREA TO XINGANG, CHINA

WEIGHT: ET-WEIGHT: 99.521MTS

GROSS-WEIGHT: 100.51621MTS

SHIPPING MARK: N8TB336

XINGGANG CHINA

VALUE OF SHIPMENT: USD41 301.21 CFR XINGANG

2. 模拟训练单据——预约保险起运通知书

中国人民保险公司

国际运输预约保险起运通知书

被保险人

编号　　字第　　号

保险货物项目 (唛头)	包装及数量	价格条件	货价 (原币)
合同号	发票号码		提单号码
运输方式	运输工具名称		运费

本通知书填写一式五份保险公司。保险公司签章后退回被保险人一份。

开航日期	年 月 日	运输线路	自	至	
投保险别		费率	保险金额		保险费
中国人民保险 年 月 日		被保险人签章 年 月 日		备注	

（三）审单

1. 审单资料1——N8TB336号进口合同下信用证

Form of Doc. Credit	＊40 A：	IRREVOBLE
Doc. Credit Number	＊20：	1709021198
Date of issue	31 C：	170701
Expiry	＊31D：	DATE 170821 Place TIANJIN CHINA
Applicant	＊50：	HUAXING IMP. ANF EXP. TIANJIN COMPANY 10，XINGAN ROAD，HEXI DISTRICT，TIANJIN，CHINA
Beneficiary	＊59：	HANSOL CORPORATION 9TH FL,，KWANGHWAN BLDG.，211
Amount	32B：	Currency USD Amount 41500.00
Available with/by	＊41D：	ANY BANK BY NEGOTIATION
Drafts at	42C：	SIGHT
Drawee	42A：	BANK OF CHINA TIANJIN （TIANJIN BRANCH）
Partial shipments	43P：	PROHIBITTED
Transshipment	43T：	PROHIBITTED
Loading in Charge	44A：	KOREA MAIN PORT
For transport to	44B：	XINGANG，CHINA
Latest Date of Ship.	44C：	170731
Description of Goods	45A；	CONTRACAT NO.：N8TB336 COMMODITY：DUPLEX BOARD WITH GREY BACK BRAND：HANSOL HI－Q SUBSTANCE：250 GSM

SIZE: 31" X47" L. G

QUANTITY: 100MTS (+/-2%)

UNIT PRICE: USD 415/MT

PRICE TERM: CFR XINGANG, CHINA

PACKING: EXPORT STANDARD PACKING IN CONTAINER.

SHIPPING MARK: N8TB336

XINGANG CHINA

Documents required   46A

   SIGAND COMMERCIAL INVOICE IN TRIPLICATE

   FULL SET (1/3) CLEAN ON BOPARD OCEAN BILLS OF LADING MADE OUT TO ORDER OF BANK OF CHINA (TIANJIN BRANCH) TIANJIN CN AND BLANK ENDORSED MARKED FREIGHT PREPAID AND NOTIFY APPLICANT.

   PACKING LIST/WEIGHT MEMORANDUM IN TRIPLICATE.

   CERTIFICATE OF QUALITY SIGNED BY SELLER

   CERTIFICATE OF ORGIN SIGNED BY SELLER

Additional cond. 47A:

   BOTH QUANTITY AND AMOUNT 3% MORE OR LESS ARE ALLOWED

Detail of Charges 71B:

   ALL BANKING CHARGES OUTSIDE THE OPENING BANK ARE FOR

   BENEFICIARY'S ACCOUNT

Presentation Priod 48: 15DAYS

Confirmation   49: WITHOUT

Instructions   78:

   ALL DOCUMNTS ARE TO BE PRESENTED TO US IN ONE LOT BY 1ST AVAILABLE AIRMAIL THROUGH BANK OF CHINA. SEOUL. THIS CREDIT IS SUBJECT TO THE UNIFORM CUSTOMS AND PRACTICE FOR DOCUMENT CREDITS 1993 REVSION I. C. C. PUBLICATION NO. 500 WE HEREBY UNDERTAKE THAT ALL DRAFIS DRAWN UNDER AND IN COMPLIANCE WITH THE TERMS OF THIS L/C WILL BE DULY HONORED ON PRESENTATION

2. 审单资料2——大宇公司汇票

Drawn under BANK OF CHINA, TIANJIN (TIANJIN BRANCH)

L/C or A/P No. 1709021198

Dated 990701

No HSC170723/1 ... Exchange for USD 4,150,000   SEOUL, AUG 06, 2017

At ＊＊＊ sight of this FIRST of Exchange (SECOND of exchange being unpaid), pay

To the Order of COMMERCIAL BANK OF KOREA

The sum of SAY US DOLLARS FORTY ONE THOUSAND FIVE HUNDRED ONLY

To BANK OF CHINA, TIANJIN (TIANJIN BRANCH)

HANSOL CORPORATION

3. 审单资料3——大宇公司发票

COMMERCIAL INVOICE

Shipper/Exporter DAYU CORPORATION 9TH FL, KWANGHWAMUN BLDG, .211 SEJONE - RO, CHONGRO - KU, SEOUL, KOREA		No. & date of invoice HSC990723/1 JUL. 23, 2017		
Applicant HUAXING IMP. AND EXP. TIANJIN COMPANY 10, XIANAN ROAD, HEXI DISTRICT TIANJIN, CHINA		No. &date of/L/C 1009021198 JUL. 14, 2017		
Port of loading BUSAN, KOREA	Final destination XINGANG, CHINA	Remarks		
Carrier VICTORY STAR 805W	Sailing on or about JUL. 24, 2017			
Marks and No. of PKGS	Description of Goods	Quantity/Unit	Unit price	Amount
N8TB336 XINGANG CHINA	CONTRACT NO.: N8TB336 COMMODITY: DUPLEX BOARD WITH GREY BACK BRAND: HANSOL HI - Q SUBSTANCE: 250GSM SIZE: 31" X 47" L. G. QUANTITY: 99.521MTS (+/-2-%) UNIT PRICE: USD415.00/MT PRICE TERM: CFR XINGANG CHINA TOTAL AMOUNT: USD41301.21 PACKING: EXPORT STANDARD PACKING IN CONTAINER			

HANSOL CORPORATION

4. 审单资料4——大宇公司装箱单

PACKING LIST/WEIGHT MEMORANDUM

Shipper/Exporter DAYU CORPORATION 9THFL, KWANGHWAN BLDG., 211 SEJONE – RO, CHONGRO – KU, SEOUL, KOREA	No. &date of Invoice HSC170723/1　JUL. 23, 2017
Consignee TO ORDER OF BANK OF CHINA (TIANJIN BRANCH) TIANJIN CN	Remarks L/C NO：1009021198
Notify Party FUSHENG PACKING IMP. AND EXP. TIANJIN COMPANY 107, XIANGYANG ROAD, HEBEI DISTRICT TIANJIN, CHINA	

Port of loading BUSAN, KOREA	Final destination XINGANG, CHINA	
Carrier VICTORYSTAR 805W	Sailing on or about JUL24, 2017	

Marks &NO. of PKGS	Description of goods	Quantity	Net weight	Gross weight	Measurement

N8TB336　　　　　　CONTRACT NO.：N8TB336
XINGANG CHINA　　COMMODITY：DUPLEX BOARD WITH GREY BACK
　　　　　　　　　　BRAND：HANSOL HI – Q
　　　　　　　　　　SUBSTANCE：250GSM
　　　　　　　　　　SIZE：31" x 47" L. G.
　　　　　　　　　　QUANTITY：99.521MTS（+／-2-%）
　　　　　　PACKING：EXPORT STANDARD PACKING IN CONTAINER
　　　　　TOTAL QUANTITY：NET WEIGHT：99.521MTS
　　　　　　　　　　　　　CROSS WEIGHT：100.5162MTS
　　　　　　　　　　　　　　PACKAGES：167PLTS

　CONTAINER　SEAL　SUB　SIZE　REAM　QUANTITY　@ NET WEGHT @ CROSSWEIGHT　PLT NO.

NO.	NO.	(GSM)	(INCH)	(/MT)	(PALLETS)	(MT)	(MT)	
SKLU4533967/48725		250	31×47	5.0	38	22.346	22.56946	202-239
SKLU4533479/48340		250	31×47	5.0	38	22.346	22.56946	240-277
SKLU4433124/60760		250	31×47	5.0	38	22.346	22.56946	278-315
SKLU4313520/17624		250	31×47	5.0	25	14.701	14.84801	316-340
		250	31×47	5.4	11	6.986	7.05586	341-351
SKLU2320427/60653		250	31×47	5.4	17	10.796	10.90396	352-368
TOTAL					167	99.521	100.51621	

（四）进口通关模拟训练单据——进口货物报关单

中华人民共和国海关进口货物报关单

预录入编号：　　　　　　　　　　　　　　　　　　　　　　　海关编号：

进口口岸	备案号	进口日期	申报日期
经营提单	运输方式	运输工具名称	提运单号
收货单位	贸易方式	征免性质	征税比例
许可证号	起运国（地区）	装运港	境内目的地
批准文号	成交方式	保费	杂费
合同协议号	件数	包装种类	毛重（千克）	净重（千克）
集装箱号	随附单据		用途

标记唛码及备注

项目	商品编号	商品名称、规格号	数量及单位	原产国（地区）	单价	总价	币制	征免

税费征收情况

录入员　　录入单位　　兹声明以上申报无讹并承担法律责任　　海关审单批注及放行日期（签章）

	审单	审价
报关员		
单位地址　　　　　申报单位（签章）	征税	统计
邮编　　　　电话　　　　填制日期	查验	放行

CHAPTER 11
第十一章 国际贸易方式

> **本章指导**

通过对本章的学习,要求能够了解目前常用的国际贸易方式,着重掌握经销与代理、招标与投标、拍卖与寄售、加工贸易、补偿贸易等程序,运用所学知识重点学会:

1. 经销代理方式的基本做法;
2. 如何进行招标、投标;
3. 拍卖和寄售的基本做法;
4. 加工装配业务的基本做法。

第一节 经销和代理

随着国际分工的不断发展,分工所带来的专业化优势促成了国际贸易中大量经销商和代理商的涌现。通过经销商或代理商的介入,可以极大地节约"交易成本",并可减轻国际贸易中供货商与进口商之间存在的"信息不对称",使跨越国界的商品交易得以顺利进行。实践表明,经销商和代理商已经并将一直对我国企业开展对外贸易起巨大作用。

一、经销(distribution)

经销是指经销商(distributor)与生产厂家或供货商(supplier)达成协议,在规定的期限和地域内购销指定商品的一种贸易方式。经销通常又称分销,经销商在购入供货商商品后,自主经营,自负盈亏,自担风险。

国际贸易中所采用的经销方式,根据经销商所有的权限不同,可分为一般经销和独家经销。一般经销下,经销商没有对应产品在约定区域和期限内的专营权,出口企业可在同一区域内指定数家经销商共同完成指定产品的销售,但这种做法有很多弊端,最明显的比如各经销商可能同时经销其他企业的同类竞争产品。从而可能影响出口产品在指定区域的销量;此外,各经销商之间极易产生"搭便车"现象。比如,在市场调研,营销推广等工作中,会有部分经销商企图无偿利用其他经销商所获取的市场。而独家经销商对约定产品享有在约定期限和区域内的专营权。在此我们主要介绍独家经销:

(一) 独家经销的含义

独家经销(sole distribution),也称包销(exclusive sales),是指出口企业通过协议,把约定商品在约定区域和期限内的专营权给予国外某经销商的做法。采用此种做法,在协议期限内,对于约定区域内协议商品的经营,包销商享有排他性权力。这种做法区别于单边逐笔售定的是:供货商可以通过协议与包销商建立起一种比较稳定的购销关系。

(二) 独家经销协议

独家经销协议一般只是原则地规定双方当事人的权利义务和一般交易条件,协议下每批货物交付时再依据具体买卖合同确定价格、数量、交货期、贸易方式等具体交易条件。独家经销协议通常应包括下列内容:

1. 协议双方当事人名称、地址、签约日期与地点
2. 协议双方当事人的关系

明确双方买卖关系,而非代理或其他法律关系,避免以后出现不必要的争议。

3. 经销商品范围

出口方经营产品范围一般较广,所以要在协议中明确规定经销商享有经销权的商品的品种、类别及型号。确定经销商品的范围时,应充分考虑选定经销商的经营能力、资信状况、经营范围等,通常刚开始范围不宜订的过宽。若商品范围包括供货方全部商品,还应注明对于停止生产的产品和新开发生产的产品如何适用协议。

4. 经销区域

经销区域亦即经销商行使经销权的地理范围。具体可以是一个国家,或者几个国家,或是一个城市或几个城市。经销区域的确定,通常要考虑下列因素:经销商的规模,经营能力及其销售网络;商品性质及种类;市场差异程度,包括消费习惯,消费心理及文化、宗教、民俗等;政治区域划分,地理和交通条件等;还应尽量避免与已有客户和市场区域交叉重复。经销区域大小掌握应适度,既要能充分调动经销商的经营积极性,充分利用其销售网络,又要避免区域过大,超过经销商经营控制能力。通常还应规定经销商不得跨越指定区域销售,防止侵占其他经销商和出口方自有的销售区域,影响其产品销量。对于经销区域能否扩大也应规定清楚。

5. 经销期限

独家经销商的专营权期限长短应明确规定。经销期限过短,不利于调动经销商的积极性因为对于广告宣传等促销费用的投入,往往需要一定时间后才能收到效果。期限过长,难于应对市场的各种变化,也容易使我出口方陷入被动。另外,对于期限的延长及终止条件亦应订明。一旦出现协议规定的终止条件时,即可终止协议,避免损失。

6. 经销商的专营权

独家经销协议中出口商授予经销商的经销权具有排他性质,即在同一区域和协议期限内出口商不得通过其他经销商向该区域投放产品,这实际上就是独家经销商所享有的垄断专营权。但为了保障出口商的利益,一般也会在协议内规定经销商不得在同一区域经销与供货商指定商品相竞争的商品。对于此项规定,应注意的是不应违反经销商所在国"禁止独占"等相关法律。

7. 经销数量或金额

独家经销商在协议期限或每一时期内所应负责采购的商品数量或金额也是协议的重要内容。一般应结合经销商的销售能力进行商订。通常的做法是协议中规定包销商所应采购的最少数量或最低金额,一方面约束经销商必须完成既定数量或金额的承购,另一方面也意味着供货商(出口方)应供货方最低数量、金额保证。

8. 经销商的其他义务

在独家经销协议中,通常还应对特殊情况下经销商的相关义务做出具体、明确的规定。

例如:

(1)为了便于扩大销路,开拓市场,包销商应负责在该区域内采取必要的促销手段;开展市场调研活动等。比如:广告宣传、举办展览会,以及向出口商反馈该区域的销售状况、市场环境及市场动态等,但对于这些工作所投入的费用应由哪方负责,最好在协议中明确规定。

(2)对于经销商品的售后服务及技术支持,在供货商提供零部件的前提下,也应由经销商负责,费用要明确规定。

(3)经销商一般还应负责在经销区域内对所经销商品的工业产权和知识产权采取适当保护措施,发现有侵权事件及时向供货商汇报。

(三) 独家经销的利弊

在我国出口贸易中,独家经销是一种较为常用的经营方式,因为独家经销方式对出口方的确有许多好处,比如:通过包销协议,可建立起稳定的购销关系,可以更好地完成交易商品的宣传推广工作,完善售后服务,从而提高品牌知名度和顾客忠诚度,扩大销量,稳定市场,这主要是由于出口商授予经销商指定区域内的专营权调动了经销商的积极性。但是，独家经销也有弊端，原因也正在于专营权，如果使用不当，就会使出口商经营受损，经销商可能会凭借享有的专营权压低采购产品价格，经营不积极，或同时经营竞争产品等。因此，在使用独家经销这一做法时，应慎重选择经销商，并应注意同经销商的沟通，使用管理好经销商，对于经销范围、区域、期限也应规定适度，避免陷入被动境地。

二、代 理

代理（agency）是国际贸易中十分常见的做法，现在国际贸易的各个工作环节几乎都有了各种各样的代理，比如：运输代理、保险代理、广告代理、采购（销售）代理等。我们在此只介绍在国际贸易中，我出口企业广泛采用的通过国外代理商销售产品的销售代理。

（一）代理概述

1. 代理的定义及其性质

《中华人民共和国民法通则》将代理定义为："代理人在代理权限内，以被代理人的名义实施民事法律行为。被代理人对代理人的代理行为承担民事责任。"这一概念同大陆法系的直接代理基本相同，强调代理人必须以被代理人名义实施代理行为。在此我们所指的国际贸易中的代理，是指我国出口企业与国外代理商达成协议，规定由后者代为推销的商品，销售区域和权利期限，并向第三人招揽生意，订立合同或办理同交易有关的其他事宜，同时对代理商支付佣金作为报酬的一种贸易方式。代理同经销不一样，在代理业务中，我国出口企业同国外代理商的关系是委托与受托关系，而不是买卖关系，所以代理商不需动用自己资金购买商品，不负责盈亏，不承担风险，只获取佣金，以此我们可以看出，代理同经销的区别（仅就直接代理而言）

（1）行为的自主性。代理人（代理商）只能在委托人（出口商或供货商）的授权范围内，代表委托人从事商业活动，经销商完全自主经营，只要不违反关于专营权的约定。

（2）各当事人的关系。代理人一般不以自己的名义与第三人（买主）签订合同，买卖合同关系的当事人是委托人与第三人；而经销商与供货商或出口商以及与买主之间均为买卖合同关系。

（3）收入来源。代理商收入仅取自佣金，而经销商的收入则来自买卖价差。

（4）责任、风险承担。代理商无须承担风险，仅负责介绍生意，招揽订单，自己无须承担履约责任，经销商则风险、责任自担，自负盈亏。

2. 代理的种类

国际贸易中的销售代理，根据委托人对其授权的大小，可分为总代理、独家代理和一般代理。

(1) 总代理(general agent)。

总代理是指代理人在指定地区内,不但有独家代销指定商品的权利,还有代表委托人从事商务活动和处理其他事务的权利,其实就是委托人在指定区域内全权代表。在我国外贸业务中,通常指定我国驻外贸易机构作为我国外贸企业在该地区的总代理。

(2) 独家代理(exclusive agent; sole agent)。

独家代理是指在协议规定的地区和期限内对指定商品享有专营权利的代理人。委托人一旦在某一区域选定独家代理后,即负有不得在约定期限时此区域指定其他代理人的义务,并且一般还规定,委托人自己也不得越过独家代理直接向该区域投放产品。即使委托人自己直接在此区域销售产品也同样应按约定比例向独家代理支付佣金,并将已售数量或金额计入独家代理应完成的最低代销额度但为了平衡双方的权利义务,协议中还应规定独家代理在协定期限内负有不得经营同类竞争产品,及不得跨区销售的义务。

(3) 一般代理(agent)。

一般代理又称普通代理,不享有相应商品在指定区域内的专营权,委托人在同一代理区域和期限内,可选定数家代理人代理销售同一种商品。一般代理根据推销商品的实际金额或根据协议规定的办法和百分率向委托人计收佣金,故一般代理也叫佣金代理(commission agent)。其佣金幅度,一般以发票净值计算,即发票价格中扣除运费、保费、包装费及进出口税后的价值。通常为净值的1%~5%。委托人也可以直接与该区域的买主交易,无须向佣金代理支付佣金。目前我国出口业务中,较多使用此类代理。

(二) 代理协议(agency agreement)

代理协议是用以明确委托人与代理人之间权利义务关系的法律文件,就销售代理协议而言,其主要内容包括:

1. 协议双方当事人的名称,地址及订约时间

应明确委托人与代理人之间的法律关系、授权范围,写明双方当事人的名称、地址、法律地位、业务范围及注册日期、地点等。

2. 代理商品范围

写明具体的商品名称及种类。

3. 代理区域

即代理人有权开展代理业务的地区。具体规定方法同前述独家经销协议相同。

4. 代理人的权限

若为一般代理,通常规定委托人保留在协议期限时代理区域同买主直接交易的权

利,即代理人不享有专营权。若为独家代理,则要规定提供专营权条款。一般规定委托人在协议期间不得在此区域指定其他代理商或直接与买主成交,如委托人对此权利有所保留,则通常仍应按约定比例向代理商就成交金额支付佣金。

5. 代理期限及终止条款

代理期限的规定方法亦同于独家经销协议,协议中还应明确规定:任何一方在协议期间不履行协议义务,另一方有权终止协议。

6. 佣金条款

佣金条款是代理协议中十分重要的条款,要在条款里要明确规定计算佣金的基础、佣金率、支付时间和支付方法。

代理协议中,应明确是以成交额还是实际成交额或以发票金额为基础计算佣金,同时还应注明是按 FOB 价还是 CIF 价计算。佣金率也要写明规定方法,一般比率为 1% ~ 5% 左右,佣金的支付方法也有多种,如货款收回后逐步支付,定期结算支付,协议终止时一次付清或者代理人直接将自己应得的佣金从付给委托人的货款中扣除。

7. 非竞争条款

所谓非竞争条款是指代理人在协议期限内无权提供购买与委托人的商品相竞争的商品,也无权为该商品做广告,无权代表协议区域内的其他相竞争的企业。

8. 委托人的权利与义务

委托人的权利和义务一般包括:

(1) 关于接受和拒绝订货的权利。代理人在区域内收集的订单,代理人根据委托人的授权与客户订立的买卖合同转交给委托人后,委托人对于代理人送来的订单,可以予以接受也可以拒绝,但是对于代理人在授权范围内订立的合同,委托人必须保证履行。

(2) 委托人应负有维护代理人权益的义务,为了维护代理人的利益,委托人应保证不主动向代理区域发盘,并应及时将收到的此区域发盘转交代理人。由于委托人的原因使代理人蒙受损失的,委托人应予以补偿。

(3) 代理协议中应规定,委托人有义务向代理人提供广告资料、样品、目录等。委托人应及时向代理人支付佣金,并对代理人代表委托人对当地客户违法行为进行诉讼所付出的费用予以补偿。

9. 代理人的权利与义务

(1) 协议必须订明代理人的权利范围,只是交易中介,还是有权以自己名义订立合同。

(2) 应订有最低成交额条款,以此调动代理人的积极性,一旦写入协议,代理人即有义务在约定期限内完成最低成交金额,此类条款多见于独家代理协议。

(3) 代理人负有向委托人提供客户资信状况、市场情报、广告宣传,保护委托人工业产权,以及对委托人的商业秘密不得泄露等义务。

(三) 代理的作用及缺陷

代理的作用同经销基本相似，可以减轻一般买方卖方之间普遍存在的信息不对称，节约交易成本，利用其销售网络扩大交易量。但在独家代理方式下，也同样存在着独家经销中的弊端。因此，对于独家代理的选择必须慎重。

第二节 寄售与展卖

寄售与展卖都能在一定程度上保证买主直接见到交易商品，便于买主选购，因此，也是国际贸易中常见的方式。

一、寄售（consignment）

寄售是国际贸易中的一种传统贸易方式，世界上许多国家和地区在推销手工艺品、轻纺产品、土特产品以及小型机械设备等，都会采用此种方式交易。

(一) 寄售的概念和性质

寄售是一种委托销售的贸易方式，是指出口商将拟售商品运至国外寄售地，委托代销人（consignee）按寄售协议规定的条件，在当地市场代寄售人（consignor）出售，然后代销人扣除各项寄售费用和佣金后将货款汇付给寄售人的一种贸易方式。寄售人又称委托人或货主，代销人也叫受托人，可以是货主在国外市场的代理，也可以是其他的专门从事此类中间业务的中间商。

寄售方式下，寄售人与代销人根据寄售协议确定双方各自的权利义务。两者之间并非买卖关系，本质上属信托关系，因此寄售协议属信托合同性质。

(二) 寄售贸易方式的特点

寄售贸易方式与通常贸易方式相比，有以下特点。

（1）寄售人先将待售货物运至国外寄售地，再凭实物进行现货买卖，不同于售定方式那样货物是先成交，签订合同再发运。

（2）如前所述，寄售为信托性质，故寄售人与代销人之间不是买卖关系。代销人无需垫付资金，不承担货物起运至售出前的风险和费用，不负盈亏，收入仅靠获取佣金，在货物售出前的风险和费用均由寄售人承担。

（3）国际贸易中采用寄售方式通常是由待售商品自身特点所决定的，对于一些难以凭文字说明和样品成交商品或需抢行就市的商品，适合采用这种贸易方式。

（4）寄售方式中，代销人虽以自己名义进行买卖，但货物在售出前所有权仍属寄售人，代销人有权在目的港（地）代寄售人收取和保管货物。

（三）寄售的利弊

1. 寄售方式的优点

（1）有利于扩大销路。寄售方式为实物买卖，故国外买主可直接见到现货，对于一些仅凭文字说明和样品难于全面准确表示其品质的商品极为有利，买主可以当场对货物进行挑选，而且对于手工艺品、轻纺产品、土特产品等，可以起到"投石问路"的作用，便于日后此类产品打入该市场。

（2）价格可以随行就市，灵活调整。在售定方式下，从成交到商品支付常常有较长时间间隔，在此期间价格涨落是常有之事。而采用寄售方式，寄售人可以根据寄售地市场价格情况及供求关系，灵活地指示代销人以较为有利的价格售出商品，买方也可消除订约到履约期间价格变动的顾虑。

（3）代销人不须承担风险和费用，有利于调动其经营积极性。

2. 寄售的缺点

（1）出口方风险大，费用多。由于商品从出运到售出前的所有风险和费用均由寄售人承担，因此寄售人将面临更大风险和资金压力。

（2）资金回收周期较长，而且收汇不安全。寄售协议履约期限长，在商品售出前，资金一直被占用，而且货物的实际占有人为代销人，因此若对于代销人选择不当，就可能面临货、款两空的危险。

（四）采用寄售方式应注意的问题

寄售方式是一种较积极主动的贸易方式，若使用的好，可以扩大出口商品在寄售地市场的销路，在运用中，对于一些具体问题必须加以注意，否则难以达到预期目的。

1. 合理选择寄售地点

寄售方式下，寄售人承担较大资金压力和风险及相关费用，所以在选择寄售地点时，应综合考虑该地区的消费习惯和生活水平、销售渠道、市场动态以及政府对市场、进出口、外汇、关税及其他税收方面的管理情况，通常应选择商品进出境、外汇转移相对自由，税费较低的地区作为寄售地点。

2. 根据商品特性，合理选择寄售商品

并非所有商品均适合并且有必要采用寄售方式，寄售方式下交易的商品一般是品质、性能等。仅凭文字说明和样品难于成交的商品，如小机电设备、手工艺品等。但还应调查研究当地市场对此类产品的潜在需求，亦即此类产品在寄售地是有销路的，但采用通常贸易方式难于成交。

3. 谨慎选用代销人

寄售方式能否进行顺利,安全收汇,真正发挥这一方式的优势,与选对代销人的选择关系很大。对代销人的信誉、经营能力、经营作风、销售渠道要做全面的调查。若选用不慎,一则会影响商品的销量,二则可能安全收汇也难于保证。

4. 订好寄售协议

寄售协议是确定双方当事人权利义务的依据,因此,在寄售协议中须对双方权利义务及相关问题做出明确具体的规定。

(1) 商品售价。

寄售方式的一大特色就体现在成交价格的确定比售定方式灵活,为了使产品具有竞争力并获得较好售价,实际业务中常采用下列定价方法:

①协议中列明最低售价,超过限定售价以上部分可由代销人根据市场供求状况灵活掌握,低于限价则应取得寄售人同意;

②价格完全由代销人自主掌握;

③商品出售前先征求寄售人意见。

(2) 佣金与费用。

在寄售协议中应具体规定,商品销售中所耗费用如何分担,佣金如何计算及佣金比率等。此项规定也很重要,对于寄售人而言,在考虑所获利润的同时,还应确定合理的佣金以激励代销人。

(3) 货款结算。

主要考虑收汇的安全性,兼顾货款回收速度、结算费用等问题。为了保证收汇安全,必要时也可要求代销人提供银行保函等担保。

(4) 寄售期限及保管责任。

明确规定寄售期限及情况紧急时代销人应采取适当的货物保全措施。

二、展卖(fairs and sales)

随着信息产业不断发展及因特网在各个领域的逐渐普及,网上交易的便捷已引起了传统贸易方式的很大变化。展卖作为一种极其古老的交易方式,不仅丝毫未见逊色,而且在近年随着国内企业接连走出国门,会展经济在经济发展中所起的作用已不容低估。展卖这种贸易方式也将是国际贸易中的一种重要方式。

(一) 展卖的含义及其作用

展卖是利用展览会和博览会及其他交易会形式,对商品实行展销结合的一种贸易方式。实践中利用展览会、博览会、交易会、洽谈会、订货会等各种方式对商品边展边销,以展促销的形式在各国商贸会领域已十分普遍,而且也逐渐形成了一些颇具规模和影响力的国际博览会与国际展销会。究其来源，现在各种各样名目复杂的展卖方式其实是在早期一些区域性集市或庙会的基础上，不断扩大、发展，成为国际性、综合性的国际贸易方式。展卖所体现的最主要特点就是：通过展览，使客户或潜在的客户可以直接全方位接触产品，从而推销产品，达到当面成交或吸引客户日后成交的目的。

这种展销结合的贸易方式所起的作用是很明显的，具体有以下4个方面。

(1) 为来自世界各地的上家提供集中、全面、广泛的交易平台，既有更多的选购余地，还可节约交易成本。

展卖活动在展期内，集中世界各国、各地区的客户，为其提供交流的场所形成规模经济效应，可以节约大量的涉及谈判及各环节的交易费用。就参展的客户而言，若采用展会以外的其他交易方式，则通常要花费大笔费用在寻找客户和与客户交流，以及利用媒体进行广告宣传等方面。展卖方式可以避开中间商，缩短销售渠道，从而降低交易费用。

(2) 有利于宣传出口商品、扩大销路、招徕潜在买主。

展卖中买主可以直接接触到产品实物，从各个方面了解展出产品的品质及性能。参展商可借此机会宣传推广自己产品，很多卖主可能在展卖结束后陆续接到大量订单。

(3) 利用展卖收集市场信息，开展市场调研，以便更有效地掌握市场动态，交流技术，改进产品质量，增强出口商品竞争力。

(4) 通过举办国际性展览会扩大知名度，达到招商引资的目的。我国近年举办的许多中小型展览会，其作用既体现在扩大出口商品交易，同时又可借展览会使国外参展商了解当地投资环境，达到吸引外资流入的目的。

(二) 展卖的类型

目前国际上各种各样的展卖，从不同角度可分为不同类型。如：从性质上可将其分为展品主要为生产资料的贸易型展卖和展品主要为生活资料、日用消费品的消费型展卖；按举办时间可分为定期展卖和不定期展卖。在此，我们只介绍从参展商品类别分类的两种主要展卖形式。

1. 综合性世界博览会

又称"水平型博览会"，各种商品均可参展，并洽谈交易的博览会。当前，世界著名的此类博览会有：智利的圣地亚哥、意大利的米兰和叙利亚的大马士革、德国的莱比锡、法国的巴黎等国际博览会。这种博览会规模大、展期长、产品齐全，而且对公众开放。

2. 专业性世界博览会

又称"垂直型博览会"，参加展出和销售的仅限于某类专业性产品，规模相对较小，会期也较短。比较著名的有：纽伦堡玩具展览会、慕尼黑体育用品展览会、法兰克福消费品展览会，以及科隆博览会等。

（三）我国展卖概况

1. 在我国举办的展卖

我国自 20 世纪 50 年代举办广州中国出口商品交易会以来，在全国各主要城市相继举办了一些自己的小型交易会，这一贸易方式在我国将继续对进出口贸易起很大的促进作用。

（1）中国出口商品交易会（Chinese Export Commoclities Fair，CECF）。

又称广州交易会（Guangzhou Trade Fair）或广交会，我国于 1957 年春举办了首届广交会，此后每年与春秋两季个举办一次，分别为 4 月 15 日~5 月 5 日的"春交会"与 10 月 15 日~11 月 5 日的"秋交会"。40 多年来，我国利用"广交会"定期邀请国外客户前来我国集中谈判成交，根据"平等互利、互通有无"的对外贸易原则，以出口为主，进出结合，有买有卖，形式多样，极大地促进了中国的对外贸易发展，加深了中国同世界各国的经济联系。

（2）其他影响较大的展卖。

①中国华东进出口商品交易会。创办于 1991 年，会址为上海国际展览中心或上海世界贸易商城。2000 年开始向进出结合，专业化办展的方向改革，以消费品为重点，设纺织服装馆和轻工、工艺馆两个专业馆，另设一个综合馆和一个境外馆。主要展品包括：食品土畜、轻工工艺、纺织服装、机电五矿、医保化工等产品。

②中国天津进出口交易会。创办于 1990 年，会址为天津市体育展览中心，主要展品有：机电、轻工工艺、化工、纺织服装、丝绸、医疗保健、地毯、土畜、粮油食品和五金矿产等产品。

③中国大连进出口商品交易会。于 1987 年创办，地点在大连市国际会展中心，主要展品有：机械设备、电子、冶金、汽车、五金矿产、石化、纺织服装、土畜产、粮油、轻工工艺、医疗保健、非金属类产品。

④中国昆明出口商品交易会。1993 年创办。地点在昆明市国际贸易中心，展品：机电、轻工工艺、化工、纺织服装、丝绸、医疗保健、地毯、土畜产、粮油、五金矿产品。

⑤中国国际电子家电信息技术博览会。又称中国青岛对外经济贸易洽谈会。1984 年首次举办，会址在青岛市国际会展中心，主要产品有：数码信息、通信技术及产品、数码音响、多媒体技术及产品、家庭数码和娱乐产品、智能、家电、软件等产品。

⑥中国哈尔滨贸易洽谈会。创办于 1990 年，地点在哈尔滨市哈洽会会馆，展品主要有：粮油、五金矿产、纺织服装、土畜产、轻工工艺、机械设备、电子、医疗保

健、石化、建材、林木、工艺美术、旅游服务等。

除此之外，较有影响力的还有中国乌鲁木齐对外经济贸易洽谈会、厦门举办的中国投资贸易洽谈会、深圳的中国国际高新技术成果交易会。上述展卖会除展销商品以外，均不同程度地涉及国际经济合作等领域。另外还有某些商品产地或出口口岸举办的专业性小型交易会，简称"小交会"（minifair）。

2. 在国外举办的展卖

除我国举办的各类展销会及参加国外的国际博览会外，我国还有企业到国外参展，支持外商举办或与外商联合举办展卖会。

第三节 拍卖与招标投标

与其他贸易方式相比，拍卖和招投标通常更能体现竞争性买卖的特点。正是由于这两种方式成交条件上所体现的竞争性，所以在一些特定的领域或针对一些特殊商品，这类交易方式更有利于商品发现价值和实现价值增值，在国际贸易中，也是一类经常使用的交易方式。

一、拍卖

拍卖（auction）是由专营拍卖业务的拍卖行接受货主的委托，在一定的地点和时间，按照一定的章程和规则，以由众多买主公开叫价竞购的方式，最后由拍卖行把货物卖给出价最高的买主的一种现货交易方式。

采用拍卖方式成交的商品，通常是品质难于标准化，或难于久存，或按传统习惯以拍卖出售的商品，如：毛皮、原毛、鬃毛、牲畜（主要是马匹）、羽毛、烟草、茶叶、纸张、热带木材、水果、蔬菜、花卉、象牙、古董、艺术品等。并且此类国际商品拍卖大多已经历史地形成了固定的拍卖中心，其中原毛和茶叶的拍卖，已逐步转向主产地进行。

（一）拍卖的形式

目前存在的拍卖形式主要有：

1. 增价拍卖（ascending-price auction）

增价拍卖也称"买方叫价拍卖"或"英式拍卖"（english auction），是最常见的一种拍卖方式。由拍卖人（auctioneer）对拍卖物品宣布预定的最低价格，然后由竞买者（bidder）竞相加价，直至叫价最高时，拍卖人击槌宣告交易达成，从而出价最高者获得拍卖物品。

2. 减价拍卖（descending-price auction）

减价拍卖又叫荷兰式拍卖（dutch auction）。由拍卖人宣布拍卖物品的预定最高价格，若竞买者中无人接受，就逐渐降低叫价，直至有竞买者表示接受时击槌成交。这种方式多用于鲜活商品、水果、蔬菜等的拍卖。

3. 密封递价拍卖（sealed bids；closed bids）

密封递价拍卖也叫招标式拍卖，由拍卖人事先公布拍卖物品的具体情况和拍卖条件，然后由竞买者在规定时间内将其出价密封递交给拍卖人，再由拍卖人在规定时间统一开标，选择条件最适合的成交。这种拍卖方式公开性差、选择性小、透明度低，通常用于某些国家的政府或海关在处理库存物资或没收货物时，另外，在美国政府发行国债、国际货币基金组织、出售黄金时也都采用这种拍卖形式。

（二）拍卖的程序

1. 拍卖前的准备阶段

参加拍卖的货主要把拍卖物品运到拍卖地点，存入仓库，委托拍卖行进行整理、挑选、分类、分级、分批编号，将参拍物品按分批编号汇编拍卖目录。拍卖目录中一般应列名商品种类、批号、等级、规格、数量、产地、拍卖次序及拍卖条件，接下来分发拍卖目录并进行广告宣传。

2. 查看拍卖物品阶段

拍卖是一种现货买卖，所以竞买人在参加拍卖前会查看拍卖物品，以便按质论价。

3. 正式拍卖阶段

正式拍卖是在预定时间和地点，按照拍卖目录规定的次序，逐笔减价成交，拍卖行必须严格按照拍卖公告中的各项规定举行拍卖会。竞买者入场前要先登记个人简况，缴纳一定的保证金，领取牌号进场就座，拍卖开始后，拍卖师当众宣布拍卖方式，简要宣读拍卖规则，然后按拍卖目录次序逐一拍卖。

4. 成交与交货阶段

拍卖成交后，买主应在标准合同上签字，按约定付款，提货，买方付款中除拍卖物品价款外，一般还包括支付拍卖行的佣金（commission）或经纪费（brokerage）。拍卖结束后，拍卖行会在报刊上公布拍卖结果，以显示拍卖物品的市场行情及国际市场价格，供商人交易参考。

（三）拍卖相关问题说明

1. 关于拍卖的原则

拍卖的基本原则即所谓的"三公一高：公平、公开、公正，价高者得"。这是保障拍卖方式经久不衰的主要原因。

2. 拍卖合同订立的程序及相关法律制度

一般的买卖合同订立必须经发盘和接受（亦即法律上叫的要约与承诺）两个步骤，在此需说明的是：拍卖是一种特殊的交易方式（各国均有相关的法律对其操作程序、规则、拍卖人资格认定等作出专门规定。我国也于1997年11月1日正式颁布实施了《拍卖法》对这一方式下当事人的权利义务等作出调整）。按照各国有关合同的立法，拍卖中的拍卖公告并非发盘（要约）只是邀请发盘（要约引诱），拍卖人的出价及最终成交时买主的应价才分别为发盘和接受（要约和承诺），对这一法律性质应加以注意。

二、招标与投标

招标投标在国际贸易中常用于国家政府机构或者公用事业单位部门的物资采购，国际承包和劳务合作以及国际上政府贷款援助项目和世界银行等国际机构的贷款援助项目等操作中。可以利用这一贸易方式公开竞争，降低成本，规范操作，以提高透明度等优势，使招标方能获得最有利的成交条件。

（一）招标投标的含义及类型

招标（inviation to tender）是指招标人（买方或工程承包中的业主，发包方），在规定的时间、地点，以某种特定的方式发布招标公告，表明自己对特定的商品、工程或服务采购的规格、条件和要求，同时邀请相关的投标人（供货商、服务的提供方或工程建设项目中的承包商）参加投标并按照规定程序从中选择成交对象的一种交易行为。

投标（submission of tender）是指投标人应招标人的邀请，根据招标公告或招标单的规定条件，在规定的投标时间内向招标人递盘的行为。由此可见，招投标是一种贸易方式的两个方面。

目前，国际招投标的方式主要有以下几种。

1. 国际竞争性招标（international competitive bidding，ICB）

招标人邀请众多投标人参与投标，从中选择招标人认为最为有利的成交。根据其公开程度又可分为：

（1）公开招标（opening bidding）。

招标人在有代表性的宣传媒体上刊登广告宣布买主进行采购，并广泛地邀请供应商或承包商前来参加投标。公开发表招标公告，凡愿意参与投标的公司，都可领取（或购买）详细的介绍资料和资格预审表，只有通过资格预审的公司才能购买招标文件和参加投标。开标采取公开方式，中标结果也公开发出。政府采购物资，利用国际金融组织贷款采购的物资等，大都采用这一方式。

(2) 选择性招标（selected bidding）。

也叫有限竞争性招标或邀请招标。采用这种方式招标，招标人不在报刊上刊登招标公告，而是根据自己具体的业务关系和情报资料由招标人有选择地邀请客商，通过资格预审后，进入投标。此种招标程序适用于技术复杂或专门性货物，工程或服务，因此类商品或服务的供应范围有限，或者是采购价值低，出于经济效益考虑而采用这种方式。

2. 谈判招标（negotiated bidding）

谈判招标不是通过一次招标和开标来确定合同，而是由招标机构在开标后，和任何一个投标人通过谈判的方式磋商合同的具体条款，然后再来确定中标人。相对于一次完成的招投标有一定的灵活性，多用于金额巨大，投标人实力相当的项目招标中。

3. 两阶段招标（two-stage bidding）

是综合公开招标和选择性招标的招标方式。第一阶段：招标机构就拟采购的目标货物或工程的技术、质量或其他特点以及就合同条款和供货条件等广泛地征求建议（除合同价款外），并同投标人进行谈判以确立目标货物或工程的技术规范。此阶段结束后，招标机构可最后确立技术规范。第二阶段：招标机构依据前一阶段所确立的技术规范进行正常的公开招标程序，邀请合格的投标商就包括合同价款在内的所有条件进行投标。

（二）招投标程序

招标、投标业务的基本程序包括招标，投标、开标、评标、中标，签订合同四个阶段。

1. 招标

招标阶段具体工作一般包括：发布招标公告，制定招标文件，对投标人进行资格预审等。

(1) 发布招标公告（announcement of tender）。

凡采用"选择性招标"或"谈判招标"方式时，一般不发招标通知。若采用"公开招标"或"两段招标"，则通常在国内权威报刊或杂志上刊登招标广告。有些招标广告还应根据相关规定在国外指定刊物上刊登，或向驻外商务机构或驻本国的国外商务机构发出，以使国内外更多客商均可参加。招标通知与招标广告内容差不多，主要介绍招标项目的主要内容，要求条件和投标须知等。

(2) 制定招标文件（bidding documents）。

招标必须事先制定好招标文件，招标文件又称"标书"或"标单"，其中主要列明招标的贸易条件和技术条件，此项条件由招标人自己或由专业化咨询公司或工程建筑公司协助制定。投标人对此没有讨价还价的余地，招标文件还须列明投标人须知，例如列明投标人资格、投标日期、开标日期、寄送"标书"的方法、地址等。此外，招标单中还要求规定投标人缴纳投标保证金及履约保证金的条款。其中以保证金金额的交付、保证方式等作为投标担保。

(3) 对投标人的资格预审 (prequalification)。

资格预审是公开招标前的一项重要工作，它是预先确定投标人的资格条件，以确保其在各方面有投标能力的关键工作。所谓预审是指由招标人对投标人的基本情况、财务状况、供应与生产能力、经营作风及信誉进行全面预先审查，预审合格方能取得投标资格。

2. 投标

投标人参加投标时必须做好下列工作。

(1) 研究标书，做好投标前的准备工作。

投标人参加投标前，要做的准备工作，关键是认真分析研究标书。若是工程建设项目还应亲临实地考察。要对招标文件中的商品、成套设备的质量要求、技术标准、运输条件、保证金条款等认真分析，做到量力而行。投标在法律上被认定为"要约"，对"要约人"（投标人）有约束力，即在投标期内不得撤标。所以投标人对价格、交货期、招标人所在国的税收、法律等相关问题都要仔细研究。

(2) 编制投标文件和提供保函 (L/G)。

投标人经过慎重考虑后，一旦决定参加投标，就要根据招标文件的规定编制和填报投标文件。为防止投标人撤标或中标后不与招标人签约，招标人通常要求投标人提供投标保证金 (bidding security) 或称投标押金 (bid bond)。投标保证金可以缴纳现金，也可以由投标人提供银行保函 (L/G) 或备用信用证 (Standby L/C)。保证金额至少不低于投标金额的 1.5%，一般为 2%~5%。若投标人中途撤标或中标后不签约，则招标方没收上述保证金或要求相应银行支付保证金。如果投标人落标，则开标后，招标人退还保证金给投标人。

(3) 递送投标文件。

投标文件必须在投标截止日期之前送达招标人，逾期失效。递送投标文件，应密封后挂号邮寄，最好采用专人递交。

3. 开标、评标、中标

(1) 开标 (opening of tender)。

招标按照预先规定的时间和地点，当众拆开密封的投标文件，宣读内容，所谓公开投标，不公开投标是由招标人自行选定中标人，投标或其代表不参加。国际招标大多采用公开开标的方式，开标时所有报价应登记在案，有招标委员会签字，在评标和授标时，不得修改报价。

(2) 评标。

评标就是招标人对投标书的各项条件进行综合评审、比较。评审的主要内容包括：研究对比投标报价；投标文件是否符合标书规定；投标的履约能力等。

（3）中标（award）。

招标人对投标人经过上述一系列评审后，在所有投标人中选出报价最优惠，各项条件最符合招标条件的投标人为中标人。招标方根据定标意见以书面形式通知中标方，此通知具有"承诺"效力。并向其他投标方发出落标通知，退还投标保证金。

4. 签订合同

通常招标文件中已附有明确的合同条件及合同格式，而且中标者明确表明接受标书中的条件，并承认在规定投标期限内其投标书有约束力，但招标人与中标人在签订正式合同前，双方仍可就合同条款进一步澄清。签约前，中标人一般要在规定期限内向投标人提交一份履约保函，由招标人接受的银行开立。

按照国际惯例，如招标人在评标过程中，认为所有的投标均不理想，不能选定中标人，也可宣布招标失效，拒绝全部投标，将所有投标都作为废标处理。我国2000年1月1日施行的《招标投标法》第42条第1款亦有类似规定，一般出现以下情况，评标委员会可以否决所有投标：

（1）最低标价大大超过标底或合同结价，招标人无力接受投标；
（2）所有投标书均与招标要求不符；
（3）投标人过少，没有达到预期的竞争性。

第四节 国际加工贸易

随着经济全球化的在深度和广度的不断演进，国际分工不断发展加工贸易已不断逐渐成为一些发展中国家利用外资，发挥本国比较优势，解决就业的重要贸易政策。韩国、新加坡等新兴工业化国家正凭借这一政策发迹，并完成了国内产业的升级换代。我国在改革开放以后，伴随着外贸体制的几轮改革，各地政策，法规的纷纷出台，加工贸易也在各个领域逐步扩大。近年来，在东部沿海地区、辽东半岛、山东半岛、长三角、闽南地区以及珠三角，加工贸易在国际贸易各方式中所占比例逐步攀升。据统计，自1996年以来，加工贸易出口总额已超过我国每年进出口总额的50%。

一、国际加工贸易概述

（一）国际加工贸易的含义和特点

国际加工贸易是指利用国外资源在本国进行加工、装配和制造，再将产品销往国外的贸易方式。本质上是一种以商品为载体的劳务出口。从各国经济发展的进程看，国际加工贸易是一种初级的国际经济合作方式。在我国，广义的加工贸易包括来料加工。根据外经贸部颁发的《加工贸易审批管理暂行办法》的解释：所谓的加工贸易是指从境外保税进口全部或部分原辅材料、零部件、器件、包装物料（下称进口料件），经境内企业加工或装配后，将制成品复出口的经营活动，包括来料加工和进料加工。传统意义上的加工贸易主要指来料加工和进料加工。但伴随着"走出去"战略，国内企业逐步开展的境外带料加工业务亦应属于国际加工贸易。

来料加工（processing with customers materials）是指我国国内厂商（加工承揽方）保税进口国外厂商（委托方），包装材料。有时也用专用设备，按双方合同中约定的规格、款式、技术和商标等进行加工生产，将制成品按约定时间交付委托方。我国国内厂商收取加工劳务报酬，进口料件及出口成品可以合作，也可进口料件时暂不计价，而出口成品时由外商支付工缴费，实际业务中所见，以前者居多。若委托方提供的是原件，零部件和技术，或相关设备，由我加工方根据设计、工艺和技术要求进行装配，则此种业务就叫来料装配（assembling with customer's components and ports）。

进料加工（processing with imported materials），也就是习惯称的"以进养出"，指国内厂商从国外购进原料，加工生产出成品再销往国外。这种贸易方式下，进口原材料主要是为了扶持出口。我国开展的"以进养出"业务，除了包括进口轻工、纺织、机械、电子等行业的原材料、零部件加工，制造或装配成成品出口外，也包括以国外引进农、牧、渔业的优良品种，经种植或繁育出成品再出口。

加工贸易相对于传统的进出口贸易而言，国家政策及管理方面存在着一些区别：如国家对加工贸易合同实行审批制度，并须登记备案，加工贸易方式下进口料件享有暂时免税的优惠，故由海关对其实施严格监管或者把加工企业引入出口加工区进行集中监管。同时还有配合海关监管的加工贸易银行保证金台账制度。成品出口须经海关对《登记手册》核销及银行对加工贸易保证金台账的核销。在来料加工与进料加工之间亦有一些区别：

（1）有关进口原材料、零部件。在来料加工业务中，进口料件的所有权属于国外委托方；而进料加工因双方的买卖关系，故所有权归属于国内承接方。

（2）收入来源不同。来料加工业务中，我方只负责加工业务，实际占用自有资金，故只收取工缴费（来料加工中为加工费用，来料装配中为装配费用），而进料加工下我方可获取产品的原料加工成成品的附加值。

（3）产品销售情况有别。来料加工虽有原料的运进和产品运出，但实质为同一笔交易，原料的提供者（委托方）即为成品的接受者。我方不用考虑原料来源和成品销路，无商业风险。所以，此种方式比较适合于劳动密集的中小企业；进料加工中原料的进口和成品出口一般分别为两笔不同的交易，我方购进原料，自筹资金，自寻销路，自担风险。故要求企业具备一定的销售渠道和销售能力。

（二）国际加工贸易的作用与不足之处

1. 国际加工贸易的作用

国际加工贸易业务中，加工方通常为外汇资金短缺，技术不十分发达，但劳动力资源丰裕的发展中国家。就我国而言，开展此项业务有以下作用：

（1）有效利用外资。

由于我国自1994年，收入外汇的结售汇制取代了外汇留成制后，企业进口所用外汇很大程度上无自主权，而开发展加工贸易，尤其是来料加工、来件装配，可以基本不动用外汇及资金。从而大大减轻我国内企业的资金压力。

（2）发挥本国生产潜力及利用国外市场，提高资源配置效率。

通过开展国际加工贸易，亦可利用国际、国内两个市场，有效地配置资源。改革开放以来，不少企业存在生产能力过剩，设备闲置，尤其是转轨时期的国有企业，通过开展国际加工贸易可在一定程度上扭转这一局面；目前国内就业压力仍然很大，开展加工贸易可有效地缓解就业压力。对于国内原料短缺的行业，可以进口国外原材料；而国内丰裕的原材料，可以在来料加工中争取提高国内用料比例。多层次、多角度利用国际市场提高我国资源配置效率。

（3）可提高我国内企业技术及管理水平，便捷地获取国际市场信息，扩大出口规模。

来料加工业务中，委托方为了降低风险的考虑，常常会派遣专家对加工方进行技术指导和培训，也可能提供相关先进设备，这对于加工方汲取国外先进生产管理技术是极为有利的。我国东部沿海地区在近20年的加工贸易中，有不少是通过这种方式发展壮大起来的。如广东一带的机械、电子、服装等加工贸易已卓有成效。通过开展来料加工，我方可及时了解国际市场的动向，捕获市场信息，有利于促进国内企业生产更多适销对路的产品销往国外市场。

（4）可促进我国经济结构调整和产业升级。

以国际分工和跨国公司国际生产为背景的加工贸易，是促进我国商品结构和产业结构升级的有效途径。在这方面，新加坡、韩国走在了我们的前面。而我国也正在逐步实现从劳动密集型主导产品出口逐步向资金、技术密集型转变。同时，随着我国加工贸易的不断发展，还可以推进沿海到内地经济结构的逐步调整。

2. 国际加工贸易的不足之处

（1）对成品要求品质规格的主动权掌握在外商手中，我方处于被动地位，限制我方企业业务的拓展。

在对外加工装配业务中，商品的所有权由外商控制，在成品的质量检验及销售过程中，若外方来料不足时，我方也会很被动，且是我方接受外商委托加工而生产，对我企业拓宽业务范围也有诸多不利。

（2）可能会造成对同类产品正常出口的冲击。

虽然目前我国已设有许多出口加工区，但仍然有许多区外的加工贸易企业，各企业间的制定上不能完全统一，造成同类的恶性竞争；另外，由于受原产地规则及被动配额的影响，若有不慎常给一般贸易下的同类种商品的出口同一国家带来挤压。

（3）企业加工贸易业务，恶化外贸经营秩序，并影响外贸企业的声誉。

加工贸易在我国虽然已经过 20 多年的发展，但外贸企业相关的制度并不十分健全。不法商人利用加工贸易走私贩私，利用合同欺诈。近年来，加工贸易有些年份占了大头，这给我国对于加工贸易的监管提出了挑战。

二、国际加工贸易的业务程序

我国目前开展加工贸易有多种形式。但总体而言，可分为直接承接加工业务和通过外贸公司开展。不论在哪种情况下，对外加工贸易合同签订之后，必须按国家有关规定办理批准备案等手续。办理批准备案手续的部门为国家外经贸部，自治区、直辖市及计划单列市的外经贸委或他们的授权机关。

就加工方而言，开展加工贸易，通常有以下几个阶段：

（一）签约前的准备阶段

国际加工贸易是一种比较复杂的涉外经济贸易活动。同一般贸易前期准备工作的不同之处主要是项目和客户的选择及工缴费的确定等。

1. 确定项目

在选择确定项目过程中，必须要综合考虑各方面的因素：

（1）符合国家有关政策，比如我国按商品类别将加工项目分为：限制类和允许类；将对外贸易企业分为 A、B、C、D 四类，其中：A 类为区内加工贸易企业或区外由海关保税监管的企业，不实行银行保证金企业账制度；B 类实行银行保证金台账"空转"制度；C 类为银行保证金台账"实转"制度；D 类为受到取消加工贸易经营权处理的企业。

（2）要从引进先进技术的角度，选择加工贸易项目。

（3）要注意发挥企业现有生产能力。

（4）产品在国际市场长、短期的供求状态，对加工方国家原先大量出口的产品以及在国外市场已占优势的产品，不应作为开展对外加工贸易的项目。

加工贸易禁止类商品：

（1）进口料件属于我国禁止进口商品（包括旧服装，含淫秽内容的废旧书刊，含有害物、放射性的工业垃圾等）；

（2）返销制成品属军民通用化学品、易致毒化学品；

（3）返销制成品属我国加入国际公约并对外作出数量承诺的商品（如锡等）；

（4）废旧汽车、摩托车及其主要部件拆解翻新；

（5）国家明令不许开展加工贸易业务的其他商品。

限制类：

（1）两纱两布（棉纱、棉坯布、棉涤纶纱、棉涤纶坯布）；

（2）漂布（棉漂布、棉涤纶漂布）；

（3）阿拉伯袍裤；

（4）蚕丝类；

（5）抽纱；

（6）兔毛；

（7）珍珠（打磨、穿孔、穿串）；

（8）纯羊毛地毯；

（9）盐水蘑菇和蘑菇罐头；

（10）皮制劳保手套；

（11）钨制品；

（12）氧化锑、锑；

（13）含氧化钇稀土制品；

（14）供应港澳的卫生纸、瓦楞芯纸、麻纱、麻坯布；

（15）对港澳出口实行配额的鲜活冷冻食品；

（16）外国对我国实行进口配额限制的商品；

（17）糖类。

允许类：

除禁止类和限制类以外的商品。

2. 客户的选择

加工贸易具有"两头在外"的特点，在实际业务中，对客户的选择尤为重要。加工贸易通常不是只有一次交易就结束了。少则半年，多到三、五年，甚至更长。在选择客户时除了应注意工缴费水平外，更应考虑对方资金实力、信誉、技术水平以及经营能力。目前，同我国开展加工贸易业务的外商，主要有厂商、贸易商、经纪人。三者中应首选厂商，因其掌握产品相关技术和生产工艺流程，而且在日常生产经营中已形成固定的原材料供应渠道和销售网络；其次是贸易商，尤其是原来一直经营我出口产品的贸易商，虽无技术，但有推销能力。对于经纪人一定要严加警惕，防止上当受骗。当然，最主要的还是客户的资信情况及经营作风。

3. 加工贸易项目的可行性研究

加工贸易项目的可行性研究，因制成品及交易特点而异。对于进口少量料件，一次性出口成品并收取加工费的加工项目，加工方在签订合同之前只需对自己的生产能力，原材料用料产品优劣及工期控制。财务状况做简单预测即可。但对于目前以跨国公司主导的大中型加工贸易项目；因进口料件数量大，成品分批出口，甚至还需投入其他辅料和辅助设备，就必须对其进行严格的可行性研究。在对于项目的选择上，应尽量避免承接因对方国家产业调整而转移到发展中国家、地区生产的一些环境污染严重的产业。近年来，在某些地区不时出现从国外进口污染严重的工业垃圾进行回收。例如：废旧塑料制品的回收，运回漆包线回收铜丝等。另外，对于一些加工期较长的产品，必须考虑到因市场变化可能带来的风险，如：成品出口时因市价变动外方借口质量、规格的某些细小问题，拒绝收取货物，导致产品无法返销或延迟返销。除此之外，对加工贸易中使用的货币、利率、汇率、设备价格和产品价格之间的整体关系也要认真加以分析，综合考虑以上各方面因素，避免因开展加工贸易导致对外商品的过度依赖。

（二）谈判签约阶段

加工贸易合同与一般贸易合同有很大差别，以进料加工为例，在订立合同主要条款时，应考虑以下方面的问题：

1. 关于加工贸易业务下的来料来件

来料来件是进料加工的基础，对方能否按时、按质、按量供应料件决定了我加工企业能否按规定完成成品的交付。来料来件的品质条款，必须明确订明其名称、规格、等级、标准、品牌等。必要时亦可留有复样，作为品质纠纷的重要依据；来料、来件的运输，必须订明交货期、交货地点。对于根据生产进度，分批供应料件的，还应合理预测生产能力、加工周期、以保证供料与生产的顺利衔接，避免出现停工待料或无法如期完成加工任务。合同中为了明确责任，还要规定好出现上述情况时的补救措施及费用的负担。如果加工中使用料件国内可廉价购买，在能保证品质的前提下，可同外方协商订入合同，以增加外汇收入。

2. 成品质量

委托方为了保证成品在国际市场的销路，对其质量要求比较严格，为了使成品质量符合合同规定，加工方应对技术生产流程各环节的监督控制。合同中关于成品品质的条款规定应该明确具体，选择易为双方接受的，国际上公认的检验机构对品质进行检验，并出具证书。必要时，应留有复样或封样。对于一些工艺复杂，品质等要求高的产品，有时委托方会派遣专家对加工方进行监督和指导，如是则应在合同中加以订明。

3. 单耗及残次品率

单耗，亦即耗料率，原材料消耗定额，指单位成品消耗原材料的数量；残次品率是不合格产品占成品的比率。这两个指标的确定应当合理，订购过低，则加工方履行合同会有困难。若物料不足，只能自己承担。实际残次品率高于所订比例，则委托方有权拒收；若订得过高，委托方可能会受损。因此，这一内容也是加工贸易合同中的关键之处。基于此，委托方在提供原材料及零部件时，应根据约定的单耗和残次品率相应增加提供物料的数量。同样也应订明不符合规定条件时，各自应该承担的责任。

4. 工缴费

（1）工缴费的确定。

工缴费就是委托方应支付给加工方加工装配产品的劳务费用。这是加工贸易合同中双方都十分关心的问题，也是合同的重点。加工方在确定工缴费时应考虑到委托方所在国家或地区加工费水平和对来料件进行加工、装配所投入的各项费用开支，如：工资、管理费、仓储费、设备厂房折旧费、动力费、产品包装费、港杂费、税金利润以及可能己方提供的原料价款，依此为基础，订立有竞争力的费用水平。在确定工缴费时，还应考虑到市场行情的变化和货币汇率的变化等因素，对于期限较长的加工贸易合同，加工费用不宜订约过死，亦可订立相应外汇保值条款。

（2）工缴费的支付。

国际加工贸易工缴费的支付结算中有两种做法：一种是来料、来件、成品运出均不计价，成品出口后由委托方支付工缴费；另一种是进口料件、出口成品各作各价，两者的差额即为委托方应支付的工缴费。因前者双方风险难于平衡，实务中多采用后者。具体可由加工方在进口料件时以远期信用证或托收远期付款（承兑）交单方式作为支付方式，而出口成品时要求委托方以即期信用证或托收即期付款交单方式支付。若双方为老客户，也可能会采用汇付方式由委托方预付部分或全部工缴费。以上付款方式只是原则，实际当中应灵活搭配选用，但一般须遵循"先收后付"的原则，合理考虑两项支付时间差和加工周期，尽可能避免占用加工方自身外汇资金。

5. 料、件及成品的运输与保险

由于来料加工贸易中进口料件、出口成品所有权均系委托方所有，之间并未发生过所有权的转移，故原则上一进一出的运输和保险都应由委托方自理，但鉴于实际操作的方便，尤其是考虑到成品出运及加工期间的保险，委托方办理可能不便较为。故通常可将其中某些工作交由加工方协助办理，但应计入工缴费一并由委托方付给加工方。中国人民保险公司为适应来料加工业务发展的需要，开设了来料加工一揽子综合险，投保这一险别，即可有保险公司承担两段运输及加工期间的相应风险。

6. 加工装配产品的产地证和配额

在合同中应对加工装配产品的原产国（或地区）加以议定，避免加工贸易产品与本国一样，贸易产品的配额，也可在合同中订明不得占用我国被动配额。按照我国出口货物原产地标准，对于不符合该标准的，可根据外商要求向我签证机构—外经贸部及其指定机构（贸促会等）申领加工装配证明书。

7. 有关工业产权的问题

加工贸易中常涉及的工业产权有商标和专利，对于委托方指定的商标、图纸、外观设计等,加工方应加以注意,以防侵犯第三方的相关权利。慎重起见,可要求对方提供有关商标或专利的注册文件或其他足以证明其有合法所有权或使用权的文件,或者争取在合同中订明相应免责条款。如对第三方造成侵权,责任概由委托方承担,与加工方无关,加工方因此而受损失应由委托方赔偿。

8. 其他

加工贸易中除以上内容外,其他与一般贸易合同类似。但还应注意合同期限及合同履行中的奖惩办法。

(三) 合同报批阶段

现阶段,我国加工企业在对外加工贸易合同签订之后,必须按照国家有关规定办理批准备案手续,以获取《加工贸易批准证》,向海关申领《加工贸易登记手册》以及在银行开设加工贸易保证金台账。这一步骤主要是国家为了使海关实现对加工贸易在原材料进口、加工期间、成品出口前整个过程全面、有效的监管。开展加工贸易业务的企业必须遵循国家对加工贸易所制定的相关法规。国家主管部门对报批的加工贸易合同主要审查其进出口原辅料件和产品是否涉及国计民生的大宗商品、战略物资;是否涉及进出口配额和许可证管理的商品;此外,还要审查项目是否属国家政策的许可范围;是否有利于本国产品出口和经济发展;是否会造成环境污染等。只有按规定取得批准备案证明后,加工进口料件才能办理有关进出口手续及获取免税优惠。

(四) 合同履行阶段

1. 进口料、件时的相关手续

加工方在原材料进口环节应按国家规定完成上述向海关登记备案等手续,获取《登记手册》,否则货物进口时不能享受相应优惠。除此之外,还必须在来料、来件到港时,凭《登记手册》填写加工贸易专用报关单,向海关提交相应单证(发票、装箱单、提单),及时向海关申报,并接受海关检查,有关料件自进口之日起到加工成品出口之日止,均受海关监管。

2. 成品出口的履行步骤

(1) 备货;

(2) 催证、审证、改证;

(3) 运输与保险。

主要工作有:向外运机构办理托运手续,订立舱位和出运日期,CIF合同还应办理保险。其中出口报关与一般贸易有所不同,向海关申报出口时,除了填写规定份数的报关单和提交相关单据外,还应提交《登记手册》以便向海关办理查验手续。

(4) 核销结案。

货物出运后,我国加工企业须在规定期限(合同约定期限或最后一批货出运后1

个月),持《登记手册》,填写好实际用料情况,办理核销结案手续,解除监管。而后到相应银行办理银行保证金台账核销。

加工贸易下的进口料、件均系保税性质,未经海关允许不得将其出售、转让、调换、抵押或移作他用。合同履行完毕后,由于改进生产工艺和改善经营管理而剩余的料、件或增产的成品,在核发批准文件(或合同备案证明书)的审批机关核准转为内销时,经海关审核情况属实,可对合同金额的2%部分予以免税。

(5) 制单结汇。

第五节 国际电子商务

一、电子商务的含义

国际电子商务的出现是全球经济一体化的最新形式,是信息化、网络化条件下国际贸易手段和新方法,随着信息技术在国际贸易领域的广泛应用与发展,电子商务已成为国际研究和实务领域关注的焦点。国际电子商务是电子商务活动在跨越国界范围内的延伸,所谓电子商务,是指在技术高度发达的现代社会里,掌握信息技术与贸易规则的法人,系统化运用电子工具,高效率地从事以商品交换为中心的各种活动的总称。简单地说,电子商务就是电子化的商务对于电子商务的研究,可以从经济的角度,分析商务电子化过程中的效率、费用的经济性及商务活动在电子化条件下的基本特征与操作变化,从技术的角度,商务电子化研究的是商务交易活动的信息化,最为突出的就是安全模式下的电子数据交换技术的开发电子商务,还可以从法学的角度进行研究,主要分析电子数据交换过程与商品物流的法律权利与义务的关系,尤其是网上交易的可靠性与安全性的法律保障问题;另外,涉及贸易、电子技术、法律关系的电子商务活动具有较高的综合性和特殊性,因此也有从对信息和网络条件下的商务活动新方式进行研究,认为电子商务更多的是一种商务管理模式。

二、电子商务的分类

从不同的角度进行划分,常见的分类有以下几种。

(一) 根据是否有支付的划分

1. 电子事务处理是无对价支付的电子商务活动

例如:通过网上招标、网上磋商、网上签约、网上报税等,可以提高工作效率,增加交易的透明度和交易的公平性，尤其是与政府管理机构之间的网上办公，有利于提高政府工作的透明度，促进政务公开，增强政府的公信力。

2. 电子贸易处理是有对价支付的电子商务活动

也就是说，在电子贸易处理中涉及购物、付款、缴税等价值交换和对价物交付的贸易活动，而这些活动都可以通过信息化、网络化技术进行。电子贸易处理有利于减少交易环节、降低企业交易成本、增强企业的竞争力。同时，也有利于方便消费者，扩大消费选择，减少消费支出，提高消费的满意程度。

（二）根据参与电子商务活动的对象的划分

1. 企业对消费者的电子商务（B2C）

这种电子商务形式一般表示为 B2C，表示从商家到消费者的意思，是商户与个人客户或商户与消费者之间的电子零售商务。常见的具体形式就是网上购物或电子购物。网上购买的商品可以是有形的邮票、书籍、花卉、日常用品、家用电子产品等，也可以是无形的服务，如电子软件、网上影院、商务信息等。

2. 企业对企业的电子商务（B2B）

这种电子商务形式是商业机构（企业、公司）与商业机构之间的电子商品交易。这种交易使用互联网或各种商务网络进行订货、付款、报税等电子商务活动，是电子商务领域发展最早和发展规模最大的一种电子商务形式，也是国际电子商务的主要形式。常见的具体形式就是国际电子贸易、电子招标、电子采购、电子资金调拨（EDD）等。国际上发展最快的 B2B 网络是增值网络（value added network，VAN），电子数据交换（EDI）就在该网络上运行。增值网络上的电子数据交换技术应用使得企业与企业之间的电子商务得到了迅速的扩大和推广。

3. 企业对政府机构的电子商务（B2G）

这种电子商务形式是商业机构（企业、公司）与政府机构之间的电子商务活动。这些活动有相当一部分属于电子事务处理，但也有企业与政府机构之间的电子商务处理活动。作为电子事务处理的电子商务实际上就是现在流行的电子政务活动。比如，网上报税、网上报关、网上申领营业许可等，另一些企业对政府机构的电子商务活动则类似于 B2B 或 B2C。例如，政府的网上采购、网上招标、网上产权交易等电子商业交易活动。

4. 消费者对政府机构的电子商务（C2G）

通过这种电子商务形式使政府可以把电子商务活动扩展到个人税收申报与缴纳、社会福利发放等商务活动中来。既提高了政府的办事效率，又增加了政府工作的透明度。

另外，从商业活动的运作方式看，根据是否完全通过电子商务方式完成整个商业交易将电子商务划分为完全电子商务与不完全电子商务。对于有形商品贸易，尤其是国际贸易来说,都包含有商品的包装、保管、运输、配送等物流环节,所以是不完全电子商务。根据电子商务信息网络范围,还有本地网络电子商务、远程国内电子商务和全球电子商务等划分。

三、电子商务的特点

(一) 交易虚拟化

通过 Internet 为代表的国际互联网,贸易双方可以在电子世界里虚拟出一个真实的贸易平台环境,在这个平台上,商品交易者无须见面,就可以完成贸易谈商、商务合同签订、运输协议安排、电子报关、网上银行支付等交易活动。尤其是视频聊天、商务网络中心等技术和形式的出现,可以在网络上虚拟现实(virtual reality),使得网上贸易交易更具有现实性。

(二) 交易成本低

电子商务可以大大降低双方的交易成本。

第一,网络传输具有比信件传输或传真更低的成本、比电话交谈的费用低,又具有文件形式的可靠性。同时,电子数据处理可以缩短交易过程的时间,减少重复的数据录入,大大降低信息处理的费用。

第二,网上直接交易,不需要中介的参与,减少了交易环节和中介的费用。

第三,通过互联网进行产品介绍,可以减少大量印刷品宣传推广材料的费用,而且通过多媒体手段,宣传手段更加形象生动。

第四,电子商务属于"无纸贸易",可以减少 90% 的文件处理费用。

第五,互联网提供了即时信息,使无库存生产和销售成为可能,有利于降低库存成本。

第六,内部网的无纸办公,也有利于降低企业管理费用、节省时间,提高企业内部管理的效率,从而达到降低企业产品成本的目的。

(三) 交易效率高

在现代电子化商务活动中,原料采购、产品生产管理、商品的销售、市场供给与需求的变化、金融信贷、国际汇兑、运输、保险、报关等许多交易环节和过程,可以在无人员干预的情况下,通过电子报文的即时传输和计算机信息内动处理,在极短的时间内按照事先设定的标准化程序正确地完成。电子商务文件处理的标准化、格式化和及时传输性,使得电子贸易克服了传统贸易方式的易出错、人工成本高、处理速度慢等缺点,极大地缩短了交易的时间,提高了交易的效率。

（四）交易透明化

由于交易洽商、合同签约、装船订舱、保险、商检、进出口报关、货款支付、货物配送安装等环节均可以通过网络进行。一笔交易只要进入电子数据处理平台，凡与此平台联网的相关各方通过电子密码可以对整个过程进行监控。使交易双方、商检、保险、货运、银行、海关等相关机构可以清楚地了解该笔交易进展的实际情况，减少了暗箱操作的可能性，提高了交易的透明度。

电子商务也具有交易过程的信赖和交易者身份合法性认定、交易的安全性、交易的规范性和标准化等需要进一步解决的问题。

四、互联网条件下的国际贸易

（一）电子数据交换与国际贸易

1. 电子数据交换的含义

电子数据交换（EDI）是由数据标准化、电子数据交换软件与硬件、信息传输网络等要素构成的建立在电子化技术平台上的商务活动的规范和业务流程。它是目前应用最为广泛的国际贸易领域单证数据处理的核心技术系统，EDI 传送的贸易文件主要有订单、回执、发货通知、运单、提单、装箱单、保险单、收据发票、报关单、进出口许可证、商检证、配额证等，EDI 系统是标准化无人值守操作系统，可以通过 EDI 数据处理中心和有关各方的计算机终端系统运用专用计算机软件和硬件直接传输和交换贸易文件资料，避免了人工操作的重复录入与输入错误，提高了操作的效率和数据传送的正确性。

EDI 的构成要素是数据标准化、EDI 软件与硬件、通信网络。标准化数据是电子数据交换的基本元素，通过转换软件、翻译软件、通信软件，可以将用户自己信息库系统的数据资料转换为计算机可以识别的 EDI 标准格式，提供给计算机网络系统进行传输交换，EDI 标准是由各个企业、各个地区的代表共同制定的电子数据交换共同标准，EDL 软件与硬件由计算机技术人员根据国际贸易特点进行应用研究开发。EDL 使用的计算机通信网络是专用增值网（VAN）。

2. EDI 的特点及其对于国际贸易的影响

EDI 的特点主要表现为以下五个方面：

第一，使用仅限于具有固定格式的贸易业务信息和具有经常业务联系的客户和单位之间；

第二，传送的资料仅限于与贸易业务有关的票据资料，不包括一般性的共享信息；

第三，采用共同的标准化格式，区别于 E-mail 的灵活性特点；

第四，无须人工介入操作过程，由收发双方的计算机系统直接传送交换；

第五，与电子传真或电子函件不同，不需要人工阅读判断和重新录入，可以有效地减少人为介入的错误。

EDI 的应用大大提高了国际贸易交易文件的传递速度。据统计，运用 EDI 系统可以提高文件传递速度 81%，降低文件处理成本 38%，减少操作错误损失 40%。具体地说，国际贸易中 EDI 系统的运用具有缩短交易时间、提高交易效率、节约交易成本、节约库存和文件投递费用等优点。同时，运用 EDI 系统，还具有促进企业管理模式和管理手段的改进，使企业的管理结构、系统、过程，以及与客户、供应商的关系发生革命性的变化有利于提高企业的管理水平和经营效率。

EDI 系统也有一些不足，具体表现有两点：一是需要使用专用增值网，成本较高，限制了中小企业的进入，因此，一定程度上限制了企业合作的范围。同时 EDI 只限于 B2B 类型的电子商务活动，专用网限制了一般消费者的介入，使企业不能直接面对普通消费者，二是 EDI 的标准化格式和特殊的数据交换协议，限制了现实交易的多样性和灵活性，同时也缺乏一般性共享信息的运用。

（二）互联网与国际贸易

1. 互联网的含义

互联网从广义上说是通过现代计算机技术和通信网络将全世界不同地理位置的功能相对独立的数以亿万计的计算机系统互连起来，以功能完善的网络软件（网络通信协议、网络操作系统等）实现网络资源共享和信息数据的交换的网络系统。互联网从狭义上说是国际互联网的简称。又叫因特网（Internet），它是建立在计算机信息处理系统基础上的一组全球信息资源的总汇，是互联网中影响最大应用最为广泛的网络系统。Internet 以相互交流信息资源为目的，基于一些共同的协议，并通过许多路由器与公共网络系统互联而成，是一个信息资源和资源共享的集合。计算机网络只是互联网信息传播的载体，而 Internet 的优越性和实用性则在于信息资源与资源共享本身。

2. 互联网 + 国际电子商务的优点

互联网具有开放性、全球性、无国界性。从互联网诞生伊始，就具有民间广泛参与的色彩。所以，基于互联网的电子商务系统是一种适用面宽、用途更为广泛、更具有竞争潜力的电子商贸系统，事实上，通过 IP 地址和网络协议，各个企业的内部网（Internet）和公共电子数据交换系统或其他外部网（Extranet）都可以集成到全球互联网中，从而使得企业无论大小，都可以方便地进入互联网参与国际贸易活动并进行电子数据交换。

和 EDI 相比较，互联网 + 国际电子商务系统具有以下几个特点。

第一，费用低廉，覆盖面广，一般说来，EDI 用户要支付增值服务商两笔费用，一是邮箱租金，二是报文传输费用。前者以时间（年或月）为单位收费，后者以信息流量（千比特）为单位计量收费。互联网一般只收月租金，不计流量，且月租仅为 VAN 的 1/4 左右且有下降的趋势。另外，互联网遍及全球各个角落，用户通过电话线就可以拨号上网，方便与其他贸易伙伴进行信息交流和文件传输。所以，对于中小企业和普通消费者来说，互联网更有利于他们参与到电子商务活动中来。

第二，使用更为灵活，不受特殊数据交换协议的限制。互联网上的传输文件可以是格式化的标准模式文件，也可以是用户任意使用的任何文件形式。不必受 EDI 形式下的标准化格式限制，也不必受特殊的数据交换协议的限制，任何人可以通过电脑直接输入与纸面文件格式完全相同的传输文件，不需要特殊的翻译软件和转换软件，任何人都可以看出并直接使用。

第三，功能更为全面，国际互联网可以全面支持不同类型的用户实现不同层次的商务目标。用户可以在网上发布电子商情进行在线洽商，建立网上虚拟商场，进行网上购物，网上银行付款甚至通过专用免费软件，进行网上股票交易等不同层次的电子商务活动。

第四，市场模型由卖方市场向买方市场转化，有利于全球一体化市场的良性循环，在 EDI 中主要是 B2B 电子商务，企业还没有直接面对消费者，而且仅为商务文件数据交换，没有更多的商情信息，在互联网中，企业直接面对最终消费者，消费者的选择更为多样性，企业的竞争更为激烈，从而使得市场类型由传统的以企业为中心的生产者驱动市场转变为以消费者为中心的消费者驱动市场，这一转变，有利于企业紧密切合消费者需求，改进技术和管理，降低生产成本+提高生产效率，实现生产与交换的良性互动。

3. 互联网+国际贸易存在的问题

互联网具有开放性、低成本等特点，使得任何人都可以轻而易举的进入这个信息资源共享的平台。因而产生了互联网商业交易过程的信赖和合法性问题、安全性问题和标准与规范的问题。

具体表现有以下几个方面：

（1）买卖双方身份如何确定；

（2）卖方是否具有销售所述商品和服务的权利；

（3）买方是否具有支付所购商品与服务的能力；

（4）交易机制和支付机制是不是可靠的、合法的；

（5）与商品或服务交易相联系的物资流与资金流是不是安全的；

（6）交易过程中文件的标准化与规范化。

互联网尽管有很多优点，但也存在一些至关重要的问题。有关可靠性、安全性、合法性问题已经逐步解决，有些问题还需要努力，所以，目前互联网的运用主要是交易前的准备，交易过程中洽商，以及非标准化文件的传输，涉及签约、支付、保险、报关、商检等问题,在国际贸易中大多数还是应用 EDI 基础上的增值服务网。实际上许多国家针对贸易环节不同,已经分别设置了金融支付网络、贸易交易与结算网络、海关报税系统网络以及相互据以联网交换信息的公共互联网络等。

五、互联网+国际电子商务(跨境电商 B2B)实务操作程序

(一)交易前的准备

交易前的准备,主要包括信息收集和信息发布两个方面,是买卖双方从事国际商务活动的一个重要阶段。这个阶段的主要活动包括交易双方通过互联网广泛寻找交易机会和交易伙伴,进行价格和成交条件的对比,了解市场信息,了解有关国家或地区的贸易政策、政治和文化背景,发布企业供给或需求商品与服务的信息,通过互联网进行企业和产品的宣传等。

(二)交易过程中的基本程序

交易双方在充分了解市场信息的基础上,决定通过电子数据交换进行贸易活动后,进入标准化电子商务应遵循的基本程序。具体环节如下:

(1)需求方向供货方提出商品报价请求(REQUOT),说明想购买的商品信息;

(2)供货方向需求方回答该商品的报价(QUOTES),说明报价信息;

(3)需求方向供货方提出商品订购单(ORDERS),说明初定购买的商品信息名;

(4)供货方对需求方的商品订购单做出应答(ORDESP),说明有无该规格、型号、品种、质量的商品信息;

(5)需求方根据供货方对商品订购单的应答提出是否变更请求(ORDCHG),说明最后确定购买商品的信息;

(6)需求方向供货方提出商品运输说明(IFTEIN),说明运输工具、交货地点等信息;

(7)供货方向需求方发送发货通知(BESADN),说明运输公司、运输设备、交货地点、包装等信息;

(8)需求方向供货方发回该商品的收货通知(RECADN),报告收货信息;

(9)供需双方收发汇款通知(REMADN),买方发汇款通知,卖方报告收款信息;

(10)供货方向需求方发送电子发票(INVOIC),买方收到商品,卖方收到货款并出具发票,完成交易。

（三）互联网＋国际电子商务履约及其优越性

在实际合同履约中，对于买卖双方来说，中心是货、证、船、款四个字。

（1）备货。许多贸易公司，往往是在合同签约后才开始备货，包括采购、包装、境内运输、仓储等。在电子商务平台上，国内的采购、包装、装运、仓储都可以通过互联网或电子数据交换系统进行安排，以求得最佳的采购计划和运输方案，以达到成本最低、效益最好的经营目的。

并且，通过互联网，尤其是标准化的 EDI 系统，可以实时跟踪合同执行进度，实时把握合同履约的具体进程。

（2）报验。对出口货物进行检验，既是对买方负责，也是对卖方负责，如果货物不符合合同的规定，会导致拒付或其他损失。实际商品的检验过程必须人工干预，但商检报验的预约、报验单据和商检证书等都可以通过电子商务系统自动生成。相关技术检验数据，根据检验仪器的先进程度，有的也可以直接转换为电子数据为有关单证所使用。

（3）催证、审证、改证。在电子商务系统中，催证、审证、改证等人的脑力劳动工作都可以由电子商务系统自动完成，而且比人工复核的效率和准确性更高。

（4）租船订舱与报关装运保险。在运输方式选择和保险投保过程中，电子商务技术可以用计算机计算做出费用最低的安排。并通过电子商务系统，完成租船订舱、电子报关、装运卸载安排、保险、商检和签发提单等工作，而且比人工作业更好更快。

（5）制单结汇。结汇过程的各种票证单据的制作也可以通过电子税务系统和与之联网的银行结算系统来完成。在信用证支付方式中，因为信用证的独立与自足特点，决定了合同、提单、信用证、发票汇票等内容应严格做到"正确、完整、及时、简明、整洁"，并且要求"单单一致，单证一致"。人工作业经常会出现不一致的错误，轻则需要反复改证或重制单据，重则会导致拒付。而在电子商务系统中，由于通过计算机系统联网作业，相关数据一经输入，根据有关标准化格式文件，会自动生成内容完全一致的相关单证，从而大大提高了单据的正确性和制单的效率，保证了收汇的安全。

英文参考教程

Traditional and New Trade Forms

A. Traditional Trade Forms

In our country, traditional import and export business may be carried on in various ways and forms according to the international trade requirements.

1. Free Trade by Contract

Free trade by contract includes distribution and fixed distribution, exclusive sales, commercial agency, etc.

1) Distribution: Distribution means the distributor allocates and sells the goods on behalf of the exporter. It belongs to reselling trade which is widely used in international trade. Distribution may be divided into 2 cases; one is that the distributor buys the goods from the exporter on sales contract basis and sells on the market freely. The relationship between the exporter and the distributor is that between the seller and the buyer, which is terminated after the two parties have fulfilled the duties stipulated in the sales contract. In a broad sense, common importers and commission merchants are all distributors. In this case the distribution agreement is unnecessary. The other case is that the exporter entitles the distributor to sell the provided goods in a certain area abroad within a period of time on the basis of the distribution agreement by which the distributor; shall abide.

2) Fixed distribution: Fixed distribution means that the exporter chooses several distributors in a certain foreign market within a period of time and allocates the same goods to – the appointed distributors for their distribution to whom the exporter will give some preferential treatments in prices, terms of payment or discounts. But the distributor does not enjoy the exclusive rights.

3) Exclusive sales

a) The term "exclusive sales" means that the exporter entitles the foreign distributor to sell a certain kind of commodity exclusively in a certain area within a period of time on the exclusive sales agreement basis. The right of exclusive sales mean that the exporter makes offers of a certain kind of commodit only to the exclusive distributor in a certain territory within certain period of time while the exclusive distributor shall purchase and sell or otherwise deal in any articles of the kind as similar to or competitive with the commodity in the territory. The distributor shall not act as agent of distribute for any other person firm other than the seller.

b) The features of exclusive sales are; The relationship between the exporter and the exclusive distributor is solely that of the seller and the buyer. The distributor is not the agent or representative of the seller and is to have no authority to contract in the name of, and to create any liability against, the seller. The exclusive sales agreement is the contract made between the exporter and the authorized distributor which stipulates the rights and obligations of the two parties and determines the juridical relationship between the two parties.

The main contents of the exclusive sales agreement are the name of the agreement and the relationship between two parties;

The name of the agreement shall be in accordance with the nature and contents of the agreement.

In the exclusive sales agreement, we shall stipulate clearly that the relationship between the seller and the distributor is solely that of the seller and the buyer. The distributor is not the agent or representative of the seller and has no authority to act on the seller behalf.

2. The right of exclusive sales and counter condition

After the seller has authorized the buyer to act as his exclusive distributor, he shall not make offers of the specified goods to any other party in the agreed territory except the authorized exclusive distributor. The seller may ask for the counter right as well and stipulate that the distributor shall not directly or indirectly, purchase, sell or otherwise deal in any articles of the same kind as similar to or competitive with the products in the territory and that the distributor shall not act as agent or distributor for any other person, firm other than the seller.

- Commodity, territory and time limit The two parties shall stipulate clearly the description, specification, etc. of the goods in the exclusive sales agreement. The scope of the exclusive commodity shall be determined according to the business purpose of the exporter and the operation ability and credit standing of the exclusive distributor. The scope of the exclusive commodity should not be too large.

It will be beneficial to both parties to choose a reasonable territory. The usual method is to choose a small territory first, then to extend to a larger territory according to the exclusive sales turnover. Furthermore, in order to protect the benefit of the seller, the exclusive sales agreement also stipulates that the exclusive distributor shall not resell the products outside the territory during the effective period of the agreement. As to the term of validity of the agreement it is no good being too long or too short.

- Quantity and amount: The minimum purchase amount is a main condition on which the seller shall authorize the buyer to act as his exclusive distributor. The minimum purchase amount is determined according to the capacity of the market and the standard to which the exclusive distributor may get through his effort. In case the distributor fails to fulfil the task, the seller reserves the right to cancel the agreement.

- The relationship between each individual contract and exclusive sales agreement?

The exclusive sales agreement itself is not the contract instead it is the agreement which stipulates the rights and obligations between the seller and the exclusive distributor which is carried out by signing individual contracts separately. The agreement shall stipulate clearly that the quantities, prices and shipments of the products shall be confirmed in each transaction teach individual contract under the agreement shall be subject to the terms and conditions prescribed in the agreement.

4) Agency. A vast amount of international trade is handled not only by direct negotiations between the buyers and the sellers but also by means of agencies. An important reason for appointing a foreign agent is that he has all necessary knowledge of local conditions and of the market in which he will operate. He knows what goods are best suitable to his area and what price the market will bear. In developing foreign trade, agents and intermediaries of ten play a very important role.

Agency means that the agent signs contracts with a third party on behalf of the principal or does other matters relating to the sales in compliance with the instructions from his principal, while the principal shall be responsible for the agent's business activities and the obligations incurred therein. The rights and obligations of both parties are determined by the agency agreement. Their relationship is that of sales on a commission basis.

Agencies abroad appointed by our export enterprises are generally commercial agencies through which agreements are entered into between the export enterprises and the agents abroad in order to stipulate the commodity, validity, territory, minimum purchase amount, payment terms, terms of price, exclusive. rights and obligations remedial measures for breach of the contract, market information, etc.

As far as selling transactions are concerned there are mainly three types of agencies: the commission agency, the sole agency and the general agency. The commission agent may be a firm or a person who acts upon the instructions from his principal to sell goods on the best terms obtainable. He charges a certain amount of commission for his services under some kind of agreement or contract.

The sole agent is similar to a commission agent, who may be a firm or a person acting exclusively for one foreign principal with exclusive (or sole) agency rights to sell on a commission basis-certain commodities in a certain area in accordance with the agreement concluded. The general agent is regarded as the representative of the principal and in general the acts of the agent are taken as those of the principal. The sole agency agreement mainly includes the commodity, territory, validity, exclusive rights, commission, minimum turnover, etc., which is similar to the exclusive sale agreement but it has some specific features.

Name of the agreement; The name of the agreement shall be exclusive agency agreement.

* Limits of authority and obligations of sole agency; In order to avoid acts of the sole agent which are unfavorable to the principal, the sole agency agreement often stipulates the limits of authority of the sole agency, for example, the sole agent is only entitled to solicit buyers for the principal and sign contracts with them. The sole agent shall act in good-faith and upon the instructions of the principal.

* Authorization of sole agency right and counter right; After the principal authorizes the sole agent the right of exclusive sales the principal may ask the sole agent to undertake certain obligations as counter conditions on which the sole agent shall not directly or indirectly sell or deal in any articles of the same kind as, similar to, or competitive with the product in the territory.

* Agency commission; Agency commission is the reward given by the principal to the agent for his services and is a main obligation of the principals The sole agency agreement shall stipulate the specific rate the calculating basis of commission, and the method of payment.

The commission rate is determined by the feature of commission marketing amount, competitive degree etc. The calculating basis of commission is the invoice value, or FOB price or FCA price.

* Market report is in order to keep the seller well informed of the prevailing market conditions, the sole agent shall undertake to supply the seller, at least once a calendar quarter or at any time when necessary, with a market report concerning the information on the changes of local regulations in connection with the importation and sales of the commodity covered by the agreement, the local market tendency and consumers' comments on quality, packing, price, etc. , of the goods supplied by the seller under the agreement. The sole agent shall also supply the seller with quotations1 samples and advertising matters of similar commodities of other suppliers.

* Exception; The transactions concluded between the governmental bodies in the countries of the seller and the sole agent shall not be restricted by the terms and conditions of the agreement nor shall the amount of such transactions be counted as part of the turnover mentioned in the agreement. The exclusive sale and the sole agency are different. The relationship between the two parties is that of sale by proxy as to the sole agency, while the relationship is that of sale on fixed distribution as to the exclusive sale. The exclusive distributor will purchase and sell the goods in his own name, and assume solely the responsibility for his own profits or loss. As to the sole agency, the agent resells the goods in the agreed territory according to the trade terms stipulated by the principal. The agent charges a certain amount of commission and does not undertake any risks. After the exclusive distributor has purchased the goods, he shall open an L/C by himself or pay the purchase price by other methods. In the case of sole agency, after the agent has introduced the goods to the buyer, the actual buyer shall open an L/C to the principal.

3. Auction

Auction is a kind of spot transaction in which the auctioneer is entitled to sell the goods according to certain principles and regulations. By auction, the buyers bid publicly and finally the auctioneer sells the goods to the buyer whose bid price is the highest.

1) Kinds of Auction

a. Mark-up auction: The auctioneer declares the lowest expected price first, then the buyers bid their higher prices until someone makes the highest bid for the goods. Finally the auctioneer beats the mallet to declare the conclusion of the transaction.

b. Mark-down auction or Dutch auction: The auctioneer offers the highest price first, then he deducts a small amount from his offering price gradually until someone declares that he accepts the offer. Dutch auction is often applied to the sales of fresh or live commodities.

c. Sealed bids or closed bids: The auctioneer declares the particulars of each lot and the conditions of auction first. The buyers shall submit their sealed bids to the auctioneer within the stipulated time limit at the named place. The auctioneer will choose the most suitable one and conclude the transaction with him.

2) General procedure of auction

Preparation: The cargo owner delivers the goods to the warehouse appointed by the auctioneer who will arrange to classify and lot out the goods, prepare and print auction catalogues, set together with the seller the price and sales terms.

a. Inspection by the buyers: Since auction is a spot transaction that the buyers should have reasonable opportunity to examine the goods carefully. They may either check the sample provided by the auctioneer or survey the whole lot in the warehouse.

b. Formal auction: Formal auction is carried out at the time and place stipulated according to certain principles and regulations. When the auctioneer believes that no higher price will be bidden, he will beat the mallet and declare the conclusion of the transaction.

c. Making payment and taking delivery of the goods: After the conclusion of the auction, the auctioneer usually sends a written confirmation of sales to the buyer for verification, then the buyer shall sign and sum it a purchase confirmation to the auctioneer as a written evidence, and pay for the goods against the warehouse receipt and take delivery of the goods within the time limit according to the stipulations.

4. Consignment

Consignment means that the consignor delivers the goods to the place of consignment abroad first, then entrusts the consignee with the task to sell the goods according to the conditions and methods stipulated in the agreement of consignment.

1) Features of consignment

The consignor shall first deliver the goods to the commission agent or consignment agent.

a. Before the commission agent sells out the goods, the title to the goods still belongs to the consignor.

b. The commission agent is commissioned to sell the good; for the consignor and he will deal with the goods according to the order of the consignor only.

c. The consignment agent will not undertake any risks and expenses and he only charges commission for his service.

2) Advantages of consignment

a) By means of consignment, the seller may sell spot goods or newly-developed products at the local market abroad, thus, the seller may avail himself of the opportunity of marketing according to the supply and demand of the market.

b) The consignment agent does not need to undertake any risks and expenses nor to pay for the goods in advance.

3) Consignment agreement: The consignment agreement is a written document concluded between the consignor and the consignment agent, which stipulates the rights and obligations, conditions and methods of consignment. The agreement of consignment mainly includes the following contents.

The name of agreement, rights and obligations of the two parties: The agreement shall stipulate clearly that before the goods are sold out, the title to the goods still belongs to the consignor and the risks and expenses are generally undertaken by the consignor. After the goods are sold out, the title to the goods will be transferred from the consignor, to the buyer directly.

4) Territory of consignment and commodity of consignment:

These two items must be carefully determined on the basis of thorough investigations.

a. Methods of determining price. There are 3 ways to determine the price.

b. The consignor stipulates the lowest price. The consign-ment agent can only sell the goods at this price or at a price higher than this one.

c. The consignment agent determines the price according to market quotations by himself.

d. The consignment agent determines a price which shall be approved by the consignor.

e. Commission: The consignment agent will charge commission for his service.

5. Invitation to Tender and Submission of Tenders

The invitation to tender and the submission of tenders are the two aspects of one mode of trade by which the inviter sends out an announcement of tender in order to call bidders to bid within the time limit. The bidders fill in applications for tenders within the time limit and submit tenders through an agent. Finally, the inviter chooses the most suitable bidder and concludes the transaction with him.

1) Procedure of invitation to tender

a. Draw up invitation document! The contents of the invitation document mainly include the requirements of invitation format of contract clauses of contract, illustration of commodity and technical requirements.

b. Issue announcement of tender: The inviter will put an advertisement in the important local newspapers so that the lawful and competitive companies or enterprises may have chance to take part in the submission of tenders.

c. Prequalification: The inviter will examine the credit standing, business experience, business scope, capital position, etc. of bidders in advance. Only those qualified bidders may take part in the submission of tenders.

2) Procedure of submission of tenders

Obtain and study the tender document. The bidders shall study the contract conditions, mainly including quality and specifications, price, time of delivery, and all other technological requirements listed in the invitation document carefully. Because the submission of tenders is in fact a firm bid whose validity is long, it cannot be withdrawn before the award so the bidders must take into consideration the changes of the market price and various expenses.

The invitation document or document of inviting bids, including instructions for bidding tender document or contract conditions, etc. are in fact a firm offer whose validity will be extended to the date of opening of tender whose contents shall be definite.

3) Provide bid bond: In order to prevent the bidders from withdrawing their bids orrefusing to sign the contract, the inviter usually requires the bidders to provide a certain percentage of bid bond which may be made available by cash, L/G or stand-by L/C.

Submit application for tender: The tender document shall be sent to the inviter before the terminal date, otherwise it will be invalid.

4) Opening of bids and award of bid: There are two ways of opening of bids, i. e., the public opening of bids and non-public opening of bids.

By the public opening of bids, the inviter opens and reads out all the sealed tender documents. All bidders may amend public representatives to keep watch over the opening of bids. By the non-public opening of bids the inviter will decide the successful bidder by himself. The award means that the winning bidder is chosen as the subject for signing the contract. When concluding the contract, the bidder is usually required to pay the performance bond, or establish the performance L/G with his bank.

6. Futures Trade at Commodity Exchange

1) Brief introduction of commodity exchange: The commodity exchange is an organized market at which futures contracts of particular commodities are sold according to its regulations

at a stipulated time. It is a special market consisting of committed members. The commodities dealt in at the commodity exchange are mainly primary products, e. g., non-ferrous metal, grain oil, foodstuffs, cotton etc. The two largest centers of commodity exchanges are the New York Commodity Exchange and London Metal Exchange.

2) Futures contract: The futures contract is a standard contract drawn up by the individual commodity exchange. It usually stipulates the unified trading unit, basic grade general requirements for packing and other terms. On the basis of the futures contract, the buyer and the seller may only negotiate the price, date of delivery, and number of contract at the stipulated time.

The futures contract of commodity exchange is different from that for general trade. The forward contract for general trade is suitable for future delivery of the actual commodity. The seller fulfils his duty of delivery only if he delivers the goods to the buyer actually according to the terms and conditions, including quality, quantity, packing, time of delivery, etc. stipulated in the contract. While the futures business at the commodity exchange is only the transaction of futures contract itself which does not involve actual transferring of the goods. So the futures contract business also called paper contract business.

3) Hedging: Hedging means that when the seller (buyer) sells (buys) the actual commodity, he will buy. (sell) The futures contract of the same amount at the commodity exchange. From the view point of a long period of time prices at the commodity exchange are almost the same as those at the actual commodity market, so the loss or profit in actual commodity business may be compensated or offset by the profit or loss in futures business at the commodity exchange.

Hedging includes selling hedging and buying hedging. In addition to the above-mentioned forms barter trade, transit trade and frontier trade are also included in traditional trade patterns.

B. New Trade Forms

The new trade forms are either the combination of sale and purchase or that of products, accommodation and technology transfer, e. g., processing with customer's materials, assembling with parts supplied by clients, counter trade, lease trade, etc.

1. Processing and Assembling Trade

Processing and assembling trade includes assembling with parts supplied by customers and processing with customer materials, processing with customer drafts and processing with customer samples.

1) Features of processing and assembling trade

a. Processing and assembling trade is different from general import and export trade, because the latter belongs to the scope of commodity trade? while the former does not. Although processing and assembling trade involves the import and export of raw materials and parts, the titles to the goods still belong to the principal, the trustee only provides service and charges the agreed reward for processing and assembling.

b. Processing and assembling trade is different from the processing of imported materials. As to the processing of imported materials, our enterprises purchase raw materials from abroad. process them into products and sell them to the markets abroad. The import of raw materials and export of products are not so related closely as the former. As to processing and assembling trade factories abroad provide raw materials or parts and accept qualified products. Our enterprises are not responsible for losses and profits nor undertake risks of sale.

So it is a transaction that combines import of raw materials or parts with export of products.

2) Contract of processing and assembling trade

The main contents of the processing and assembling contract are:

a. Stipulations on quality, quantity and time of arrival of customer's materials or parts.

b. Stipulations on requirements for quality of products?

c. Stipulations on quantity of products and date of delivery?

d. Stipulations on assembling or processing fees.

3) Stipulations on terms of payment

There are two methods used to calculate the reward for processing and assembling. One is that the principal pays the reward according to the progress of processing or assembling or the quantity of products irrespective of the prices of materials, parts or products. The other is that the prices of materials or parts and the factory prices of products are calculated respectively. The difference will be the reward. As to the terms of payment for the labour remuneration, in most cases we may accept the reciprocal L/C or remittance as the modes of payment.

2. Counter Trade

Counter trade is a mode of trade which makes use of the agreed commodity or service as a mode of payment for the equipment technology imported from abroad.

The forms of counter trade are various but the basic forms are barter trade and compensation trade.

1) Barter trade: Traditional barter trade is generally carried out by means of commodities of the same value. It neither concerns the payment by cash nor a third party, so it is also called direct barter. The two parties only conclude a contract which includes the specifica-

tions, descriptions, quantities of the goods to be bartered. Traditional barter trade is an individual transaction, and the performance is simple. But this kind of traditional barter trade cannot be comprehensive used, because the goods bartered shall be needed by both parties and shall be of the same value. At present, barter trade is mostly carried out through the reciprocal L/C i. e. the two parties conclude a barter trade contract which stipulate that the export and import commodities of both parties should be paid by means of L/C according to the agree prices. The L/C is opened by one party on condition that receives the L/C of the same value opened by the counter party. Therefore, modern barter trade often concerns a third party.

2) Compensation trade: Compensation trade means that on party provides the other with equipment and technology, the payment of which is made by the goods manufactured within the equipment and technology, or by other goods. This kind of transaction generally embodies the balance of import and export trade between two parties.

Forms of compensation trade mainly include:

Products buy-back. This involves an exchange of interrelated goods. For example when imported textile equipment is paid for by a Chinese enterprise with textiles manufactured with the equipment or when payment for licence. Fees is made with licensed products, the buy-back percentage may be various. Where the value of buy-back amounts to 10 percent or even exceeds the value of the imported equipment or technology or service, it is called full compensation. Where the value of buy-back is less than 100 percent of the value of the imported equipment or technology or service, and the foreign firm agrees that the equipment or technology or service can be compensated by part of payment in cash and the remainder in goods manufactured with the equipment or in licensed products, it is called partial compensation.

Counter purchase. It happens sometimes that the foreign exporter does not need the products manufactured with the equipment he provides, or that his equipment, such as hotel equipment, transportation vehicles, medical apparatus, does not produce tangible goods, the two sides may agree to resort to other goods for the payment for the equipment. This gives rise to another type of compensation trade.

3. Lease Trade

By lease trade, the lessor delivers the equipment to the lessee and entitles him to use it within a period of time on the basis of the lease contract entered into between the lessor and the lessee. The lessor collects a certain sum of money as rent. Lease business in modern economic activities mainly refers to equipment lease which combines commercial credit and financial credit. In case the lessor and the lessee are in different countries this kind of lease trade is international lease trade.

1) Features of typical international lease trade

a. The lessee obtains the right to use the equipment instead of raising money to purchase the equipment by himself.

b. Within the period of the lease the title to the equipment belongs to the lessor, the right of use belongs to the lessee.

c. The period of lease is usually 3 – 5 years, while it may be as long as more than 10 years; the rent may be average periodically or be decreased successively.

d. After the termination of the contract, the equipment shall be returned to the lessor, but usually by means of consideration. The lessee will pay a little sum of money and get the title to the goods.

2) Kinds of Lease Trade

According to the purposes of lease trade, it falls into two kinds: **financial lease and operating lease.**

Financial lease is the basic form of equipment lease, the purchase of which by the lessor is financing. The features of a typical financial lease contract; It is irrevocable within the period of lease. Both parties are not entitled to withdraw the contract. Full payout must be made within the period of the lease. The equipment is only leased to one customer. The total amount of rent usually consists of the price of the equipment, interest and other formality expenses. After the lessee pays off all the rent, the title to the goods is transferred to the lessee.

（资料来源：宋秀峰．国际贸易（双语版）［M］．中国发展出版社，2010.

Alan E. Branch．国际贸易实务（第五版）［M］．孔雁，蔡荣生译，清华大学出版社，2007．）

➢ 本章小结

在经销方式下，双方当事人通过包销协议建立了一种较为稳固的购销关系。货物由经销商购买、销售、自负盈亏。代理是指由出口商作为委托人与国外的代理商达成协议，授权代理人推销其商品、签订合同。寄售是按双方签订的协议进行的，寄售人和代销人之间是委托与受托关系，寄售协议属于行纪合同（又称信托合同）性质。

招标和投标是国际贸易中比较常见的一种贸易方式。招投标程序基本上包括招标，投标，开标、评标和中标，合同的签订等四个阶段。拍卖是指以公开竞价的形式，将特定物品或者财产权利转让给最高应价者的买卖方式。

参加展览会是企业最重要的营销方式之一，也是企业开辟新市场的首选方式。国际国内有许多形式的展览会，企业应该根据租金的目标选择合适的展览会并做好参展的后续工作。

加工贸易是一种新型贸易形式。加工贸易的形式主要包括来料加工和进料加工两种贸易方式，此外，近年来我国企业在海外投资中开展的境外加工贸易方式，也被视为加工贸易的新形式。在我国，对等贸易包括易货贸易、记账贸易、补偿贸易、互购贸易、转手贸易、抵销贸易等。

国际电子商务用数字化电子方式进行商务数据交换和开展国际贸易活动，是一种创新的国际贸易方式。它将成为未来国际贸易的重要方式之一。但利用电子商务方式所进行的国际贸易方式，企业在线交易系统，如在线采购管理等已经成为从事国际化经营的企业的现实选择。

➤ 本章名词

经销　包销　经销协议　代理　独家代理　寄售　招投标　国际竞争性招标　拍卖　密封递价拍卖法　来料加工　进料加工　境外加工贸易　对等贸易　易货贸易　记账贸易　补偿贸易　互购贸易　转手贸易　B2B　B2G　B2C

➤ 理论思考

1. 如何鉴定独家经销协议和独家代理协议？
2. 经销、代理和寄售的区别是什么？
3. 拍卖和招投标方式适用于哪些商品？为什么？常见的招投标和拍卖商品有哪些？这两种方式对于交易双方有什么好处？
4. 如何确定某一项目是否适合采用补偿贸易方式引进？
5. 加工贸易中应注意哪些问题？
6. 怎样鉴定加工贸易合同？
7. 课外调研：走访几家开展过加工贸易或补偿贸易的企业，了解实际业务中碰到的具体问题，思考并简要分析。

参 考 文 献

［1］徐宣全，宋秀峰．国际贸易实务［M］．杭州：浙江大学出版社，2003.

［2］保罗·克鲁格曼，奥伯斯法尔德．国际经济学［M］．第五版．北京：中国人民大学出版社，2002.

［3］曹建明，贺小勇．世界贸易组织［M］．第二版．北京：法律出版社，2004.

［4］陈安．国际经济学［M］．北京：北京大学出版社，2001.

［5］陈同仇，薛荣久．国际贸易［M］．北京：对外经济贸易大学出版社，2003.

［6］陈宪，程大中．粘合剂：全球产业与市场整合中的服务贸易［M］．上海：上海社会科学院出版社，2001.

［7］刘玲．UCP600与信用证精要［M］．北京：对外经济贸易出版社，2003.

［8］陈岩，国际贸易理论与实务［M］．北京：清华大学出版社，2007.

［9］董瑾．国际贸易理论与实务［M］．北京：北京理工大学出版社，2005.

［10］国际商会．跟单信用证统一惯例（UCP600）［M］．北京：中国民主法制出版社，2006.

［11］海闻，林德特．P．王新奎．国际贸易［M］．上海：上海人民出版社，2003.

［12］华欣，张雪莹．国际贸易实务［M］．北京：清华大学出版社，2003.

［13］兰箐．国际贸易理论与实务［M］．北京：清华大学出版社，2003.

［14］黎孝先．国际贸易实务［M］．北京：对外经济贸易出版社，2001.

［15］黎友焕．国际贸易［M］．北京：中国商务出版社，2003.

［16］李凯，郁培丽，刘德学．国际贸易理论与实务［M］．大连：东北大学出版社，2003.

［17］李湘．国际贸易教程［M］．上海：上海财经大学出版社，2004.

［18］李左东．国际贸易理论、政策与实务［M］．北京：高等出版社，2006.

［19］刘厚俊等，国际贸易新发展——理论、政策、实践［M］．北京：科学出版社，2003.

［20］刘伟．国际贸易［M］．北京中国发展出版社，2006.

［21］马野青，张二震．国际贸易学［M］．南京：南京大学出版社，2003.

［22］毛筠，孙琪．国际贸易理论与政策［M］．杭州：浙江大学出版社，2003.

［23］屈韬. 外贸单证处理技巧［M］. 广东：广东经济出版社，2000.

［24］祝卫. 出口贸易模拟操作教程［M］. 上海：上海人民出版社，2002.

［25］商务部编写组. 国际贸易［M］. 北京：中国对外经济贸易出版社，2007.

［26］陶明，吴申元等. 服务贸易学［M］. 太原：山西经济出版社，2001.

［27］童宏祥. 外贸单证实务［M］. 上海：华东理工大学出版社，2003.

［28］涂永式，江虹，欧阳北松. 国际贸易理论与实务［M］. 广东：广东高等教育出版社，2005.

［29］汪素芹. 国际服务贸易［M］. 北京：机械工业出版社，2007.

［30］汪五一，封定一，刘莉. 国际贸易实务［M］. 合肥：中国科学技术大学出版社，2002.

［31］王俊宜，李权. 国际贸易［M］. 北京：中国发展出版社，2006.

［32］王文举. 国际贸易理论与实务［M］. 第二版. 合肥：安徽大学出版社，2003.

［33］吴百福，徐小薇. 进出口贸易实务教程［M］. 上海：上海人民出版社，2007.

［34］徐进亮. 国际结算惯例与案例［M］. 北京：对外经济贸易出版社，2007.

［35］许宁宁. 中国—东盟自由贸易区［M］. 北京：红旗出版社，2003.

［36］仲鑫. 国际贸易实务［M］. 北京：机械工业出版社，2005.

［37］薛荣久. 世界贸易组织（WTO）教程［M］. 北京：对外经济贸易大学出版社，2003.

［38］卓俊. 国际贸易理论与实务［M］. 北京：机械工业出版社，2006.

［39］姚东旭. 现代国际贸易［M］. 北京：经济管理出版社，2006.

［40］叶德万，陈原. 国际贸易实务案例教程［M］. 广州：华南理工大学出版社，2003.

［41］尹翔硕. 国际贸易教程［M］. 第三版. 上海：复旦大学出版社，2005.

［42］袁永友，柏望生. 国际贸易实务案例分析［M］. 北京：中国商务出版社，2004.

［43］翟江南. 货物贸易理论与实务［M］. 北京：对外经济贸易出版社，2007.

［44］张坚. 国际贸易实用手册［M］. 北京：中国纺织出版社，2004.

［45］张曙霄，李秀敏. 国际贸易——理论、政策、措施［M］. 北京：中国经济出版社，2001.